The Political Career of
W. Kerr Scott

The Political Career of

W. KERR SCOTT

THE SQUIRE FROM HAW RIVER

JULIAN M. PLEASANTS

UNIVERSITY PRESS OF KENTUCKY

Copyright © 2014 by The University Press of Kentucky

Scholarly publisher for the Commonwealth,
serving Bellarmine University, Berea College, Centre College of Kentucky,
Eastern Kentucky University, The Filson Historical Society, Georgetown College,
Kentucky Historical Society, Kentucky State University, Morehead State
University, Murray State University, Northern Kentucky University, Transylvania
University, University of Kentucky, University of Louisville, and Western
Kentucky University.
All rights reserved.

Editorial and Sales Offices: The University Press of Kentucky
663 South Limestone Street, Lexington, Kentucky 40508-4008
www.kentuckypress.com

Cataloging-in-Publication data is available from the Library of Congress.

ISBN 978-0-8131-4677-5 (hardcover : alk. paper)
ISBN 978-0-8131-4678-2 (epub)
ISBN 978-0-8131-4679-9 (pdf)

This book is printed on acid-free paper meeting
the requirements of the American National Standard
for Permanence in Paper for Printed Library Materials.

Manufactured in the United States of America.

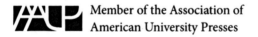 Member of the Association of
American University Presses

CONTENTS

INTRODUCTION

William Kerr Scott was the most controversial, polarizing, and successful North Carolina politician of his age. When Simmons Fentress, a writer and astute observer of North Carolina politics, evaluated Scott at the end of his four-year term as governor, he referred to him as "the century's most cussed governor": "Columnists and commentators attacked him as a political accident, a notorious spender of other people's money, a dangerous liberal tied to Harry Truman's coattail, a governor of only half of the people." The man who changed the face of the state was, according to Fentress, "as plain as a plow point, as candid as a school kid and as stubborn as an Alamance mule and just as unpredictable." While many would be glad to see him go, "the gladdest are the men in the front offices of the big utilities." Fentress concluded that Scott would be remembered as a builder but that "he was, essentially, a needler, a provoker, a builder of fires under the foot-draggers and the indolent," but always for a "good cause." The governor brought a new level of political courage to Raleigh, a brand of effrontery that had him "delineating the ills of the legal profession before an audience of lawyers and cursing private power companies at a power plant dedication." In a profession where everyone avoided controversial issues and parsed each sentence, Scott was an anomaly who always spoke his mind. He never understood the value of no comment. In summary, Fentress praised Scott for stubborn and fearless commitment to his goals.[1] Scott's impressive achievements changed the course of the Old North State and led to an industrial revolution and improved living conditions for all its citizens.

Up until 1948, North Carolina had been dominated by a powerful machine organization, known as the Shelby dynasty or the Gardner machine. Led by what V. O. Key Jr. called the *progressive plutocracy*,[2] the machine consisted of an oligarchy of bankers and industrialists who dominated the state's political and economic decision making. The Shelby dynasty favored sound, conservative government and maintained power by controlling the elective and appointive offices of the state administration. For twenty years, its members had, in effect, chosen the governor of the state. They

Governor W. Kerr Scott with his ever-present cigar. Photograph by Hugh Morton, North Carolina Collection, University of North Carolina at Chapel Hill Library.

were believers in the status quo and had access to the political funding that would keep them in power.

Kerr Scott, a folksy, plainspoken, ambitious candidate, changed the power structure in the state in 1948 by winning one of the greatest political upsets in the state's history. When he announced as a candidate for governor, very few gave the Alamance dairy farmer much of a chance, but he effectively mobilized his supporters with a populist attack on big business and a constant denunciation of machine politics. Farmers and the poorer element in the state believed that they had not been given their fair share of state largesse and grew tired of the conservative, business-dominated political system. Kerr Scott believed that, in a land of forgotten people, what was bad for two-thirds of the state was bad for the entire state. He understood the needs and desires of the state's less fortunate citizens and rode their demand for improvement in their lives to victory in the race for governor. His defeat of Charlie Johnson, the state treasurer, ended a twenty-year reign of conservative machine politics in the state and changed the face of North Carolina politics. If Johnson, the chosen candidate of the "progressive plutocracy," had prevailed, then North Carolina would be a far different state than it is today.

This book is focused on the contributions of Kerr Scott as governor from 1949 to 1953, but it is also the story of North Carolina's dramatic progression from a state not far removed from an introspective, backwater, segregated society dependent on tobacco and textiles into a vibrant, diversified global economy and the center of the industrial, banking, and information revolution in the South. Many of these changes took place during the ten-year period 1948–1958, when Kerr Scott held political office. When he took office, North Carolina had a per capita income that ranked forty-fifth of the then forty-eight states, an average school completion of 7.9 years, and a major problem with illiteracy. Sixty-six percent of the population lived in rural areas, and only one city had over 100,000 in population. There were no interstate highways, and only sixteen thousand miles of the state's sixty-three-thousand-mile road system were hard surfaced. The state had no regional hospitals, no community colleges, and very few opportunities for advancement for those who lived in rural areas. Most of the rural folk lacked medical care, suffered from inadequate schools, and were isolated without telephones and electricity. In the legislative session of 1949, Governor Scott's progressive legislation to improve roads, schools, and medical facilities set in motion the changes that would lead to the state's rise to prominence.

In 1948 the state had begun to change in many ways. There was a new mood of optimism among returning veterans and young people just beginning to vote. The state government had a large surplus accumulated during World War II to spend on citizens' needs. World War II had a transformative effect on the state and set the stage for Scott's legislative successes. The massive government spending in the state for the purchase of farm and manufactured goods, along with the building of army and marine bases, gave a significant stimulus to the economy. The increase in shipbuilding and manufacturing led to many skilled jobs and a burgeoning urbanization.

Kerr Scott's story is also the history of the factional struggles that distinguished state politics in the 1940s. There was a sharp ideological split in the Democratic Party between the conservatives and the progressive/populist wing led by Scott. This clash of ideas over race, culture, and the purpose of government has been the essence of North Carolina politics from 1948 to the present. Voters have elected liberals such as Governors Terry Sanford and Jim Hunt while at the same time choosing hard-line conservative US senators B. Everett Jordan and Jesse Helms. The epic struggle between Jim Hunt and Jesse Helms in 1984 for the US Senate pitted Hunt, the inheritor of the Scott mantle for progress, against the congenital naysayer and arch-conservative Jesse Helms. The Helms-Hunt race marked the beginning of the end to one-party politics in the South and, along with victories by Strom Thurmond in South Carolina and other southern Democrats who had switched parties, was a seminal example of the increasing influence of the resurgent Republican Party. The 1984 Senate contest was another in a long line of political fights for the mind and heart of the region. Helms won by a narrow margin and pushed the state toward a more conservative posture.

During Scott's term as governor, the bitter ideological clashes between the two factions in the state were most evident in election contests: the gubernatorial elections of 1948 and 1952; Frank Graham's defeat by Willis Smith in the 1950 Democratic senatorial primary, the most contentious and bitter conflict in the state's history; and Scott's victory in the 1954 Senate race, often referred to as the *third primary*, where he gained revenge on those conservatives who had defeated Frank Graham in 1950.

Kerr Scott defeated the machine in 1948 and 1954 when he ran for office, but he could not transfer his popularity to candidates he supported—Frank Porter Graham and Hubert Olive in 1952. He had a huge success in the 1949 state legislature with his "Go Forward" program but fared badly with the recalcitrant 1951 legislature as a lame duck governor. In his confrontations with the conservative wing of the party, despite the losses of Graham and Olive, he won the major and most meaningful confrontations by prevailing in the gubernatorial race in 1948 and with his 1949 legislative successes.

The period from 1948 to 1958 also encompasses the state's attempt to maintain its moderate stance on race, "The North Carolina Way," in the face of many controversial Supreme Court decisions and violent resistance in a South threatened by an end to segregation. North Carolina did not have any demagogues like Strom Thurmond or the Talmadges and did not close the state schools like Virginia. It had a reputation as the most progressive state in the South largely because it was generally free from political corruption and boasted of sound government practices. It did not exhibit the white racist demagoguery of the Deep South during this period, but its claim to be a national model of race relations was undermined by the racist campaigns of 1950 and, to a lesser degree, 1954. Scott, Frank Graham, and Jonathan Daniels represented the belief that interposition was not the way to resolve race issues. They improved communication between the races and fought injustices in education, employment, and voting. They believed that men of good faith and optimism could eventually lift up those who had been discriminated against, to the benefit of all the citizens of the state. In the end, however, these moderates on race did not embrace integration and failed to build up support for a gradual change in race relations.

Exactly who was this political phenomenon, Kerr Scott? A man of the people? An uncouth, semiliterate dirt farmer? When one mentioned Kerr Scott in 1948, his name evoked two totally different reactions. The Branch-head Boys, those isolated rural dwellers who lived at the "head of the branch" of the creek and on the star routes, admired him for his integrity and his work ethic and saw him as one of their own—a farmer, a man of the soil. They innately knew that he understood their yearning for a better life and their urgent need for roads, schools, electricity, and telephones. They liked him because of his outspoken and charismatic personality. He could be articulate and urbane when he needed to be, but he never forgot his roots.

The middle- and upper-class urban dwellers, led by the better-educated business leaders in the state, had a totally different, elitist view of Scott. The country club set never cottoned to him, partly because of his crude language and country drawl. They saw him as a rude intruder—a poorly educated, crass, unsophisticated rube who, with his radical views, would turn the state upside down if he ever came to power. Not only did they dislike what they perceived to be his blunt-spoken, brash personality, but they also feared his liberal politics. Ultimately, his critics made the mistake of underestimating his intelligence and vote-getting ability—to their great chagrin. With Kerr Scott, as with collards, people either liked him or hated him—there was usually no middle ground.

Scott could be as down home as he needed to be, but, in fact, he was college educated and a sensible, practical, highly intelligent man who was as comfortable with university presidents as with a crossroads gathering of tobacco farmers griping about farm prices. He could deliver a commencement address, or milk a cow, or chair a session of the Presbyterian elders at his church. He was, as the state would learn, a canny, resourceful politician—far more dangerous than the state's progressive plutocracy could ever have imagined.

Most observers did not expect the extraordinary success that Kerr Scott would have as governor. His critics initially dismissed him as an uncouth farmer, but he proved to be an astute politician and a true visionary. He reformed state government with his Go Forward program, and, during his four years in office, he made great progress in correcting the inequities between the haves and the have-nots. He engineered the passing of two statewide bond issues on roads and education. The education bond money resulted in 8,000 new classrooms, 175 gymnasiums, and 350 lunchrooms. He put in a school health program and insisted on giving pay raises to teachers. His road program ended up paving 14,810 miles of new roads and upgrading and improving thousands of miles of highways. This transportation revolution enabled the state to begin its move toward greater industrialization and enabled the farmer to get his goods to market. Scott's commitment to improved health care in the state led to a new medical school and teaching hospital at Chapel Hill and a number of regional medical centers. During his watch, funding for public health programs, nursing homes, mental health programs, and old-age assistance increased dramatically.

The first governor to recognize the long-term significance of water resources in North Carolina, Scott came up with the first comprehensive plan for water and soil conservation. He began a modernization of the state's prisons, he sponsored a bond issue for the construction of modern port facilities in Wilmington and Morehead City, and he was by far the most prolabor governor of his era. His constant prodding of the electric and telephone companies led to the installation of some 31,000 rural phones and 150,000 new electrical connections. Despite the adamant opposition of conservative state legislators, he managed to push through an astonishing array of game-changing bills in the 1949 legislative session by appealing to the public, by shrewd bargaining, and by hard-hitting leadership.

Scott was one of the most colorful governors in the state's history, and his controversial personality excited his followers and angered his critics. He was forthright and candid to a fault; no one ever doubted where he stood on any issue. He had the courage to confront his critics face-to-face: as noted, he excoriated lawyers at a legal convention and cursed private power companies at a power plant dedication. He was often self-righteous and stubborn, but he disliked the status quo and wanted immediate change. He was an agitator and a provoker of the foot-draggers, the indolent, and those who got in his way. He usually prevailed.

As governor, Scott struck blows for women's rights by appointing the first female superior court judge. Fifteen percent of his appointees to state offices were women. He chose the first black ever selected to the state Board of Education, opened a dialogue with Negro leaders in the state, and worked tirelessly to improve Negro schools.[3] He was never a demagogue, but, despite his moderate stance on race, he consistently defended segregation in the state.

Scott served as a US senator from 1954 to 1958 and achieved some success in that office, but, as a junior senator, he did not have a significant effect on the Senate. He frequently complained about the inability of one man to get much done in the Senate and bemoaned the slow progress of any legislation. He did cast some important votes, including the censure of Joe McCarthy, and worked hard for farmers, especially tobacco growers, as well as for water power and soil and water conservation. His proposal for a world food bank was visionary, but much of his time was spent grappling with *Brown v. Board of Education* and civil rights. His senatorial career was too short for him to establish a distinguished record, so the discussion of the years 1954–1958 is relegated to one chapter.

Chapter 1 has limited coverage of Scott's early life, but it is essential to give the reader a sense of his history, where he came from, and how family, place, and faith contributed to and informed his political career. Kerr Scott was one of the most effective commissioners of agriculture ever to serve in that post in North Carolina, but the coverage of those years is restricted to how that experience prepared him for and affected his term as governor. This book is more of a political history than a full-length biography, and the focus is on Scott's contributions to the state from 1949 to 1953. His electoral victories and his achievements and effectiveness as governor paved the way for other progressive leaders in the state, including Terry Sanford and Jim

Hunt. I have concluded, on the basis of his achievements and the long-term effect of the reforms he advocated, that Kerr Scott was one of the most influential governors in twentieth-century North Carolina.

Writing in the *Greensboro Daily News,* Bill Snider saw Scott's gubernatorial administration as a time of spirited moving forward and his idea of combining rural living with modern industrial society as an important blueprint for the future. Scott wanted to redress the balance between farmers and lawyers and between the people and the moneyed interests. Snider compared him to Harry Truman: "Scott and Truman were alike. Their hearts were in the right place and they were sound on many large and memorable issues. They were sometimes wrong, and petty, on small ones." Scott, continued Snider, had a mind open to new ideas and was the epitome of North Carolina's independent spirit: "He was a bulldozer, not a diplomat, a doer, not a philosopher. He never plowed under false colors." Snider concluded that Scott was as near a symbol of the state's motto, "To Be Rather Than Seem," "as we have had in this century."[4]

This book has been written essentially from primary sources. In many instances, however, the primary material was simply not sufficient for a full explanation of events, so secondary sources were needed to flesh out the story. While a variety of newspapers gave broad coverage to North Carolina politics from 1948 to 1958, I have used the *Raleigh News and Observer* extensively during Scott's term as governor since the Old Reliable covered events in the legislature more thoroughly than any other paper.

The state Department of Archives and History in Raleigh has Scott's gubernatorial papers and his Senate papers. Both sets of papers were reasonably well organized and enabled me to gain some insight into Scott's thoughts and his judgments on political activities. Both collections, however, especially the senatorial papers, were thin on key decisions as Scott was careful not to include his innermost thoughts in his personal writings. Nonetheless, his correspondence helped ascertain his views on state and world events, if not always his motivation for certain decisions.

Other than the Kerr Scott collections, the most helpful papers were those of William McW. Cochrane, Roy Wilder Jr., Terry Sanford, William B. Umstead, Luther Hodges, Capus Waynick Jr., Clyde R. Hoey, and Harry Truman. The *Congressional Record* was a valuable resource for Scott's speeches and votes while in the US Senate. The North Carolina Collection at Chapel Hill, as always, provided a rich collection of varied and relevant sources.

This study would not have been as complete without access to a significant number of valuable oral histories. These remembrances of Kerr Scott supplied the details and the anecdotes that gave the study a greater understanding of the man and a richer, fuller overview of his life. Oral histories are not infallible. Each person brings a mind-set and a bias into each conversation. In some cases it was not possible to verify the details of these recollections, but in most cases I have tried to ascertain whether the information was accurate. The most useful of the interviews were those with Robert W. Scott, Ralph Scott, Roy Wilder Jr., Terry Sanford, William Friday, Lauch Faircloth, and Frances Reesman, who gave me a precise description of Scott in the governor's office. The same is true of Roy Wilder Jr., who had inside information on Scott's activities in the Senate.

1

THE EARLY YEARS

William Kerr Scott began his journey to the statehouse in Raleigh on April 17, 1896. Born in a farmhouse in Haw River, Alamance County, North Carolina, Kerr was the eighth of the fourteen children of Robert Walter Scott (July 24, 1861–May 16, 1929), a prosperous Hawfields community farmer, and Elizabeth Hughes, a former teacher and a pious daughter of a pioneer Orange County family. The Scott family first arrived before the Civil War, traveling among the adventurous Scots-Irish families who made their way to North Carolina via the Great Wagon Road from Pennsylvania. These pioneers carved out small family farms in the Piedmont and scratched out a living with tobacco and cotton. The Scotts represented the best qualities of the rough-hewn, unpretentious, independent farmers in the state. They were typical in that they wore brogans and loved cornbread, but they were also enlightened and believed strongly in education.[1]

Kerr Scott's father, commonly known as "Farmer Bob," established a family dynasty destined to affect the state for the rest of the twentieth century. Robert W. Scott married Lizzie J. Hughes in January 1883, and, of their fourteen children, eleven lived to maturity. Led by Farmer Bob, a state legislator and leader of the Farmers' Alliance, the family produced two governors, Kerr Scott and his son, Robert W. (Bob) Scott II. Kerr Scott went on to the US Senate. Influential Scott family members also included Ralph Scott, a state senator of impressive influence for many years; Samuel Floyd, a beloved physician in Alamance County; Elizabeth Scott Carrington, a nurse and the chair of the committee that founded the School of Nursing at the University of North Carolina; and Meg Scott Phipps, the daughter of Governor Bob Scott, who became the state commissioner of agriculture.

Robert W. Scott, Kerr's father, was born in Hawfields in 1861, the son of Henderson and Margaret (Kerr) Scott. Robert W. Scott's father, a farmer and merchant in Mebane prior to the Civil War, eventually settled in Hawfields. Robert W. got his schooling at the local Hughes Academy and later at Broughton School. He had to leave the University of North Carolina in 1878 to take over the family farm, which had fallen into disrepair. Intent on developing and utilizing new farming techniques, he visited prosperous farms in New York and Pennsylvania and brought new technology and innovative farming methods to Haw River.

Hailed as the first master farmer in the state, Farmer Bob was a pioneer in agricultural innovation. He had a reputation as a "book farmer" as well as a practical one who studied, practiced, and encouraged others in crop rotation and diversified farming. He became a leader in the Farmer's Alliance and later developed an intense interest in politics as a way to improve the lives of the poor in the state. He developed an intimate friendship with Charles B. Aycock, North Carolina's education governor. Aycock visited in the Scott home on many occasions, and his zeal for expanding public education made a profound impression on Kerr Scott, then a lad of twelve. Governor Aycock appointed Farmer Bob to the state Agricultural Board, where he served from 1901 to 1929. Voters elected him—in 1889, 1891, and 1903—to three terms in the state House of Representatives, where he was a member of the roads committee. He also served two terms in the state Senate in 1901 and 1929. Robert W. Scott backed Aycock's education program, campaigned for tax support for the Hawfields public schools, and joined the leadership that established the North Carolina Agricultural and Mechanical College (later North Carolina State University), where he was named a trustee.[2]

Robert Scott had an extraordinary influence on his son's values and his career. All the Scott children learned the importance of hard work at an early age. It was understood that they were to keep their word and honor all their obligations. Each child had his or her assigned daily chores, which their father expected them to perform efficiently and with good cheer. A devout Presbyterian and elder in the Hawfields church, Kerr's father insisted that all the children be in church on Sunday and admonished them to observe a high moral and spiritual code on a daily basis. From his father, Kerr inherited traits of stubbornness, tenacity, sternness, good business judgment, and a compelling urge to help people help themselves. Bob Redwine, who knew the family well, wrote that Kerr's Go Forward program of better schools and roads was the program Farmer Bob had worked for all his life. From his mother, Kerr inherited a gentleness of nature and a sentimental streak that was not always visible to those outside the family. He also learned from the Hugheses, his mother's side of the family, a deep appreciation for history and literature as many in her family were educators, preachers, and doctors.

There was never any question about what Kerr Scott wanted to do with his life. He wanted to be a farmer and a good one. Contrary to later public opinion, he was not a poor dirt farmer. He had been born into an important local family with large landholdings and at least a middle-class income. After completing Hawfields High School in 1913, he enrolled at North Carolina A&M and graduated in 1917 with a ninety-two grade-point average and a B.S. in agriculture. At State he excelled in track, YMCA work, and debating. As one professor noted: "[Kerr] listened more intently than any other student I had." His willingness to learn and his hard work were characteristics that enabled him to achieve great success in his life's endeavors. Dr. Floyd Scott, his older brother, recounted: "Kerr was born with tremendous energy. He could do more work than any two men in the field and he used his head. He arrived at practical solutions sooner than the rest of us."[3]

After graduation, Scott worked briefly as an emergency food production agent for the US Department of Agriculture. After World War I began, he enlisted as a private in the army and served in the field artillery at Camp Taylor, Kentucky. Four months later, just as he was about to enter officer training school, the war ended, and he was discharged from military service. He returned to Haw River and, after borrowing $4,000 from his father, purchased 224 acres and began clearing the land and raising a few head of sheep and cattle.

His father had advised Kerr early on that, since he was the only one in the family with political ambitions, he should buy some land and develop it into a successful business. Then, when he ventured into politics, he could sound off on what he thought was right on any issue. Other politicians could not speak forthrightly for fear of losing their jobs. Kerr need not be afraid to blast away because he could always return to his farm.

Needing a partner in life, Kerr became engaged to Mary White, a neighbor's daughter. They both attended Hawfields High and Hawfields Presbyterian Church and had been lifelong sweethearts. Scott and "Miss Mary," as he always called her, were married on July 2, 1919. Mary quit her position as a teacher in Haw River and helped Kerr clear the land and build their first house. The energetic Scott and the gentle, soft-spoken Miss Mary cut their own timber and, with the aid of a "jack-leg carpenter," built the seven-room house he occupied until his death. He and Miss Mary had three children, Osborne, Mary Kerr Loudermilk, and Robert W. (Bob) Scott II.

Kerr, always devoted to his wife, depended on her for many things, and observers noted that there was a softness in his voice whenever he referred to her. Although quiet and reserved, Mary was an equal partner and her husband's confidante and adviser in all important matters during his career. She served as his anchor and his compass and calmed him down when he let his emotions get out of control. Her sense of purpose was as strong as his, and, when Kerr became commissioner of agriculture, she assumed the responsibility of business agent and resident manager for the farm. The wife of one governor and mother of another, sometimes referred to as "Queen Mary of Scotts" by her friends, she was loved for her "poise, friendliness, and wholesomeness of manner."[4]

Kerr and Mary's son Bob Scott admired how hard his parents had worked to develop their farm and dairy business: "Like so many North Carolina farmers he [Kerr Scott] was an entrepreneur." He remembered that his father and mother took some old worn-out land covered with gullies and built up its fertility over the years: "When you build something like that you put your soul in it and you don't give up." His parents, he noted, "had roots very deep in the soil of Alamance County and in their farm and the community." When Kerr Scott was commissioner of agriculture, he drove back and forth to Raleigh each day so that he could live at home and get work done on the farm. Bob Scott also recalled that all the Scott brothers had a sense of humor: "They believed that you should be able to laugh at yourself ... don't take yourself too seriously. It was a natural humor—not contrived."[5]

A year after he married, Kerr Scott took his first public job when he became the farm agent in Alamance County. For the next ten years, he traveled by horse, buggy, and Model T from one end of the county to the other, advising and assisting farmers with various problems. He used money from his salary to buy additional land in Haw River and practiced on his own farm what he preached to his neighbors—soil conservation and soil improvement.[6] Terry Sanford later described Scott's life as a farm agent: "The Jersey herd was growing and Kerr was rising at 5:00 A.M. to help milk, and taking the milk to the market in his pick-up truck as he went to his office. His first desk was a nail keg, in his office in the basement of the old Courthouse in Graham, and there he worked those first years without an assistant. . . . Any time off the job was spent in pushing some special project at the farm."[7]

In 1930 the North Carolina State Grange elected Scott grand master, a post he held for three years. During that time the Grange experienced its greatest membership growth. In the dark days of the Great Depression,

Scott became one of the first in his state to advocate rural electrification. He caught the attention of Franklin Roosevelt, and, when the president called a meeting of national farm leaders at Warm Springs, Georgia, Kerr Scott was the only southerner invited. Shortly thereafter, Roosevelt appointed Scott as an investigator for the Farm Credit Administration and later selected him as the regional director of the newly created Farm Debt Adjustment Administration. Scott's region included five southern states, and the Tar Heel administrator helped save numerous farmers from mortgage fore-closures. "Those were both heart-rending and happy days for me" recalled Scott. "Heart-rending because of the misery, want and hunger we saw on every side; happy because of the fear we were able to lift from the eyes of thousands of men, women and children."[8]

By 1936 Scott decided that his experience as a county agent, his leader-ship of the Grange, and his work for the federal government qualified him for the post of commissioner of agriculture. The family version of events was that, on his deathbed, Farmer Bob asked Kerr to run for commissioner and make his department the best in the country. Farmer Bob had vied for the office unsuccessfully in 1908; he had been defeated by the father of the cur-rent holder of the office, William A. Graham. Scott, as would be his modus operandi in the future, waited until only three months prior to the primary election to announce against the incumbent. Graham had been in office since 1923, and no one expected the upstart Scott to have a chance. Despite his late entry, Scott waged a vigorous campaign and won the Democratic primary by 227,808 to Graham's 207,750.[9] Scott won reelection by large margins in 1940 and 1944 and served as commissioner for eleven years.[10]

As commissioner, Scott completely reorganized the Department of Agri-culture and, as he did throughout his career, traveled the state preaching rural electrification. He helped expand agricultural marketing facilities in North Carolina, as the state had encouraged increased production without assisting the farmers in marketing their products. He compelled feed and fertilizer manufacturers to eliminate the use of sawdust and sand in their products. He fought against bovine tuberculosis in farm animals and became the first commissioner to operate the state fair without a financial loss. On a national level he led a successful campaign to obtain congressional passage of the Research and Marketing Act of 1946, which provided federal assis-tance to farmers in the marketing of their goods.

While building a state and national reputation in agriculture, Scott expanded his own farm from 224 to 1,300 acres. By 1948 he had 200 cows,

350 acres of pasture, 700 acres of corn, wheat, and alfalfa, and large areas committed to timber. His son Osborne, with significant assistance from Miss Mary, ran the operation along with fifteen farmhands and tenants. Kerr Scott primarily worked as a dairy farmer, supplying milk to Guilford Dairies, a cooperative in Greensboro.[11]

As commissioner of agriculture, Scott had incurred the wrath of the electric power industry as well as the powerful feed and fertilizer groups. The consensus was that he could be reelected as commissioner as long as he wanted but that his political future would be limited to that post. Scott, however, had higher ambitions than his current post and, despite the prevailing opinion, decided that he had the ability and the contacts to be elected governor. He then embarked on a quest for higher elective office and a political career that would result in some of the most dramatic and compelling political races in the history of the state. In the most significant contest, the Democratic primary of 1948, he would achieve a momentous upset that would spell the end for the Gardner machine in the state.

2

THE ELECTION OF 1948

The First Primary

Why did Kerr Scott, a dairy farmer with limited statewide name recognition, no real political organization, and a dearth of wealthy supporters, suddenly, in early 1948, decide to run for governor against the entrenched Gardner machine? O. Max Gardner, a resourceful textile executive from Shelby, North Carolina, had been elected governor in 1928 and quickly constructed a powerful political organization. He combined the remnants of the old Furnifold Simmons machine with the leaders of the business community in the Piedmont. The leading bankers, utility and tobacco company executives, and textile mill owners were aided by effective courthouse organizations around the state. Gardner's machine, known as the Shelby dynasty because two governors, Gardner and Clyde R. Hoey, were from Shelby, dominated state party politics from 1928 until 1948. The Gardner machine selected future governors ahead of time, and its candidates usually managed to win elections by significant margins.

The governors from 1928 to 1948 in North Carolina were part of what V. O. Key Jr. called "the progressive plutocracy." The historian George Tindall referred to these leaders as "business progressives." Writing in 1949, before he had a chance to absorb the significance of Scott's 1948 victory, Key presented North Carolina as a state with a reputation for progressive action on education, industrial development, and race relations. The financial and business elite, "an aggressive aristocracy of manufacturing and banking," controlled the state's economic and political life. According to Key, this oligarchy ruled with a strong sense of community responsibility, favoring funding for education and road building, and with a conscientious, business-like efficiency. The machine maintained power by controlling the elective and appointive offices of the state administration and took great care to ensure that those officials were fundamentally in harmony with the machine's overall point of view. In short, the Shelby dynasty favored sound, conservative government and had easy access to the political funds essential for maintaining its supremacy.[1]

It became increasingly apparent by 1948, however, that some elements in the state, especially the farmers, were beginning to tire of a conservative, business-dominated political system. Although the Democratic Party controlled statewide elections, in reality North Carolina had the appearance of a two-party state. There was an ideological split between the conservative, status quo machine wing of the party and the more democratic, that is, more liberal wing. There had always been a decidedly sectional character to North Carolina politics, and many in the eastern part of the state, mainly farmers and low-wage workers, believed their needs were ignored in Raleigh.

Over the years, these ideological and sectional factions had, with one or two exceptions, coalesced around one candidate, and the Shelby dynasty managed to maintain control until 1948. The machine had been challenged on a few occasions, mainly by Ralph McDonald in 1936, but with limited success. By 1948, however, the political landscape had changed. The machine's leaders, O. Max Gardner and Senator Josiah W. Bailey, had died without leaving successors. After World War II there appeared two large groups of new voters, returning veterans and a cohort of young men and women who had come of age during Roosevelt's New Deal. Neither group had any allegiance to the machine. The opposition to the Shelby machine thus became centered around this new group of voters, aided by the small shopkeepers and tobacco farmers in the east who continued the Populist tradition of suspicion of entrenched government.[2]

Kerr Scott had come by his Populist views honestly. His father had been a leader in the North Carolina Grange and had participated in the Farmer's Alliance, a political protest organization designed to represent the protests of disaffected farmers from all over the country. The late 1880s and early 1890s were difficult times for North Carolina farmers. They faced deflated prices for farm goods, felt victimized by high railroad rates, especially when there was no alternative means of transportation, complained about high interest rates charged by the banks, and faced a never-ending struggle against insects, soil erosion, floods, and droughts. Feeling isolated and ignored, they had very little bargaining power and turned to the Farmer's Alliance for help. The rural element understood that they could not influence a society run by big business and corrupt politicians unless they created a third party. They began to call themselves the People's Party or Populists. The Populist Party achieved some national political success in 1892, but its ideas were eventually absorbed by the Democratic Party.

In North Carolina, the Farmer's Alliance had grown quickly and by 1890 had some 100,000 members. The Populist Party managed to elect fourteen members to the North Carolina state legislature in 1892 by using antibusiness slogans and by appealing to farmers. The local leader, Marion Butler, decided to form a coalition with the overwhelmingly black Republican Party, and the "fusion" took control of the state legislature. Once in power, the new coalition passed laws increasing democracy with the popular election of local officials and significantly expanded the state education system—all reforms designed to undermine the Jim Crow system and the authority of the white supremacists. The Democrats, in the vicious "White Supremacy" campaigns of 1898–1900, regained power, repealed the fusionist reforms, and established a permanent system of white supremacy. The Democrats, in league with the corporate interests of the state, would thus control state politics for the next half century.[3]

Scott had inherited from his father, from his own work in the Grange, and from his experiences as a farmer the Populists' animosity toward big business along with their demand for a more democratic society, greater economic development, and increased aid to farmers. He accepted the premise that, for the state to prosper, the black community had to prosper but had difficulty achieving this goal so long as the corporate leaders and the conservative members of the Democratic Party used white supremacy to stay in power. Nonetheless, his Populist rhetoric and concern for the rural poor were significant aspects of his political success. Many historians would judge Kerr Scott as the most Populist of the state's governors.

While V. O. Key Jr. saw North Carolina as a progressive state, he admitted that, on many economic indices, the state ranked far down the ladder, even among southern states. The median income for families in 1950 was $2,121, and in rural areas the average was $1,304. Fifty-three percent of the state's population had incomes of less than $2,000, and 66 percent of those lived in rural areas. The state's main industries—textiles, furniture manufacturing, and tobacco—paid notoriously low wages, and labor unions had been vigorously suppressed. In 1947 some 42 percent of the workforce was engaged in farming-related industries, and 28 percent was employed in manufacturing jobs. While unemployment for whites was low, at 2.1 percent, the unemployment rate for Negroes was 5.3 percent. Illiteracy was a major problem, especially in the mountains and in rural areas. Citizens over twenty-five had completed an average of only 7.9 years in schools. For Negroes, that number was 5.9. There were no regional hospitals, no community colleges, no interstate highways, and very few opportunities for advancement for those in rural areas—many of whom had to live without telephones, electricity, and paved roads.

North Carolina's population had increased from 3,571,623 in 1940 to 4,061,929 in 1950, a gain of 490,306. Some of that increase came with an influx of new residents from the North. Many came with the military and stayed; others were attracted by retirement communities, resort developments, education opportunities, and jobs in manufacturing and textiles. There was also the beginning of an in-state migration as Negroes and farmers moved to the cities for better jobs. This migration marked the beginning of a trend toward urban growth. In 1950, Charlotte, with 134,102 inhabitants, was the only city in the state with a population over 100,000. The other five largest cities were Winston-Salem (87,811), Greensboro (74,389), Durham (73,368), Raleigh (65,679), and Asheville (58,437). The median age in the state was twenty-five, and only 5.5 percent of the state's citizens were over sixty-five. The foreign-born population was listed at 16,134 for the entire state. Nonwhite residents numbered 26.6 percent, and by every standard—jobs, education, voting rights, and health care—their opportunities were limited, and they languished behind whites in almost every category. Kerr Scott looked at these numbers and realized that the state had to expand services for its citizens, even if it meant raising taxes, and knew that the state would not budge from its low economic ranking unless there was a strong push for new roads, better schools, and a more industrialized society.

World War II had a major effect on all these statistics and helped move the state toward a stronger economy and a more democratic electorate. A large number of Negroes migrated to the North during the war years for jobs and better living conditions and returned with a new attitude toward civil rights. North Carolina soldiers had traveled all over the world and come home with a less parochial outlook and a more enlightened view of politics and a rapidly changing society. In 1948 the University of North Carolina, while regionally significant, had not yet achieved national stature. The state system had been favorably changed by a large influx of World War II veterans, who came to study on the GI Bill. These veterans were mature, hardworking students, eager to get their degrees and begin their business or professional careers. Clarence Mohr notes that the war greatly democratized access to southern colleges and universities. Southern universities expanded in both numbers and in quality and moved into the national mainstream. Attitudes among whites were modified by the war as well. Jim Cobb argues that the changes set in motion or intensified by the war had rendered W. J. Cash's version of the southern mind obsolete as southerners were now more heterogeneous, less exclusionary, and more democratic.[4]

The ideological dimensions of the war exposed weaknesses in the South's views on white superiority. The war had been waged against Germany, whose views of Aryan superiority and an end to democracy had motivated thousands of Americans to defeat the evil menace of Nazism. Now that the war had ended, what about the rights of Negroes in the South? Blacks were aware of the double standard and wanted a Double V—victory over tyranny in Europe and victory for civil rights in America. Tim S. R. Boyd demonstrated that the significant changes finally wrought by the 1960s civil rights movement were "largely the product of myriad social and economic developments that were already well under way by the end of World War II." All these changes undermined the basis for a one-party system in neighboring states like Georgia and eroded the economic underpinnings of white rule.[5]

North Carolina was considered to be more progressive on race than other southern states and did not exhibit the rigorous and confrontational approach to preserving white supremacy that the Deep South states did. With more enlightened leadership the state was less likely to resort to demagoguery and would be more amenable to changes in racial politics and economic development. While the state maintained a powerful commitment to the traditionalism of the South and remained distinctly southern, its expanding entrepreneurial spirit, its flexibility on race issues, its pursuit of improved education opportunities, and its progressive tendencies made it different from other southern states. Nonetheless, it had a history of white supremacy dating from the 1898–1900 racist campaigns, and the conservative element of the Democratic Party, by and large, wanted to maintain existing conditions and practiced segregationist politics.[6] Race remained a crucial issue in state politics, and candidates like Scott had to tread lightly on the subject as the majority of whites in the state were as yet unwilling to accept integration and their views would be revealed in the bitter Senate race of 1950.

The enormous military mobilization from 1941 to 1945 also created new opportunities for women. As Judy Barrett Litoff has explained, southern women joined women from throughout the nation in contributing to war bond drives, volunteering for military service, and assisting the Red Cross. Women seized new economic opportunities by taking over jobs vacated by men leaving for service. As Litoff notes, the war improved "the way women thought about themselves, expanding their horizons and affording them a clearer view of their capabilities."[7] As a result they became stronger and more self-reliant, and many of them supported Scott in 1948 and 1954 because he recognized their new status and believed in their drive for equality.

By any standards, World War II had a transformative effect on North Carolina, perhaps as significant as any event since the Civil War. In economic terms the reshaping of the state was dramatic. Sarah Lemmon, e.g., reported that, in addition to massive government spending ($2 billion alone for the purchase of manufactured goods in the state), North Carolina expanded its industrial base with shipbuilding (merchant marine ships, submarine chasers, ship repair stations), the production of furniture products, and the manufacture of rockets, radar components, machine-gun belts, airplanes, tents, blankets, towels, bandages, uniforms, hosiery, underwear (P. H. Hanes Knitting Co.), and other items for the war effort. The industrial expansion led to many skilled jobs outside agriculture and a burgeoning urbanization as farm workers moved to the cities or to work in the textile mills. As in many southern states, the population became more urban and less rural, and the balance of power shifted to the Piedmont. Farming remained an important part of the state's economic base, and the state's farmers responded to the great demand for their goods by tripling production during the war years.

The years from 1941 to 1945 brought greater wealth to the state as newly hired workers and GIs spent money on local goods and services. As the nation mobilized an ethnically diverse population into a military force, men and women from different cultures and backgrounds were brought together into a temporary melting pot. New factories were erected, and construction boomed, especially with the expansion of Fort Bragg, the largest artillery base in the world, and the building of the Cherry Point and Camp Lejeune marine bases. A total of fourteen new bases were constructed across the state during the war.[8] As a result of the economic revolution, the state began the transformation from a rural backwater into a modern, industrialized society.

Jennifer Brooks further expanded on the effect of World War II by concluding that the powerful forces of change put economic, social, racial, and political relations in flux, generating a political instability that permeated the postwar era at every level, eventually leading to greater political competition. In North Carolina, the war experience politicized and energized many of the returning GIs, who wanted to improve political and economic opportunity in their state. Their disenchantment with the status quo led to activism on the part of veterans, liberals, blacks, and labor unions.[9] These groups, yearning for a more democratic and equitable government, formed the vanguard of Scott's fight against machine politics.

Even with these momentous changes buffeting the political landscape, why would Kerr Scott, a relative unknown, challenge twenty years of effective machine control? Despite the population changes, one could not predict how active the new voters would be or how they would vote. There was increasing disquiet among farmers and activity on the part of veterans, blacks, and labor unions, but could those constituencies be organized? How would conservative Democrats react to aggressive action by blacks and labor unions?

Despite the uncertainty, Scott realized that change was in the air, and he believed he was in a position to take advantage of the unsettled conditions in the state. To begin with, he had much greater ambition than even his closest friends realized. He knew from experience that he was a capable politician and an inventive political strategist. He had run successfully in three statewide elections and had proved to be an efficient administrator as commissioner of agriculture. He was intelligent, honest, and hardworking and exuded a certain folksy charisma—people liked and trusted him. He already had in place a legion of followers around the state, cultivated while he was commissioner of agriculture. He did not command a political organization per se; rather, he counted on a loyal group of friends and advocates for aid and support.

Scott had traveled extensively around the state and recognized the rising unrest over a conservative government and the growing displeasure over the disparity between the rich and the poor. He himself had grown weary of rule by lawyers and bankers and thought the people felt the same. He realized that farmers and those in rural areas considered themselves to be treated as second-class citizens. He heard numerous complaints on his journeys and knew instinctively that there was a burgeoning movement clamoring for change. He believed that he could be the architect of that change. He truly wanted to better the condition of the poorer class in the state, and he would be their champion—their spokesman. This revolution, in Scott's mind, was not simply class warfare. As a committed progressive reformer, he became convinced that his leadership and ideas would prove beneficial to all citizens of North Carolina.

Ralph Scott once asked his brother why he wanted to run for governor. Ralph said: "You're a layman. I can see where a lawyer would run, it gives him connections of one kind or another. And he can help his practice. You can't get nothing out of it." Kerr replied: "I want to go to Raleigh to represent those people that don't have any lobbyists down there. That's my main reason for wanting to go. I have no objections to Duke Power and Carolina Power and Light and the telephone people making money, . . . but they've got a franchise to serve an area and I want them to give service to those people . . . out in the rural areas."[10] His son, Bob Scott, remembered that these issues of rural roads, phones, decent schoolhouses, and electricity affected him so strongly because he had grown up in Hawfields, a rural area where families, including the Scotts, had fought for years, often without success, for those same essentials.[11]

It might seem unusual for Kerr Scott, born and raised in a hidebound cultural tradition in an isolated rural area, to be a visionary, but he was. Although limited in his perspective, he realized that, after World War II, the state had huge possibilities for growth. Bob Scott later recalled that his father had impeccable timing in his quest for the governor's office. Kerr Scott perceived that the needs of the state had been neglected during the war years, 1941–1945. Bob Scott noted: "They [North Carolina] had a huge surplus backed up in the state treasury. So my dad proposed spending the money for services—schools and roads and telephones. . . . That was his platform. He struck a real note with people."[12] Kerr Scott concluded that the state would not progress sufficiently if the conservative, status quo Shelby dynasty stayed in power. The Squire of Haw River realized that Charlie Johnson, the state treasurer and the machine's next pick for governor, would continue the moderate, stand-pat policies of his predecessors and had to be defeated.

For Scott's reforms to succeed, the state had to restore the rural population to a status of equality in terms of opportunity. Only when the less fortunate were given better education, better health care, and better roads would the entire state prosper. In 1953 Governor Scott explained that he became a candidate for governor "because of . . . two convictions, . . . that rural North Carolina was a land of forgotten people and that what is bad for two-thirds of the people is bad for all."[13]

On January 10, 1948, Kerr Scott surprised the state when he announced that he would not be a candidate for reelection as commissioner of agriculture. He did not offer an explanation for his decision other than to say, "I just thought it was time for a change." He indicated that he did not plan to run for any other job but expected to return to his dairy farm in Alamance County: "I have 200 cows there and I don't have to hunt for a job."[14]

Few observers believed that Scott intended to retire from public life. After hearing of his decision not to run for reelection, Lynn Nisbet, an influential political commentator, remarked: "Now, I know who is going to be the next governor of North Carolina."[15]

The following day, the *Durham Morning Herald* quoted Scott as insisting: "I did not resign with the intention of running for governor." He then grinned and added: "So many of my friends have been stirring it up over the past two days that I may give it some consideration."[16] In the next week or so, many friends contacted Scott, encouraging him to run. E. B. Jeffress, the owner of the *Greensboro Daily News,* pointed out that the state was not progressing as it should, that the people were looking for a new leader, and that Scott seemed a good one. Jeffress feared that North Carolina would lapse into complacency and would be too conservative to meet the expanding needs of the state. While agreeing with Jeffress's views, Scott felt reluctant to declare his candidacy. Jeffress thought that Scott had the key elements of leadership and could "arouse people to his cause" and hoped that Scott would change his mind.[17]

Scott remained undecided, but pressure mounted in early January 1948 for him to declare. The *Raleigh News and Observer* predicted that he would announce for governor within ten days. Scott, still on the fence, observed: "I've had some requests that I run, but not 400,000 of them yet."[18]

It turned out that Scott had been contemplating running for governor for some time. He kept putting off a final decision, wondering whether the timing was right, whether he could raise enough money, and whether he could beat the chosen candidate of the Shelby dynasty, Charles Johnson. Johnson had a huge head start as he had declared his candidacy in April 1947, thirteen months before the date of the Democratic primary. Scott, who understood the political power structure in the state, went to see Robert M. Hanes, the wealthy, influential president of Wachovia Bank, now the de facto leader of the Gardner machine. He wanted to determine whether he had any chance of becoming governor. Hanes told him that he had no chance and could not win for two reasons—Johnson had already been anointed, and Scott was from the western part of the state. Since Governor R. Gregg Cherry had been from the west, the next governor should reside in the east. Thus the selection of Johnson, who was from Burgaw, in the east. Hanes noted that the state had a long-standing tradition that the governor's office rotated from west to east and back again each election, and he respected that tradition.[19]

Although Hanes had discouraged Scott from running, some observers felt that Hanes and the Shelby dynasty were not very excited about Charlie Johnson and thought Scott might have a shot.[20] Others, like Capus Waynick, were unsure about his chances. Waynick asked former governor J. C. B. Ehringhaus whether Scott had a chance in 1948. Ehringhaus replied: "He hasn't a chance in a thousand. No chance in the world of being governor."[21]

Still unwilling to take the plunge, Scott faced dire political circumstances if he waited much longer to announce. Charlie Johnson had already been campaigning for nine months, and the political pundits considered him a shoo-in. All he had to do was put his name on the ballot. Even more daunting, there were two other viable and attractive candidates hard at work, R. Mayne Albright, a World War II veteran, and Oscar Barker, a state representative from Durham. Another possible opponent, attorney Willis Smith, had been deterred by the seemingly insurmountable position held by Johnson. Scott benefited when William B. Umstead, at the time the most favored and formidable candidate of the machine, had been appointed to the US Senate in 1946 on the death of Senator Josiah Bailey. Umstead was running to keep his Senate seat, not for governor.[22]

While Scott vacillated, Charlie Johnson had been building an effective and extensive organization throughout the state. He had already obtained the backing of the majority of the state legislators as well as many mayors, county commissioners, and appointed officials. Selected as state treasurer by Governor O. Max Gardner in 1932, Johnson had been reelected three times and had an unblemished record. The Pender County native had spent his life in public service and had long desired the governor's office. The machine, however, had asked him to wait his turn until 1948, and now Johnson believed the office would at last be his.[23] He organized a fifty-member advisory committee to help in his campaign and eventually selected the current speaker of the House, Tom Pearsall, as his campaign manager.[24] He had also already received significant money and assistance from some of the most powerful businessmen in the state, including Robert M. Hanes and the textile magnate Charles Cannon.[25]

At this point most Tar Heels assumed that Johnson would be the next governor. Albright was too young and inexperienced, and Oscar Barker did not have the money or the name recognition. Scott's cause seemed hopeless. Even if he announced immediately, in late January 1948, he would have only four months to set up a viable campaign organization, raise money, and hit the hustings. Facing an established opponent with money, connections, and machine support, he had, everyone agreed, slim chances indeed.

The cigar-chomping Squire of Haw River remained interested but continued to equivocate. Scott decided to seek advice from the longtime political leader Major L. P. McLendon. McLendon, an influential Greensboro attorney and the son-in-law of Charles B. Aycock, encouraged Scott by explaining that North Carolina was ripe for a "ground swell" against the machine as he believed the people of the state no longer would permit their governors to be named in advance by political "big wheels"—it was time for the people to speak.[26]

Other prominent leaders who disliked Johnson and favored Scott also thought it was time for a change. Capus Waynick reported hearing a conversation between a judge and a state supreme court justice in Raleigh that, he assumed, reflected the general opinion in the state: "I'll tell you this Judge, Charlie Johnson will be elected by the biggest vote in the history of North Carolina. He has every county commissioner, every county officer and their employees working for him. He is known all over the state and worked for the counties so long that he is just unbeatable." Waynick interrupted the conversation: "Gentlemen, you may be correct, but Charlie Johnson should not be governor of North Carolina and if I can help it he is not going to be."[27]

Encouraged by McLendon's words, Waynick's support, entreaties by his friends, and a sense that North Carolinians resented having their governor chosen for them, Scott took a major step by deciding, on January 21, that he would announce for governor "if the home folks here in Alamance want me to get out there and fight." A committee of Alamance citizens, led by the textile manufacturer B. Everett Jordan of Saxapahaw, agreed to take an informal statewide "honest poll" and report back to Scott in a week. "We're going to find out how things stand." Jordan noted that, if Scott decided to run, he would "fight for him all the way."

Scott, speaking before a gathering of local supporters, promised "a grand and serious fight if you want one," but he recognized that the effort would require substantial financial backing. "I understand," he noted, "that my major opponent has all the money he needs and that he can get more." He also alluded to the other difficulties he faced: "I'm mindful that time is short. Lots of folks say that all the commitments have been made that are necessary. That doesn't bother me a bit." He was confident that, "if the people want it done," he could quickly gear up the race for governor: "It's now or never." He knew that it would take hard work, a good manager, a publicity man, and an effective get-out-the-vote grassroots effort. If the people wanted him to run, he promised to "put on the damndest campaign you ever saw."[28]

After hearing Scott speak, many of his advocates at the Alamance meeting hoped that he would soon declare. The superior court judge Leo Carr called him "a man . . . who has the political courage to express his mind." Carr declared that there were many people in public office who were too concerned about public opinion: "Scott is not like that. He is governed by what he thinks is right."[29]

Sensing that Scott was leaning toward entering the race, the public clamor for his candidacy increased exponentially with a flood of letters, phone calls, and personal entreaties. Johnson's backers, alarmed by the rising tide of support, suggested that Scott run for lieutenant governor instead. When informed of this recommendation, Scott rubbed his chin thoughtfully and added: "Of course, all that's for the purpose of keeping me out of this race. I don't know a lot about politics but I know a little and catch on right quick." Johnson's proponents then hinted that Scott might want to wait for four years and run for governor in 1952. When these suggestions did not take, Tom Pearsall paid a personal visit to Scott, urging him not to run. Scott thanked him for the visit but refused his request.[30]

According to one report, the survey conducted by B. Everett Jordan and friends indicated that Scott would have great difficulty defeating Johnson and probably could not win. Ralph Scott asked Kerr what he would do if he did not run, and Scott responded by saying that he would return to the farm and continue in the dairy business. Ralph said: "Well, a race won't delay that but six months. Let's go."[31]

After a series of all-night conferences with family and advisers, Scott announced: "We decided that I ought to get in there. These folks have surveyed the state and decided my chances are good." On February 6, 1948, he made the announcement many had expected for several weeks: "I have decided to become a candidate for the Democratic nomination for governor in the 1948 primary. I shall resign immediately from the office of Commissioner of Agriculture because I feel that no man occupying a high state office can serve the people while campaigning for the governorship. The people are entitled to know—adequately and without a doubt—the essential facts about a candidate and the things for which he stands. I intend to guarantee them this opportunity and right."[32] R. Mayne Albright concluded that Scott's entry made it a new and vastly different race.[33]

Scott's decision to resign his position as commissioner of agriculture was the opening salvo of the campaign and immediately put Johnson on the defensive. The *Durham Morning Herald* pointed out that Johnson had stated that he had no intention of resigning unless it so happened that he could not give proper service to the treasurer's office. The paper surmised that the people of the state would welcome Scott's honesty in resigning his post and would condemn Johnson for not taking similar action. It was unthinkable, concluded the paper, that one could wage an industrious campaign and still be worth as much to the citizens in his job as he would otherwise. The Johnson clique in Raleigh greeted Scott's announcement with studied disdain, and Johnson had no comment. Mayne Albright judged that Scott would need some real money if he expected to defeat Johnson because "Cholly" was "trained under the Shelby system and has been eating off the state training table for years."[34]

Editorial comments from around the state welcomed the prospect of a real campaign for governor as there had been little interest in the contest up to this point. The *Raleigh News and Observer* found Scott's entry a "wholesome development" and good for democratic government.[35] The *Durham Morning Herald* conjectured that, while Scott might have been a reluctant candidate in the beginning, very encouraging reports from across the state and opposition to Johnson pushed him into the contest. The election was now no longer a walkaway.[36] Scott's hometown paper, the *Burlington Daily Times News,* praised him for taking on the Shelby dynasty and its propensity for picking governors a decade ahead. That concept was too restrictive and did not allow for "open field" running. The paper quoted Lynn Nisbet, the head of the North Carolina Association of Afternoon Newspapers, as stating that Scott would surely run an offensive campaign and that the fireworks were about to begin. One wag observed that Johnson's supporters' attempts to eliminate any significant opponent had worked with Lindsay Warren, Willis Smith, and Kenneth Royall, who decided not to run, but what they had done "was to drown a bag full of kittens and now they've got a live wildcat on their hands."[37]

Although well imbued with Presbyterian values and a strong believer in thrift, honesty, and family values, Scott occasionally resorted to salty language to get his points across. As the campaign commenced, his advisers, understanding that he often spoke his mind without concern for the consequences, had to scrutinize his comments and speeches carefully. One example of his straightforwardness came when he was asked why he waited until February to announce for governor. He replied: "You can't keep a hard on for nine months."[38]

Roy Wilder Jr., a Scott adherent, well understood Scott's use of the vernacular. In his book *You All Spoken Here,* Wilder discussed the use of southern speech: "Here in the South . . . , we aren't inhibited in our talk. We turn the spigot on and let it burble. . . . In our flow of talk there often are phrases full of humor, of poetry, of beauty. . . . There is speech irreverent and impertinent, brash with bogus insults and mock abuse. Country humor is found in much of our talk, often earthy and seldom subtle, for pallid and insipid observations aren't inherent in our make of expression."[39] This is how Scott spoke; it was who he was. Even if his sometimes coarse verbiage offended or upset the privileged class, he had to be true to himself, or he would lose the approbation of the Branchhead Boys. On the other hand, his handlers had to keep a close watch on his activities lest he lose votes with unappreciated verbal blasts. Standing up for what one believed was fine, but an overdose could send voters scurrying into one's opponent's camp.

Scott's home folks celebrated his decision to run by turning out to give him an enthusiastic send-off. Scott said: "I'm ready to go and I'm going to need your help. You realize I have a big handicap by getting in so late, but I think it can be done." The locals announced that they were for him 100 percent and seemed pleased he was finally in the contest.[40] On February 8, W. Kerr Scott paid his $150 filing fee, which he noted was "the price of a good cow," and the race was on.[41]

Johnson made the first strategic move in the campaign when he came out in favor of a $100 million bond issue for the purpose of financing the improvement of rural roads—a blatant attempt to gain support from the farmers—Scott's largest constituency.[42] Johnson divulged that the other candidates had talked about doing something for rural roads but noted: "They haven't offered a solution." He thought it better to borrow the funds now than wait "for current revenues to do the job." This proposal was not in character with his traditional fiscal views, but he hoped that the idea would benefit him politically.[43]

While Johnson progressed with his platform and organization, little had been heard from Kerr Scott. He did manage to open his campaign headquarters in Raleigh at the Carolina Hotel on February 16,[44] but he explained that he would not get out and make any speeches and planned to stay "as close as possible to Raleigh." He was so far behind in campaign organization that he had to spend his time setting up the necessary apparatus.[45] He limited his active campaigning, but by March 1 he still had not picked a campaign manager,[46] and those backing his campaign became antsy. What was he doing? Where were the attacks on machine politics? When would he get into full campaign mode?

Behind the scenes Scott had picked Charlie Parker as his publicity agent[47] and had begun writing letters asking for political help and financial aid. Ralph Scott, Kerr's younger brother, did much of the letter writing in search of help to run the race. He penned a note to Staley Cook on February 16, 1948, in which he made clear that most of the dairy farmers in the state would back Kerr and described things as "very encouraging" so far. He expected his brother to lead in the first primary.[48] Ralph wrote many letters to other possible adherents, explaining that Kerr's success would depend on their help and that he would appreciate anything they could do.[49]

During much of January and February 1948, Johnson maintained a low-key campaign and ventured out only infrequently, making speeches to carefully chosen audiences. Johnson, like Governor Thomas E. Dewey in the November 1948 presidential race, knew he was the prohibitive favorite and tried not to make any egregious mistakes. "We do not believe," he said, "that the people of the state are particularly interested in what the several candidates think about each other; therefore we do not intend to engage in personalities."[50] This statement, of course, came when Johnson and the machine arrogantly assumed victory: they would later change their tune.

Mayne Albright and Oscar Barker energetically careened around the state seeking votes. Albright, a favorite of labor and World War II veterans, established mobile headquarters in a trailer, and by early February he had already visited seventy-one of the one hundred counties.[51]

Even at this juncture the real battle was between Johnson and Scott, and Barker quickly faded from view. One small-town newspaper, The Elizabeth City Independent understood the changing political attitudes in the Tar Heel state and early on predicted problems for the Gardner machine. The paper described the current machine as "a ship without a rudder" and opined: "Never has the machine been threatened with such formidable opposition as Scott offers it." The paper, very prescient in its prognostication, foresaw that voters would lean toward Scott because of his forthright honesty and ability to get things done. Why did the people like him? "[He] will no more hesitate to put his foot into the backsides of a big politician than he will the smallest employee of the state, if he thinks that man isn't doing his job."[52]

In late February Scott finally showed a little life in a talk before the Business and Professional Women's Club of Durham. He did not present a detailed platform except to say he was for better roads, schools, medical care, and the development of the state's natural resources. He declared emphatically that he was the candidate of all segments of society. He noted that he had not originally intended to run for governor when he resigned public office but that an overwhelming swell of public support persuaded him to enter the race. What he called the "crown princes in state politics" asked him to wait four or eight years: "They told me they had already picked your governor for you. They are asking you now to confirm their choice in the Democratic primary on May 29. I say to you that you ought to be allowed to choose your own governor."[53]

Scott dithered about choosing a campaign manager, and this delay created worry and consternation among his constituents. He finally decided to run his own campaign—a highly unusual and risky maneuver since no candidates in recent years had run without an outside manager. He said one advantage was that he would make his own commitments and not be beholden to a campaign manager's promises.[54]

While Scott struggled with managerial problems, Johnson stayed on a straight and steady course. He repeated his view that the state needed all-weather highways for rural routes to serve school buses and called attention to his desire to put any bond issue to a vote of the people. The state treasurer wanted taxes held at the current level, described the state's finances as excellent, and noted that the state would have a large surplus at the end of the fiscal year.[55]

Scott responded to the treasury surplus by telling an audience of Granville County farmers that either the surplus should be "used to render service to the state" or taxes should be reduced. He did not, however, want to reduce taxes. He wanted to meet some of the demands for increased public service in the state, that is, money for education, roads, and medical care. His view was that there was not a surplus in funds but a deficit in public services.[56]

On Monday, March 15, over a month after he officially entered the race, Scott hit the hustings in earnest. The Squire of Haw River opened with a radio speech carried over the Tobacco Network. In his talk he emphasized the essence of his message to the people—increased teacher salaries and lower teaching loads; increased state aid for school buildings; better rural roads; and better medical care. Scott said he would favor the complete program recommended by the state Medical Care Commission, including a four-year medical school and teaching hospital at the University of North Carolina in Chapel Hill—a proposal he had previously criticized.[57]

Aspirant Scott's initial foray into the political battleground created barely a ripple as newspapers gave his speech perfunctory treatment. As his own campaign manager, Scott had failed to effectively promote his candidacy. A critical juncture in his quest for office was at hand. Fortunately, after a long and difficult process, Scott managed to persuade Capus Waynick to come on board as assistant campaign manager and the éminence grise of the group. He acknowledged that he was glad to have Waynick with him because of his experience in state government. Waynick had served in both branches of the General Assembly, had been chairman of the state Highway Commission, and had been editor of the *High Point Enterprise*. He was from the Piedmont and had excellent contacts around the state.

Waynick agreed to aid Scott "because it is apparent that the candidate needs to be relieved of duties in his Raleigh headquarters in order that he may carry his candidacy directly to the people all over the state." He asserted that in his fifteen years in state government he had not seen "a more resolutely competent person enter public administration" than Kerr Scott, who would end the lag in public service and put to rout those men who were in government for personal gain. At the same time as he got help from Waynick, Scott appointed a woman, Estelle T. Smith, as associate manager in charge of women's issues.[58]

More intriguing than the public comments made by Waynick was the inside story of how he came to the aid of Scott and saved the campaign. In a letter written to Kerr Scott on February 20, 1955, Waynick spelled out the sequence of events leading to his commitment to Scott's campaign. Scott had approached Waynick on several occasions to join his team, but he refused. Waynick did not think Charlie Johnson should be governor of the state, but he was not sure that Scott could win. Scott came to Waynick, knowing that his campaign had bogged down, and said: "I have a funny feeling that if you'll join me, I'll win and if you don't, I can't."[59]

Waynick recalled that he took the job knowing it was a gamble as Scott's chances of winning were slim, but he did so without hope of personal gain because of what Scott could do for the public good.[60] When Scott replied to Ambassador Waynick's 1955 letter, he agreed with Waynick's recollection of the events: "I believe you stated the case about as it was or I recall it. I appreciate what you did."[61]

Now that he had some assistance in Raleigh, Scott went out to line up

Ad for Scott in the 1948 gubernatorial campaign. Kerr Scott Papers, courtesy of the State Archives of North Carolina, Raleigh.

his county managers. Lauch Faircloth remembered his part in the 1948 campaign and his view of Charlie Johnson—"the most pompous son-of-a-bitch I have ever in my life seen." Faircloth, a twenty-year-old who had been working on his father's farm, had heard of Scott and knew "he had a lot of appeal." Scott asked Faircloth to manage his campaign in Sampson County, but Faircloth said he didn't know anything about political races. Scott said: "Son, you can do it. All you have to do is nail up a couple of placards." Faircloth agreed: "When I left that night I was the county manager."

As Faircloth began to work for Scott, he made a discovery: "I found out that I was a fool because everybody in the county was for Charlie Johnson. It was already predetermined that he was going to be governor. The county Democratic organization was for him." One businessman called him an idiot for getting into something he knew nothing about and predicted that "the cow milker wouldn't get any votes." Nonetheless, he dutifully posted placards, talked to some people, and raised a little money. And that was how Lauch Faircloth, later a US senator, got into politics.[62]

While Johnson expanded his selection of new managers into fifteen counties, Scott spent a week "politiking" down east. After a visit to Manteo, he exhibited his wry sense of humor. The locals told him that he was "the first candidate who ever came down that way and left without promising them a bridge."[63] Back at headquarters, the Waynick-led team mounted an attempt to raise badly needed funds. Scott sent out a form letter asking for suggestions and monetary contributions: "I would much rather be elected governor of all the people than go in there with just a few rich men contributing to my campaign, thereby making me feel under obligation to them when matters came before the governor to be acted on affecting all our people."[64] His control central also sent out a postcard dated March 28, 1948, presenting him as "The People's Candidate for Governor," a slogan much repeated during the coming months. The mailing, with the heading "Go Forward with Scott," stressed that Scott had resigned his state position and was not running for governor at the taxpayers' expense. He had become an office seeker only when asked by "thousands of North Carolinians who are fed up with having a political machine pick their candidate for them."[65] This theme became the emphasis for the remainder of the race, since a contest between the people and machine politics gave Scott the best chance for victory. The election was always about the haves versus the have-nots, rural versus urban, and Scott versus the Gardner machine.

Ralph Scott and other staff members acknowledged that black voters would be crucial in a close contest and early on began a surreptitious effort to woo Negro leaders. Ralph Scott wrote the influential T. J. Hamme, asking him to use his contacts throughout the state to get out the vote for Scott. Hamme replied immediately and offered to "serve any way I can." He later met with Kerr Scott in Raleigh and set up a group that would solicit votes from "the Negro citizens of this state." He advised Ralph Scott to advertise in The Carolinian, the black newspaper in Raleigh.[66] The Scott forces continued to work with Negro leaders throughout the campaign but kept these contacts secret so that the solicitation of black votes never became a campaign issue.

On March 30, Charlie Johnson officially opened his campaign at a rally in Burgaw. He denied, without using the specific word, that he was the candidate of any machine or political faction or group. He was running in his own right and would make no commitments to any group that would in any way limit his "fullest liberty of action."[67] However, the very fact that the state revenue commissioner, the conservation director, the paroles commissioner, the state highway commissioner, and the utility commissioner attended the rally provided resounding proof that he was at the very least the candidate of the establishment.

His formal platform differed little from what Johnson had covered in previous speeches. Increased salaries and reduced classroom loads for teachers, a school health program and new school buildings, a referendum on a bond issue for secondary roads, a reasonable expansion of state services, and increased emphasis on establishing industry in rural areas. All this, he surmised, could be obtained without "additional taxes and without departing from the principles of sound fiscal administration."[68]

In Burgaw the Johnson backers handed out leaflets raising the east-west issue. In North Carolina, tradition mandated that the governor, the speaker of the state House of Representatives, and the US senators be rotated every election cycle between the east and the west. The time-honored agreement was not in the state's constitution but over the years had become a gentleman's agreement. The original line, drawn up around 1835, was between what Albert Coates called the "agricultural East" and the "industrial West," but the line had fluctuated over the years. The need for such a line came about because of inequities between the two regions. Initially, the western part of the state felt left out in a state legislature dominated by the agrarian interests of the east. Later, with the industrialization and urbanization of the Piedmont region, the influence of the west increased and put the agricultural and poorer eastern part of the state in fear of a limited influence on state government and reduced largesse from the state. There was also always a racial and cultural component to the east-west issue since the great majority of blacks resided in the eastern part of the state.[69]

By 1948 the east-west tradition was less significant as an issue than it had been in previous years, but it was still important. In 1948 it was the east's turn to have a governor, and Charlie Johnson, the eastern candidate, opened his campaign by accusing Scott of being from the west: "Preserve Party harmony—Give the East Its Governor. By the terms of the rotation agreement, Alamance has always been considered in the west."[70] Scott, however, went to great lengths to persuade voters that he was an easterner. He declared that Alamance County was twenty miles to the east of the geographic center of the state, that the population center was thirty miles west of his home, and that his home county of Alamance was in the eastern judicial district.[71] These arguments put to rest any lingering controversy over whether Scott was an easterner. The *Burlington Times News* ran an editorial denouncing the idea of putting geography before men. The so-called east-west tradition merely perpetuated the trading of the governor's office between political leaders.

This idea, wrote the paper, put a limit on the right to run and should have been discarded years ago.[72]

By the end of March, Lynn Nisbet pronounced that the race had narrowed to a contest between Scott and Johnson, although Albright and Barker would get enough votes to force a second primary. Albright, in particular, had run a vigorous and effective race. Few gave him a chance to make the runoff, but he would be in a strategic position to influence the winner in a second primary.[73]

In early April, Scott stepped up his activity in his quest for the governor's mansion. He spent two days in the Wilmington area and spoke in Charlotte and at the Kiwanis Club in Kings Mountain. In Southport, he lamented the "unwholesome conditions" in state schools, where teachers were paid less than farmhands. The state had to act quickly, he warned, to keep the school system from "falling apart."[74]

As the hype surrounding and the attention paid to this important race increased, North Carolina residents enjoyed a moment of levity when the *Raleigh News and Observer* did a feature on the most obscure participant in the contest—Olla Ray Boyd, a pig-breeding political perennial from Pinetown who had run for governor in 1944, garnering some 2,069 votes statewide. Despite the paucity of votes, he decided to run again in 1948 as the publicity helped his pig business and shrub sales. At six foot four and 277 pounds, he advertised himself as the "biggest hog breeder in the state," a title no one disputed. A bachelor, Olla Ray lived with his mother and admitted to never having had a love affair but also to being open to opportunity. Not only was he proposing a 40 percent pay raise for teachers; he was offering "any of them a chance at being the first lady of the state."[75]

Scott, of course, paid no attention to Olla Ray; he concentrated on his most important problem—raising enough money to keep the campaign on track. The campaign had only about $5,000 available for radio time, newspaper ads, and transcription costs.[76] To replenish the coffers, Charlie Parker prepared the mailing of some seven thousand letters to "Fellow Democrats," asking for help to elect Kerr Scott, "who will be governor of all the people." The appeal lamented the fact that Scott's opponent had three of the richest men in the state aiding his effort and that the Scotts simply did not have as much money as the Johnson crowd. More money was needed to run a viable campaign.[77]

The intervention of B. Everett Jordan helped save the Scott crusade. Jordan had been an effective fund-raiser for the Democratic Party, and Mary,

Kerr Scott's wife, was one of B. Everett's favorite cousins. As Ralph Scott told the story: "[Jordan backed Kerr up] in every way he could; not only with his own money but he got his friends to contribute, and that meant so much. I doubt that Kerr would ever have been governor if it hadn't been for Everett and folks like him." Ralph recounted visiting headquarters in the early days of the election and discovering that they did not even have enough money for postage: "[Jordan] gave me $4,000 to take down to headquarters—$4,000 at that time was a whale of a lot of money, but such things like that saved the day for Kerr."[78]

Bolstered by the infusion of cash, Scott stepped up his appearances and planned nine talks for April 5–9.[79] As soon as Scott expanded his operations, Mayne Albright charged that "more than one" candidate was trying to buy the election. The Haw River farmer reacted by saying that he did not expect to exceed the $12,000 first primary limit set by state law. Scott defused Albright's charge with humor, adding: "Over at Spring Hope they have put up a big street sign, 'We're Hot for Scott.' I didn't tell them to put it up and I didn't pay for it, but I don't intend to ask them to take it down."[80]

In Confidential Bulletin no. 2, the Scott organization listed the candidate's schedule for the week of April 11–17, which included appearances at the Rotary Club in Roanoke Rapids and speeches in High Point, Chapel Hill, Durham, and Newton. The bulletin told Scott workers that their candidate had "exploded the first in a series of bombs" in Wilmington, the headquarters of the Tidewater Power Company. Scott claimed that the area was being "strangled economically by excessive electric power rates and as governor he would use all his power to relieve the area of this disabling condition." He pointed out that the Tidewater Power Company rates were higher than those offered by a comparable company in another part of the state. That differential was a direct loss to the customers, and the high rates also retarded industrial development in the area when cheap rates would provide great economic benefits to everyone.[81] It was a typical Scott maneuver—bearding the lion in its den—and he benefited from the publicity stirred up by such brash confrontations. Capus Waynick said that Scott liked "to change things . . . do unusual things." He acted as a catalytic force and ignored traditional methods and attitudes.[82] Lynn Nisbet agreed: "[Scott] is reverting to type as an iconoclast and rampager, in contrast with his dignified and sedate conformity to custom during previous weeks."[83]

Scott headquarters had finally gotten up to speed. The hierarchy sent out samples of revised Scott campaign pamphlets and posters and mailed out suggested radio spots for local stations as well as advertising copy for newspapers.[84] In addition, full-page ads appeared in small-town newspapers, labor periodicals, veterans' publications, and health-care centers all over the state, touting the man from Haw River as a patriotic veteran and a dependable and courageous leader.[85]

Scott revisited the east-west issue in a speech in Alexander County. He knew the previous importance of the issue but tried to downplay its significance in 1948: "[The] machine in Raleigh is spreading the misinformation in the east that I am a westerner because they are desperate. They haven't got a strong candidate and they haven't gotten any response to the real issues they have raised so they are trying to manufacture an issue out of geographical inaccuracy. The people of North Carolina won't swallow that one any more than they will a candidate for governor handpicked for them by a machine eight years in advance."[86]

Charlie Johnson continued to believe that he would win easily, apparently unaware that he was losing his big lead to the fast-charging Scott. As the fifty-seven-year-old, white-haired treasurer traveled the state, it became apparent to voters that he was not a very good public speaker. His talks lacked humor, and he relied too much on logic backed by facts rather than rhetoric, but he got his points across. He continued to run on his record of public service and his extensive knowledge of state finances: "I would like to wind up my career as Governor. . . . I wasn't drafted by anybody; I didn't ask anyone if I could run. The Governor's office is the highest in state government and it is natural for one to aspire to it."[87]

Johnson headquarters sent a pamphlet to potential supporters, proclaiming his expertise and experience in improving municipalities in the state. The pamphlet quoted favorable editorials by several state newspapers. The *Charlotte Observer* praised him as having one of the best minds in the state, and the *Albemarle News and Press* noted that his advice and counsel to local governments over the years had been most helpful. The *Greensboro Daily News* wrote: "Tradition and precedent are with Mr. Johnson." The pamphlet also listed Johnson's qualifications for office. He had served as a sergeant in World War I, had been chairman of the state Banking Commission, and was a deacon in and the treasurer of his Presbyterian church. Johnson was eminently qualified to be governor.[88]

On paper, Johnson looked great—more experienced than Scott and a sure winner—but elections are not decided by résumés. And, in this election, Johnson's experience as treasurer would backfire on him as Scott's analysts focused on what would prove to be one of the decisive issues in the campaign. Capus Waynick spied the opening—the failure of state deposits in banks to earn interest—and recommended an assault on Johnson based on it. Seeking specific information about state deposits, Waynick persuaded Don L. Spence, a Republican, to write Treasurer Johnson and request information about where public funds had been deposited and what interest had been earned.[89] The six-page report Johnson sent to Spence showed that 239 banks and branches in all one hundred counties had been used for state deposits of up to $171 million—all without earning interest. Johnson explained that the state treasurer had very little discretion as to how or where state funds were invested since state regulations specified that only state or federal bonds could be purchased for investment of state funds.[90]

Scott immediately pounced. He asserted that Johnson "has been losing a million dollars a year for the taxpayers" by not investing millions of dollars of surplus state funds into interest-bearing accounts instead of leaving them with state banks as demand deposits at no interest. Furthermore, continued Scott, state law allowed Johnson to put these funds in interest-bearing securities that were readily convertible to cash.[91] Scott hit Johnson in a vulnerable spot. Since Johnson was running on his expertise and judgment as state treasurer, Scott wondered why he had not invested state funds to gain interest? Did he not know the law? Was he favoring large state banks that would profit by using state funds without paying interest? If the law did prohibit him from investing in interest-bearing notes, why did he not push to have the law changed? Scott made it appear that Johnson was the machine candidate and a treasurer who favored wealthy bankers. Lynn Nisbet maintained that Scott's strategic shift from the early "lamb-like" Scott to a more aggressive stance put Johnson on the defensive, and although Johnson remained the front-runner, the attacks hurt.[92]

Throughout his odyssey, Scott repeatedly emphasized his key issues. He challenged the state to develop the potential and skills of its young people through a revitalized and expanded school system; otherwise it would never go forward: "My judgment is that the best tax dollar is that transmuted into public service, whether used in building a farm-to-market road or paying a competent person to teach a child."[93] Scott urged that more money, "now piled up in banks without interest," had to be invested in N.C.'s most important crop—"its oncoming generation of boys and girls."[94] He considered the education situation so dire that he urged Governor Cherry to call a special session of the General Assembly to "deal with the crisis in public schools."[95]

Two ads designed by the Scott campaign attacking Scott's opponent, Charles Johnson, the state treasurer, for his constant changing of positions and his failure to earn interest from state bank deposits. Kerr Scott Papers, courtesy of the State Archives of North Carolina, Raleigh.

Capus Waynick organized a backbreaking schedule for Scott as the candidate worked to get his message to the voters. On April 18, Scott spoke in Union County in the morning, had lunch in Stanly County, and spent the afternoon in Cabarrus County. He then flew to Wilmington on April 20 for the Azalea Festival before returning to Mt. Airy for an afternoon rally.[96] The next week saw more of the same—first Charlotte, then back to Wilmington, and by the end of the week visits to Laurinburg, Onslow County, Moore County, and Lee County and a return trip to Charlotte.[97]

On his visit to Charlotte, Scott, with characteristic vigor, insisted that he was not antimachine but the candidate of all the people. He managed, with a wry smile, to divulge that, after his criticism of $171 million in surplus state funds not being invested properly, suddenly Governor Cherry put $15 million into federal government bonds. Why did the governor wait until now, and why should Johnson continue to control these funds?[98]

Scott's strategists worked hard to get the women's vote and the farm vote, knowing that these constituencies could spell the difference between victory and defeat. Waynick welcomed the support of Mrs. Sarah L. Avery, who described Scott as "a good man," noting: "We need some changes in the direction the state government is moving."[99] Waynick rejoiced when Susie Sharp, later appointed by Scott as a superior court judge, rejected Johnson and came out for the maverick Scott because of his sympathy for the farmer and the "little man."[100] Terry Sanford recalled that Scott recognized that he could not take the farm vote for granted and needed more votes in rural areas outside Alamance County. Scott thus increased his emphasis on rural electrification, telephones, and roads in pursuit of those votes[101] while repeating his allegations that the exorbitant costs of electricity had retarded industrial development in the state.[102]

Scott campaigned differently in those isolated outposts in eastern North Carolina than did Johnson. As Bob Scott recalled him saying: "Well, the way I campaign, I go into a county and I don't go to the courthouse the first thing like most of them do to pay my respects to the powers that be. I go up to the head of the branch. And I start working back down. By the time I get to the courthouse I've got my votes. It's the boys at the branch head that got me elected. I don't have to pay any attention to the folks in the courthouse. They weren't working for me."[103]

At a fish fry for his fifty-second birthday, Scott got a little het up about the campaign and predicted that he would be nominated and elected,[104] but this campaign bluster, typical of most politicians, did not serve him well as

Scott campaigning for governor in 1948. Note the blacks in the crowd. Courtesy of the State Archives of North Carolina, Raleigh.

he was far removed from any hope of victory in the first primary. While he had made tremendous progress, the best he could expect at this juncture was to make the runoff and prevent Johnson from getting a majority.

While Scott whooped around the state in April exuding passion and energy on behalf of his cause, Johnson seldom attacked Scott, nor did he bother to answer his challenger's charges. He continued to concentrate on courthouse rallies and civic clubs while trumpeting the fact that he had county managers in all but two of the one hundred counties.[105] His cautious approach and overly optimistic attitude a month prior to the voting was beginning to put his election in jeopardy as the energetic Scott was gaining ground every day.

The Burgaw native tried to steal back some of the headlines from Scott by advocating a huge state appropriation of $85 million, some $21 million more than was currently budgeted, to meet present-day education needs.

Realizing that Scott's demand for meeting the state's necessities had gained traction among voters, Johnson now shifted to Scott's position, arguing that the surplus should be used for increased public services. Use of the surplus, he believed, would eliminate the need for new taxes.[106] Later, Johnson called for all-weather roads, the expansion of state facilities for the mentally ill, and increased funding for tourism.[107] The eastern candidate also urged the expansion of library facilities and books as the state's expenditure on libraries was just thirty cents per capita and the national average was fifty-two cents per capita.[108]

By the end of April 1948, one month before the May 29 primary, voters had a difficult time determining the liberal candidate in the race.[109] The platforms of Albright, Scott, and Johnson were virtually indistinguishable. With the exception of Scott's denunciation of Johnson's road bond proposal, the three shared similar views about education, roads, and health care. Albright and Scott urged a minimum-wage or a wage-hour law; otherwise, the platform differences were minimal. The race would be decided not by policy positions or ideology but by Albright's and Scott's charge that Johnson was committed to and controlled by the machine and big business. If Johnson was ineffective in defending his independence, the election was up for grabs.

Scott refused to let up on his fusillade against Johnson. Once again commenting on the state treasurer's failure to get interest on state surplus funds, he reminded listeners that he had never charged Johnson with dishonest or illegal activities while treasurer, saying only that he "has proved himself a very poor businessman from the taxpayers's standpoint."[110] Wherever Scott spoke, he reminded listeners that Johnson was the hand-picked candidate of the machine and that he had received both orders and cash from the bankers and wealthy manufacturers in the state. He also explained that he himself was an experienced administrator who, unlike Johnson, had the integrity to resign his office after announcing for governor and that he would not be subservient to the dictates of big business. He wanted a new day in North Carolina, a state "so long burdened by the tyrannical machine."[111]

Trying to solidify support from state employees, the Johnson hierarchy warned state workers that, if Scott were elected, there would be a drastic turnover of state jobs. In reply Scott wrote a letter to state employees stating: "No capable state employee with a recognition of his responsibilities to his employer ... has anything to fear from me." He would advocate, he said, on behalf of "capable employees" for better pay and working conditions. Of course, Scott being Scott, he could not resist adding: "Any employee who does not have these virtues [loyalty, faithfulness and efficiency] will find me tough and hard to get along with."[112]

Hearing rumblings of discontent from his followers around the state, Charlie Johnson belatedly began to realize that his once-insurmountable lead had melted away and that Scott's criticisms had gained him a growing audience. For the first time, Johnson felt it necessary to lash out at Scott and defend his integrity and record as state treasurer. He emphatically denied that his failure to invest public funds had cost taxpayers millions of dollars and insisted that he had violated neither the letter nor the spirit of the law in regard to the investment of public monies. Scott, however, had "violated the Ninth Commandment": "He has borne false witness against his neighbor." Johnson asserted that the assaults on his integrity showed that Scott, who lacked a constructive platform, had "turned in desperation to a campaign of criticism to blacken [his opponent's] name and divert attention from his own incapabilities": "The people will not be deceived."[113] Johnson's decision to respond to Scott's accusations indicated that the thrust had hit home.

The *Durham Morning Herald* defended Johnson and upbraided Scott for his "rash charges," which would end up hurting Scott more than Johnson. Scott, declared the paper, was too heavy-handed in his attacks and did not care where the blows fell.[114] The *Wilmington Morning Star* agreed that Scott's charges would boomerang since Johnson had answered them effectively and had administered his office with "a high degree of business intelligence and indisputable integrity." Johnson, wrote the paper, had been restricted by a 1943 law regarding investing surplus funds and had survived fifteen audits. Only in a political campaign would his record be challenged.[115]

Other papers disagreed. The *Elizabeth City Independent* had, in an earlier editorial, observed that, after Scott's initial accusations, Governor Cherry put $15 million of surplus state money in government securities, earning $1.5 million: "Scott was saving money for the state before he even became governor. . . . [It] makes one wonder how much more money lying in the banks should be . . . put to work earning interest."[116] The *Washington Daily News* added its voice to the debate by reminding its readers that the state was still "dominated by the money interests." Scott, it noted, believed in free enterprise but opposed "state policies that reward rich banks and millionaire donors at the expense of the farmers and working class."[117]

As all good political campaigners do, Scott instantly responded to Johnson, charging: "The state treasurer is trying to hide behind legal technicality and charges of mud-slinging to gloss over his deficiencies as a businessman and custodian of the taxpayer's money. This is the oldest device of machine politicians." He denied that he had made any charges of personal dishonesty; rather, he had merely offered his opinion that Johnson was a "poor businessman on the basis of his record as state treasurer." He thoughtfully suggested that perhaps Johnson had been too busy campaigning to pay attention to his duties as treasurer and renewed his call for Johnson to resign his post.[118] The gloves were now off, and the last three weeks of the campaign would be a slam-bang affair, highlighted by negative character assassinations.

Picking up on a dramatic change in voters' attitudes, the *Raleigh News and Observer* explained that, "as the gubernatorial campaign reache[d] a peak of anger with one candidate in polite but unmistakable terms calling the other a liar," the race was generating "not only heat but light." It concluded that voters were not content with the way things were and wanted to move forward in a progressive manner. North Carolina, it maintained, had been lagging for years with underfunded schools, worn-out roads, inadequate libraries, and no law to prevent the pollution of its streams. Regardless of who occupied the governor's chair, the people wanted a resumption of progress.[119]

Taking a cue from the Raleigh editorial, Scott and his associates renewed their push for education reform. On May 5, Capus Waynick sent a letter to each teacher in the state, listing Scott's views on education: "Kerr Scott means what he says about schools, he has always been a school man; he always has kept his promises." The mailing included a letter from Dr. J. Y. Joyner, the former state superintendent of public instruction and a man highly regarded by educators. Joyner promoted Scott's candidacy because he believed him "to be the best qualified of gubernatorial candidates to give the state an aggressive, progressive, constructive, independent, liberal administration."[120] Grace Furman, a campaign worker, remembered toiling "mighty hard" in the basement of the Carolina Hotel in Raleigh to get out thousands of these letters[121] as they would be essential to Scott's victory in a closely fought campaign.

While Dr. Joyner's endorsement was a major coup, Scott added to his education portfolio by sending a series of pamphlets to newspapers. The pamphlets emphasized that he came from a family closely identified with schools and teachers and included his "constructive program for schools": "Reduce classroom size to 30; increase the base salary of teachers from $2,400 up to $3,600. The state of North Carolina cannot afford NOT to pay these salaries; compulsory attendance; more school buildings; expansion of federal aid administered under strict local control; and more school buses."[122]

Not to be outdone, Johnson outlined a program for education remarkably similar to Scott's proposals. The main difference was that the treasurer, once a very conservative custodian of state monies, now asked for an immediate appropriation of $25 million from surplus funds to build and refurbish school facilities.[123]

As Scott struggled to overcome Johnson's lead, campaign finances remained a problem. The campaign constantly had to find new sources of revenue to keep the bills paid. Despite dwindling coffers, Waynick and others managed to produce some powerful ads and place them in state newspapers. One example, "The Deadly Parallel," compared Scott's record to Johnson's and delivered a lethal body blow to Johnson (paraphrased sections do not carry quotation marks):

> SCOTT–resigned state job to run for governor. JOHNSON–hanging on to state job and campaigning at taxpayers' expense. SCOTT—people's candidate. JOHNSON—machine candidate. SCOTT–knows what it is to meet a private payroll and to PAY taxes. JOHNSON—always on public payroll. SCOTT—hasn't gone about the state promising political jobs for support. JOHNSON–"would have to enlarge capitol if he made good on all the promises made for him." SCOTT–hasn't promised roads for votes. JOHNSON—his henchmen demand support for machine in exchange for roads built with taxpayers' money. SCOTT—"Will revitalize state government, open the windows and let in fresh air in Raleigh." He will scrape off the political barnacles. JOHNSON—would have to keep the old-guard tax eaters and increase their number.

The ad reminded voters that Johnson, not Scott, was backed by big business and that Johnson had cost them millions by letting state funds pile up without interest.[124]

Several key points of this political comparison resonated with voters, especially the idea that Scott would go to Raleigh and let in some fresh air. The people were clearly impatient with the conservative, status quo state government and wanted change and some new faces in Raleigh. While Johnson may or may not have promised roads for votes, the state Highway Commission had been a cesspool of petty corruption for many years and had been building roads on the basis of political connections. Scott knew a slow-moving target when he saw one. He promised to replace state Highway Commission members engaged in "political road building" with men of vision who recognized that all the people, not just the politically connected, needed better roads. He consistently insisted that a key priority for the next governor would be to help the state get out of the mud and to provide roads with all-weather accessibility for both markets and schools. Scott would be the best man for that job.[125]

While the two heavyweights on the main card sparred with each other, Mayne Albright reclaimed some of the voters' attention by reviewing his case for the governor's chair. He surmised that he could attract 200,000 voters because "bickering" among "certain other candidates" had turned many votes in his favor.[126] He called the machine "bankrupt in vision and leadership," ruled by the dead hand of the past, and charged that the Shelby dynasty therefore "cramps, discourages, and hinders political thought and action throughout the state."[127] Every time he trained his guns on machine politics, he helped Scott's cause enormously.

As election day approached, Scott increased his activity in his unrelenting pursuit of victory. He knew that the path to success lay in a constant barrage of criticism against Johnson, tying him to the machine, and castigating him about state bank deposits. He announced that, if Johnson had been a good businessman, he would have "obtained statutory authority" to invest state reserve funds in interest-bearing securities instead of leaving them as "inactive balances." Referring to the $105–$171 million deposited in 234 banks, he explained that the state could have earned $1 million with safe investments. The banks were making such investments, and they, not the taxpayers, earned all the profits.[128]

Editorials in several papers indicated that Scott's attack on the deposit of state funds in banks was paying dividends. The *Duplin Citizen* discovered that four banks in Duplin County had almost $760,000 in state deposits on which they paid no interest. These charges were not "mud-slinging," argued the paper, and it praised Scott for exposing public records that every citizen had the right to know about.[129]

Kerr Scott crisscrossed the state, strengthening his farm support, and working hard to convince women to go to the polls. Estelle Smith, Scott's associate manager, wrote a letter, "Dear Scott Worker," asking recipients to "round up the women in your county" and get them registered. Smith maintained that 1948 was a year in which, by voting for Scott, women would get better schools and better teacher pay and elect a man who believed "that women should receive equal pay for equal service."[130]

Scott worked vigorously at getting out the rural vote. At a farm bureau meeting he contended that agriculture was the backbone of the state and noted that he was the "only candidate who has lived on a dirt road all his life." The majority of citizens lived in rural areas, he continued, but the current government has not been sympathetic to their needs. While on his feet, he hammered the Tidewater Power Company for excessive rates and slammed telephone companies for their failure to expand the system.[131] In Kenansville, he repeated his desire to build more rural roads since it was a severe economic penalty when large numbers of citizens were handicapped in getting their goods to market and their children to school.[132]

In Campaign Bulletin no. 5, Charlie Parker crowed that Scott had come off a big winner in the exchange over Johnson's handling of taxpayers' money. Scott was not guilty of mudslinging—he merely discussed the state treasurer's public record. Parker then announced that Scott had taken the lead.[133] Despite this optimistic appraisal, Scott did not in fact lead at this juncture, and the Scott forces faced much deeper cash-flow problems than did Johnson. Nonetheless, Scott had narrowed the gap and forced Johnson to make additional promises to the voters.

On May 14, Johnson sent a letter to all state employees reminding them that *he* was also a state employee and favored salary increases for all.[134] Implied in this missive is that, if elected, he would not resort to the wholesale firings that would be de rigueur if Scott assumed office. Only one day elapsed before Scott came up with his own plan for pay increases for all state employees. With increased services demanded by the people, the state needed, he declared, a better workforce, but low salaries were "starving its most efficient employees out of public service." He was aware that the "political machine" had been circulating reports that he would fire state employees who did not vote for him. "This is ridiculous," he snarled.[135] State workers, aware of Scott's past record of dismissing employees, knew better and generally favored Johnson.

With only one week to go before the primary, Charlie Johnson confidently predicted that he would win outright. He surely must have known that he would be high man, but, despite reports from adherents that he was rapidly losing votes, he refused to accept the possibility that he might not get even 50 percent of the vote. Rather than attack Scott and defend himself more forcefully, Johnson reverted to his initial strategy of staying above the fray and, in a new ad, reminding voters of his achievements.[136] One would have thought that at this juncture in the race he would not call attention to

Scott acting as the auctioneer in the North Carolina Harvest Festival. Campaign for governor, 1948. Courtesy of the State Archives of North Carolina, Raleigh.

his controversial time as state treasurer, and this bland, ineffective ad contrasted sharply with the vigorous, energetic campaign run by Kerr Scott.

The Democratic Party held its state convention in Raleigh on May 20 at the height of the gubernatorial contest. More than three thousand delegates, including Scott, Johnson, Albright, and Barker, gathered at the biennial meeting. Not only did the candidates have to interrupt their schedules, but the party also had to consider what stand to take on President Harry Truman's civil rights program. Civil rights had not been of any consequence in the race to this point, but the issue could lead to a split in Democratic Party ranks if not handled properly. Tasked with defusing the race issue in the state party platform, the resolutions committee, in a carefully worded compromise, decided on sending an uninstructed delegation to the national convention in July.

There had been much opposition in the state to Truman and his civil rights agenda, and the party thought that an uninstructed delegation was the best way out of the dilemma as there would have been a fierce fight over any endorsement of the president. The members of the delegation were to be given the authority to "use their own judgment on how they shall vote on all matters coming before the convention and without any instructions from this convention." At the same time the state party praised the national Democratic Party without mentioning Truman and issued a strong statement in favor of states' rights without any reference to civil rights.[137] Since the goals of each of the three major candidates were so similar, neither the party platform nor the convention had a measurable effect on the race.

Back on the hustings, Scott and Johnson launched their final push for the nomination. Johnson focused on the eastern part of the state, while Scott put the finishing touches on his campaign with a schedule that took him from Northhampton County in the east to Asheville in the west.[138] By the end of his run the Squire expected to have visited ninety-three of the one hundred counties and traveled some sixteen thousand miles by car and plane. He had, according to Roy Wilder, worked extremely hard to gain the nomination: "[He had] made more than 50 arranged speeches, held uncounted meetings, flown at least 5,000 miles, made 17 radio broadcasts. One day in Charlotte he spoke to 6 different audiences, held a conference with campaign workers and that night made a speech in Monroe."[139]

Scott persevered in his tireless tirades against Johnson as a machine candidate and as a friend of the bankers. An ad in the *Sampson Independent* praised Scott as a God-fearing, forthright leader and viewed with alarm the attempts to "saddle on the backs of the people of North Carolina a boss controlled government."[140] In Roxboro, Scott said that he opposed his opponent's idea for a huge bond proposal to build new roads. He did not want a single bond issue until the surplus "now piled into banks without interest is put to work for the purpose for which the money was collected." The times demanded a governor "who is more than a one talent man." Johnson, he opined, was not even very good at his one talent.[141] Although Mayne Albright claimed that he had first raised the issue of "unused funds and unmet needs," it was Scott who had seized on it. Albright conceded that Scott's focus on attacking Johnson for "letting those favorites take a free ride on the public's money" had "proved to be a most significant boost to his campaign."[142]

Albright tried a last-ditch attempt to gain support by pointing out that the "big-money candidates," Scott and Johnson, had each spent over

$100,000 trying to buy the election, an amount vastly over the legal limit of $12,000.[143] Of course Johnson and Scott had overspent the legal limit. No one had paid the slightest attention to these rules for years, and everyone knew it. It was a standing joke in North Carolina political circles. Johnson reported spending $11,260.32, while Scott admitted to $11,769.16, both sums just under the limit. These figures did not come close to covering the cost of the radio spots and newspaper ads, let alone staff salaries, rental on state headquarters, and all the other expenses necessary for a winning campaign. For example, the cost of a hotel room at the Carolina Hotel for Waynick was $605.00, and the June bill for local ads was $499.80. After his 1954 race for the U.S. Senate, Scott admitted that the cost just for running his state headquarters in 1948 amounted to over $62,000. The actual cost, including ads and radio broadcasts, had to be over $150,000.

A partial list of contributors found in the Capus Waynick Papers was instructive. Robert W. Scott gave $5,000; Nello Teer, who ran a road-paving company, contributed $2,000; W. P. Saunders, a Southern Pines textile executive, put in $1,000.[144] When Scott made his final report for the first primary, those names were conspicuously missing from the list of contributors, and he listed donations of $11,407. The contributors listed in Waynick's papers accounted for $13,000 in donations, so any final accounting in terms of both names and numbers was far from the truth.[145] The voters, however, were totally uninterested in such duplicity and paid little attention to this issue.

During the last few days of the contest, Scott headquarters, via Campaign Bulletin no. 6, notified workers that Scott was pulling ahead. Charlie Parker observed that the Johnson camp feared a second primary and that, if Johnson did not win the first primary outright, he would be a "gone gosling."[146] A full-page ad in state newspapers claimed that only Scott had the "true devotion to the public good" and that his opposition, whose camp had boasted it had the election "in the bag," now worried that the bag had been slit wide open and that the votes of the masses were not for sale. The voters wanted change and knew Scott was the man who would lead the great masses forward.[147] An ad featuring "The Deadly Parallel," which had been successful earlier in the race, also appeared in full-page format.[148]

In the last-minute fusillades, each side tried to shore up its base and make inroads into its opponent's core support. Johnson characterized agriculture as the state's greatest resource and promised more funds for research, teaching, and marketing,[149] while Scott proposed a three-point plan for financial relief of cities and towns.[150] In his last attempt to persuade the voters, Johnson ran lengthy ads repeating his platform, extolling his virtues, and explaining that his program was sound and practical and could be put into effect only by a man with his experience and training. The headline ran: "A Vote for Johnson Is a Vote in the Best Interest of Our State."[151]

Many of the state's newspapers endorsed Johnson. In Charlotte, the home of bankers and the largest urban area in the state, the *News* picked the state treasurer because he had wider government experience and would have more clout with the legislature: "The tradition of good government would be safe in his hands."[152] Of course, Scott had his editorial support as well, but not from the *Raleigh News and Observer*. Although the paper had written favorable editorials about him and he shared the publisher Jonathan Daniels's political philosophy, it had a policy of not endorsing candidates in the Democratic primary.[153]

In his final address, Scott declared that the most important issue to be decided was whether citizens would "vote for things as they are, or elect a ticket that will give assurance of a change in policy-making and policy-makers." Johnson merely said that he had conducted his quest on a high plane without reference to personalities: "I want to win the nomination on merit and ability."[154]

The final results of the first primary showed, as expected, Johnson in the lead with 170,141 votes and Scott a close second with 161,293 votes. For a man who started late and lacked the money of his heavily favored opponent, Scott had upset the prognosticators and almost outpolled Johnson. Mayne Albright received 76,281 votes, and the three lesser-known candidates accounted for approximately 15,000 votes. Johnson carried fifty-one counties, Scott forty-one, Albright seven (all in the east), and Barker one (his home county of Durham). Johnson ran well throughout the state, especially in the west, winning Buncombe and Burke Counties by 4–1, and he excelled in urban areas, prevailing in Mecklenburg County by 2–1. Scott outpolled Johnson in most of the rural, eastern counties but fared remarkably well in counties such as Wake, Guilford, and Forsyth. In Wake County, he came in first and Johnson third, a significant marker for the runoff. He won his home county, Alamance, by a huge margin, taking 6,115 votes as opposed to Johnson's 591.[155] Several editorialists and commentators were disappointed with the small turnout—fewer than 400,000 voters when some had predicted 600,000.[156]

Immediately after the final results were posted, Scott exercised his right to call for a runoff. Capus Waynick was delighted with the returns and predicted that "Kerr Scott would be the next governor of North Carolina." The Johnson forces showed less enthusiasm but tried to exude some confidence. Johnson issued a statement that, since he held a commanding lead in the first primary, he had the utmost confidence that he would prevail in the runoff.[157] He was whistling in the dark. He was finished politically unless his supporters could mount an aggressive and effective fight or Scott made some egregious error. The momentum was now with Scott, and Johnson's failure to win outright in the first primary doomed his chances. Scott's attacks had paid off. Now he needed more of the same. Johnson's campaign seemed disorganized, and Scott's surprising showing led to increased financial contributions and added enthusiasm on the part of his supporters. Scott, however, cautioned his advocates against overconfidence and predicted a hard fight.

One key to victory in the second primary would be which candidate could corral the Albright supporters. Albright early on said he had not decided on whether to take an active part in the runoff, but he added that both Scott and Johnson had congratulated him on his campaign and suggested conferences with them.[158] Aware that he was close to one of the most momentous political upsets in state history, Scott was taking no chances and planned to campaign just as hard in the runoff as he had in the first primary.

3

THE SECOND PRIMARY, 1948

Both sides began the renewed battle very quietly with organizational meetings and fund-raising while publicity managers prepared new copy and flyers. As the *Burlington Daily Times News* described it: "The first week of the second campaign was the time for preparing the fields, overhauling machinery, etc. The second week . . . is planting time." The next weeks would see the "peak of cultivation activities followed by a brief ripening period, culminating in the harvest of votes June 26."

Thomas J. Pearsall, Johnson's campaign manager, claimed that he was pleased with the first primary results and predicted an intensified campaign in the runoff. Mayne Albright, wooed by both Johnson and Scott, quickly declared neutrality. He would not try to influence the vote of his supporters and asserted: "I would not trade any influence I may have for present or future personal or political gain." Oscar Barker, the fourth-place finisher, came out for Johnson.

Scott praised Albright for a "clean and vigorous" race, urged Albright's supporters to back him in the second primary, and quickly signed up four former Albright staffers.[1] He also sought the approval of labor, Albright's main constituency. The Scott forces persuaded William Smith, the North Carolina director of the Congress of Industrial Organizations (CIO), to send a letter to all his members, urging them to back Scott. In his letter, Smith asked his members to organize committees to get out the vote and to work with union locals: "There are to be no public statements or public endorsements of any candidate—and particularly that of Kerr Scott. Do not give anything to the newspapers."[2] Cognizant that the imprimatur of labor was the kiss of death in North Carolina politics, Waynick had wisely asked Smith to keep his assistance under wraps. Ralph Scott recalled that, if there was a strong candidate like Scott, labor would work with its own crowd, keep its support private, and, thus, be a significant asset.[3] After observing meetings between the American Federation of Labor, the CIO, and independent unions, the *Raleigh News and Observer* confirmed that word had gone down through the ranks of organized labor that Scott was the man to support in the runoff.[4]

Before any real progress could be made in renewed political activity, Scott had to shore up his finances. Capus Waynick told Ralph Scott that they needed $10,000 to begin the second primary. Scott went to a loyal supporter and asked for the money. The man, who had already given $300, thought that was enough. Ralph told him: "If we wake up on Sunday morning and find that [Kerr] lost by just a few votes, we'll never get over it." After a long pause, the donor said he would be good for $5,000.[5] This initial gift proved to be essential for the second primary start-up.

Charles Parker formulated the strategy for the runoff by sending Campaign Bulletin no. 7 to personnel in the field. Scott believed the tide was now running in his favor, but much needed to be done, and the campaign could not slow down in its efforts. Parker effusively praised the women's vote as an important factor in Scott's success and urged all the organizers to work hard for the veterans' vote.[6]

Johnson and his advisers knew that the strategy employed in the first half of the battle would not suffice this time. With only an 8,848-vote majority, they had to be more aggressive and avoid being constantly forced on the defensive. Many of Johnson's backers were upset and angry with his less than energetic performance in the first primary. Others backed him because they feared the ascendancy of Kerr Scott. According to the *Coastland Times* in Manteo: "The people of Dare County have gone crazy; they were damn fools to vote for Kerr Scott."[7]

As the runoff began, the Johnson campaign exhibited a major shift in strategy by unleashing the state senator Rivers Johnson to snipe at Scott. Rivers Johnson accused Scott of costing taxpayers $100,000 for the runoff "just to see if he can overtake Mr. Johnson's lead." He said that Scott was "a master at reversing himself" on issues, especially when it came to his support of the good health program, which he initially opposed. He mentioned that Scott himself had been on the payroll for twenty-seven of the last thirty years but still had the audacity to talk about Charlie Johnson being a state employee of many years.[8] This initial assault was, at best, thin gruel.

The *Zebulon Record*, a Scott paper, thought that, if Rivers Johnson's diatribe was the best the Johnson gang had, they were hard up for ammunition. Apparently the Johnsonians had now decided they could not win on merit and would resort to mudslinging.[9] The *News and Observer* pronounced the "new look" attack strategy of debatable value.[10] The *Elizabeth City Independent* reminded Johnson that he initially promised to conduct the election on a "high plane." That, however, was when he was confident of winning. Now that the Johnson camp smelled defeat, it had desperately resorted to lambasting Scott.[11]

Undeterred, the Johnson juggernaut had just begun its "New Look" strategy. The campaign had H. H. Baxter, the mayor of Charlotte, write a letter to all the other mayors in the state, praising Johnson for his commitment to home rule and for advocating "more aid to the cities from state funds." City residents, continued Baxter, paid more taxes than those living in rural areas, and cities needed more financial aid from the state. If Scott were elected, state aid to cities would be set back ten years.[12]

In the second primary Johnson relied heavily on his cronies in the state Highway Commission to get out the vote. Department leaders roamed around the state pledging roads for votes, and Johnson himself, in a letter to Rex Wilson, promised to pave a road near his home if Wilson would aid the cause.[13] A. H. "Sandy" Graham, the chairman of the Highway Commission, made it clear that he and many other highway workers and state employees thought they would forfeit their positions with a Scott triumph.[14] The *Durham Morning Herald* confirmed that the Highway Commission had sent mimeographed letters to employees implying they would lose their jobs if Scott won.[15]

Johnson himself leaped into the fray, giving his adversary a dose of his own medicine by accusing Scott of being the machine candidate. He condemned Scott for developing a "political ring" in the Department of Agriculture. That ring "is now at work," he announced, as agriculture employees "are riding day and night in state-owned cars, promoting and fostering the interest of my opponent." Johnson vigorously defended his tenure as state treasurer, denying that he neglected his duties while campaigning, and chastising Scott for deceiving the public about investing state funds. Scott apparently wanted Johnson to speculate with taxpayer money, but Johnson would have no part of it: "You have not lost one penny of your tax money. All cash subject to investment has been invested."[16] He recalled that Scott had bitterly attacked the merchants and civic clubs in the state and had initially been strongly opposed to the good health program. Now he was best friends with the civic clubs and the biggest advocate of the good health plan. The Johnson clique even trotted out that old warhorse, former governor and stemwinder Cam Morrison. Morrison denied that there had ever been a political machine in the state, insisting that Johnson had a "stainless" public record and that Scott had created ill will and prejudice by pitting county against town and the poor against the rich.[17]

The first flurry of the "new look" attack strategy concluded by denying that Johnson had any machine connection and pointing out that 77 percent of the state legislators favored him: "Isn't this a good indicator of what those familiar with state government think of Charlie Johnson?"[18] The *Durham Morning Herald* wrote an editorial defending Johnson's position on the deposits of state money. The paper argued that he was not required by law to invest the funds and that the law demanded that funds always be accessible. However, it did admit that Johnson was a machine candidate since he had aid from previous governors and the "courthouse gangs."[19]

Scott, slow to respond to these new tactics, reiterated his earlier campaign themes. He persuaded Ferd Davis, the editor of the *Zebulon Record,* to blast away at the failure to gain interest on the deposit of state funds in local banks. Davis checked on deposits in local banks and discovered that one bank had invested $500,000 in state funds and earned interest from that investment. He asserted that there was no statute preventing the investment of state funds under reasonable safeguards and referred to Johnson as an inept financier, "either astoundingly ignorant of the most elementary financial knowledge or deliberately confusing the facts." He divulged that he had been approached by Johnson supporters who offered to make it worth his while if he did not print the facts and figures about deposits of state money without interest.[20] He ignored the entreaties and published the material anyway.

The Alamance County dairy farmer kept up a drumbeat of accusations about Johnson being the handpicked candidate of a "few powerful men." He said that North Carolinians did not want to adopt the "Russian system under which you can vote for or against only one man for each office." These "king makers" had made a mistake in trying to dictate to the people, as demonstrated by the first primary vote, when the machine got only 40 percent of the vote and 60 percent indicated that they opposed Johnson and wanted change.[21]

Both sides made an all-out effort during the last week to secure the nomination. Scott set out on a whirlwind final tour, confident of victory. His concluding ads emphasized his experience in government administration and portrayed him as a man who knew how to economize and enjoyed the confidence of the people.[22] They insisted that he had a sound, sensible, progressive program. He wanted to keep the state marching forward and to keep the governor's office as the office of the people.[23] One effective ad inserted in the *Fuquay Springs Independent* listed the first-primary vote in Alamance County—Scott 6,115, Johnson 191—and the vote in Wake County—Scott 8,656, Johnson 5,386—for a total of 14,771 for Scott and 5,977 for Johnson: "It's nearly 3–1 with the people who know the candidates best."[24]

As the voting date of June 26 loomed, Scott unlimbered a few final salvos. Brandishing Charlotte mayor H. H. Baxter's letter asking for support from city mayors, he alleged that this was one of several "secret covenants" made by Johnson, who was "bidding frantically for votes—with the people's money." Not only had Johnson promised to return sales tax and gas tax money from the state treasury to the cities, but he had also made so many promises of appointment to the Highway Commission that he would have to announce a plan to increase its size: "Never in the history of state politics have such numerous and unpublished pledges been made. If kept, they would leave the state with an unprecedented number of jobholders and empty the state treasury."[25] In addition, Scott continued, machine backers were trying to buy the election for Johnson with a "slush fund" collected from banks "which have huge sums of taxpayers' money in them without interest."[26] He revealed that political pressure had also been put on state employees, who had been "bludgeoned" with threats of cuts in pay or loss of jobs if they did not get behind Johnson.[27]

Johnson quickly denied making any secret covenants and wondered why Scott was so desperate as to use "sly and subtle insinuations" against him. He once again went into a long and technical explanation of why many state funds did not draw interest, but his response was vague and ineffectual. In his penultimate radio address, he finally used terms that voters could understand. He called Scott a "hatchet man," not in reference to his attacks during the campaign, but because he had fired so many qualified employees when he became agriculture commissioner.[28] Too little, too late. Johnson never did mount a clear and competent response to Scott's claims about the state deposits and had very little ammunition to put Scott on the defensive. Calling him "sly" just did not get votes in North Carolina politics.

On the day prior to the vote, both camps exuded confidence. Johnson thought he would win by as many as thirty thousand votes because the people believed in good government. Scott said that the "people are going to see to it that the ring's political machine is hauled away to the junkyard

WARNING!

SOMEBODY'S LIABLE TO GET CAUGHT HOLDING THE BAG

An ad pointing out Charles Johnson's overconfidence in believing that he had the election sewed up while Kerr Scott was "liberating voters" and gaining momentum. Kerr Scott Papers, courtesy of the State Archives of North Carolina, Raleigh.

Saturday."[29] Just prior to the vote, Capus Waynick, certain of a decisive win, wrote a supporter that Scott's cause would be triumphant.[30]

One wonders what Charlie Johnson was thinking when he predicted victory by thirty thousand votes. In the final tabulation, he lost by almost thirty-two thousand votes—217,620 (54 percent) for Scott compared to 182,684 (46 percent) for Johnson.[31] The 400,000-vote total was far above expectations, demonstrating how intense the battle had become in the runoff. Saying that he had run a clean, hard campaign, Johnson conceded defeat and pledged his support to the party in November. Scott felt very "humble" as he joined the voters "in this tidal wave movement to keep N.C. going forward."[32]

Letters of congratulation poured in to Capus Waynick, the key organizer of victory. Excelle Rozzelle, a black minister in Winston-Salem, congratulated Scott for a great victory and hoped that he would be successful in revitalizing the state.[33] Rozzelle and other Negroes had worked diligently behind the scenes for Scott, and the black community certainly did its part in helping him into office. John Lang wrote that Scott's victory would usher in a new day in North Carolina politics and that the days of "KING FIXING" should be over.[34] J. Walter Lambeth called the vote "the most remarkable demonstration of popular support without demagogic appeal" that he could recall in North Carolina. The people had confidence "in the fundamental integrity of Kerr Scott."[35] Luther Hamilton, a superior court judge, confessed that he did not vote for Scott but had admiration for his "character, industry and vision—and certainly now for his political leadership." He also lavished well-deserved praise on Waynick for being a master organizer and an excellent publicity man.[36]

The Squire of Haw River, only the second farmer ever elected to the state's highest office (the first was Elias Carr, who served as governor from 1893 to 1897), reveled in his triumph. Since the law establishing runoffs had been promulgated in 1916, Scott became the first candidate who had been the runner-up in a primary to win the runoff. Pleased with the outcome of his four-month effort, the weary warrior returned to Hawfields to rest and greet supporters. Always recharged by his visits to the farm, he loved to walk alone across the fields in the early morning sunlight. However, before the sun was up, and before he could take a victory lap, visitors began streaming to the farm. Squire Scott sat in a chair under the shade of a tree in front of his one-story farmhouse and greeted hundreds of guests.

While relaxing at home, Scott commented to the press on his successful run for office. He was aware that he still faced a challenge from the Republican nominee, George Pritchard, in November, but in North Carolina in 1948 the Democratic nomination was tantamount to election, so the November race was not on his mind. He wearily noted that he was thankful there was not a "third primary." He had no specific plans other than meeting with his staff, visiting Governor Cherry in Raleigh, and attending the Democratic national convention in July.[37]

In analyzing the results, several conclusions are obvious. The majority of the Albright-Barker supporters had voted for Scott, thus accounting for the winning margin. Scott prevailed in all seven counties won by Albright in the first primary. He won by large margins in Durham and Guilford Counties and took Wake County by 2–1. While he had done poorly in the mountain areas in the first primary, he did much better there in the runoff. Johnson did well in the west and the urban areas, but several eastern counties slipped from his grasp, and sixteen counties switched from Johnson to Scott. The reality was that Johnson had reached his maximum vote in the first primary when he garnered 170,141 votes. Despite all the hard work and money spent, he was able to increase his total to only 182,684, a gain of 12,543. Scott, however, expanded his total significantly, from 161,293 to 217,620, an addition of 56,327.[38]

State newspapers immediately recognized the long-term meaning of Scott's victory. The *Raleigh News and Observer* thought the most salutary effect was that it ended for a long time "the unwholesome practice of picking governors months and years in advance." The paper saw the contest as one of personalities and the race as essentially a choice between those who thought the old-line politicians had done a good job and those who wanted a change. This was a victory for the people, and Scott succeeded because he persuaded the voters that his fight was their fight. The Old Reliable presciently concluded that the long, hot political fight had ended but that the greater campaign for the continued progress of North Carolina was just beginning.[39]

The *Charlotte News* had endorsed Johnson but reasoned that Scott would make a sound and progressive governor. He won because of solid support from labor and because the antimachine vote went to him.[40] The *Asheville Citizen* observed that the keys to Scott's victory were the large turnout and his winning of the Albright and Barker advocates. Although the *Citizen* thought the machine issue was fabricated for political advantage, it worked well for Scott.[41] One of the better commentaries came from the *Henderson Daily Dispatch*. The paper agreed that at one time there might have been a machine but felt that by the present day it had lost its power to function effectively and that Scott merely attacked a straw man. The Johnson organization never caught its stride and did not get out its message, and Johnson's poor showing in the first primary "took the wind out of [his campaign's] sails." The conservative wing had been in power too long, and a transition toward more liberal government was in the cards.[42]

The *Greensboro Daily News* noted that Scott made political history with his decisive triumph: "The Scott victory . . . broke the apostolic succession, real or mythical." Those opposed to conservative, status quo government rallied around Scott. He managed a more vigorous, effective, and aggressive fight than previous candidates, while Johnson was "not on a par as a campaigner" with previous machine choices. The *Daily News* reckoned that an important factor in Scott's victory was the growing feeling that the state's cumulative surplus could not be justified—the state was either overcharging or underservicing its citizens.[43]

Professional historians later noted a significant trend in southern politics after World War II as a series of moderate to liberal neopopulists gained elective office. Jim Folsom became governor of Alabama in 1946, while Earl Long of Louisiana, Sidney McMath of Arkansas, and Fuller Warren of Florida, along with Kerr Scott, became chief executives of their respective states in 1948. Also in 1948, two New Dealers, Estes Kefauver of Tennessee and Lyndon Johnson of Texas, gained seats in the US Senate. For a short period of time, the populist politics of economic class and leftover New Deal ideology gained a precarious foothold in the South.[44] This limited success would not last as the Red-baiting and racial hatred that destroyed the candidacies of Frank Graham in North Carolina and Claude Pepper in Florida in 1950 were a harbinger of things to come. After *Brown v. Board of Education* in 1954, race would split the Democratic Party and be one factor leading to the rise of the Republican Party in the South. Even so, the election of a few populist and progressive leaders in 1948 was an important, if temporary, shift in southern politics.

In the final analysis, the main ingredient in Scott's victory was the citizens' demand for change from the conservative, staid, machine politics of the past. Voters had tired of the so-called Shelby dynasty's control of state politics, and they finally found the right candidate in Kerr Scott. Even if there was no longer an effective Shelby dynasty and by 1948 it was more of a remnant of the older machine, Scott's strategy worked brilliantly. He said that citizens voted for him because of one fundamental question: Can the people choose their own governor, or "must they rely on a few politically and financially powerful individuals to pick a governor for them"?[45] By consistently denouncing the machine and the influence of rich bankers and textile owners, he stood up for the rights and opportunities of the poor farmers and workers in the state—a classic case of populist politics. Squire Scott knew his base was with the rural element, and he did not focus on nor did he expect much help from bankers or lawyers. With his characteristically barbed sense of humor, he remarked: "Not enough lawyers supported him to prepare a decent will."[46]

Another crucial factor proved to be the unrelenting assault on Johnson's decisions in regard to the deposit of state funds in local banks. The Federal Deposit Insurance Corporation had, in 1937, during the Depression, freed banks from paying interest on demand deposits of public funds, and state law did not authorize the state treasurer to require banks to pay interest on state deposits. Nonetheless, by placing state funds into private banks without drawing any interest, Johnson appeared to favor the wealthy bankers who were among his most important backers. Scott constantly reminded everyone that his failure to invest state funds had cost North Carolina millions.

This issue caught voters' attention partly because, shortly after Scott raised it, Governor Cherry immediately invested $15 million of surplus state money in US government bonds. Why had this not been done before? Johnson hid behind technicalities in an emotionally charged campaign, and his dry, obtuse responses to Scott's complaints failed to persuade voters. Scott advocates used the term *lazy money* to describe the lack of paid interest, and that term resonated with voters. W. T. Bost, a Johnson acolyte, wrote in the *Greensboro Daily News* that Scott's charge that state funds did not draw interest was "one of the best tricks in the campaign" and "the heaviest load" that Johnson had to carry.[47]

Johnson's team suffered from overconfidence from the outset as its candidate assumed it was his turn and he would win easily. Thad Eure, the secretary of state, said at the beginning of the race that there was no way Scott could beat Johnson, that the Hawfields farmer was just tilting at windmills. Then, after Johnson announced, Eure commented that he "never got out of his chair" and that "Scott beat the lard out of him."[48] On the night of the vote, a black Raleigh elevator operator summed up Scott's victory: "I done figured this out. Mr. Scott got in there to run for governor. Mr. Johnson, he just walked, but Mr. Scott he ran."[49] Terry Sanford recalled that Johnson was "so certain of election that he had already ordered a new Cadillac" and that

Scott's upset win over the "establishment tore it all to pieces and it's never been the same."[50]

Johnson ran a flawed campaign. Already under fire for his close association with big business, he made a big mistake by publicly praising the state's bankers and textile owners, who provided him with large sums of money and campaigned extensively for him. He thought that having the legislature, the judges, most public officials, and the bankers for him was the path to success. Unfortunately for him, that scenario proved to be the problem, not the solution. The average citizen already distrusted big business and its excessive influence over state politics. In addition, the Johnson campaign started politicking far too early, spent money needlessly in the early days, and eventually ran out of steam. Johnson was hurt in the first primary when some members of the Shelby machine worked hard to elect William B. Umstead to the US Senate and did not devote as much time or money to Johnson, thinking that the effort would not be needed. Johnson erroneously spent most of his time voicing platitudes and visiting those who already supported him.

During the heart of the contest, Scott seized the initiative and raced around the state slamming Johnson and the machine at every opportunity, while Johnson played a prevent defense the entire first primary. When Johnson did go after Scott, the issues were either irrelevant or so lame as to be dismissed by most thoughtful observers. After failing to win outright in the first primary, Johnson managed to hit back at his opponent, but with limited success. Charlie Johnson, however, did not lose the election; Kerr Scott won it.

Scott's organization, strategy, and tactics were superb, and much of the credit goes to Capus Waynick's skillful handling of the campaign. The Scott team struggled mightily to raise enough money to run a competent race, and Waynick admitted that the campaign was "conducted on a financial shoe string": "We were forced to make it a contest of a cause against money."[51] Nonetheless, Scott's organization had enough money to prevail.

Scott won the race through hard work and effective planning, but the key to his success came because he competently used the two main issues— machine politics and state deposits—to his advantage. He was able to secure the women's vote and haul in the black vote while receiving a major contribution from labor. The Textile Workers Union, working with the Congress of Industrial Organizations and the American Federation of Labor, claimed to have "played a pivotal role in Scott's run-off victory."[52] Scott won the 1948 election partly because of his grassroots appeal. He won most of his votes by speaking to small groups and by using his charm and straightforward manner in one-on-one conversations with voters.

Scott, of course, overwhelmingly won the rural and farm vote. In 2012, with North Carolina a successful, diverse state, it is hard to realize that, in 1948, 66 percent of the state's residents lived on farms or in towns of fewer than twenty-five hundred. North Carolina had more farmers than any other state save Texas. Many of the farms were small, and the residents barely managed to eke out a living, making the state one of the poorest in the nation in terms of per capita income. Tobacco accounted for almost 65 percent of all cash crop receipts, and this two-crop (cotton and tobacco) system tied the farmers and their sharecroppers to the soil and kept them indebted to the banks and the town merchants. In addition, many of the nonfarm population—those who worked in textile mills and operated small businesses—were also from rural areas. The economic progress of the state in 1948 depended to a large degree on success in farming, textile manufacturing, and furniture production. Scott's populist views appealed to workers in each of those areas. The rural farm-to-market roads were in deplorable condition, many of them impassable in rain or winter conditions. In July 1948 only 66.4 percent of the state's farms had electricity, and those farmers without power were eager to get hooked up. The telephones-to-persons ratio in the state was 1–8, and over 100,000 people in rural areas demanded phone service.[53]

Scott understood the plight of the rural poor and promised to get the farmers out of the mud by paving roads and to provide them with telephones, electricity, better schools and teachers, and improved health care. As Bill Friday observed: "You are not going to vote against a man who tells you that." Friday judged that the statewide network Scott set up while he was commissioner of agriculture was decisive in his campaign. Everything was local, and that was essential to his success. According to Friday, Scott had a special sensitivity to poor people and farm people "that was as honest as the day is long." Raised to value integrity, decency, straightforwardness, and honesty, Scott "knew who he was—what his origins were—his church and his farm." He conveyed this to the have-nots. They liked him and voted for him. He saw that by paving the roads and improving schools and health care he would lift the state into the industrial age, and he persuaded his constituents to follow his dream. Friday called him "the most skilled populist political figure this state had ever seen."[54]

The combination of rural and progressive forces finally coalesced behind a populist candidate to usher in a New Deal for state politics—a new era of a more open government and greater opportunities for all. The election of Kerr Scott still ranks as one of the great political upsets in North Carolina history, and Scott's win changed the future of the state in dramatic ways.

By the early fall, Tar Heel Democrats had become resigned to living under Kerr Scott as governor, but some writers, like W. T. Bost, argued that Scott's victory was not a revolution and that his "impressive" win was due only to the deterioration of the machine and the skill of those "cunning publicists, Charles Parker and Capus Waynick." Despite his large win, Bost correctly predicted that Scott would have a difficult time getting his program through a conservative legislature.[55]

Meanwhile, after a short rest, realizing his path to success would be strewn with obstacles and opposition, Scott began to work on his agenda as governor. He reached out to both opponents and supporters, asking for their help. He wrote to the newly elected lieutenant governor, H. Patrick Taylor Sr., a Johnson supporter, whose contacts and influence he would sorely need during the legislative session, asking for Taylor's cooperation as he "approached the final test of the people's willingness to turn over to our hands the responsibility we have sought."[56]

Scott's first foray into national politics came with the Democratic national convention in Philadelphia in July. As the North Carolina delegation arrived in the City of Brotherly Love, many southern delegates, greatly disturbed by Truman's candidacy and his civil rights platform, vowed to oppose his nomination. Although the North Carolina representatives had been sent to the convention without any instructions as to how to vote, the overwhelming majority favored Georgia senator Richard Russell. Russell's adherents included Senator Clyde Hoey, William Umstead, and the more conservative party members. The progressive wing of the state Democratic Party, including Scott and Jonathan Daniels, courageously came out for Truman.

The simmering conflict over civil rights erupted on July 14, when Minneapolis mayor Hubert Humphrey advocated a stronger civil rights plank than the mild and ambiguous one favored by party leaders. Humphrey wanted an end to the poll tax, an end to lynching, and an end to segregation in the armed forces, and he favored fair employment legislation. The party hierarchy feared a walkout by the southern delegates, which would be a blow to whatever chance Truman might have in November. A bare majority of the delegates voted for the strong civil rights plank, and the entire Alabama and half the Mississippi delegation marched out of the convention. Governor Cherry grabbed the North Carolina banner to keep his state from joining the walkout. It took the full power and prestige of both Scott and Cherry to hold even a minority of North Carolina delegates for Truman. The Democratic Party eventually nominated Truman on the first ballot by 947½ votes for Truman to 263 for Russell.[57] There was no move to make the motion unanimous for fear of further alienating the South.

Although the North Carolina delegation had not bolted the convention, party politics were polarized around Truman and the race issue. Conservative Democrats feared that the entire ticket might lose in 1948 with Truman as the presidential nominee. Leaders like William B. Umstead warned Capus Waynick, whom Scott had selected as the new state Democratic Party chairman, that he could not carry the state for Truman because people told him they would never vote "for that civil rights S.O.B."[58] Congressman "Muley Bob" Doughton told Waynick he should not try to help Truman. If he did, he could get the whole ticket beat.[59] Waynick, however, as head of the state party, praised Truman's ability to lead and went around the state calling on voters to mark a straight Democratic ticket.

Many Democrats were reluctant to campaign for Truman but knew better than to abandon the party ticket as it might lead to significant gains by the Republicans and could threaten their power and influence in Raleigh and Washington. Some, like Senator Hoey, gave lip service to the national ticket but worked laboriously for the state candidates. Although he had cast his vote for Richard Russell at the convention, Hoey wrote a constituent that he had closed ranks and made speeches on behalf of the party and for Truman's reelection. He thought the Dixiecrats would not do well in the state or carry more than three to four states nationally.[60] Scott, while enthusiastic for Truman, did not often mention his name while conducting his own campaign for governor.

The problem became more troublesome with the appearance in the state of J. Strom Thurmond, who in July had been named as the presidential candidate for the States Rights Democratic Party, known as the Dixiecrats. In his two-day, five-hundred-mile swing through the state, Thurmond preached states' rights and white supremacy. He alleged that Truman's civil rights program was the first step toward the creation of "a totalitarian, socialistic government," that a federal police force would make whites go to school with blacks, and that the Democratic Party had been taken over by "pinks and subversives." When he spoke to students at the University of North Carolina, he was greeted with derisive laughter, especially when he declared: "I have no racial prejudice."[61]

Robert Taft, Strom Thurmond, Henry Wallace of the Progressive Party, Harold Stassen, Alben Barkley, the Democratic vice-presidential nominee, and President Harry Truman all made visits to the state during the fall, making it a memorable campaign season. All four parties—Republicans, Democrats, Progressives, and Dixiecrats—mounted very aggressive efforts in the state. Recognizing voters' strong dislike of Truman's policies, the local Republicans thought they had a real chance to make some inroads into Democratic control of the state. George Pritchard, their candidate for governor, predicted a victory and a return to a two-party system since the evil effects of a state clinging blindly to a one-party system would attract voters to the Republican Party.[62]

Scott made at least seventeen speeches during fall gatherings, while the Democrats held rallies in every congressional district. Scott stressed that his promises in the Democratic primary would be his program in the governor's mansion. Only Congressman Thurmond Chatham dared to lavish praise on Truman. Whenever he did so, there was prolonged applause from the audience.[63]

President Truman's appearance on October 18, the highlight of the fall campaign, was the first presidential visit to the state since Teddy Roosevelt's in 1905. The president arrived on his four-motor plane, *The Independence*, and an estimated twenty-five to thirty thousand well-wishers greeted his motorcade as it traveled from the Raleigh-Durham airport to the Sir Walter Hotel in downtown Raleigh. Truman officially opened the state fair before a friendly crowd of seventy-five thousand. His speech was nonpolitical, but he did take a swipe at the do-nothing Eightieth Congress and earned Scott's approval when he said the real issue in the campaign was the people versus the special interests. Kerr Scott met Truman for the first time at the fair,[64] and, since they were cut from the same cloth and were running similar campaigns, they became fast friends and confidants. The *Raleigh News and Observer* predicted that Truman would easily carry the state, although it realized that some who greeted him on his visit would never vote for him.[65]

On the day prior to the November 1948 vote, Scott and Waynick made an appeal for voters to turn out for Truman since, as Scott put it, North Carolina's problems had never been understood or helped by national Republican politicians.[66]

On November 3 Americans learned that the experts had been wrong and Harry Truman had achieved the political upset of the century. He had 303 electoral votes and 24,105,812 popular votes and carried twenty-eight states, compared to Dewey's 189 electoral votes, 21,970,065 popular votes, and sixteen states. Strom Thurmond won in four southern states with 39 electoral votes. As David McCullough described it: "The President who had had to fight just to get the nomination from his own party . . . [beat] the opponent everybody had said was unbeatable. It was not only a supreme moment of triumph in a long political life, but one of the greatest personal victories of any American politician ever."[67]

In North Carolina governor-elect Scott won a huge victory over the Republican George Pritchard: 570,995 votes to 206,166. Perhaps most surprising was that Truman carried the state 459,070 votes to 258,572, a margin of victory second only to that he had achieved in Texas. Few observers expected Dewey to win North Carolina, but the size of Truman's vote, after the heated controversy over his civil rights program, astonished many prognosticators. Strom Thurmond received only 69,652 votes, and Dewey's and Thurmond's totals combined were 130,000 votes shy of Truman's. This was the opposite of many southern states, for example, Florida, where Thurmond's and Dewey's combined totals exceeded Truman's.[68] North Carolina had lived up to its reputation as a progressive state. The *New York Times* praised the state's mild reaction to Truman's civil rights program and its strong support for the president, declaring: "North Carolina is generally recognized as the most liberal and progressive state in the South."[69] The state did not succumb to the racist appeal of Strom Thurmond, and the 1948 vote shored up its reputation as moderate on race. The race issue had been avoided for the time being, but the state's moderate reputation would be shattered in less than two years in the brutal 1950 Senate race.

The popular Scott outpolled everyone on the Democratic ticket, with over 100,000 more votes than Truman. Scott called the national vote a "very fine tribute to President Truman" and said the farmers were the real winners in the election as agriculture would have a greater voice in Washington and Raleigh.[70]

Scott now readied himself for the huge challenge that lay ahead. He had the nominal support of the Democratic Party hierarchy—even Clyde Hoey had pledged his "complete cooperation"[71]—but he faced a conservative and recalcitrant legislature. A letter to the *Raleigh News and Observer* wisely noted that, while Scott knew the people and their real needs and desires, the "apostles of privilege" in the House and Senate would try every way possible to block his legislation. Since the governor did not have the veto power and only advisory powers, "only an aroused public can bring about Scott's proposed reforms."[72]

4

ROADS AND SCHOOLS, 1949

Governor-Elect Scott returned from a two-week vacation in Coral Gables, Florida, rested and ready for work. While he vacationed in Florida, he missed meetings of the Advisory Budget Commission, gathered to sort out the budget for the upcoming legislative session. The Advisory Budget Committee, now defunct, was an important body in 1949 as it counseled the governor on the preparation and administration of the budget. Until 1971, the governor's budgetary powers were legislative in origin, not constitutional, and could be snatched away from him at any time. Since Scott faced an adversarial legislature that could overturn his budget, he needed to make his case to the commission. Although he sent the commission memoranda explaining his budget views, his absence was significant as he was not able to push for his pet projects.

Not only that, but before he took office Scott managed to create his first major controversy by asking two public servants to step down. In a harbinger of things to come, he wrote Vance Baise, the chief highway engineer, and Charles Flack, the chief clerk of the state Utilities Commission, asking them to resign their positions. He explained that he wanted Baise out because he needed to "make a change" in the Highway Commission and that he wanted Flack out because the latter had promised to remain neutral in the governor's race but had worked hard for Johnson. "I had an agreement with Charlie in the campaign," he was quoted as saying, "and he broke it. I thought if I couldn't trust him on that I couldn't trust him on anything else." The problem was that Scott did not have the authority to fire either man—that lay with the Highway Commission and the Utilities Commission, respectively—and, not surprisingly, both Flack and Baise defied Scott's request. Flack eventually resigned; Baise did not. The heavy-handed decision brought immediate criticism.[1] The *Asheville Citizen* called it "a regrettable controversy" and wondered why Scott wanted to "enter office in an aura of recrimination and some bitterness."[2] The *Durham Morning Herald* feared the "spirit of vindictiveness" and the sense of unrest that many had hoped might be averted when Scott came to power.[3]

Scott ignored the adverse reaction and focused on the task at hand. He knew that reforming the state and implementing his Go Forward program would not be easy. The *Raleigh News and Observer* warned the governor-elect that arrogant lobbyists were already at work to save the state from his program and wanted to belittle him before he even began his work. To make his unconventional character "seem like incompetence," it noted, "seems to be the desperate plan of reactionary interests to stop a new program for the state before it begins." Although Scott was sometimes "unpressed as to clothes, language and act," he was entitled to the state's support in his attempt to achieve progress.[4]

The unconventional Scott showed the state what it could expect for the next four years in an address to the North Carolina Citizens Association, a group composed mainly of conservative businessmen. He announced that he believed in telling the truth and that, if he criticized anyone, he should do it to their face. Thus, he told his audience that he thought that their organization and their magazine, *We the People,* should be called "We the People against the People." He claimed that their goal was profit and success and that it often came at the expense of the average man. He also called out the telephone company representatives in the audience: "If you can't get telephones to the people, I'll join in with others, using any powers I have as governor to see that something is done about it." While on his feet, Scott denounced the power companies for their lack of vision and warned them that, if he had to reorganize the Utilities Commission, he would. If he needed to pull their franchises, then that would also be an option. The governor told the tax-conscious businessmen that there would have to be an increased gas tax and a bond issue to pay for the roads program. Finally he revealed that he planned to appoint rural representatives to several state boards and commissions and wanted "to see the minority race represented in state government."[5]

The Squire's tirade was totally unexpected and outraged many of the attendees, who were unaccustomed to such straightforward talk and derogatory comments. While a few business leaders saw some wisdom in his remarks, his talk not only alienated the majority of the audience but also forced them to pledge their best effort to stop Scott. The *Raleigh News and Observer* praised Scott for placing "his cards on the table" and for standing behind his pledge to provide better services to North Carolinians.[6]

In an earlier speech to the organization of state school superintendents, Scott had been just as forthcoming. He thought there would be more money for schools if counties would do their part to evaluate property fairly for purposes of taxation and noted that tuition for state universities had not been raised in several years. The counties and universities had to raise their own funds; they could not "look to the state for everything." He then stressed the need for bringing Negro and Indian schools up to the level of white schools: "If you'll be honest with yourselves, you'll agree that they aren't right now."[7]

The governor-elect weighed in on health issues when he addressed the North Carolina Good Health Association. He came out strongly for a four-year medical school and a teaching hospital for the state and encouraged physicians to support better roads and telephones to enable rural inhabitants to get better access to medical care. He called attention to the urgent need for more doctors, more county hospitals, and better care for the mentally disabled.[8]

As Scott prepared for his gubernatorial responsibilities, he made two significant appointments. He chose Charlie Parker, who was responsible for "a brilliant piece of work" during the campaign, to handle publicity. He also picked John Marshall and Ben Roney as his two private secretaries (equivalent to an administrative assistant) and began hiring secretarial staff.[9] It had been the tradition in North Carolina for the incoming governor to select the chairman of the Democratic Party, and Scott, grateful for his invaluable work on the 1948 campaign, chose Capus Waynick.[10] Scott now had his most trusted advisers on board. Like many other incoming governors, he planned to wait until the General Assembly adjourned to make appointments to major boards and commissions. This delay meant that he could get support for his legislative program from state officials who hoped to hold on to their jobs and also from legislators who coveted such posts for themselves or for their constituents.

Perhaps the governor's most important confidante for the next four years was the one person who could actually boss Kerr Scott around, his devoted wife, Miss Mary. Mary Scott, a smiling and charming woman who barely came up to her husband's shoulder, was an excellent hostess at social events and also a very capable administrator as she ran the thirteen-hundred-acre dairy farm when her husband was agriculture commissioner. A proud, religious woman, she did not try to advise Kerr on day-to-day policy as governor, but she had a strong influence when he faced moral or ethical issues. Bill Friday observed that she was a very intelligent woman and a key to Scott's

Governor Scott and his wife, Miss Mary, in the governor's mansion, Raleigh. Scott was devoted to his wife, who was his confidante and adviser in important matters. Courtesy of the State Archives of North Carolina, Raleigh.

success. "One of the silent forces in his life—all to the good as she was also driven to improve the lot of the people she grew up with."[11]

As the year 1949 dawned, the time seemed propitious for the state to achieve its much-delayed progress. The *Raleigh News and Observer* observed that the populace had rejected the leadership of those opposed to a New Deal for the state. Those "men of persuasive pessimism" would surely be counted on to exhibit a spirit of repression and reaction, but Scott, no revolutionary, would "emerge as the vital leader of a still vital state." The paper insisted that "his greatest problem will not be cash, but courage."[12]

Prior to the inauguration, Governor R. Gregg Cherry contacted Scott (although some versions have it the other way around) and said he wanted to do the governor-elect a favor. Cherry knew that Scott lived on a dirt road in Hawfields and thought it would be a shame if a future governor did not have a paved road. When Kerr became governor, he would surely pave that road, and Cherry knew that Scott would be heavily criticized for so doing. Cherry asked Scott: "Why don't you let me do it before I go out of office?" Scott agreed since he knew there would be a "hue and cry from the press" if he did it himself. Governor Cherry got the Highway Department to come in, build a new road and a bridge across a creek, and connect Scott's road to Highway 54. His son Bob said: "I never saw a road built that fast." Scott named it Cherry Lane, the name it still carries today.[13]

As the General Assembly began arriving for the 1949 legislative session, it faced the same problems as previous legislatures: money, roads, schools, and alcohol. With requests that amounted to more than twice the anticipated revenues, the legislators were left with some difficult spending decisions. House members chose Kerr Craige Ramsey, a formidable opponent of Scott, as speaker of the House. Although Democrats controlled both houses by overwhelming margins,[14] the conflicts would be on ideological lines.[15]

On January 6, a plain-spoken man of the people, W. Kerr Scott, took the oath of office in Memorial Auditorium as chief executive, North Carolina's first farmer-governor in more than fifty years. Scott reluctantly donned his inaugural dress of striped pants, a long-tailed coat, and a high silk hat, fancy and incongruous garb for a dairy farmer. He called this his "2 cow suit"— since he had to sell two cows to pay for it.[16]

On a cold, sky-blue morning in Raleigh, more than fifty thousand spectators lined the streets to observe the inaugural parade, the most expensive on record. The parade marshal said it was the biggest turnout for any inaugural parade that he had seen. Governor Cherry, Governor-Elect Scott, and the fifteen-car motorcade of family and public officials made its way to the auditorium, where Cherry introduced the new head of state and Scott took the oath of office from Chief Justice Walter Stacy. Other inaugural activities included a luncheon for two hundred at the governor's mansion, an inaugural ball, and a reception hosted by the new governor for well-wishers at

Inauguration of W. Kerr Scott as governor of North Carolina, January 6, 1949. Scott is pictured with four former governors of the state. From left to right: J. Melville Broughton, R. Gregg Cherry, Kerr Scott, Clyde R. Hoey, and J. C. B. Ehringhaus. Courtesy of the State Archives of North Carolina, Raleigh.

which some fifteen hundred turned out. There was a Scottish air to the proceedings with skirling bagpipes and a song written in the governor's honor sung to the tune of "Loch Lomond."[17]

The highlight of inaugural week was the governor's address to the state and the legislature. Claiming a mandate from the people to carry out the pledges he had made in the campaign, Scott courageously presented his fifteen-point Go Forward legislative program. His recitation of his proposals varied only slightly from his platform in the 1948 election. He began his peroration, interrupted sixteen times by applause from the crowd of thirty-five hundred, by saying he faced the future with confidence and did not fear a recession. He noted that the state was in sound fiscal circumstances but needed to spend accumulated monies to bring public services current with the needs of the times.

First on the agenda was secondary road building, "essential to the economic as well as the cultural development of North Carolina." Scott wanted to get rid of the "mud tax" and build twelve thousand miles of blacktopped roads so that both industry and agriculture would flourish. He understood that transportation was the life blood of the economy, and he wanted to link the region as an economic and cultural unit. Good roads would help industry but would require a gas tax and/or a bond issue. Second on the list was education. "The most valuable crop we raise in North Carolina," Scott said, "is our children." He proposed increasing teachers' pay to a minimum salary of $2,400 and allocating more money for new school buildings. Worried about the increasing dropout rate at institutions of higher learning, he thought the answer might be a system of junior colleges. The third most important goal was better health. Scott wanted to continue building the medical school and teaching hospital at Chapel Hill, but the state could not "fulfill its mission without the correlated development of rural hospitals and clinics." He favored a dental school and urged vastly improved hospitals for the mentally ill.

These three items formed the core of his Go Forward program, but not far behind was his demand for the immediate improvement of public utilities: "Electric power is the cheapest labor the farmer, as well as the manufacturer, can hire." He pointed out that there were still over 100,000 farms in the state without electricity and that the public utilities charged industry too much for their power. The chronic lack of telephones also retarded rural development. He reminded listeners that, while these privately owned companies were entitled to a fair profit, the laws regulating utilities were outmoded and the Utilities Commission needed to be reorganized.

The remainder of the program included a statewide referendum on the alcoholic beverage question, more aid to veterans, the repeal of the anti–closed shop law, wage-hour legislation, revision of archaic election laws, increased pay for state employees to attract and retain superior personnel, more democratic representation on boards and commissions, and more efficiency in government. Scott hoped that, with the help of the legislature, barely mentioned in his talk, his proposals would come to fruition within four years. He would not "hesitate to slash red tape or push aside tradition, if it is necessary to eliminate bottlenecks." He promised to provide "first-hand reports of [his] stewardship" to the people and ended his talk by saying: "Let's go forward."[18]

Legislators reacted with muted enthusiasm. Several senators said they would never go along with an increase in the gas tax as their constituents were against any tax increases. Others opposed any change to the closed shop statute. D. L. Ward of Craven thought the majority of Scott's program would win approval, and another senator praised Scott's desire to get utility service into the rural areas.[19] Newspaper response was generally favorable. The *Durham Morning Herald* wrote that the governor's note of confidence was contagious and applauded him for recognizing the need to meet the deficit of service in the state: "With that vision, that sense of mission, he ought to make a good governor."[20] The *Raleigh News and Observer* agreed with Scott that the time had come for the state to embark on another broad advance and portrayed him as understanding that he could not do it alone. He appeared ready to act in concert with the legislature.[21]

Scott took office at an opportune time for his progressive program. There was a large surplus of general revenue funds and also a $31 million postwar reserve fund. Tired of dealing with the economic distress of the Depression and the paucity of certain products during the war, North Carolinians were ready for the legislature to spend the surplus and hoped the spending would lead to an expanded economy. Despite Scott's cries about the lack of services and a stingy legislature, much had already been done by the Cherry administration, which had provided for a 30 percent raise for teachers, increased education spending from $38 million a year to $60 million, and legislated a 20 percent increase for state employees. Under Cherry the road conditions improved as four thousand miles had been hard surfaced, mostly rural and secondary roads.[22]

As Scott began gearing up for his legislative program, his personal secretary, Francis Reesman, described how Scott organized and ran his office. All Scott's personal mail went directly to his desk. He would open his own mail and then give individual pieces to one of his two private secretaries, John Marshall or Ben Roney, or to another staffer for action. Mrs. Reesman stated that mail was very important to Scott and that he was very good at keeping up with his correspondence.

Mrs. Reesman also portrayed Scott as "a very outgoing person" with "a wonderful sense of humor," "a nice person, you enjoyed being around him." On a typical day the governor would arrive in his office around 8 A.M., but he did not like to stay cooped up in the office. He spent as much time as possible in Haw River rather than the governor's mansion and loved going out and attending events such as the Yam Festival in Tabor City and mingling with the people.

Scott's two key administrative assistants, Marshall and Roney, wrote many of his speeches, but the governor had the final say. He listened to advisers, but, as everyone expected, he had his own ideas. Scott, remembered Reesman, was a very pragmatic politician, "very sure of where he stood": "You weren't going to change him without very, very good reasons." Reesman described Scott as an idea man, not a detail man. He had a vision for a better North Carolina and intended to achieve his goals. She thought of him as a "maverick" who "did not mind kicking up dust a little bit and got a kick out of surprising people." He believed, according to Reesman, that without active involvement little would get done, and he liked to provoke people into positive action.[23]

Reesman observed two sides to Scott. She considered him an intelligent, educated man, but he never forgot his upbringing. He could speak in an educated manner, but he enjoyed the reaction to his more colloquial statements. "I am going to plow to the end of the row," for example, was always uttered with a twinkle in his eye. His personality varied with his audience—whether he was speaking with a university president or with local folks in Hawfields. He saw himself as an outsider in politics and could get angry when opposed. He could, however, accept and learn from a setback and once told Terry Sanford: "Well, it does a man good to get knocked down every now and then."[24]

Mrs. Reesman never saw any anger or rude behavior in the office. Governor Scott treated his staff as equals and was nice to them, never demanding or ordering people around, "as kind as he could be." When Reesman had a miscarriage and was in the hospital, he sent his chauffeur every evening to the hospital "with tons of flowers from his office and the prison farm." He called every day and was "very understanding and very compassionate."[25]

Scott's staff quickly learned that, unlike most politicians, their new boss was always on time. In fact, he was so prompt that he would sometimes be so early for meetings it would be embarrassing. He would often get to parties ahead of the host. So his staff would tell him that programs or meetings began later than they actually did so that he would not arrive early. His son, Bob Scott, once asked him about his obsessive need to be on time. He replied: "Well, it's a habit and I can't break it. When I grew up roads were not good. Automobiles were unreliable. One simply started a journey allowing for a breakdown, a flat tire, or getting stuck in the mud on a rural dirt road. So you gave yourself plenty of time and you began early. Nowadays the roads are good, cars are good. . . . I still make myself start early so I won't be late."[26]

As governor, Kerr Scott became the most visible political figure in the state. Although the state constitution said that the supreme executive power would be vested in the governor, his influence was significantly limited by the lack of veto power (not obtained until 1996) and the fact that he could serve only one term (not changed until 1977). Once the 1951 legislative session ended, he was a lame duck even though he still had eighteen months left in office. As director of the budget, the governor had some power in preparing and recommending a budget to the legislature, but the legislature had the final say and could change the governor's recommendations whenever it pleased.

Although the governor did have appointive powers—Scott would end up making over seven hundred appointments to various posts, commissions, and boards—his power of appointment and removal was restricted by law. Several choices needed legislative approval, and he could not remove any constitutional official elected by the public without cause. Members of the Council of State, which included the secretary of state, the attorney general, the auditor, the treasurer, the superintendent of public instruction, and the commissioners of labor, agriculture, and insurance, were all constitutional officers and were elected by popular vote. Although the Council of State was established as an advisory board for the governor, it did not always agree with his views.

As titular head of the Democratic Party, Scott had some authority in the political realm, but from 1949 to 1953 the conservative wing of the party worked tirelessly to reduce his power and influence. Thus, he had to turn to the bully pulpit to shape public opinion and elicit support for his policies. He effectively utilized the informal powers of the governor—access to the media through public addresses, meetings with legislators and public organizations, and periodic news conferences—to publicize his agenda and sway public opinion, in effect going over the heads of the legislators. He had not only the skill but also the will to use his persuasive personality, his status as head of state, and his mandate from the people to motivate the state's representatives to pass his bills.[27]

To that end, the governor held his first news conference on January 7, 1949. The press reported that Scott "discussed appointments with candor, gave frank answers to questions about his program and impressed his listeners" as a man who believed in openness in government. His first press conference would be the model for his four years in office. He held press conferences on most Tuesdays when he was in town and almost always answered questions forthrightly. On this occasion, he promised to present a specific plan to the legislature "very early" for financing his road-building program. He challenged the press to record his remarks accurately. He believed the citizens would be wholeheartedly for his proposals if the Fourth Estate were "to give the people the facts as they are."[28]

The legislature began deliberations on Scott's ambitious fifteen-point legislative program, wondering where it would get the revenue to pay for everything. As the legislators convened, lobbyists representing the business interests in the state flocked to Raleigh to exert pressure against any expanded tax structure.[29] In his second press conference, the newly elected governor threw out an olive branch when he praised the choice of committee chairmen announced by the House and Senate. When asked whether many of the new chairmen had not been supporters of Charlie Johnson, Scott answered that they were but that that was fine with him. He wanted all factions represented and did not anticipate having any trouble working with them.[30]

On January 13, Scott presented his budget message to the legislature and explained that the budget had been drawn up by the Advisory Budget Commission with input from Governor Gregg Cherry and Scott himself. The Advisory Budget Commission, related Scott, had not explored possible new sources of revenue, but it would, he believed, be necessary to find additional funds if the state were to go forward. The legislature would have to determine whether it would be a wise decision to hold back the large surplus accumulated in World War II in the face of unfilled service needs for the citizens. In specific terms, Scott's budget included a salary increase of twenty percent for schoolteachers, expansion of mental health facilities, $27.5 million for the construction of county roads, $550,000 a year for school health programs, and an allocation of the $72 million general fund surplus for permanent improvements.[31]

Scott did not focus his energies just on the budget and legislative matters; he confronted the race issue head on. In an address to the North Carolina Dairy Products Association the verbose governor declared that it was time that the state stopped dodging the Negro question. "They came here against their will brought in chains," he said, continuing: "I am going to follow through and see that the minority race has a fair opportunity and gets the training [to fit into the state's growth]." Negroes had been handicapped by insufficient formal education, and one step toward rectifying this problem would be a $6 million building program at the Agricultural and Technical College at Greensboro, the predominant Negro school in the state. The

Negroes, judged Scott, needed to be properly trained, particularly in the mechanical trades. Although Scott seemed condescending in his remarks, his speech was praised in northern newspapers like the *New York Times* and the *Hartford Courant* as a ray of hope for Negroes in the state.[32]

By the middle of January, the Squire from Haw River had finalized his road program and presented his plan in a special message before a joint session of the legislature. He called for a $200 million bond issue and a one-cent increase in the gas tax to finance the work. The money would be applied only to secondary roads. The combination of borrowing money at low interest rates and a modest increase in the gas tax would be the most equitable and least burdensome way to get the roads built. The state, lectured Scott, had a sixty-three-thousand-mile road system, but only sixteen thousand miles of it were hard surfaced. He asserted that the state could build over twelve thousand miles of hard-surfaced roads in the next four years and also improve other rural roads sufficiently so as not to interrupt school bus service and keep the farm-to-market roads open. Money would not be allocated from the bond issue any faster than necessary to keep up with the work. Since the state constitution required a vote of the people on a bond issue, the governor asked the legislature to enact a law providing for the road bond issue to be submitted to the people "as early as possible."[33] Many politicians had not forgotten Scott's adamant opposition to Charles Johnson's suggestion of just such a bond issue in the 1948 campaign, calling the idea "ridiculous." Scott explained that he had changed his mind after consulting with gas company representatives, transportation experts, farmers, school and highway officials, and others and that the bond issue was the only possible solution for the funding of the road-building program.[34]

In a persuasive editorial, the *Raleigh News and Observer* contended that, since this was the largest bond issue ever proposed in the state, there would be a difference of opinion about the wisdom of the idea. The legislature should debate the merits of the idea, but there should not be a prolonged discussion as the "matter should undoubtedly be submitted to the people" and the real debate left to the voters, who would decide the fate of the bond issue. The one-cent gas tax did not require a vote of the people and should be decided by the legislature, but the bond issue and the gas tax should be debated together.[35]

Scott took time off to go to Washington, DC, for the inauguration of President Harry Truman, where he and his party attended the inaugural gala and observed the swearing-in ceremony. While in DC, he joined in the

Governor Scott greeting President Harry Truman on his visit to Raleigh in October 1951, standing in front of the President's plane, *The Independence*. To Truman's left is Gordon Grey, the second president of the Consolidated University of North Carolina. Scott and Truman, who shared similar backgrounds and values, became fast friends. Courtesy of the State Archives of North Carolina, Raleigh.

inaugural parade by leading the state float, which advertised North Carolina as "The Best Balanced State."[36] This was exactly what he intended to accomplish as governor, an economic boom based on a balance between agriculture and industry. He returned to Raleigh ready for some tough decisions and eager to confront a conservative legislature.

While the governor concentrated primarily on legislative matters, other events intruded on his agenda. Scott said several times that the most difficult decision he had to make as governor was to determine a man's right to live or die. In North Carolina, the governor possessed the power of executive clemency through pardon, the commutation of a sentence, the lessening of a sentence, or a stay of execution. When Scott took office, there were seven men on death row. The most sensational case was that of James R. Creech, a wealthy thirty-seven-year-old Smithfield farmer and businessman who killed his wife with two blasts from a double-barreled shotgun, the second of which "blew off the top of her head." Creech's high-priced legal defenders argued that he was overcome by the evils of alcohol and was not responsible for his acts. Despite a spirited defense, the jury found him guilty and sentenced him to death. His lawyers appealed to the North Carolina Supreme Court, which ruled 5–2 that the sentence should stand. The majority of the court determined that Creech clearly revealed "his stubborn purpose and unbending will to kill the deceased."

In a clemency hearing, the state Parole Board turned down a request to reduce the sentence to life imprisonment. Now it was up to Scott. The governor was inundated by pleas from both sides, and over two thousand people had contacted him asking for mercy. The *News and Observer* cautioned him that the case should be decided on its legal merit, not because Creech was well-to-do. Scott, a moral and religious man, was "torn and anguished by the decision over life and death." As his secretary, Francis Reesman, recalled, he had stayed up all night the day before the execution, wrestling with his decision. The following day he looked haggard and tired. He talked with his staff about the stressful process of making such a momentous choice, how he reacted to the crank telephone calls, his concern for the condemned man's family, and his sensitivity to the political repercussions of his judgment. He had already announced he would not intervene, but he considered stopping the execution up to the last minute. Creech was to die at 10:00 A.M., and the governor sat by the open telephone line to the prison. Reesman described the scene in the governor's office: "Slowly time slipped away, tension mounting in the room until we scarcely breathed. The governor glanced at his watch, at the phone. . . . A loud mournful tolling filled the room. It was the steeple clock at Capitol Square marking the hour as usual, but this morning spreading the message of death, insistently, mournfully. . . . The phone on the governor's desk buzzed. He answered briefly, then without looking up, spoke softly. 'It's all over.' The tension lifted, but the crushing burden of responsibility was his forever. After a minute or so, he rose slowly to his feet to leave. As he passed my desk, he paused to murmur. 'And I thought I really wanted this job.'"[37]

Prior to arriving at a conclusion, Scott had consulted with lawyers and other experts and determined that his decision had to be legal, not based on moral considerations. Creech had been convicted by a jury. As Scott noted: "The slaying was inexcusable. And the defendant should be punished to the degree of the crime." It was the law and the law had to be obeyed: "I don't have the last word. The last word is the law." Scott received hundreds of letters expressing "gratification" for his decision, knowing it was difficult and heart wrenching.[38] W. C. Pou congratulated him for "the courage [he] displayed in standing for justice in the Creech case."[39] In response to a man who had asked for a reprieve for Creech, he explained his judgment as best he could: "You realize, of course, that this was a trying experience and that I reached my decision only after prayer and the deepest consideration."[40]

In February 1949, Scott made two crucial appointments that would have a significant influence on his administration. He recommended Jonathan Daniels, the editor of the *News and Observer,* as the Democratic national committeeman. Although a controversial choice, since many in the state thought that Daniels was far too liberal on the subject of race, the state Democratic Committee accepted, as it always had, the governor's selection.[41] Scott now had an experienced and knowledgeable backer who had close ties to the Truman administration. The *New York Times* called Daniels, who had been press secretary to both Franklin Roosevelt and Truman, one of the South's most prominent liberals. It quoted Daniels as saying that, although reactionaries had power in the South, a great liberal leadership would come out of the region and provide social services for all its people: "North Carolina is progressive and wants to stay that way. This state believes in equal opportunities for all its citizens."[42]

The second key appointment was even more important. Scott persuaded Dr. Henry W. Jordan, the brother of B. Everett Jordan, to take the post of acting chairman of the state Highway Commission. Jordan, an industrialist, had been the Sixth District highway commissioner for the past four years and had worked closely with the current Highway Commission. In Jordan, Scott had found a man who was acceptable to both sides on the road bond issue. Since most members of the current commission had opposed Scott in 1948, Jordan was the perfect choice to bridge the differences. He professed to want nothing more than to carry out Scott's road program and asked the eight to nine thousand employees of the Highway Commission to give him their full support.[43] That was just the sentiment that Scott wanted to hear.

Scott had attempted to co-opt the dissidents on the Highway Commission by choosing one of their own while at the same time getting a proven and effective leader to implement his road program. Shortly thereafter, he shored up his support for new roads by getting the endorsement of Bob

Hanes, the acknowledged leader of the state bankers. Hanes's approval was advantageous to Scott as his opponents had hoped to use bankers to thwart the plan. Hanes proclaimed that the bond issue and tax package "is not only needed, but is necessary to the continued growth of North Carolina."[44]

As he had promised in his run for governor, Scott agreed to meet with Negro leaders in the state to hear their grievances. State members of the NAACP responded by presenting him with a seven-point list of recommendations for ending discrimination. Included were requests for equal employment, the appointment of Negroes to policymaking boards on the basis of recommendations from the NAACP, Negroes to be allowed to enter tax-supported institutions of higher learning on an unrestricted basis, the abolition of segregation on public transportation, the elimination of widespread inequalities of opportunity in secondary schools, and the enforcement of criminal sanctions against registrars who refused to register qualified Negro voters. The NAACP congratulated Scott on his election and pledged its backing for his administration. Its members had heard and read his remarks pledging full support for all the people and announced that they had the same objective, a more democratic government. Scott answered by saying he planned to name Negroes to the Board of Education and other agencies. He carefully explained that he would study each one of the seven points in the presentation and "do what is best for all the people of the state," as long as it would bring benefit without friction.[45]

The governor merely meeting with the Negro leaders in the state was an advance in race relations. The NAACP demands seem, from today's perspective, reasonable and necessary. In 1949, however, many constituents were outraged that Scott had met personally with Negroes, and for his effort the governor received several hateful and critical letters, demonstrating yet again the volatile nature of race relations. Robert Johnson conveyed that it had been "a very painful task to read that stinking, red tainted article . . . concerning the niggers in our beloved state." He continued: "You belong back on the farm you dumb clod knocker. What right have you to begin telling people how they must marry, live with and mingle with niggers in N.C."[46] Scott did not bother to reply to that letter, but he did respond to a more muted protest from a Mrs. R. L. Welsh. She did not use any derogatory terms, writing instead that integration would never work in the state. The rights the Negroes were asking for were not in "keeping with our N.C. rights": "Can you imagine anything more humiliating than a white lady being forced to sit beside a drunken Negro . . . or our children being forced to sit in class with the Negro children?" She predicted that murder and assaults would break out if Negroes got equal rights. Scott replied: "Certainly no question of social equality is to be considered seriously." He believed that the Negro should have equal opportunity for economic advancement, but even this must be achieved step-by-step to prevent conflict between the races as that would defeat the purpose he was trying to achieve—better relations between the races.[47]

T. F. Young thought Scott was leaning favorably toward the NAACP, which was mounting a "viscious [sic] attack against our way of life": "We as white people should be proud of our race and its accomplishments and not want to see it change to a molatto [sic] groupe [sic]." Charlie Parker replied to the letter and tried to mollify Young. He wrote that Scott was no tool of the NAACP: "Nor need you fear that anything he does will lead to the deterioration of the white race." Scott wanted Negroes to have the economic opportunity to contribute taxes to pay for services: "There is no question of social equality involved in the Governor's program for Negroes."[48] At the other end of the political spectrum, Scott got encouragement from L. Brooks Hays, a moderate congressman from Arkansas. Hays congratulated the governor for his "forthright" statement on the need to give attention to the problems of race relations. Scott thanked Hays and agreed with him on the need to improve the economic status of the Negro but cautioned that government should move "wisely and slowly" without "stirring up undue strife."[49]

Scott knew that racial discord could destroy his legislative program, so he managed to tiptoe carefully around this issue. He favored continuing the segregation of the races, but he was willing to meet with Negroes in the state and do whatever he could to promote economic opportunities. Although very little was accomplished in reference to the NAACP's seven recommendations, Scott's actions were symbolic, and his racial views were far ahead of most contemporary politicians in the South.

While concentrating on race relations, roads, and schools, the peripatetic Scott also pushed for utility reform. Under a bill he recommended, the Utilities Commission could order a company to provide adequate service and additional facilities if its service was inadequate or unreasonably discriminatory. The bill would expand the powers of the commission to regulate the right-of-way for telephone, electric, and telegraph lines.[50] On several occasions, the governor mentioned the importance of expanding the state's port facilities in Wilmington and Morehead City. He did not say how he would pay for such expansion beyond suggesting that a bond issue might be necessary.[51] He made it clear that he did not want to pursue the expansion of port facilities until he had solidified support for roads and schools.

One area of concern caught Scott's attention, if not his commitment. Labor leaders demanded repeal of the anti–closed shop law, which, in effect, prohibited labor unions in the workplace. Scott owed the labor unions for their support in 1948 and had urged revisions to the law, but he knew the bill had little chance of passage owing to vigorous antiunion sentiment, and he did not want to endanger the chances of passing his major legislation by pushing too hard for a labor bill. He did, however, send a letter to the house committee considering the bill and made a speech "strongly urging" passage of a bill that would have allowed voluntary union shop agreements between employers and labor. The legislature killed the measure, and, reflecting the animosity toward labor among state legislators, "Cousin" Wayland Spruill said: "We've got 'em by the throat now."[52]

Kerr Scott now turned to a subject dear to his heart—education. Everyone in the state knew that there was a desperate need for more and better schools, but the citizens did not want to have to pay increased taxes to achieve that goal. Prior to speaking on the issue, Scott gathered thirty influential Tar Heel educators to brief them on what he was planning on saying and seek their advice.[53] By reaching out to these potential key supporters of expanded school funding, he solidified his base before he made a statewide appeal. He then made an impassioned address on education before a joint session of the General Assembly, urging legislators to solve the drastic education problems facing the state. In advancing his proposals, he added that he was carrying out the recommendations of the state Education Commission and Board of Education. He asked for a $50 million bond issue to be submitted to the people and voted on at the same time as the road bond issue. He requested use of the $30 million postwar reserve fund to build new schools since the glaring deficiencies in school buildings in the state qualified as an emergency. He suggested extra taxes on cigarettes and amusements to help pay for the improvements. "There is no point in playing hide and seek with this problem," he noted. "Let's get together and thresh it out."

The reaction, as usual, was mixed. Senator J. C. Eagles remarked: "It was the most forthright speech I've heard in this legislature. I think now the people of the state will understand the problem we have." Others called the plan "sound" and "fine" and recognized that you could not have services unless you paid for them. Several solons opposed new taxes and the use of the reserve funds. Senator Lee Weathers said the bond vote was "most reasonable" while the suggested tax increases were "fantastic and unreasonable."[54]

"The Nuisance and Disturber," as it was known to many eastern North Carolinians, pointed out that some legislators had determined that North Carolina was doing well enough and did not need to sacrifice for the future. The paper favored Scott's program because better education was essential to the spirit of progressivism; otherwise, the state would slip back into the mud hole. The decision was not a "matter of the quantity of dollars, but of the quality of ourselves."[55] To move his proposals along, Scott offered to absorb some of the "cussing" that tax bills might provoke. He would be happy to introduce any tax bill and endure the negative comments so long as the legislature would not "jump all over [him] like a bunch of wolves."[56]

The governor knew that his tax "suggestions" would generate little traction and his reform agenda faced tough sledding. John Larkins, a state senator and fiscal conservative, was typical of the Scott naysayers. He remembered that, while he got along with Scott personally and Scott had some good ideas, he and other conservatives "mainly disagreed with the method of financing programs."[57] The real stumbling block for Scott's agenda, as demonstrated by Larkins, was how to persuade the fiscal conservatives to accept any tax increase or even a bond measure to pay for his program.

Scott concentrated on the road bond legislation, for, without approval of this proposal, the Go Forward program would stall. He surmised that he would get the education bond approved and that that issue would help the turnout for the road bonds as many citizens viewed education progress as essential. However, a favorable legislative vote on a statewide referendum for the road bond proposal was uncertain. The legislature talked constantly about reducing Scott's $200 million request by $50 million. Scott lamented that, if that were the case, then one-fourth of the people entitled to roads would not get them. If he could not get all $200 million, then he "might as soon" not have any.[58]

To overcome the legislature's recalcitrance, Scott focused on getting public opinion behind the bill. He held frequent press conferences and made a concerted effort to educate the voters by touting the benefits of his Go Forward agenda. In 1949 pretelevision North Carolina, he had no way of communicating directly with his supporters other than through press conferences, an occasional radio broadcast, and public addresses. During his press appearance on February 8, broadcast in this instance for the first time over forty-six radio stations, he invited listeners to attend the meet-

Governor Scott drinking milk with a farm worker. Scott never forgot his upbringing and enjoyed spending time back at his farm and socializing with what he called the "rural element." Courtesy of the State Archives of North Carolina, Raleigh.

ing of the legislature's Joint Public Roads Committee: "Let your legislators know how you feel about good roads." He asserted that he would accept no compromise on the $200 million figure and promised that the money would be spent without waste. As for financing: "You got to go after something if you want it." If you get "so tied up figuring why something can't be done, you would never get started."[59]

Some twelve hundred of Scott's supporters showed up in Raleigh at the meeting of the Joint Public Roads Committee. Thirty-seven members were in favor of the bond issue with only two against. The two opponents, however, were formidable. A. H. Graham, the recently resigned commissioner of highways, objected to the referendum because it was too expensive and the system already had enough funding. He accused Scott of playing politics with roads as the governor had ridiculed the idea when Johnson proposed a bond issue during the 1948 campaign. John Sprunt Hill, another former highway commissioner, explained that only 20 percent of the traffic was on rural byways and that the money would be better spent on primary roads, which carried 80 percent of the traffic.

Scott's supporters, waving placards and cheering, turned the hearing into a rally. Mrs. Frank Andrews allowed as to how farmwives were tired of riding "on roads that make you go bumpity-bump-bump." George Coble, head of Coble Dairies, argued that the roads were not a class matter as they would help everyone. At the very least, the people in attendance let the committee know that they wanted the right to express their opinion on road construction in a plebiscite.[60]

Heartened by the public outpouring at the legislative hearing, Scott went before the Farm Bureau at its annual convention to elicit help. Blunt spoken and gruff as always, he asked the attendees to convince legislators to provide the services they had promised when elected: "Hell, I laid it on the line and told them [the legislators] where they could get the money. Now a swarm of lobbyists are coming to Raleigh . . . to try to block anything in the way of a program. I need your help and I mean I need it. I need the help of all people who are interested in seeing North Carolina develop." The following day, the North Carolina Farm Bureau gave its seal of approval to Scott's road plan.[61] That ratification had been expected, but every group committed to the cause helped the movement for better roads.

Initially, the House Public Roads Committee approved the bill and passed it on to the Finance Committee,[62] but problems developed when the Senate passed amendments to reduce the amount to $100 million, to make the gas tax contingent on approval of the bonds, and to set the date for the vote as June 28, not allowing the governor to determine the date.[63]

Now faced with having to compromise on the $100 million Senate figure, Scott appealed to the state Highway Commission for help: "I hate to see a restricted program that would keep up the feudin', fightin' and fussin' over roads." He explained that those who got their roads fixed would be pleased but that those who did not would be dissatisfied and that the neglected roads would probably never get paved. He emphasized that the voters deserved a chance to voice their opinion on the matter. Although many members of the commission remained anti-Scott, Chairman Henry Jordan promised full support from his organization.[64]

Scott, the outsider, continued to have difficulty bucking the entrenched conservatives in the legislature.[65] He said that he had to overcome the brakes put on by the conservatives and that it took time to throw off their influence on legislative thinking. They belonged to the "Can't Do Club": "I've never been invited into that fraternity."

The momentum changed when, on March 1, the governor held a meeting in his office with every major figure in the state assembly—"it was time for a meeting of the minds." Scott realized that it was necessary to do "a little head-knocking," and, by the time the conference ended around midnight, he had the support of most of the participants. Twenty-five senators reportedly signed a round-robin endorsement of the road bond bill. The governor managed to put pressure on the legislature by remarking that he would remember the opposition to his program when they asked him for favors and appointments in the days to come.[66]

After March 1, Scott became more upbeat and confident every day as the General Assembly seemed to be "jelling" on schools and roads. Some members of the legislature began to discern a change in attitude about the road bond referendum.[67] The mood had changed because of Scott's convincing public advocacy for the plan, his personal intervention with individual legislators, and the mandate from his overwhelming victory in the 1948 campaign. Scott's strategists insisted that legislators who voted for the referendum could reduce the political fallout by assuring voters that they would not actually be voting for the bonds or for increased taxes and spending; they would merely be presenting the issues to the voters for their approval or disapproval. By early March the momentum for passage increased when, despite earlier misgivings, House Speaker Kerr Craige Ramsey and Lieutenant Governor Pat Taylor signed on, a significant boost to the possibility of success for the bill.[68]

Scott's struggle with the legislature took a brief hiatus when suddenly and unexpectedly, on March 6, 1949, only shortly after he had taken office, US senator J. Melville Broughton dropped dead of a heart attack.[69] The junior senator's death stunned North Carolinians. The state had anticipated a long and successful Senate career for the popular ex-governor, who seemed to be in vigorous health. Now he was dead. As the immediate shock subsided following his funeral on March 9, political speculation regarding his successor intensified. Papers listed the early contenders as William B. Umstead (not a real option as Scott and Umstead disliked each other intensely), L. P. McLendon and B. Everett Jordan (both early supporters of Scott in the 1948 race), Dr. Clarence Poe, Willis Smith, R. Mayne Albright, and Capus Waynick (the architect of Scott's 1949 victory).[70] Poe was certainly too old, Smith too conservative, and Albright too young. Waynick was the early favorite, along with L. P. McLendon. Indeed, some maneuvering and discussion regarding the Senate vacancy did not even wait until Broughton's interment. W. T. Bost, the dean of North Carolina political writers, remarked: "There was no way to contain a commonwealth willing enough to mourn the loss of one of the most illustrious of its modern figures, but too impatient to await the orderly selection of his successor. This isn't seemly, but it is inevitable."[71]

The newspapers in the state filled their columns with endless analysis, much of it designed to influence Scott's choice. Jonathan Daniels pinned his hopes on Waynick.[72] The anti-Scott *Charlotte Observer* favored former Senator Umstead as he had Washington experience and choosing him might ease Scott's path in negotiating his Go Forward program through a legislature filled with Umstead adherents.[73]

In his initial public statement about the vacancy, Scott declared that he would make a choice after "due deliberation." He admitted that he was overwhelmed with political advice owing to thousands of telegrams, letters, phone calls, and personal visits. "Evidently," he wryly observed, "there is some sort of campaign going on."[74]

Indeed there were several full-blown campaigns in action, and only an actual appointment could calm the waters. The longer Scott hesitated, the more agitated the posturing to influence his choice. He was clearly perplexed at the mountain of conflicting advice he was receiving about a decision he never expected to make. He began to believe that the choice of any of the top three candidates—Umstead, Waynick, or McLendon—would incense the partisans of those not chosen and might jeopardize his legislative agenda. So he considered alternative choices. Jonathan Daniels, highly regarded in Washington, was one possibility, but Daniels wanted no part of the internecine political battles in the state. It was just as well as the liberal Daniels was a divisive figure, roundly despised in many parts of the state, and probably could not win in 1950.[75]

As Scott continued to deliberate, many correspondents urged him to make an immediate appointment for the good of the state.[76] The *Gastonia Gazette* accused him of playing "nauseating" politics. There were numerous good men available, and he was holding representatives and legislators in line so that he could "ram some of his pet legislation" through the assembly.[77] Some urged the choice of a Christian leader and statesman rather than a shrewd politician.[78] One writer merely suggested that Scott seek guidance from the Heavenly Father.[79] Scott replied that he was naturally "seeking divine guidance as I approach the hour of decision."[80]

Scott got a significant number of crank letters from those who wanted the seat but were not qualified. A classic of the genre was from Ormond Fooshee, a thirty-four-year-old unmarried farmer who announced that he was qualified because he did not drink. He thought he could handle the job: "I am not a member of nothing except the church and the Farm Bureau, so I don't owe any one [*sic*] any thing [*sic*]. I don't think people would through [*sic*] you out of office if you gave me the job." Fooshee claimed he had "as good horse sense as the next man" and "could do better than some of the birds up in Washington."[81]

Fred Bonitz, an old friend, sympathized with Scott's dilemma and reminded him: "No matter who you name you will make the others peevish to say the least and you will have to hunt up jobs for all of them." Bonitz's own choice was Waynick.[82] Scott initially wanted to pick Waynick, to whom he owed much. A telephone conversation between Scott and Waynick, recalled by Waynick, was as follows: "Scott: People are saying this fellow Waynick would make a good senator. Waynick: Governor, he'd make a great senator. But if there's any embarrassment to you whatsoever, don't you name him. I won't lift my hand to get you to do it."[83] Waynick thought he had a good chance to be picked and, despite his protestations, had written a few letters extolling his own virtues and asking for assistance in getting the post.

Scott knew the political fight for the full term in 1950 would be brutal, and he wanted someone who had the strength and ability to stand for election.[84] At this juncture, he jettisoned Waynick, concerned that he would have difficulty holding the seat, and then decided to eliminate all the early favorites and begin his search anew.[85] In his March 11 news conference he publicly interred any hopes the early favorites might have had by declaring that the position was still "wide-open." Asked if there were any "dark horses," he replied: "One comes through my door every hour or so."[86] The longer he delayed, the more likely he had a sensational surprise in the offing. However, on March 15, nine days after Broughton's passing, he merely handed out a list of forty-eight names submitted to him with more than one endorsement. Asked when the final decision would be made, he blandly replied that he needed time to read all the letters and telegrams he had received and that the Senate was not doing much anyway.[87]

Scott was undeterred by the press, and his dissembling was a purposeful tactic. His delay marked a frantic effort to press into service the most unlikely of all serious candidates. For, by March 12, Scott had made up his mind to offer the Senate seat to Dr. Frank Porter Graham, the most renowned liberal in the state and president of the Consolidated University of North Carolina.

The path to Dr. Graham's selection—and his tortured acceptance—was both circuitous and difficult. It began when Miss Mary, Scott's wife, came across the list of forty-eight men in her husband's coat pocket. She asked him to read her the names, and, when he got to Graham, she said: "Well, you can stop right there. As far as I'm concerned, that's it."[88] Scott paused. For probably the first time, he thought about Graham as a serious candidate. Later that same day he conferred with Jonathan Daniels, who also suggested Graham. Scott responded: "I think that would be wonderful if you could persuade him to take the job." Daniels agreed to go at once to Chapel Hill and approach Graham.[89] Thus began a bizarre period of eleven days in which Scott and Daniels repeatedly tried to convince Graham to enter elective politics—a role he had never envisioned for himself.

Daniels's first conference with Graham was inconclusive. Despite a supporting call from Scott, Graham declined the offer. At the behest of Scott, Daniels returned the next day, and Graham capitulated—for a brief period. He later called Scott and reneged. Scott remembered the exchange: "He apparently became so overwhelmed with the thought of taking on such a task and leaving the university that he . . . said he positively would have to withdraw his decision."[90] Most politicians would have given up at this point, but Scott continued to press Graham despite intensified public pressure to make an immediate selection. The *Gastonia Gazette* and the *Charlotte Observer* wrote that the long delay was harmful to the state, which needed both its senators, and concluded that Scott had put politics ahead of the state's welfare.[91]

Spurred by public criticism, Scott once more turned his full power of persuasion on the reluctant university president and sent Jonathan Daniels to Graham for one more attempt. Daniels argued forcefully that Graham must go to the Senate, where he could work in service to his lifelong goal, world peace, as well as his cherished domestic goals, federal aid to education and better labor-management relations. Daniels knew that the call to duty was the credo by which Dr. Frank lived his life, and Graham finally succumbed to the blandishments of Scott and Daniels and agreed to accept the appointment. Scott and Daniels had never asked Graham's opinion on any issue, and, except for a commitment to run in 1950, Scott asked only that he "go up to Washington and then be on your own."[92]

All that remained was a public announcement. Rather than call a press conference, Scott wanted to get maximum shock and surprise out of his announcement, so he decided to present his choice at the O. Max Gardner Award dinner in Chapel Hill. The selection was unknown except to a very few, who were sworn to silence. After presenting the Gardner Award, he told his audience: "While I am on my feet, I want to make the announcement here tonight that your next Senator is . . . Dr. Frank Graham." For a moment, there was stunned silence—a more unlikely choice could hardly be imagined. Then came cheers and a thunderous standing ovation for the beloved Dr. Frank. To Scott's great delight, his surprise had worked to perfection.[93]

Frank Porter Graham, the diminutive sixty-two-year-old educator and liberal activist, waited until the applause died down before arising to accept. With customary self-effacement, he observed that he had rejected Scott's importuning two or three times: "But he is a stubborn Scotch Presbyterian. I found that I would have to say yes." He confessed that it had been the most difficult decision of his life because it meant that he would have to leave the university. Scott, always one to have the last word, jumped up to confirm that Graham had indeed rejected him two or three times: "But I would not take no for an answer."[94]

The Graham appointment made sense for several reasons. Recognizing Graham as a great humanitarian, Scott admired his Christian stewardship and his identification with the dispossessed. He knew that Graham had endorsed his Go Forward program as well as Truman's Fair Deal and thought they were in agreement on every major state issue. He also liked Graham because he was not a lawyer and not a professional politician. He believed that Graham's selection would be approved by his liberal base, and he hoped this choice would expand his support among those who had elected him in 1948. Finally, it was good politics. The governor calculated that Graham's popularity and national prestige would make him a powerful and successful candidate in 1950, perhaps scaring off all rivals.[95]

Frank Graham, a native Tar Heel, had graduated from the University of North Carolina, earned a master's degree in history from Columbia University, and returned to Chapel Hill to teach history. After serving as a marine in World War I, the young Graham became dean of students. He was chosen president of the University of North Carolina in 1931 (later the Consolidated University of North Carolina) and served in that post until 1950.

In retrospect, Scott overestimated Graham's popularity and underestimated the potential for harsh disagreement with many of his liberal stands. The governor might have done well to check into Graham's membership in some controversial organizations before choosing the lifelong educator. Graham had long been a proponent of the right of labor to organize and became peripherally involved in several publicized strikes. He was a member of the Southern Conference on Human Welfare, which Communists had infiltrated, and he was careless about signing political petitions from radical leftist groups, some of which, like the American Committee for Democracy and Intellectual Freedom, were Communist fronts.[96] The *Goldsboro News-Argus* pronounced that, as expected, Scott had done the unexpected. He had ignored Graham's past associations and neatly sidestepped "any personal complications which might result from his having named a man who seriously sought the place."[97]

Graham had finally agreed to accept the nomination because he relished the challenge and the opportunity to be a spokesman for world peace and because he simply could not shirk his duty. And he did so despite the unrelenting opposition of his wife, Marian. She realized that going to Washington would take him out of his element, and she feared that politics would subject him to pressures and forces that might well destroy him.

Press and public response to the nomination gave vivid illustration that Scott's decision had the potential for spectacular political conflict. The exuberance of Graham's advocates was matched by his opponents' anger and lamentations. The loudest hosannas came from a Jonathan Daniels editorial. He wrote that "our hearts swell with gladness" (a line from the official state song) with the choice of the state's "most vital advocate of full and equal opportunity" for all the people.[98] The *Chapel Hill Weekly* stated: "[Scott] could not have found anyone better qualified for membership in the Senate by character, intellect and training."[99] The majority of the daily press in the

Governor Scott shocked the state when he made the unlikely choice of the liberal Frank Porter Graham, the president of the Consolidated University of North Carolina, to succeed the deceased Senator J. Melville Broughton in the US Senate. In a bitter and vicious campaign in 1950, Willis Smith defeated Graham in the contest for a full six-year term. Courtesy of the State Archives of North Carolina, Raleigh.

state enthusiastically applauded the pick, one paper predicting that Graham was held in such high esteem that no one could beat him in 1950.[100]

On the other hand, some papers recognized the highly controversial nature of the selection and surmised that Graham's political tenure might be brief. The *Fayetteville Observer* observed: "Committed to Truman's civil rights issue, he will find he had many friends who would go along with his advanced liberalism at an academic level, who will not be there on a legislative level."[101] The *Charlotte News*, never friendly to Scott, presciently noted about Graham: "No one inspires such fierce loyalty and devotion, no one arouses such bitter enmity."[102]

For black leaders and the black press, Graham's anointment was manna from heaven. The *Carolina Times* called Scott and Graham men of destiny who would hasten the death of the old order in the South.[103] Walter White, head of the NAACP, called the decision the most dramatic and "most heartening evidence of the political metamorphosis in the South."[104]

And therein lay the problem—Graham's liberal tendencies. While most national newspapers—the *New York Times* and the *Washington Post,* among others—approved of the choice, his detractors saw him as a dreamer with a gift for affiliating with disloyal organizations and considered him far too advanced in his views on race relations. The *Montgomery Journal* did not like his subversive memberships, his kowtowing to labor unions, or his membership on Truman's Committee on Civil Rights and predicted he would be badly defeated in 1950.[105]

After reading his mail, which revealed 88 percent favorable responses, Scott must have been pleased with the almost universal backing of his nominee. The letters came from a dazzling array of citizens from every station of life—farmers, schoolteachers, businessmen, laborers, and distinguished Americans. Harry Golden, the editor of the *Carolina Israelite,* wrote: "Now is the winter of our discontent made glorious summer by the two sons of Carolina, Scott and Graham."[106] Other tributes poured in from President Truman, Eleanor Roosevelt, and General George C. Marshall. Marshall thought: "It is the country that is to be congratulated and I think I am the best qualified witness to this view of the appointment."[107] Truman was delighted to welcome to the Senate an enthusiastic southern supporter, a man of highest character and integrity who possessed an enlightened viewpoint and was an earnest champion of the forgotten man.[108]

The critics were mainly upset with Graham's racial views and his involvement in left-wing causes. Scott received quite a few angry letters that foreshadowed the depth of racial animosity that would be revealed during the election of 1950. An anonymous postcard decried his "attitude in trying to force the nigs and whites to mingle and mix together so we are dun [sic] with you and him also not the friend we was."[109] Other correspondents sent missives to "Governor Cur Scott" accusing him of "playing drop the handkerchief with Joe Stalin"[110] and wondering why the state would want to send a socialist-Communist to the Senate: "We already have too many Reds and Pinks. . . . Why not send Graham and all like him to Moscow."[111]

Never bothered by what he considered unwarranted criticism, Scott turned his attention back to the legislature. He seized the initiative with a radio talk designed to prod a few of the "hesitants" in the General Assembly. There was talk, he declaimed, about dangerous spending that would lead to a bankrupt state. His road program was not radical but a reasonable investment in the state's future. He denounced the lobbyists for the giant oil companies for trying to kill the gas tax and for spreading propaganda about his changing his mind about road bonds. He admitted so doing, but his reversal on this important subject merely demonstrated a flexible mind.

In his address Scott told the citizens of the state that they could not plead poverty, except perhaps of the spirit, in opposing a one-cent gas tax. They spent much more on alcoholic beverages and non-essentials than the state spent "guarding the health and educating the million school children in the state." Prior to signing off, he called on citizens to come to Raleigh to attend a public hearing of the Appropriation and Education Committees and to talk to their representatives about improving schools.[112] The *News and Observer* supported Scott with a front-page editorial calling on those who wanted the state to move forward to come to Raleigh to help determine the future of the commonwealth. They should not "be held back by the timid or the tightwads, by those of little faith and those whose private interests are more precious to them than the progress of the state."[113]

Scott and the *News and Observer* got exactly what they wanted when a large crowd of five thousand citizens came to the state capitol for a rally to demand better schools. The crowd listened while sixteen speakers, including Dr. Frank Graham and those representing women's colleges and Negro education, praised Scott's education plan. The highlight of the day was a dramatic speech given by the frail, elderly Dr. J. Y. Joyner, who had been superintendent of schools under Governor Charles B. Aycock during the first renaissance in state education. Joyner favored the recommendations for public schools presented by the North Carolina Education Association because they represented the considered views of the experts, because they would raise teachers' salaries, and because the changes would increase and improve the education facilities for the state's greatest resource—its children. He asked his audience and the legislators to keep Aycock's dream alive. He finished with a flourish: "Finally I favor them because I love North Carolina. Gentlemen of the Assembly of North Carolina, our hopes, our faith, triumphant over our fears, are all with thee. Deny not the cry of a million children, crying for a better chance, crying for better schools."[114] Joyner, the grand old man of North Carolina public education, won over the partisan crowd, and the rally forced legislators at least to consider increased education funding.

Despite the successful rally, the General Assembly responded slowly to Scott's education proposals and was generally obstreperous. It refused to increase teachers' salaries to Scott's recommended $2,200–$3,100 range but came close—$2,081 for beginning teachers and up to $2,787 for experienced ones. Still and all, this was progress as it amounted to a 28.5 percent pay increase.[115] Scott reluctantly accepted this raise as the best he could get. Eventually, the legislature decided to submit a $25 million school bond issue, instead of the $50 million requested, and appropriated $25 million from the state reserve fund, instead of the $30 million Scott wanted, to aid in school construction.[116] The General Assembly refused, however, to raise any taxes for education. Scott got part of what he wanted but not enough, and the legislature missed a sterling opportunity to boost the quality of schools in North Carolina.

While her husband sparred with the General Assembly, Miss Mary, with the advice of an expert inspection team, determined that the House of the People, the old Victorian governor's mansion on Blount Street, needed major repairs. The mansion was in poor condition after years of neglect. Governor Scott invited the legislature by for a tour to see for themselves. Appalled by its appearance, in March 1949 legislators approved a $50,000 appropriation for restoration.

As it turned out, the $50,000 appropriation was not sufficient to pay for the recommended changes, and Scott could not persuade the legislature to provide additional funds. Nonetheless, the importance of preserving the historic and architectural significance of the house had been established, and Mary Scott monitored a scaled-down refurbishing project.

During their four years in the Executive Mansion, the Scotts spent much time on their Haw River farm, where the governor relieved some of the stress of his office. Despite their desire for a simple lifestyle and their populist leanings, the First Couple entertained guests with a flair. They held elaborate state dinners in their refurbished home for distinguished visitors like General and Mrs. George C. Marshall and Vice-President and Mrs. Alben Barkley. It was estimated that some 225,000 North Carolinians visited the mansion for teas, receptions, dinners, and tours during the Scotts' time in Raleigh.[117]

The governor achieved two of his initial fifteen goals when the legislature passed a bill to authorize a $7.5 million bond issue for the purpose of developing port facilities in Wilmington and Morehead City. It also agreed to his request to expand the size of the state Highway Commission. By increasing the number of members on the commission, Scott hoped to make the

The Scott Go Forward program included $7.5 million in bonds to provide facilities for oceangoing vessels at the state port facilities in Morehead City and Wilmington. The governor is shown breaking ground at the state Ports Authority at Wilmington in 1950. Photograph by Hugh Morton, North Carolina Collection, University of North Carolina at Chapel Hill Library.

commission more democratic and more responsive to the public's needs.[118] The key was that now he would appoint his own people to the commission, giving him more control of decisions made on road building.

Scott turned his attention back to the road bond issue and expressed pleasure when, on March 14, the House voted 107–2 to allow the people to vote on the bond issue and voted 87–20 to increase the gas tax by one cent. He said: "The [legislative] log jam has been broken. Some of the logs are floating toward my sawmill."[119] He still, however, had to deal with the more conservative Senate.

Scott wanted the gas tax detached from the road bonds and the gas tax levied by the legislature. The bond referendum would thus pass more easily since the antitax group had enough clout to defeat the entire measure. The Senate refused Scott's request and made the tax contingent on voter approval of the bond issue. Scott won an important victory when the Senate accepted the amount of the bond issue at $200 million. Displeased with the Senate for tying the gas tax to the bond issue, he claimed that an "obstructionist clique" in the Senate still wanted to kill the road plan.[120]

His forceful and blunt denunciation of the obstructionists in the Senate outraged many conservatives, but, by painting those senators as reactionaries unconcerned with the well-being of the citizens of the state, Scott gained statewide approbation. In a further attempt to get the Senate to move on his bills, he launched an attack on the lobbyists in the state. He called them the "Third House" and claimed that they controlled the General Assembly. He singled out Gilmore Sparger, a lobbyist for the North Carolina Petroleum Industries, for his concentrated effort to defeat the bond issue and gas tax. Scott's tirade prompted two of his supporters to sponsor a resolution to bar lobbyists completely from the floor of the House of Representatives. The resolution referred to lobbyists as "hirelings" of special interests who "worked against the welfare of the state and its people."[121] The resolution did not pass, but it did put lobbyists in a bad light and, thus, helped Scott's cause.

On cue, the *News and Observer* lashed out at lobbyists. While not all lobbyists were evil and often provided needed information for legislators, the paper claimed that they were paid to promote private interests that were always selfish. They were agents of a "greedy and ruthless invisible government which cares nothing about North Carolina or its people except the right to exploit it at the least possible cost to themselves."[122]

While these attacks against lobbyists might have helped Scott's cause with the public, they had little effect on the Senate. The upper house refused to make any compromises on the House bill and continued to delay both the education and the road bills. The essential difference between legislation proposed by the two chambers was that the House bill would raise the gas tax through legislation while the Senate wanted to have the people vote on the gas tax at the same time as the bond issue. The *News and Observer* referred to the legislature as "negative, nagging, uncreative, and entirely unimpressive." When asked when the lengthy, hectic, and confused legislative session would end, Scott responded that he did not know but assured everyone that he "was satisfied it would be before the next one convenes."[123]

Simmons Fentress, writing in the *News and Observer*, said that the steady, unrelenting opposition to Scott's program came from a group of conservatives and the economy bloc—the political diehards and "irreconcilables" who had supported Johnson in 1948. They refused to raise taxes and would vote no on almost any issue favored by the governor.[124] Some critics alleged that the conservatives were correct to challenge Scott's bills because the governor was a "little reluctant to get along with those who did not happen to vote for him in the primary."[125] Scott advocates denigrated the legislature for using every devious method possible to thwart the will of the people who had elected Scott by an overwhelming majority.[126]

Eventually, the General Assembly settled on a compromise bill, the Secondary Road Bond Act of 1949, that left the bond issue at $200 million. The gas tax would not be part of the referendum, but it would be contingent on the outcome of the referendum. If the referendum passed, the gas tax would go up one cent, from six to seven cents a gallon. The act allocated each county's share of the $200 million and left the date of the vote to the discretion of the governor. Scott was not completely happy with the compromise because it tied the bond issue to the gas tax. But, after a long and difficult conflict, he accepted it because he got most of what he wanted, particularly the $200 million figure. He called on all North Carolinians to help organize the effort to pass the referendum.[127] He now had to persuade the public to vote for the road and education bond issues. Since the Senate had made the gas tax contingent on approval of the bonds, it made his task harder. Still, if the bond referendum—the centerpiece of his Go Forward program—passed, it would be a huge victory.

The fourth longest legislative session in the state's history ended on April 23, 1949. Scott did not get all he wanted, but one adviser reckoned that he got a majority of his progressive reform program to increase public services for the citizens of the state. In addition to the $25 million school bond issue, the $25 million for school construction, and a pay raise for teachers, the legislature provided $177 million, $9 million more than requested, as a general appropriation for running the schools. State employees got a 20 percent pay raise and $900,000 to be used for merit raises. The assembly agreed to Scott's reorganization of the state bureaucracy with a new personnel department responsible for establishing equitable salary scales and for reviewing the responsibilities and duties of every state employee. In addition to the general fund, the legislature designated $120 million for the highway fund, $2 million for the agricultural fund, and $73 million for permanent improvements, with the university system getting one-third of those monies.[128]

In the health field, Scott managed to achieve almost all his agenda. The legislature funded the Medical Care Commission, begun in 1944, and designed to provide an overall plan to improve medical care in the state. The commission already had a four-year plan under way, and, when completed, the program would, in the immediate future, provide forty-three new hospitals, most in the underserved rural areas. This expansion would add three thousand additional beds in new hospitals, nursing homes, and health centers. Funds allocated for the medical school and the teaching hospital, then under construction at Chapel Hill, would help relieve the shortage of doctors and nurses. Scott's hope for a dental school at the University of North Carolina also eventually became a reality. The General Assembly earmarked $800,000 for local health departments, over $7 million for the treatment and prevention of tuberculosis, and monies to the state Health Department for a new building and for research and educational programs.

Scott had challenged the legislature to improve state humanitarian services, and it responded favorably. Payments for old-age assistance increased, as did unemployment benefits and aid to dependent children. The assemblymen accelerated the building program at state mental institutions and set up a separate program for the treatment of alcoholism. Scott had requested prison reform and received the funds to create a first offender training center to provide vocational education to young prisoners.

The governor placed a priority on having the state develop and preserve its natural resources, especially forest reserves. He obtained approval of a bond issue for the new port terminals in Wilmington and Morehead City, but the legislature turned down his proposal to establish a commission to control water pollution. He claimed a victory, however, when the state Utilities Commission was increased from three to five members and he was able to choose the two new members.

Scott did not achieve some of his minor objectives. The legislature ignored his desire to change labor laws and rejected every tax proposal he made.[129] The governor considered these setbacks as inconsequential. He was lukewarm on labor reform and did not want to be blamed for any new taxes. He got the essential parts of his program—roads, schools, and health—and was pleased with the results. Lynn Nisbet, an astute and experienced journalist, wrote that, despite serious opposition, Scott's "record of legislative achievement has not been surpassed, seldom equaled, by any governor in recent years."[130] Legislative reporters concluded that he got well over 50 percent of what he wanted, while some of his inner circle saw the figure as close to 80 percent[131]—a remarkable achievement considering the virulent opposition to his proposals. His legacy, however, would depend on the outcome of the bond issue referendum.

Scott succeeded partly because of the times. There was a surplus of funds after the war, and he had won a mandate in the election from a rural electorate tired of business as usual. There was a sense of promise in the state's future, and the people demanded new and better services, telephones, electricity, and improved schools and roads. Legislators could not completely ignore the groundswell of reform. Scott shrewdly used his powers of persuasion to change some minds and met privately with key legislators to explain exactly why they needed to go along with him. His attack on the lobbyists, his frank and broad-ranging press conferences, his persuasive public addresses, and his bulldog tenacity helped turn the tide. He was often tactless and rude in his comments about legislators, but his candor and passionate advocacy appealed to the masses.

As the legislative session drew to a close, the governor redeemed one of the promises he made during the campaign, to appoint minorities to state boards. He chose Dr. Harold L. Trigg, the president of St. Augustine's College in Raleigh, as the first black ever appointed to the state Board of Education. He picked Trigg because he was "well-qualified" and because "it was time the state recognized its Negro citizens and accorded them a voice on state boards." The News and Observer praised the choice as Trigg clearly had the credentials for the post and his appointment set a precedent for the future. The St. Louis Post-Dispatch noted that Scott was a governor to watch: "If he puts as much thought and independence into all his appointments as he has in these [Graham and Trigg], the country is going to hear from him."[132]

As expected, there were howls of protest as well as a surprisingly large number of letters praising the decision. Phone calls and telegrams, some of them bitterly racist, poured into the governor's office. A representative letter came from J. S. Davis. He had supported Scott in 1948, Davis explained, and had "nothing personal against the colored race": "But my honest opinion is that we have enough good white men that are capable of filling the offices of our state." He warned Scott that this choice would cost him white votes in the bond election.[133]

A positive response came from O. Max Gardner Jr., the son of the former governor. He wrote that Trigg's appointment "gives encouragement and lifts the morale of the close to a million Negro citizens in North Carolina."[134] In the same vein, the attorney Curtiss Todd agreed that Trigg was "eminently qualified" by training and practical experience to render a great service. He ended with the following: "May you continue to follow the dictates of your heart and conscience in matters affecting the welfare of all the people of this great State."[135] In July, the Executive Committee of the Southern Regional Council praised the selection of Trigg as a "hopeful sign of such an extension of democracy in the South."[136]

The governor gave gracious and well-reasoned replies to those who disagreed with his appointment of Dr. Trigg. He responded to J. S. Davis: "We have two races living side by side here in our State . . . [and have usually lived in] friendly cooperation. I want to do what I can to promote the kind of helpful relations among the people, and it seemed to me that justice called for somewhat better representation of the minority race in our public affairs." He asserted that he was not a radical on race relations and had chosen Trigg because he was a "man of sane views about race relations": "He has no disposition to hasten change of the established customs with respect to separate education of the races in this State."[137] Scott continued to favor segregation but thought that an outreach to minority citizens was not only fair but also constructive and would help improve the dialogue between the races.

Scott also kept his campaign promise to let a little fresh air into Raleigh. After the legislative session ended, just as his enemies had predicted, he asked for the resignation of several key state employees of long standing, many of whom had supported Johnson. One wag called Scott's housecleaning a "demonstration of crop rotation." He chose a new leader for the state Paroles Commission, a new director for the state Department of Conservation and Development, a fresh face as head of the state Highway Patrol, and a new leader as the director of prisons. He made D. S. Coltrane, an old college chum, assistant director of the budget, a decision he would later regret. Edwin Gill resigned after eighteen years as commissioner of revenue to be replaced by a Scott supporter. The insurance commissioner's post went to Scott's campaign manager in Randolph County. The governor retained only two special superior court judges while appointing seven new ones. The same policy was used with the state Board of Agriculture, the Board of Education, trustees of state colleges, and the appointive members of the Advisory Budget Commission. Scott ousted all the current members of the Highway Commission and picked nine new commissioners.

In the end, only a handful of state officials escaped the ax wielded by the governor. When he had finished with his housecleaning, there were new faces everywhere and many more farmers, women, and businessmen on state boards, many of them Branchhead Boys and stalwart supporters of Scott.[138] Scott put his stamp on the state bureaucracy and dramatically increased his influence by use of his appointive power. His retention of Dr. Henry Jordan as chairman of the Highway Commission turned out to be a brilliant decision in light of the difficulty in getting the road bond issue passed.

By July 1949 Scott had made some 280 assignments to boards, offices, and commissions. Almost everyone he selected had campaigned for him in 1948. He made his appointments usually without notice and ignored any recommendations or protests.[139] There was, of course, some criticism of and objection to some of his choices, especially those who were viewed as political hacks rewarded for past assistance in his campaigns. If state officials had supported Johnson in 1948, their fate was sealed.[140]

The *Fayetteville Observer* criticized the governor's actions and charged that Scott had cost the state millions of dollars by replacing good and efficient public servants "for no reasons other than political ones." His actions told state employees: "Your jobs do not depend on your efficiency. Your jobs depend on guessing who will be the next governor and doing efficient political work for him." C. G. Davidson also protested Scott's highhanded and arbitrary actions and thought: "The present administration is obsessed with the idea of political vengeance." Scott replied by explaining that many state government personnel were unable to do their jobs and "should take advantage of their retirement status and give way to more active, vigorous leadership[141]—a weak excuse for what was a political purge.

Capus Waynick heard rumblings of discontent about Scott's harsh decisions on firing longtime state employees. He realized that there is "a strong likelihood that the Governor will consult his impulses in these matters [i.e., appointments] and ride roughshod over tradition and practice."

He concluded that, as long as he was assured of Scott's high purposes, an "occasional outbreak of ruthlessness" could be accepted.[142] Scott, however, saw no problem with his methods. His appointees were doing an excellent job, and he had promised the people "that for 365 days of the year there shall be no dull moments."[143] He was certainly right about the latter statement as he seemed always to be in the middle of some controversy. After his drastic reordering of the state bureaucracy, he now prepared to take on his most important mission, securing a favorable vote on the road and school bonds referendum.

5

THE REFERENDUM

Although Scott painted a bleak picture of North Carolina's rural roads, the state had a history of being the "Good Roads" state. As far back as 1915, the legislature established a state highway commission and, in 1921, went into the road-building business. North Carolina constructed and maintained a highway system of fifty-five hundred miles of hard-surfaced roads running through towns and cities of more than three thousand people that connected all the county seats. Interestingly, in 1921 the roads were financed by issuing a $50 million bond issue secured by a one-cent per gallon tax on gasoline and automobile license fees. The state kept up its roads through auto, bus, and truck licenses, gas taxes, and federal funds. By 1949, there were 10,351 miles in the state system, mainly primary roads, and 51,031 miles of county roads maintained by the state, but only 14,635 miles of these rural roads were hard surfaced.[1] Thus the need for a new bond issue.

Much of the success on the road bonds vote would depend on the support of the new state Highway Commission. All the members had now been appointed by Scott, and the new board expressed enthusiasm for the bond issue.[2] There were fourteen highway divisions in North Carolina with each division responsible for a designated geographic part of the state. Each division had its own highway commissioner, and it was here, on the local level, that the groundwork would be done to persuade voters to accept the bond issue. Dr. Henry Jordan, chairman of the Highway Commission, campaigned throughout the state and delivered more than fifty speeches urging voters to get behind the bond referendum. Because of his status and integrity, plus his personal knowledge of road building, Jordan was a major factor in arousing support for the bond issue.[3]

Keenly aware of the long-term significance of the vote, the governor used all his energy and political savvy to get the bond issues approved. As required by the bill, Scott determined that the election would be held on June 4, 1949—sufficient time for him to set up an organization to get out the vote.

He planned to "go all out" in the campaign. As he reasoned: "Good roads are important to good schools and good schools are important to North Carolina."[4] For his main focus, he planned to use facts and figures aimed at showing how poor roads crippled state development and how good roads would help all Tar Heels, both rural and urban: "The state moves forward on its transportation facilities."[5]

On April 26, Scott incorporated a statewide, nonprofit citizens committee, Better Schools and Roads, Inc., to persuade North Carolinians to embrace his vision. He selected John Marshall as the executive secretary and picked an executive committee that included educators, women, labor leaders, farmers, and some powerful politicians.[6] In retrospect, the governor's decision to establish Better Schools and Roads was the turning point in the fight. The organization geared up quickly and disseminated information in a timely fashion. Without an effective headquarters providing relevant information and getting out the vote, the road bond issue might have failed.

Scott began his quest by explaining in great detail why both the education and the road bond issues should be approved. He repeated these views over the next five weeks in several radio addresses and during numerous rallies, luncheons, and visits to every part of the state. Scott explained: "[Both schools and roads] have been close to my heart all my life." His experience living on a dirt road and depending on poor rural schools made him cognizant of the need to develop both.

Scott appealed to those in urban areas who enjoyed good roads and schools to understand the plight of a large number in the state "who suffer inequalities and disadvantages in school equipment and school services." He hoped that the tradition of unselfishness and strong community spirit would help people heed his appeal. He reminded citizens that, every time North Carolina made an investment in its physical properties and its people, the state made great progress economically. When the state dispensed the blessings of prosperity to the economically weaker sections, "the result was splendid." Failure of the state government to act in recent years had resulted in increased poverty and a widening of the gap between the rich and the poor.

Knowing that the education bond issue would be more popular than the road bond issue, Scott early on combined the two issues as if they were one referendum. Although the legislature had given teachers a pay raise, he determined that that increase was not sufficient. The state could not withhold a living wage from the twenty-six thousand public school teachers without great cost to the entire state. Scott asked citizens not to forget "that our richest possession is the great army of children ... who are with us as citizens of the future." Schoolchildren needed inspiration from teachers who knew that "the people regard their work as honorable and valuable." School buildings had deteriorated and become overcrowded, and the bond issue would enable the state to meet the increased demand for new classrooms.

As for highways, Scott argued that he had a mandate from the people to improve secondary roads. The bond issue would not be a "wild adventure," as some critics had charged, but a sound investment since the Highway Commission, which was opposed to waste, would spend the money wisely and every county would get its proper share. The commission would not allow the primary roads to deteriorate as the bond issue would free up regular funds to restore principal highways to first-rate condition. North Carolina would once again be known as the "Good Roads" state. There could be no progress without this kind of investment in the state's infrastructure.[7]

Scott opened the most intensive phase of the drive with a radio address on May 10 in which he emphasized the need for both bond proposals if the state were to advance to greatness. The *News and Observer* backed him up, reasoning that he had made "a convincing case." The paper thought the time was right, the money would be spent wisely, and the voters should accept their responsibility. If this attempt were defeated, there would be a long delay before any progress could be made.[8]

Better Schools and Roads carried the fight across the state. On May 13 the organization sponsored simultaneous rallies covering nine highway divisions and fifty-six counties. Scott barnstormed the state with a schedule reminiscent of his 1948 election campaign. On May 11 he spoke first to the student body at East Carolina Teachers College, then to the Better Schools and Roads group in Greenville, and finished off the day with a talk in Tarboro. On May 10, while dedicating the Morehead Planetarium in Chapel Hill, he managed to get in a plug for the referendum.[9]

Scott received some much-needed help when Lieutenant Governor Pat Taylor decided to participate actively in the campaign. Taylor, influential with the conservative wing of the party, realized that most people wanted something done about roads and schools, and he vowed to help. Scott wrote Taylor and thanked him for his assistance, explaining that this kind of effort would carry the program to victory on June 4.[10] Even George Pritchard, Scott's Republican opponent for governor in 1948, came out in favor of the bond issue.[11]

The education establishment pitched in with major contributions to the school bond fight. The state Parent Teachers Association became a "most militant advocate," and Scott later singled it out for praise.[12] Clyde Erwin, the state superintendent of public instruction, commended both bond issues as essential as they would "break the shackles of isolation and ignorance in many communities."[13] A. C. Dawson, a past president of the North Carolina Education Association, likewise advocated for both bond issues while calling Scott "the staunchest friend of education that has been in the capitol during my lifetime."[14]

On May 15, John Marshall made his initial report on the activities of Better Schools and Roads to the governor. He informed Scott that the response from all sections of the state had been strong and that committees had been formed in every county except two. He explained that the remarkably quick organization was due to the able assistance of the state highway commissioners. He warned that the opposition had opened headquarters in Raleigh and that Better Schools and Roads needed to use the enthusiasm of the people to offset this high-powered challenge from the oil companies and the cities. He concluded that the probond forces' trump card was "a state-wide organization which they cannot hope to match."[15]

Marshall then released a detailed explanation as to how each county would benefit from the bond issues. He also put out newspaper ads featuring prominent state leaders supporting the bonds. Individuals showcased in the ads included Lieutenant Governor Taylor; church, labor, education, and farm leaders; prominent members of women's clubs; and Gurney P. Hood, the state banking commissioner. One ad read: "You can depend upon the people, leaders and outstanding forces of N.C. to rally behind the fight for a better state. . . . This is no partisan, racial or sectional fight. Good schools and good roads are good for everybody."[16] These ads proved to be a powerful tool as most citizens of the state knew and respected many of the people listed. The diversity of the supporters, especially church leaders and businessmen, helped persuade some citizens who might not otherwise have bothered to vote.

Better Schools and Roads added to its arsenal a fact sheet sent to newspapers throughout the state. The fact sheet included the date of the election, a sample ballot, and the information that those already registered to vote did not need to register again for this special election. It added some important figures that would not generally be known to the public. Only one mile in four of the state's roads was paved, and there were forty-seven thousand miles of unpaved roads. (The figures on paved and unpaved roads varied significantly depending on which source was cited.) Only one-third of the mileage traveled by school buses was over paved roads. Good roads would benefit the cities as many industrial workers lived outside the city limits and needed good roads to get to work. The same was true for shoppers who needed to get to the larger cities for necessary goods.[17]

The probond group also supplied another pamphlet to citizens, "Fifteen Questions and Answers about Governor Scott's Road Program." One pertinent question was, "When would the bonds be paid off?" The answer was that the bonds would mature in twenty years and the gasoline tax would contribute $7 million of the $14 million annual carrying charge. With more hard-surfaced roads, there would be more travel and, thus, increased revenue from gas taxes. The remainder of the annual interest charges would be made up from the state highway fund. The pamphlet made it clear that the Highway Department was gearing up to handle the increased production by doubling the number of its personnel, doubling the number of its facilities, and obtaining the materials needed for the roads.[18] This document succeeded in its purpose because it answered questions that most citizens might pose in a very direct, logical manner without recourse to exaggeration or propagandistic verbiage.

Scott continued to be the focal point of the campaign as he raced around the state. In Asheville, he told the audience: "[Those of us] out in the mud have been helping you pave these primary roads for the past 25 years. Now we're asking you to come over to Macedonia and help us." He reminded his listeners that many rural children had to wait over an hour or so for school buses to arrive when in bad weather the roads were muddy. The resultant overexposure to the weather led to colds, flu, and sometimes pneumonia.[19] The following day he reported that the campaign was "coming along fine" and that attendance had been very good at the various rallies.[20] At this juncture, Scott's advisers had determined that the school bond issue would pass without much difficulty. Approval of the road bond was still in doubt.

The oil companies created the Petroleum Industries Committee, set up headquarters in the Sir Walter Hotel, and embarked on a concerted drive to derail the road bond issue by distributing negative literature and advertisements all over the state. Oil lobbyists made several public addresses and emphasized that the approval of the road bond would mean a public debt of $217 for each family of four in the state. Only the oil industry had made a careful study of the proposal and "forthrightly set out figures certified by a public accountant in Raleigh," figures that "have never been refuted."

The committee argued that the state already had enough revenue to build new roads without going into debt. There would be $420,000 in interest charges, and the debt would be paid through increased taxes. The committee contended that the proposed tax increase and bond issue would lead to the greatest debt in the state's history and were "fundamentally unsound, unnecessary and undesirable."[21] The Petroleum Industries Committee essentially opposed only the gas tax, but, in order to defeat the tax increase, it had to marshal arguments against both bond issues since they were linked.

Several state newspapers, primarily those in Charlotte and other urban areas, joined the oil companies in rejecting the road bond proposal. The *Charlotte News* agreed with the Petroleum Industries Committee that the state Highway Commission already had more than enough money to build the necessary roads without the bonds or the gas tax. To oppose the bonds would indicate not a lack of faith or vision but merely "plain ordinary common sense."[22] The *Durham Sun* alleged that Scott's real reason for backing the bond issue was to build up his personal power and advance his political ambitions.[23] The Petroleum Industries Committee sent postcards around the state stating that the road bonds would increase the state's debt so much that there would be the possibility of new state taxes on land and personal property.[24] A full-page ad allegedly paid for by citizens of Anson County pointed out that this unsound and "reckless measure" would damage the state's reputation for steady and progressive government. The ad ended by telling citizens that they should vote for school bonds and against road bonds as they were two separate issues.[25]

Although the oil industry arguments undoubtedly persuaded some voters, Scott capitalized on the outside intervention by the oil companies and used them as a whipping boy to stir up his followers. He called the oil companies "carpetbaggers sent down to tell North Carolinians how to run their own business" and warned voters not to let these carpetbaggers trick the state out of better schools and roads.[26] He later suggested that the oil industry should be regulated by the state Utilities Commission since it "is just as much a monopoly as telephones and electricity." The oil companies had been raising prices without any notice or explanation, and no one could do anything about it.[27]

As was his wont, the governor invaded Charlotte, the center of those who disapproved of the bond issue. In a meeting of the city's business leaders, he called their resistance "damnable," and he especially resented the effort of those employed by the oil companies to kill the bond issue. He repeated his contention that the bonds would pay for themselves and that they represented a sound investment in the state's future: "I'm a Scotch Presbyterian and I never let anybody throw away my money. And I'm not going to see any of the state's money thrown away."[28]

Scott's election strategy hit a snag when Kelly Alexander and the state NAACP picked what was, at least for Scott, an inconvenient time to file a discrimination suit against the Durham school system. The suit demanded equal schools and equal facilities for Negro institutions from elementary school through college. Alexander said that this was a suit not against segregation but against discrimination as white schools were vastly superior to Negro schools. At a news conference, Scott, fearful that the lawsuit might jeopardize the bond vote, declared: "[It] was a pity to have to be forced into it. We should have beat them to it." He gave a boost to the hopes of the Negro leaders by promising that the school bond issue would lead to major improvements in the Negro school system.[29]

In the end, the lawsuit did not affect the bond vote. Kelly Alexander wrote Scott to inform him that the North Carolina State Conference of the NAACP appreciated "the interest [he was] taking in improving the conditions of Negroes in North Carolina." He specifically thanked Scott for selecting Dr. Trigg and three other Negroes for the forty-seven-member Resource-Use Education Committee. The NAACP supported the bond election, and Alexander included a flyer sent out to its members in which the organization asked them to contact Negro voters and unite behind the governor's program. "Negroes of North Carolina have a wonderful opportunity to show appreciation for the liberal program of the Honorable Governor Kerr Scott," the flyer noted, by supporting the bond issue, which would be of great advantage to all citizens: "We cannot overlook the fact that Governor W. Kerr Scott is proving to be the best Governor we have ever had in North Carolina."[30] Bayard Rustin, a distinguished educator who worked for the Fellowship of Reconciliation, an organization trying to improve race relations in America, wrote Scott: "My heart has greatly been stirred by your courageous appointment of Dr. Graham." He also approved of the choice of Dr. Trigg. He sympathized that Scott had a difficult legislature to deal with: "But it is good to know that despite this fact, you are carrying on in that liberal tradition which is to me, America."[31]

The governor launched a final flurry of speaking and handshaking in an attempt to close out his campaign on a favorable note. On a visit to Sanford, the local moderator called the gathering a "get-together of progressive-minded and barbecue-minded citizens" and introduced Scott as a "crusader of progress." Scott said he came to Sanford on "behalf of a movement that is truly a citizen's movement" and expected Lee County would respond with a resounding yes vote. He concluded: "It would be a tragedy if we failed."[32] The governor had made numerous speeches in every part of the state and felt like he had done his best to win over voters. This was his fourth state-wide search for votes in one year (the first three being the two Democratic primaries and the November election), and much of his previous election apparatus was still in place. He called on his past adherents and asked them to cast their lot with him one more time.

The *News and Observer* promoted both bond issues but concentrated on why the road bonds should be approved. If the road bonds were ratified, all the present highway revenues could be used for the primary roads. If the bond were defeated, the highway budget would be divided between primary and secondary roads, and neither job would be properly done. The state had never been able to make improvements without going into debt, and now was the time "to go forward again" with a sound investment.[33]

As the countdown approached, Scott found "sentiment overwhelmingly for the bond issues" despite the fact that opponents were putting out "a lot of false statements." He repeated his often-stated explanation that there would be no increase in property taxes, only a one-cent gas tax that would pay off the bonds. He urged everyone to get to the polls "as we need all the help we can get in the rural areas."[34] In a letter to a constituent, the governor admitted that there had been a hard fight over the road issue but said that he firmly believed that "there is nothing that the forward-looking people of North Carolina cannot accomplish when they set themselves wholeheart-edly to the task."[35]

Two other individuals closely connected to Better Schools and Roads viewed the impending vote favorably. Lieutenant Governor Taylor pre-dicted that the school bonds would be accepted by an overwhelming vote and the "road bonds by a very safe margin."[36] John Marshall's greatest fear was "too much optimism on the precinct level," but he nonetheless foresaw a victorious day.[37]

By the last week, it was obvious that the support for both bond issues was very strong. Speaking into a battery of microphones that carried his voice to forty-four radio stations, Scott made one last simple, direct appeal, requesting that voters help remove the significant bottleneck the state had so that "progress in the next 25 years will be the greatest in North Carolina's history." Rural people needed help now, and "the state could not afford to veto this great proposal for physical progress."[38]

The people listened. On June 4, more than 400,000 voters—a larger turnout than expected—gave Scott a smashing victory by passing the school bonds by a more than 2-1 margin, 273,663-122,460. Despite organized resistance by the oil companies, the road bonds also passed comfortably, 229,493-174,647. Scott did not appear too surprised by the margin as he had predicted the road bonds would succeed by 30,000-50,000 votes. He admitted that the contingent gas tax increase hurt the vote somewhat as it was put in deliberately for that purpose "and the very group that did it will be the ones to squawk the most in later years on account of it."[39]

Scott gained overwhelming majorities in the rural areas, and in general, the smaller and more isolated the precinct, the larger the affirmative vote. Deep River in Moore County, a rural precinct without a single paved road, voted 112-0 for the road bonds. In Kannapolis, where Charles Cannon, the president of the giant Cannon Mills, ruled the town, there was a different outcome. Cannon opposed both issues because it would impose a heavy tax burden on him and his millworkers. The Kannapolis voters obeyed Cannon and turned back both proposals—the road bonds by 3-1 and, in an unusual turn of events, the school bonds by a resounding 4-1 margin.

The road bond vote divided essentially on a rural-urban basis with the greatest resistance, as expected, from the urban areas. The bonds were defeated in Mecklenburg, Forsyth, New Hanover, Guilford, and Buncombe Counties. Mecklenburg, New Hanover, and Forsyth voted against both bond issues. Scott had not been very successful in persuading the urban areas that secondary roads would be as beneficial to them as to the rural areas. Although conservatives, Johnson supporters, and Republican-leaning newspapers led the fight against the bonds, Scott won over blue-collar and rural voters partly because they believed he had their best interests at heart.

While celebrating his victory, the irascible Scott could not pass up a chance to lambaste the negative attitudes of the big city dwellers. He started out by criticizing civic clubs in the state: "Your civic club member is all right on little peanut things when it comes to cooperating with the farmer, but when it comes to doing something big for the farmer, he's not worth a damn. Too many had rather skin than be skint."[40] Carey P. Lowrance rebuked Scott for castigating civic clubs as a group as his remarks were a "definite slander to many fine clubs." Scott owed them an apology. Lowrance chided Scott for his use of the word *damn,* "such unbecoming and profane language" being

As governor, Scott had many public and social duties around the state, including crowning beauty queens. Some governors saw these responsibilities as a drudgery, but Scott reveled in the experience. Courtesy of the State Archives of North Carolina, Raleigh.

an insult to the state. Scott, of course, was unrepentant. He refused to back down from his opinion of civic clubs, although he did admit there would be a few exceptions. He conjectured that his interpretation of profanity differed from Lowrance's view, but he would be willing to change *damn* to "not worth a dad-blame." Otherwise: "When I stated that their efforts were not worth a damn, I was sincere and still stick to this, but do not feel profane in doing so."[41]

Scott had won another major victory, and his successes in the 1948 elections, in the recent legislative session, and now with the referendum garnered him national attention and increased his prestige and power in the state. He had once again used all his political skills and inexhaustible energy in winning the fight. To achieve his goal, he had traveled five thousand miles, made fifty arranged speeches, given seventeen radio addresses, and visited with everyone within shouting distance as he made his way across the state, denouncing "carpetbaggers," and pleading for progress in North Carolina. Whether at church meetings, press conferences, or barbecues or making telephone calls or crowning beauty queens, he never failed to put in a plug for the bond issues.

Both sides spent heavily to win their arguments. The oil industry paid for publicity men, typists, radio spots, and advertisements. Better Schools and Roads also spent large sums getting its message out. It has never been clear as to where all the organization's funding came from, but the consensus was that money flowed in from the dairy industry, trucking companies, highway contractors, and some industrialists while small contributions came from those who had supported Scott in the past.[42]

A torrent of congratulations flowed into the governor's office from all over the state. J. M. Walker was thrilled by Scott's "sweeping victory." Walker saw a "real new day for the country boy and girl"; they would be the state's future farmers and produce North Carolinians' daily food.[43] The *Road Builders News* praised Scott and the citizens of the state for having "the courage required for self-imposition of additional taxes" because they recognized that more and better roads cost money but led to tangible benefits for the state.[44] The *News and Observer* complimented Scott and bemoaned the unfair charges made by opponents that he was intent on political power for himself rather than the welfare of the state. The editorial urged all parties to work together to end any divisions between the rural and the urban areas of the state.[45]

Once the hubbub over the bond issues had subsided, Scott returned to his gubernatorial duties. On June 6 he made several significant appointments. He added three Negroes to the Board of Trustees of Greensboro A&T College, bringing the total number to five. He selected Mrs. Roland McClamroch, a founder of the League of Women Voters, as the first woman on the state Board of Conservation and Development.[46] He named another woman, Hilda G. Carpenter, as acting assistant commissioner of paroles.[47] The choice of Mrs. McClamroch and Mrs. Carpenter demonstrated his commitment to providing women a greater say in state government and served as a precursor to one of the more important decisions he would make as governor, picking Susie Sharp as the first female superior court judge in the history of the state.

In her splendid book on Susie Sharp, *Without Precedent,* Anna Hayes chronicled the relationship between Sharp and Kerr Scott from the time she supported him in the 1948 gubernatorial contest until her appointment. Judge Allen H. Gwynn of Reidsville joined with Jim Sharp, a Reidsville lawyer, and his daughter Susie in bucking the establishment and coming out for Scott. Miss Sharp had never met Scott and was surprised when Scott headquarters called and asked her to manage his campaign during the second primary, but she accepted the challenge.

Susie, her father, and Judge Gwynn worked hard for Scott in the runoff. Scott carried the county with 60 percent of the vote and took notice of Susie's fine work. Anna Hayes explained: "[Susie Sharp] had backed a candidate on principle, not party politics, and had unexpectedly been catapulted into the winner's circle. It changed her life."[48]

Susie Sharp's name was now in play for some position of importance in the Scott administration. The Rockingham attorney Hamp Price spoke with Scott and told him that the time had come to recognize women's participation in state politics. Women had been instrumental in Scott's electoral victory, and he might want to consider being the first governor to select a woman for the bench. Knowing Scott's penchant for surprises, Price noted that it would attract national attention and even went so far as to propose a candidate, Susie Sharp. Scott responded that Price might be on to something and promised to think about it.[49]

An earlier, important missive to Scott from the former dean of the University of North Carolina Law School, Maurice T. Van Hecke, also recommended Sharp. Professor Van Hecke had seen indications that Scott was considering nominating a woman to the superior court and suggested he give serious consideration to Sharp. She would, in his judgment, make an excellent judge: "She would rank with the best of the men on the Superior Court in ability, insight, courage and wisdom. Ultimately she would deserve a place on the Supreme Court." Scott replied that he held Miss Sharp "in the highest esteem" and that she would "receive every possible consideration in this respect."[50]

Miss Sharp's name first appeared in print in the *Greensboro Daily News* in February. Tom Bost wrote: "Judge Susie would be a natural for Governor Scott. He likes to do things never done by anybody else."[51] Scott asked several knowledgeable observers to test the reaction to such a nomination. One respondent reported that both men and women alike favored her appointment, but another report found reactions ranging from "hearty approval" to "equally hearty disapproval." Everyone thought Susie a good and smart lawyer, and there was no question about her integrity, but some

Governor Scott selected Susie Marshall Sharp as the first female superior court judge in the state's history. He believed that women could perform as well as men and appointed women to several significant positions in the state administration. Photograph by Hugh Morton, North Carolina Collection, University of North Carolina at Chapel Hill Library.

wondered about the ability of women "to act in an impartial and judicial manner." Scott favored putting a woman on the court but would pick Sharp not just because she was a woman but only if she were better qualified than the other candidates.

Keenly aware of the political nature of the appointment, Miss Sharp was unsure whether she would accept the post if offered as she was uncertain whether the state would accept a female judge. Nonetheless, when her name appeared on the list of new superior court judges, she agreed to serve. In writing to thank the governor, she expressed just the right sentiments: "I am fully conscious of the honor you have done me, but I am even more keenly aware of my responsibility to you and to the women of the state because I know that when you honored me you were honoring them. In making this appointment I know you took a risk, and I promise that I shall do my utmost not to let you down or to disappoint the women of the state. I only hope that my best will be enough."

Press reviews of the nomination were largely positive, and, when Sharp took her oath on July 1, 1949, the governor expressed confidence that she would "fill the office with credit."[52] The *News and Observer* praised the choice and commented: "[Those] who know Miss Sharp are confident that as Judge Sharp she will make a record that will dispel any doubts that may still exist as to the fitness of women to hold judicial offices."[53] Once again, Scott had done the unexpected, and he relished being in the spotlight. The significance of this nomination went far beyond the surprise choice. Scott struck a blow for women's equality by breaching what had been a men-only club and by expressing his belief that women could serve in public office as well as or better than men.

In July, Scott turned his focus to two areas of concern. First and foremost, he continued to prod the utility and telephone companies to "put a little more speed behind [their] work" in providing phones and electricity to rural areas. He called a meeting of the five utility commissioners in his office and asked that they obtain from each utility company a study of their underserved areas and that the companies come up with the cost of completing the job of supplying electricity to these areas. He criticized private utility companies for their "negative approach" in impeding progress in the state. Incensed that rural people were doomed to wait years because the companies would not give them service, Scott observed: "If we had to depend on these people to win a war, we'd never win one." The governor not so subtly warned: "If the private companies won't supply them, then the government will have to." He declared that there were 268,000 farm families who needed electricity but could not get it and 100,000 families waiting for phone service. He asked those who needed phones and power to write and "tell [him] about it."[54]

State residents responded in large numbers. Their letters, often scrawled on notebook paper and lacking proper grammar, graphically spelled out their needs and frustrations. Scott had put as much pressure as he could on the phone and power companies. He had threatened them with government intervention, had urged the Utilities Commission to investigate, and now made public these letters asking for help as proof of the rising demand for service.

To increase the state's industrial capacity, the governor gave his approbation to the Army Corps of Engineers' plan for extensive development of public water power by constructing ten dams on state rivers. The plans for river basin development fit in with his Go Forward program as industrial development and farm improvement would need additional electric power. The state had been growing so rapidly that there would be an increasing shortage of electric power. Scott expected the power companies to oppose the plan but thought that would be short-sighted because, as the state developed industrially, there would be more business for private utility companies. He sarcastically noted that there was nothing to prevent the private companies from building their own dams and plants if they opposed the government program.

Scott sought help from the federal government to promote the building of the dams. On a trip to Washington, DC, he had a thirty-minute visit with President Truman, who had apparently issued him an open invitation. In their meeting, the two discussed politics, especially the rugged campaigns they both fought in 1948, the Rural Electrification Administration, Senator Frank Graham, and the possible dams in North Carolina. When asked whether the president was in a good mood, Scott nodded yes. However: "I'd hate to have tried trading mules with him. For he certainly would have skinned me." There was some speculation that Scott was going to Washington to confer with Truman about being secretary of agriculture. Scott laughed that off: "I would no more go in that direction [resigning as governor] until the impeachment committee says so." He continued: "[The president] would rather I stayed in North Carolina and work in my own garden."[55]

Scott followed up his meeting with Truman with a letter to the president in which he expressed his interest in increased appropriations for the completion of the Buggs Island dam on the Roanoke River in Virginia. He contended that the dam would supply cheaper and more abundant power and would promote greater industrialization with a better-balanced economy between industry and agriculture. Truman replied that he was pleased to note Scott's interest in the dam but could not make a commitment: "I wish it were possible to give everybody everything they want."[56]

The governor's other area of immediate concern was increasing government efficiency and fulfilling his promise to get the "dead wood" out of government service. Scott calculated that the state could save as much as a quarter of a million dollars on what he called "petty graft" by cutting out unofficial use of state-owned cars, private telephone calls at state expense, and use of state postage stamps. Since the state had embarked on its greatest spending program, it had become necessary to save everywhere possible in the "interest of economy and efficiency."[57] The governor called a meeting of the heads of all the departments to emphasize that it would be essential for state employees to "get value received for every dollar spent" and to plug any leaks existing in the expenditure and collection of revenues.[58] Most employees complied with the new austerity directives, but not without a sense of humor. One state worker placed the following sign on a water cooler in the state capitol: "NOTICE: Do not drink ice water after 4:30 P.M. to assure that you do not take state property with you."[59]

Both as a candidate and as governor, Kerr Scott demonstrated a strong belief in unions and in collective bargaining between labor and management. Despite his favorable attitude toward unions, he reluctantly became involved in several labor disputes, the most prominent of which was the Hart Cotton Mill strike in Tarboro. After a lengthy and contentious impasse over a new contract, the union gave up its demands for a new union contract and agreed to a renewal of the old one. At the last minute, however, management came up with changes to the previous contract, including a no-strike clause. The absentee mill owners had determined that, since the mill no longer made a profit, it would be cheaper to shut it down than to operate it. They deliberately forced a walkout by making outrageous demands that were unacceptable to the workers. Without any other recourse, five hundred workers called a strike on May 12, 1949.

The strike, which would last for seven months, early on developed a siege mentality. The company tried to undermine the morale of the strikers by threatening to evict them from company housing. The Textile Workers Union of America (TWUA) gave large sums of money to support the workers, but they faced enormous odds since the company did not want to settle and had obtained a court injunction that drastically limited picketing.[60]

Initially, the governor planned to take no action other than to suggest that the company and the union submit their dispute to arbitration. The union agreed, but, as expected, management refused.[61] A few days later, Scott publicly denounced the conduct of the company and stepped up his pressure on management to end this "destructive economic warfare" by divulging that the dispute had brought "hardship to the townspeople, the workers and the employer." The company ignored the governor's pleas and refused to budge.[62] The *News and Observer* lauded Scott for his efforts and sided with the union, blaming the mill owners for the impasse by "steadfastly and obstinately" refusing arbitration.[63]

Violence flared at the mill in September when a TWUA member assaulted Marcus Carter, the plant manager.[64] Worried about the increase in acrimony between the two sides, Scott called the participants into his office in Raleigh, remarking that the company wanted to "bust the union." The meeting ended in failure. Scott asked state and federal labor officials to intervene and declared that the situation had reached such proportions that it affected the entire state and should not continue. He continued to believe that the issues could be settled amicably, but, the day that the governor invited federal intervention, a striker was badly beaten by three Tarboro policemen. The union called on Scott to investigate "the unwarranted brutal beating" and to bring an end to police violence in the city. Scott put the Highway Patrol on full alert but did not order it into the fray. Instead, he once again called on both mill officials and strikers to do everything possible to avoid additional conflict.[65]

Scott continued his efforts to mediate by traveling to New York to meet with the company president, Frank Leslie, and the national head of the TWUA. Scott and Leslie got into a heated argument, with the governor calling the company's attitude "uncompromising" and "inflexible." Scott asked that the mill continue operations under the old contract, but Leslie refused. Disappointed once again, Scott summed up the problem: "Fundamentally the trouble is that the company just doesn't believe in unions and the union does." When, on October 29, a free-for-all broke out between police and strikers, Scott reluctantly ordered in the Highway Patrol.[66] Eventually, the strike failed, although the National Labor Relations Board (NLRB) had found the owners of Hart Mill guilty of unfair labor practices and ordered them to comply with arbitration. They ignored the order and appealed the ruling to the US Circuit Court of Appeals. The court set aside the NLRB's order, concluding, in a startling decision, that the company had met its obligation to bargain collectively and that the union should have signed the original contract. The company had won and, in effect, had busted the union. The union leaders had no choice but to call off the strike, and the striking employees voted to return to work without a contract. The union's only option at this point was to try to reorganize the plant, but workers voted against the TWUA 357–236, and the plant was never unionized.[67]

Kerr Scott's intervention in the Hart Mill strike was significant for two reasons. First, his many public calls for mediation broadened knowledge of the strike and the issues at stake both statewide and nationwide. Second, for the first time in recent memory, a governor had essentially taken the side of the strikers. Previous North Carolina governors had supported the company position, often sending in troops to break strikes.[68] Scott was the most prolabor governor in a generation and had, to some degree, paid his political debt to labor by backing the union in the Hart Mill controversy.

Although distracted from party politics and the duties of state by labor-management conflicts, the governor realized that before the end of the year he had to begin the process of strengthening the Democratic Party's organization in time for Senator Graham's bid for the four years remaining in Broughton's US Senate term. Capus Waynick had resigned as chairman of the state Democratic Executive Committee in May to become the US ambassador to Nicaragua. Scott expressed deep regret at the resignation and thanked Waynick for his excellent service to the state and his personal assistance: "You have been a true friend and a wise counselor."[69] In a surprise move, he selected B. Everett Jordan, his old friend and a key campaign supporter in 1948, as the new state chairman. Many were perplexed at the choice because Jordan was more conservative than Scott and, as a mill owner, could prove to be a political liability for Graham.[70]

Scott chose Jordan partly out of appreciation for his financial and strategic help in the election of 1948. But Jordan also offered Scott entrée into the business world, and Senator Graham would need aid and funding from the business community in 1950. Plus, almost everyone recognized Jordan as an organizer par excellence. According to Congressman Horace Kornegay, Jordan turned out to be one of the best state chairmen the party ever had: "He was available, he was interested, he was practical, he was straightforward and, I think, highly respected. He was a good fund-raiser and well-connected to the business community." The only criticism that Kornegay heard was that Jordan was too conservative.[71]

After all the crises with bond issues, labor unrest, and state appointments, Scott devoted some time to his personal correspondence. As noted earlier, he took his mail seriously and tried to respond to as many letters as possible with advice or a solution to a problem raised. Most correspondents clamored for roads, phones, or electricity or all of the above. Herman Parker announced that he had voted for Scott and for the bond issues. Now he needed assistance with getting his road paved since it was often impassable; also, he had been begging for electricity for five years "but got nothing but promises." Scott responded by assuring him that he would have his complaints investigated. The governor observed that he had been receiving thousands of such missives and that it would take some time to look into all the requests: "So please be patient, with the assurance that I am doing everything possible to improve these conditions as rapidly as possible."[72]

The majority of letters to the governor consisted of legitimate questions, complaints, requests for help, invitations, and comments on state politics. As did all public officials, Scott received letters from what his staff referred to as the "crazies." Letter writers frequently asked Scott to get them jobs, cure illnesses, transfer their sons to a prison closer to home, fire various public officials, eliminate sin, etc. The governor's assistants lumped all these queries, which could not possibly be fulfilled, into one file, called File 13.

The following communiqués are representative of some of the more unusual demands. Mrs. Inez Brickell asked Scott to get her a ton of coal because the weather was cold and she had "arthritis and sinus trouble bad."[73] Bessie Reid contacted the governor complaining that she and her children were "living with a man can't read or write." Furthermore: "He is mean as a snake. Please help us."[74] After hearing that the school bond issue passed, Joseph Miller requested that Scott sell him a used forty-eight-passenger school bus.[75] Thurmond Sain wanted the governor to see "Captain Curtis" (unidentified) to get him to give Sain his job back.[76]

Captain Thomas Hall issued the bizarre request that Scott get rid of the "devilish booze" and the "damnable tobacco" in the state: "When you smoke tobacco you are burning incense to the devil." Hall insisted that tobacco was "the cause of polio, spastics, criminals, arsonites [sic], insanity, criminals, whores, and pimps." He asked the governor to eliminate "all tobacco growing, curing, auction, storing, grading, shipping, smoking" and put all the acreage into "cereals, foods, fruits, eggs, cotton, etc." for the great famine that was coming because "the curse of Almighty God is upon the state."[77] Obviously, there is no answer for such a letter, and Scott simply ignored such outrageous but entertaining dispatches.

One letter that certainly did not qualify to be placed in File 13 but should be noted for posterity was an almost inexplicable epistle from one Jesse Helms, then the news director of WRAL radio station in Raleigh. "As far as I am concerned," wrote Helms, "[the present governor] is the first North Carolinian in my lifetime who has the vision and the ability to become president of the United States. And he may represent North Carolina's only chance for that honor in my lifetime." He urged Scott to "have a heart-to-heart talk with the governor in the hopes that he may set his cap for that accomplishment." Helms observed that Scott had a way of getting along with the little man.[78]

Scott replied: "I hardly know how to answer your letter . . . other than to say I do deeply appreciate the spirit of the letter and your feeling in the matter." He noted, however, that he had several important programs under way and wanted to give full time and energy to them. He would do the best he could as governor and leave to others to judge whether he should undertake anything else: "As you have perhaps observed, too much ambition is dangerous and has killed a great many persons."[79] One wonders what possessed Helms to write such a letter. Clearly, he must have had some favor in mind because the two men were natural enemies and would be at each other's throats in the bitter Senate campaign of 1950.

In addition to marshaling legislation through the legislature, stumping for bond issues, and running the state, the governor had to perform the civic functions of his office by attending ceremonial and social activities around the state. In his book on government and administration in North Carolina, Robert Rankin noted that the typical governor had to devote large amounts of time to interviews, speeches, and trips. While in Raleigh he would be "besieged by a continuous stream of people" seeking favors and suggesting policy. He would have to meet and greet high school graduates, the Boy Scouts, the Daughters of the American Revolution, and other groups who wanted to shake hands or have their pictures taken with him. All this took time, but the governor "must keep in close touch with the people of the state." Rankin made it plain that he was expected to make countless trips around the state to be closer to the people and get a sense of the pulse of his constituents: "Speeches must be made to engineers on stream pollution, to beauty shop operators on cosmetics and to farmers on hog cholera." Since his presence lent prestige and dignity to ceremonies, the governor was expected to give commencement speeches and Fourth of July addresses, judge beauty contests and answer a myriad number of requests.[80]

Rankin listed Scott's schedule for October 1949 as an example of the responsibilities of a governor. On October 2 he made a speech to the North Carolina Association of the Deaf and attended the Tennessee-Duke football game. He spent two days at home in Haw River before going to Democratic political meetings in Reidsville and Whiteville in preparation for the November elections. He was in Washington for Farm Day on October 8 and then had political meetings in Carthage, New Bern, and Tarboro. On October 14 he visited the Yam Festival in Tabor City and spoke to cotton manufacturers in Pinehurst. He was at the state fair in Raleigh on October 21, and the rest of the month was taken up with political speeches, Farm Day in Clinton, and a meeting with the Grange on October 28.[81] This list does not include all his engagements, nor does it include making time for personal meetings, reading and signing letters, ruling on paroles and death sentences, and intervening in labor disputes. Scott, of course, could not keep such a schedule during the legislative session, but October 1949 was fairly typical of his monthly calendar during his tenure as governor except for trips outside the state to Washington, DC, to governors' conferences, and to Democratic Party gatherings.

Scott was a big football fan, especially enthusiastic about his alma mater, North Carolina State, and loved the pageantry and the crowds at college games. When introduced at a North Carolina State–North Carolina game at Chapel Hill in September 1949, he was booed by the crowd. The *Greensboro Record* thought the incident "disgraceful," but the Tar Heel fans said it was all in jest and not an insult. They were just responding in kind to a Scott joke about the University of North Carolina hospital. Billy Carmichael, the university comptroller, said that the two most-talked-about individuals in North Carolina were the football player Charlie "Choo Choo" Justice and Kerr "Boo Boo" Scott.[82]

When Governor Scott watched him play in the fall of 1949, Justice was at the peak of his college career. Number 22, the slightly built, 165-pound hero of the Tar Heel football team is perhaps the most famous athlete in the state's history. No North Carolina athlete was more admired and lionized, and no one quite captured the imagination of the state like Charlie Justice. Justice had an extraordinary, legendary career at Chapel Hill from 1946 through 1949. A triple-threat tailback, he gained 5,176 yards rushing, scored thirty-nine touchdowns, and passed for twenty-six more. He averaged 42.5 yards on 251 punts, and he returned 74 punts for an average of 16.2 yards per return. He was a first-team All-American in 1948 and 1949. In an editorial celebrating Justice's football career, the *Raleigh News and Observer* quoted Frank Leahy, the Notre Dame football coach: "I have long been one of your strongest admirers, because when a young man can receive as much publicity as you have for four years and remain as level-headed as you have, he becomes a tremendous credit to intercollegiate football."[83]

While Justice ran wild on the gridiron, a basketball revolution was taking place in Raleigh. In 1946, North Carolina State College hired Everett Case, a high school coach in Indiana, as its head basketball coach. When Case arrived, sports fans in the state were basketball illiterates. That did not last long as Case's teams were an immediate success. The Red Terrors, as they were then known, used Case's fast-paced offense and full-court defense to blow away the opposition. Case's success forced all the other basketball coaches in the state to improve their teams and match his innovative style.

In his marvelous career at North Carolina State—377 victories and 10 conference championships—Case helped push basketball to the forefront of the national imagination, igniting a passion and excitement that made Tobacco Road (North Carolina State, the University of North Carolina, Duke University, and Wake Forest University) one of the hotbeds of basketball in America. Everett Case, "the Old Gray Fox," was the first coach to cut down the nets after a victory, the first to turn down the lights during player introductions, the first to use pep bands, and the first to set up formal basketball camps. He inaugurated the Dixie Classic, at the time the foremost regular season tournament in the country. Governor Scott was a huge fan and reveled in State's successful 29–3 record in 1949. Case upped the ante on his opponents on December 2, 1949, with the opening of the 12,400-seat William Neal Reynolds Coliseum, the largest basketball facility in the South. Basketball in the state would never be the same.[84]

As Scott grew in power and influence with the success of his programs, he came under attack by those who thought he had too much authority and was rapidly becoming a dictator. As Arthur Leseane wrote in the *Baltimore Sun*, not only had the governor upset precedent and toppled the party organization in charge of North Carolina politics, but his Go Forward program also left the stand-patters and conservatives fearful for the future.[85]

The governor, of course, rejected the negative comments and continued to make intemperate remarks about conservative groups in the state. His ill-considered criticisms heightened the unrest. In a speech to the North

Carolina Confederation of Labor convention, Scott told the group that the Chamber of Commerce was not interested in developing the state and had fought every measure to help the farmer. The US Chamber of Commerce reacted to this invective with a letter disparaging Scott's remarks and championing its work as among the "most constructive influences" in supporting worthwhile projects. It asserted that it tried to create an atmosphere where management and labor could work happily together. Scott brushed off the letter by remarking: "Not a single man I have talked to has taken sides with the U.S. Chamber of Commerce."[86]

A reprimand by Thurmond Chatham was not as easy to ignore. The congressman was "sick and tired" of Scott complaining about civic clubs and the Chamber of Commerce because by so doing he had arrayed class against class. Scott, unruffled, chuckled in characterizing Chatham's comments as "interesting" and explained that the congressman was a good-hearted fellow but got excited sometimes. He denied condemning civic clubs as such and argued that his program was designed to close the breach between country and city people, not to make it deeper.[87] When Scott lashed out at Kerr Craige Ramsay, the speaker of the House, for opposing some of his Go Forward legislation in the 1949 session, Ramsay's muted but effective reply ended with a word of caution: "The General Assembly is a coordinate branch of government and was never intended to rubber-stamp the executive."[88] T. C. Johnson wrote Capus Waynick that Scott still talked "impetuously at times" but "retain[ed] most of his strength among the people."[89]

Newspapers and conservative politicians added to the tumult. The *Shelby Daily Star* slammed the governor for his criticism of the General Assembly, lawyers, civic clubs, and utility companies and noted that he was "now singling out people [House Speaker Ramsay] who did not and do not agree with him on how to run the state government." Scott had threatened to cancel the franchises of public utility companies if they did not expand, but he had no such authority by law: "No North Carolina Governor is supposed to be a dictator over the people." Further, no governor was infallible in his views. The paper wanted "Bossman" Scott to succeed but reminded him that a divided state is a hampered state.[90] An unsigned letter to the governor followed up the sentiment of the Shelby paper: "You can't keep antagonizing large groups of people and stirring up class hate and prejudice without reaping it sooner or later. You have a wonderful opportunity to make a great governor, but I don't think you can do it by dictatorial methods."[91]

The *Charlotte News,* a Scott nemesis, gave the governor credit for his sincere and genuine concern for his fellow man and an uncommon amount of political courage, but it also found him "utterly intolerant of anyone who disagrees with him." This intolerance caused him to be surly and sarcastic, to be petulant when humor was called for, and evoked boorishness when dignity was in order. Scott could not get by forever "by insulting people and breeding animosity in those [he] would like to have on [his] side." He had spent too much time "scolding, chiding, deriding anyone who failed to genuflect toward him and pay homage."[92]

The *News* may have gone a little over the top, but the censure was appropriate and represented the feelings of a significant number of conservative citizens in the state. Scott was Scott and still believed that the way to force change was to stir the waters a bit. Nonetheless, a cult of personality was beginning to develop, and the governor knew he had to moderate his strategy. Always a shrewd tactician, he responded to the criticism because it was politically expedient to do so, not because he believed that the attacks had any validity.

Ever the pragmatic politician, Scott realized that the criticism was growing and could enervate his agenda. He did not want to alienate his base or undermine his legislative goals, so he began to change his ways. John Marshall encouraged him to "stay on an even keel and be a little more careful in his off-the-cuff speeches." Marshall reported that several members of the Democratic Party and the press had noticed a change and had complimented Marshall on his efforts to modify the governor's often-contentious rhetoric. Marshall continued to discuss controversial issues with Scott "without telling him what to do" and then "hold [his] breath and hang on."[93]

The chastened Scott illustrated his dramatic change in attitude when he threw the operating switch that sent power pulsing from the huge new steam-generating plant on the Lumber River. He praised L. V. Sutton and the Carolina Power and Light Company for a "staggering accomplishment" and "a magnificent enterprise." He told them they should be "justly proud" of their part in making electricity available to rural areas. Nevertheless, he made it clear that there was not yet enough electric power as a million citizens were still without electricity. He complained that the electric companies gathered in the Piedmont, where there was high demand, and ignored the eastern part of the state, where there was less demand. Before he sat down, he simply could not resist a dig at the Tidewater Power Company for having rates so high that they throttled industry. L. V. Sutton spoke after Scott and pointedly noted that there had never been a power shortage in his company's territory and that the company had three steam-generating plants and a fourth in the works. Carolina Power and Light maintained nine hydroelectric plants and paid $5.5 million in taxes. The *Raleigh News and Observer* agreed with Scott that the private power companies had done a big job but noted that eastern North Carolina still needed more power than the private companies had furnished.[94]

While working hard to get more electricity and telephones for the state, Scott did not forget his commitment to improve Negro schools. Speaking to a gathering of southern regional educators, he again observed that the state needed better facilities in high schools and colleges for Negroes. He touched on the fact that many Negro schools were in "deplorable conditions" and were so bad in Orange County that a lawsuit could and probably should be brought against school officials. He assured his audience that the money from the new school bonds would bring up the level of Negro schools.[95]

The governor also had Clyde A. Erwin, the superintendent of public instruction, prepare a report outlining eight areas where Negro schools were inferior to white schools. The eight areas included inadequate transportation, lack of schoolrooms and other facilities, very little vocational or graduate education, inadequate maintenance of buildings, noncompetitive salaries, and not enough teachers for the five Negro colleges in the state.[96] The state had a long way to go to equalize education for minority races and would not achieve anything close to equality for many years, but at least Scott had called attention to the problem and began spending money to alleviate some of the discrepancies. Although his efforts were paternalistic in nature, they pleased the black community and were greater than those of any previous governor.

In many ways Scott was not the typical southern governor of the day, unlike Fielding Wright of Mississippi, Eugene Talmadge of Georgia, and Strom Thurmond of South Carolina. At the Southern Governor's Conference in Biloxi, Mississippi, in September 1949, when the more conservative governors tried to turn the meeting into a Dixiecrat rally, Scott did not participate. He explained that he "was not in such hot standing down there." When asked whether he was a states' rights man, he replied that he did not support the Dixiecrats and that instead of states' rights what he stood for would be better explained by the term "states responsibilities"—if the states assumed certain rights, then they had the responsibility to supply the services the people needed.[97] As governor, Scott consistently opposed the more radical, demagogic responses to integration, and, with a few exceptions, such as Jim Folson of Alabama and Albert Gore Sr. of Tennessee, he was much more willing than other southern governors to embrace the reach of the new modern state on education, infrastructure, health, labor, and the environment. Many southern governors were more conservative and very reluctantly gave support to any major changes in education, health care, or environmental policy. They clung strongly to the Old South tradition that less government is more and that any change might undermine their political power, while Scott envisioned state government as the only entity that could rectify the ills of a region where one-third of the population was ill housed, ill clothed, poorly educated, and impoverished.

As did most governors, Scott faced some serious problems in the state prison system, which was run by the Highway and Public Works Commission. One of the major failings of the penal system was the systematic mistreatment of prisoners. On one occasion where a prisoner was handcuffed to his cell for fifty-two hours, police charged N. L. Carpenter, the superintendent responsible for the brutality, with assault. When Carpenter appeared in Judge Susie Sharp's court, the lawyers for the Highway Commission argued that he was merely carrying out his duties according to long-standing, authorized practices. The jury found him guilty of assault resulting in serious bodily injury. Judge Sharp denounced prison discipline as medieval and excessive. She sentenced Carpenter to nine months on the roads but suspended the sentence since he did not make the rules and was obeying others whose responsibility was greater than his.

This event and others like it led to a revamping of the prison system. Sharp and Scott understood that prisoners were difficult to handle and could not be mollycoddled, but the Carpenter case went beyond the pale and brought unwanted attention from newspapers and denunciation from the public. Scott ordered Henry Jordan and J. B. Moore, the prisons director, to launch a three-month study of the prison punishment system and modernize it "without delay." The report submitted by Jordan and Moore led to several changes. It recommended a full-time psychologist, an education director to improve prison education and vocational training, and better guard training and floated the idea of incentive pay for work done by prisoners. These reforms were not immediately implemented, but with Scott's urging the state began to develop a more modern prison system.[98]

From June until December 1949, Scott's major priority—building roads—was never far from his mind, especially since everyone was clamoring for his road to be built immediately. Some rural dwellers hoped for roads to be built right up to their farms. Scott disabused them of that notion: "I know some of you are going to get restless because you won't get your road right away. But you understand that it's not in the program to build a road right up to the house from a highway. If we did that, the first thing you know you'd be wanting the highway commission to sweep off your porch."[99] Knowing that citizens were anxious to have the road-building program begin, Scott had the Highway Commission put out a county-by-county report listing the roads slated for paving.[100] He affirmed that the actual building of highways and byways would begin after January 1, 1950, once the planning had been completed, engineers hired, and equipment purchased. He called on the Highway Commission to set a goal of building ten miles of blacktop road-way every day for the next three and one half years.[101]

By late October the chairman of the Highway Commission reported that there were three to four hundred highway projects under contract and that they would be completed on time.[102] In late November the state opened bids for thirty-one new projects and 210 miles of road.[103] This activity encouraged those badly in need of roads that the planning and organization were going forward, but the state had no intention of rushing to build highways without a master plan.

As the year drew to a close, Scott decided to make a report to the people. In his inaugural address he had outlined his fifteen-point Go Forward program, and he considered it his duty to report on the progress of that plan. He gave credit for the accomplishments to legislators, government officials, advisers, and others who made up his team. He began by citing the approval of the two bond issues, roads and schools. The road program would be the most ambitious in the state's history, with the goal of twelve thousand paved miles. Scott asserted that the increase of $22 million in the direct appropriation for public schools had been spent on raising teachers' salaries and reducing their loads and on better school transportation, new facilities, and a child health program. The $25 million voted for by the public and the $25 million from state surplus funds had been allocated to build new classrooms around the state.

Scott proudly pointed out the building of new hospitals, nursing homes, and health care centers, in many instances where there had been no previous facilities. The teaching hospital and medical school at the University of North Carolina were under construction, and additional monies had been spent on public health programs, four hundred additional beds for the mentally ill, and the treatment of tuberculosis. Old-age assistance and aid to dependent children had increased. The prison system had begun a process of modernization, including a first offender training center. Ground-breaking ceremonies had been planned for the new port terminals at Wilmington and Morehead City.

Scott reported progress in providing electricity and telephones to rural areas. With the cooperation of the utility companies, some 7,967 miles of rural lines had been provided. There had been an increase of 56,097 new phones, but that covered only 15 percent of rural dwellers, so more needed to be done. The governor announced that he had kept his promise by getting broader representation on state boards and institutions and by letting some fresh air into state government. He gave statistical evidence for his vigorous house cleaning: "Of the 428 appointments I have made in 1949 to various boards and commissions, only 89 or twenty percent, were reappointments." Of these 428 appointees, 15 percent were women, up from 7 percent, and he had selected fifteen Negroes. In another critical area that had been a key issue in the 1948 campaign, Scott revealed that the state had deposited cash balances from the state treasury in various financial options and had earned $1,798,111.89 in interest. He regretted failure in labor legislation but felt confident that the state budget was in good shape and that the needed public services had been provided for North Carolinians.[104]

While the *Raleigh News and Observer* did not agree with every appointment or dismissal, it congratulated Scott for achieving significant progress in his first year. "The times clearly demonstrated" the need for a new team to run state government, and, as captain, "the governor has assembled a good team." The paper decried the frequent attacks on Scott. Seldom had any public figure been abused and vilified as much as he, and the charges that he was a dictator or was bankrupting the state were silly.[105]

The farmer from Haw River had done a remarkable job in achieving his fifteen-point program. He had mastered the legislative process, had dealt effectively with many vexing problems, and, through his leadership and personal appeal, had changed the face and the future of his state. His first year in office would be the high-water mark of his political career. He had succeeded beyond expectations, but there were new problems to face—the most challenging of which would be to elect Frank Graham to a four-year term in the Senate.

6

CRUCIBLE OF LIBERALISM

Frank Graham and the 1950 Senate Race

Governor Scott knew early on that Graham might face a difficult challenge in his desire for a full term in the Senate but hoped that his personal popularity would enable him to avoid a major opponent in the Democratic primary. Much depended on his political acumen and his interest in an early and effective campaign organization. Thomas Turner, a Graham partisan, warned that the senator had to make early preparations if he expected to win. Turner told Jonathan Daniels that tough opposition to the senator would coalesce if Dr. Frank ignored his political duties and did not "awake to the political facts of life."[1]

In August 1949, aware that Graham had given no thought to a political organization, Daniels created an informal statewide correspondence network and began contacting key advocates to plan campaign strategy. He knew that the modest and self-effacing Graham would have to be pushed hard to set up his headquarters and come up with a viable campaign strategy.[2] Throughout the latter part of 1949, Graham devotees weighed in on the proper steps to be taken. Charles B. Deane urged Graham to get active in the race as soon as possible, with special attention to labor and the black vote.[3] O. Max Gardner Jr. wrote Daniels that, despite his popularity, Graham needed to get out, press the flesh, and persuade voters that he was not a racial radical and "too leftist."[4]

Many political observers surmised that, with the backing of the powerful Scott administration and the farmers plus the black and labor vote, Graham would be too strong for anyone to challenge. Graham, however, was far too liberal for many North Carolinians, and there had been some frantic activity by conservative Democrats to find a suitable opponent. Former senator William B. Umstead, a hard-line conservative, had expressed interest and would be a formidable adversary.[5] Another possibility was none other than

Robert R. "Our Bob" Reynolds, who had left his Senate seat in 1944 after two terms rather than face certain defeat because of his isolationist views. He had been out of the public eye for six years, a situation he found intolerable. Ever the crowd pleaser, he told the *Charlotte Observer*: "I'm getting a lot of encouragement to run. And I might add that I am encouraging myself to enter the race."[6] Most pundits quickly dismissed him as an insignificant political force.

Governor Scott, along with Daniels, made it clear to Graham's followers that they would do everything in their power, out of the public eye, to promote Graham's candidacy. Scott met with Congress of Industrial Organizations (CIO) leaders in August and December and asked for their assistance. The CIO responded by assigning Dave Burgess as a full-time political operative in North Carolina to increase voter registration and elect liberal candidates.[7] Burgess met with Kelly Alexander Jr., state head of the NAACP, who agreed to work with the CIO.[8] Scott wanted the help of blacks and labor, but he also wanted them to do their work discreetly.

Although Scott and Daniels had publicly declared Graham unbeatable, that opinion was for public consumption and was designed to scare off any viable opponents. As 1949 drew to a close, Daniels became more worried about Graham's chances since, despite several entreaties, the senator had not yet appointed a campaign manager. He explained to one correspondent that, while Graham was a natural politician and at ease with people, he was "a little innocent and naive in matters of political organization." He wrote Eleanor Roosevelt, who had expressed concern about Graham's chances, that the greatest danger to his election was Truman's civil rights proposals. If the senator supported such legislation, he would antagonize large numbers of people in the state. Daniels presciently concluded that the only possible way anyone "could defeat Frank, would be in a horrible 'nigger-communist' campaign."[9]

Scott disagreed with Daniels's assessment that Graham was unbeatable. If I were going to run, Scott told reporters, "I would certainly anticipate . . . opposition and would plan my campaign accordingly. No man exists on earth who can't be beaten." Scott promised that, if Graham did have opposition and a "smear" campaign ensued, then he himself would actively campaign for him.[10]

With his own prestige and future political hopes linked to Graham's senate career, in December 1949 Scott invited a group of influential Graham supporters to the governor's mansion, primarily to discuss ways in which the Scott administration could aid Graham.[11] Astonished at the political naïveté displayed, T. C. Johnson, the commissioner of paroles, cautioned the group that Graham might have serious difficulty winning the election.[12] Despite pleas from Scott and other friends, with the May 1950 primary barely six months away Graham still had not bothered to select a campaign manager or plan a strategy. Nor had he given any thought to how much the race might cost or how the money might be raised. Kathryn Folger, a friend and adviser, recalled that Dr. Frank simply assumed that, if voters wanted him in the Senate, they would march to the polls and mark their ballot for him. If left to his own devices, Folger observed, Graham probably never would have done anything to organize his campaign.[13] Eventually, tired of waiting for Graham to act, Scott, Daniels, and others simply took over the fledgling organization in precisely the same way they managed the appointment. They were not about to abandon their candidate or let the campaign languish. Nonetheless, by the end of January there was still no manager or campaign headquarters.

In early January, Graham got an unexpected boost when his most dangerous opponent, William B. Umstead, withdrew from the race for health reasons despite "an overwhelming promise of support from around the state."[14] With Umstead out, it now appeared that Graham would face only minimal opposition,[15] but Scott was having none of it. When asked whether Graham was a safe bet for nomination, he replied: "If it was me, I would run like I was being shot at."[16]

With only a little over four months to go before the primary, Graham's adherents finally concluded that they must organize the campaign even though at this point there was no serious opposition. At the very least, a sound organization might scare off viable opponents. The Clinton attorney Jeff Johnson and Gladys Tillett began the process by sending letters to encourage supporters to rally to Graham's standard, while other friends spoke publicly of his virtues.[17]

Widespread advocacy by friends was inadequate for a formal campaign, so Scott announced his enthusiastic support for Graham. He made a direct appeal for labor support: "You haven't got a better liberal in America than the Senator you've got. Let's don't slip up in this and assume that everything is all right." He illustrated the dilemma of a sitting governor when he said he could not stick his neck out too far in helping Dr. Graham: "But if given a chance I might do just a little bit more."[18]

In addition to labor and the Scott organization, a major source of strength would be the state's black voters, who saw Graham as their best friend. Black leaders began organizing to assist Graham by proposing to register some twenty-five thousand new voters for 1950.[19] The Scott brains trust had to tread very lightly in appealing to black votes as President Truman's civil rights proposals had created a strong backlash in the South. Especially troubling to the white supremacists in North Carolina was Truman's advocacy of an act proposing the establishment of a permanent fair employment practices commission (FEPC). The act would empower the federal agency to mediate disputes in which employees claimed discrimination based on race, religion, or ethnicity. Should conciliation fail, the FEPC would have enforcement powers.

William B. Umstead's withdrawal from the race had disappointed conservatives, who now resumed the search for a prominent opponent for Graham. The lack of a suitable office seeker did not discourage Graham's critics from continuing to fulminate against him. The *High Point Enterprise* and its editor, "Battling Bob" Thompson, an unrelenting foe of Scott and Graham, set the stage for later fusillades by referring to Graham as the "pink-tinted Senator." The main issues, concluded Thompson, would be the senator's radicalism, his fronting for Communist organizations, and his thinly disguised enthusiasm for socialism.[20]

On January 31, 1950, "Our Bob" Reynolds surprised Graham supporters and political observers alike by announcing that he would run against, not Senator Clyde Hoey, but Graham because Graham's views were foreign to Reynolds's thinking and not in keeping with the philosophy of North Carolina voters. Always out for the main chance, Reynolds knew he stood a better chance of defeating the controversial Graham, whose political strength was untested, than Hoey, who was popular, experienced, and conservative.[21] In vintage Reynoldsese, he confided to his law partner: "I could never defeat Hoey. I can't beat a man who goes around the state with a Bible in one hand and his pecker in the other."[22] Conservatives were not pleased with the Asheville man's entry into the contest. Holt McPherson contended that Reynolds was not a conservative but merely an opportunist and showman who could not win and would turn the race into a political carnival.[23]

Couched in his unique blend of states' rights democracy, nativism, and opposition to government largesse, Reynolds's quest was doomed from the start. Democratic Party leaders thought him an embarrassment and decried his reentry into politics. Jonathan Daniels dismissed his candidacy, calling Graham a "better citizen, a sounder man and better senator." The contest between Reynolds and Graham would give Democrats an easy choice.[24]

Despite the promise of a colorful race from one of the state's most promi-nent demagogues, the press chastised Reynolds for entering the race.[25] The *Washington Daily News* had the most thoughtful analysis of Reynolds's pos-sible effect on the race. His entry created an opportunity for a third, more conservative candidate to make a strong bid against Graham as he would siphon votes away from Graham.[26]

Because many North Carolinians could stomach neither Graham nor Reynolds, conservative Democrats renewed their efforts to find a suitable challenger to Graham. The anti-Graham, anti-Scott group found its man in Willis Smith of Raleigh. Smith, a highly successful attorney, had been speaker of the North Carolina House of Representatives in 1931 and was a former president of the American Bar Association. Initially, he indicated he had no appetite for the rigors and expense of a Senate race, but under heavy pressure he began to change his mind.[27] He thought that a major-ity of citizens in the state did not share Graham's beliefs and views. As he sampled potential support around the state, he received hundreds of phone calls and letters beseeching him to run, and he began to think that, if he did announce, he could win.[28]

The Graham camp recognized that Smith was a serious threat who could derail Graham's budding Senate career. Several of Graham's lifelong friends, including Charles W. Tillett, tried to talk Smith out of entering the contest,[29] but to no avail. Bowing to the groundswell of support and an intensive conservative push to enlist his candidacy, Smith paid his filing fee on February 24.[30]

Scott once again warned the Graham hierarchy against overconfidence: "The most dangerous statement you can make is to say you can't be beat. Folks don't like a man to say he is all-powerful."[31] Graham finally took heed of Scott's advice and opened his Raleigh headquarters on February 21, only three days prior to Smith's entry into the race. In retrospect, Graham's delay in setting up his campaign apparatus gave encouragement to the Smith forces. Daniels, Scott, and Graham had simply waited too long to choose a campaign staff and establish a headquarters. If money had been raised and the orga-nization put on a viable basis in December 1949, potential candidates like Smith might have been discouraged from entering the race since Graham would have had an insuperable head start. Without a nascent headquarters and some serious fund-raising, Scott and Daniels had failed in their attempt to convince conservatives of Graham's invincibility.[32]

With advice from Daniels and Scott, Graham chose Jeff Johnson, an astute political operative and former state legislator, as his campaign manager. The well-known, experienced, and much-respected Johnson would make up for Graham's political inexperience.[33] Johnson delayed in hiring a publicity director, a key post considering Graham's controversial past. One of the leading candidates was the young Jesse Helms, at the time the news director of WRAL. According to Helms (and he told this same story several times over the years), Scott and Graham summoned him to a meeting and tried to persuade him to serve as Dr. Frank's publicity director. Helms claimed that he was not surprised at the offer since he was on good terms with Governor Scott. But he refused the offer in "one of the most difficult statements [he] ever had to make in [his] life." He tearfully told of his affection for Dr. Frank and thanked Scott for thinking of him. He could not accept because he disagreed with Graham on some key issues and intended to support Willis Smith if he ran. Overcome with emotion, Helms "choked up," but Graham put his arm around him and told him that he understood his decision.[34] Subsequently, Graham picked Abie Upchurch for the post.

Willis Smith's entry into the race changed everything. Although out of politics for nineteen years, the Raleigh attorney still had high visibility and good connections. He represented the "progressive conservative" coalition in state politics, the group that Scott had taken to the woodshed in 1948. In him, the archfoes of Scott and Graham had a candidate who would represent their traditional southern democratic views and, they fervently hoped, depose the new liberal order in North Carolina. Make no mistake, the race was as much against Scott as it was against Graham.

Smith quickly lined up individuals and groups to sponsor his cause, especially wealthy bankers and merchants such as the Raleigh businessman A. J. Fletcher, who owned radio station WRAL, and President Louis V. Sutton of the Carolina Power and Light Company, who took great pleasure in raising money to thwart the plans of both Scott and Graham. Perhaps most troubling for Scott, B. Everett Jordan, a close friend of Smith, secured money and much-needed textile support for him. Although Jordan served as state party chairman and should have been neutral in the contest, he continued to raise money and advise Smith throughout the Democratic primary.[35] Such partisan activity marked the beginning of a fatal split between Scott and Jordan, who had previously been a strong Scott advocate. Scott saw Jordan's shift to Smith as a personal betrayal.

The press agreed that Willis Smith was a serious candidate who would provide a severe test for Graham. For those who loved a good fight, the

Asheville Citizen declared, the Graham-Smith-Reynolds contest loomed as the greatest battle of the century.[36] Wade Lucas, writing in the *Charlotte Observer,* surmised that the race would be a referendum on Graham's views and Scott's leadership. Much would depend on Graham's skill on the hustings and Scott's ability to persuade his voters to come out for Graham without creating a backlash against his administration.[37]

The Graham camp reacted gloomily to Smith's entry. Jonathan Daniels foresaw a "real fight"[38] and characterized Smith as the embodiment of the anti-Truman resistance in the South.[39] Scott remained cautious. He insisted that Smith's candidacy would serve "to prove Frank Graham to be a very effective politician before it's over."[40] He had better be as Smith would command enthusiastic conservative support. With race and communism as viable issues, Smith could launch devastating attacks against Graham's beliefs and views.

Campaign manager Jeff Johnson was the principal person running the day-to-day operations, but he received constant advice from both Scott and Daniels. Governor Scott was an active, if surreptitious, adviser from the outset. He mobilized his own followers on behalf of the senator and met occasionally with the staff to listen to problems and make suggestions. He did not visit the campaign office—such a move would be too public—but he frequently talked with Johnson by phone. Daniels concentrated on raising money, getting key endorsements, and writing favorable editorials.[41]

On the other hand, the candidate himself had almost nothing to do with campaign planning and seldom visited headquarters. Even as the campaign geared up, Graham still had no idea what his quest would cost. He once remarked that he had saved over $5,000 and thought that would be sufficient to pay for all the campaign expenses. Fund-raising was anathema to Dr. Frank, and he simply refused to ask for money, nor would he personally accept it. Neither would he ask directly for votes. The staff quickly learned that he would be a unique candidate. He would make speeches and shake hands, but someone else would have to raise the necessary money.[42]

By law, the first primary spending limit remained at $12,000. Each campaign kept two sets of books—one for the candidate and the public and one for the staff people who actually handled the expenditures. Most contributions and expenses simply went unreported.[43] All politicians, with the exception of Frank Graham, understood that the actual cost of a Senate primary would be well above $100,000, but they acquiesced in the submission of false expense reports. Graham had no knowledge that his staff had failed to report what were, by law, illegal contributions. If he had, he would not have permitted it even if following the law would have imperiled his campaign. He would not have signed the official financial report if he had known that the law was being violated.[44] How an intelligent man and a former university president could imagine that his campaign cost only $12,000 is inexplicable. Being naive is one thing, but apparently Graham deliberately avoided any specifics about finances so that he could remain pure and uncorrupted by politics. He could then sign the financial reports with a clear conscience. He was either willfully obtuse or disingenuous in his maneuvering to avoid a moral dilemma over electoral finances.

For Graham staffers, the reporting of funds was not the problem; fund-raising was. Since Graham continued to refuse to ask for money, fund-raising became the province of close advisers, notably Scott, Daniels, Johnson, and the representatives of various labor organizations.[45] Only labor seemed to understand the dire need for ready cash and quickly became one of the key suppliers of money. Dave Burgess began meeting weekly with Johnson and Scott to tender advice about the race and to discuss the best ways to pass money on to the Graham campaign.[46]

The Graham brain trust worked hard to secure the votes of black citizens in the state and met regularly, but privately, with black leaders to transform their advocacy into a massive vote for Graham. Black ministers understood the delicate touch needed to support the senator without triggering a white reaction. One minister wrote Johnson that blacks would have to run a new type of campaign, "quiet and intelligent, do a lot and say a little."[47]

Dr. Frank got endorsements from influential North Carolinians such as J. Spencer Love, the head of Burlington Industries, and many prominent businessmen, educators, and ministers.[48] These endorsements allowed Graham's advisers to present him as a patriotic, capable, middle-of-the-road candidate who commanded broad appeal. With such support Graham could demonstrate the falsity of the charge that he was a dangerous radical. Johnson could now claim with conviction that there was a deep base of support for Graham throughout the state.

Scott was in the audience when Graham formally opened his campaign on March 2, 1950. Graham presented a platform designed to defuse criticism on several issues. He told the audience that he was "not and never had been for socialized medicine." He called for economy in government and the strengthening of free enterprise as the best answer to socialism, communism, and fascism. He favored a strong national defense and repeated his support for federal aid to education, equality of bargaining for labor, a balanced budget, parity for farmers, and a "reasonable" minimum wage. He emphatically emphasized that he opposed the use of federal power in race relations, a position he claimed he had always held. Only religion and education, he repeated, could lead to permanent changes in race relations.[49]

As Graham began his complex and tortured journey to primary day, "Our Bob" Reynolds briefly captured the headlines. He began with a flair, pledging to hit every dirt road in North Carolina and to devote his time to "some politicking, some handshaking, some requesting of votes."[50] He returned to Asheville a mere twelve days later.[51] Voters did not yet know it, but his active effort to regain his Senate seat was now largely spent. His recent meanderings had raised only random clouds of red clay dust. Voters had reacted to his call for votes with the most dismissive response in public life—indifference. Reynolds understood that he could not win in 1950, but he would not withdraw and would end up being the spoiler in the race.

Willis Smith quickly set up his state headquarters and chose a staff, headed by Charles Green, the campaign manager. Smith's strategy was first to get name recognition to offset Graham's popularity and then pummel a straw man called *socialism* and tie Graham to socialized medicine. Smith's advisers denounced Scott's dictatorial control of state government and planned to exploit every pronouncement the free-talking governor might make and, thus, link dislike for Scott to his Senate appointee. Allen Langston, an experienced political operative, correctly predicted that the race would see "a lot of whispering and street corner gabbing about socialism, communism, and niggers."[52]

Smith's official campaign platform was remarkably similar to Graham's. Smith wanted a balanced budget and unfettered free enterprise. In an obvious rebuke to Graham, he opposed anyone in high office who would give aid and encouragement to "Socialists, Communists and their sympathizers and fellow travelers." He rejected an FEPC, not only because it would corrode race relations, but also because it threatened states' rights.[53] He advocated less government intrusion in people's lives and a strong adherence to a segregated society. Graham was more liberal on race, having long endorsed the eventual and voluntary elimination of segregation in the South. He endorsed full voting equality for blacks and advocated admission of qualified blacks to southern states' graduate schools where no separate provision for minorities had been made.[54] Dr. Frank's racial stances differed markedly from those of

Smith and that of the majority of North Carolinians, and that distinction would ultimately be the decisive issue in the contest.

As Willis Smith began his hectic political journey across the state, he knew that he had to make a personal appeal for votes or he would lose. On the stump, he seemed a bit stiff—"too lawyerlike," wrote one observer. His talks did not arouse strong emotion, and he was just an average campaigner, but he had a knack for names and faces. A man of conviction and integrity, he was intelligent, compelling, forceful, and articulate. The "average campaigner" was a strong candidate.[55]

Originally, the Smith counselors anticipated that Graham's association with socialist and Communist groups would be the most critical issue, but they slowly realized that attacking the senator on his racial views was more effective. They tried repeatedly to tie him to the FEPC. Smith intended to force him to admit that he had favored an FEPC in 1947, only to temporize under the heat of voter scrutiny in 1950.[56] Smith had gone on the offensive and would not relinquish his attack mode.

Graham had served on President Truman's Committee on Civil Rights in 1947 and been involved in producing its controversial report, *To Secure These Rights.* One of the report's general recommendations was the establishment of a compulsory FEPC. Although Graham signed the final committee report, he insisted that he had authored a minority report opposing a compulsory FEPC. The Smith forces said there was no so-called minority report and claimed that the senator had always favored federal intervention to end discrimination in the workplace.[57] Jonathan Daniels tried to defuse the issue by accusing Smith of stirring up "the furies of racial prejudice as a means of getting votes." He reprinted the minority report and reemphasized that Graham had consistently opposed federal intervention,[58] but his editorial did little good.

The Communist issue gained prominence with a succession of sensational disclosures, causing citizens to fear that America was under siege by spies intent on compromising national security. Against the background of the Cold War and deepening tension between Stalin's Russia and the United States, several dramatic espionage cases caught the public's attention. The most publicized was that of Alger Hiss, accused by Whittaker Chambers of being a Communist spy.[59] One month later, the British nuclear scientist Klaus Fuchs, who worked at the top-secret nuclear installation at Los Alamos, surrendered to authorities and confessed to passing American atomic secrets to the Russians. Following Fuchs's confession, nine Americans, including Julius and Ethel Rosenberg, were arrested as part of the spy ring. North Carolina's dailies reported the Fuchs-Rosenberg case as well as the Hiss trial with detailed coverage and sensational headlines.[60]

The espionage cases had profound domestic political implications as the Republican Party, desperately seeking a path to power, seized on the Communist menace as a surefire campaign issue. The accusations of treason in high places generated a highly charged political atmosphere that cast widespread suspicion on all those who were thought to sympathize with the Soviet Union, communism, or socialism. In particular, right-wing Republican rhetoric focused on the Democratic Party as composed of subversive dupes, soft on communism, and blind to the threat to American national security.

Joseph R. McCarthy, a Republican senator from Wisconsin, became the number one anti-Communist with a speech in Wheeling, West Virginia, during which he announced that he had a list of Communists working in the State Department.[61] The speech was widely reported in North Carolina.[62] McCarthy had a simple explanation of America's "decline"—it was due to a massive internal conspiracy directed by the Communists and aided by treasonous government officials. This approach was so effective that Republicans in the 1950 races around the country made communism their primary campaign issue.[63]

Daniels immediately recognized the threat McCarthyism posed to Graham's chances and predicted that the case against Graham would be built largely on the basis of his membership in alleged Communist front organizations.[64] The pro-Smith *High Point Enterprise* pictured Graham as a "softhearted" fall guy who had allowed many subversive and Communist front organizations to use his name. The columnist Bob Thompson referred to Graham as "Frank, the Front" and warned that the country "can't afford to have such a man, regardless of good intentions, in the United States Senate."[65]

Just as Graham's handlers feared, the spread of anti-Communist literature and speeches by McCarthy and others struck a raw nerve among some Tar Heel voters. Franz Krebs, for example, wrote the *Charlotte Observer* identifying Graham as a socialist planner and someone "more dangerous to our country than all the communists tried and convicted." When a person joined several front groups, Krebs continued, it seemed logical to assume that he knew what he was doing, and anyone who participated in such groups should be viewed with suspicion.[66]

Scott and others had anticipated this line of attack and called the Communist charges guilt by association, asserting that, while not calling Dr.

Frank a Communist, his critics used discredited sources to make people think that he was.[67] In rebuttal, Graham put out a pamphlet entitled "Life-Long Champion of Democracy." He again denied that he had ever been a Communist or a socialist or a member of any organization controlled by Communists or socialists. He proclaimed his unequivocal commitment to the free enterprise system. While admitting that he joined many groups, he proclaimed that he had done so to promote religion, health, education, and world peace, not socialism.[68] Unfortunately, this tepid defense did not end the controversy.

Throughout the primary, Governor Scott worked assiduously to push the Graham organization on to victory. He envisioned a great liberal triumph that would give him national prestige and more power in the state. A defeat could undermine or derail his Go Forward program, and he could not accept such an outcome. Trying hard to gain an advantage for his candidate, he made an uncharacteristic blunder in March. The Scott-appointed state Board of Elections decided to overturn the recommendations of the state Democratic chairman, B. Everett Jordan, and name election board members of its own choosing in eight western North Carolina counties, an unprecedented power grab that outraged local politicians.[69]

Press and public reaction was swift and derisive. Nearly every state paper denounced the Election Board's action. The *Asheville Citizen* called it illegal and noted that such chicanery undercut the public's faith in the political process.[70] The *Citizen,* a longtime Scott supporter, insisted that Scott's tactics bore the earmarks of justice in a totalitarian state. Scott, the Tar Heel dictator who had previously abhorred political machines, was now using the influence of his office to get his favorites elected.[71]

Besieged by reporters for an explanation of his part in the imbroglio, Scott lamely declared that the decision had been made by the Board of Elections.[72] No one who knew Scott's desire for control and his need to win the election bought his ineffective response. The next day, when the state attorney general ruled that the Elections Board had exceeded its authority,[73] Allen Langston concluded that Scott had committed a serious political blunder, "both in what was done and in the way [he had] handled the matter."[74]

The governor's interference with the function of the state Board of Elections revived an issue that would not die—Graham's relationship with the controversial and partisan Scott, a partnership that the Smith consultants continued to exploit. The governor acknowledged that Graham's opponents were trying to make him an issue in the campaign, but he insisted that he was not the issue—the records of the contestants were most important. According to Scott, once again the large corporations were trying to pick governors and senators as they were accustomed to doing—they did not want the average man to have proper representation in government.[75] This strategy might have worked for Scott in 1948, but it was of little use to Graham in the different political climate of 1950.

Newspapers favorable to Smith kept up a drum roll of anti-Scott invective. The *Durham Sun* accused Scott and Daniels of abandoning any pretense of maintaining the Democratic Party leadership's traditional stance of neutrality. Scott was an issue, the paper remarked, because of his purges and pressures and because he was trying to be North Carolina's little Napoléon.[76] The *Dunn Dispatch* and the *High Point Enterprise* likewise repeatedly pilloried Scott for aiding Graham without regard for party neutrality. They chided state Democratic officials for failing to observe the proprieties and ethics of state politics as Scott's aid to Graham included using state employees on state time in state-owned vehicles.[77] On the other hand, B. Everett Jordan, the state party chairman, who should have been neutral in a Democratic primary, campaigned hard for Willis Smith.

Smith frequently pointed out Graham's close ties to the Truman administration and harped on the fact that certain Democratic Party officials— meaning Scott and Daniels—"violated traditional neutrality." Borrowing a page from Scott's playbook, he contended that the citizens of the state would not permit would-be political bosses to tell them how to vote.[78]

Smith's claim that Daniels and Scott were aligned in a power pact to cram Dr. Frank down the throats of the electorate gained some notoriety with the publication of a series of cartoons. The "Know the Truth" Committee, an arm of the Smith campaign, produced several cartoons stressing Graham's left-wing affiliations and the influence Daniels and Scott had on Graham's political life. One lampoon depicted Scott and Daniels manipulating the strings attached to a Frank Graham puppet. Scott was pictured as saying that Graham would do their bidding and would obey the commands of northern politicians. Daniels was shown answering the phone: "Hold on, here's another order from Washington." The cartoon had Graham asserting that he had always been for the FEPC, the abolition of segregation, and socialized medicine but that as a political candidate he had to change his tune to get elected. He did not want to let Jonathan and Kerr down.[79] Another clever riposte had Graham, on his way to Washington, DC, being pulled over by a highway patrolman for driving on the left side of the highway. The caption read: "Dr. Graham, you are on the wrong side of the highway, folks in N.C. drive on the right."[80] Smith's strategy at this point was to assail Graham's social activism, pointing out that his views were incompatible with mainstream North Carolina Democrats, and to paint him as the handpicked stooge of Scott, Daniels, and Truman.

After all the complaints about his hard-line support for Graham, Scott realized that his outright and overt assistance carried a political risk. If he worked too publicly for Graham and the senator lost, it would damage his prestige in the state.[81] The governor understood that his outspoken nature was a potential problem, and he began to wonder whether he was an asset or a liability. On balance, however, Graham's inner circle believed they had more to gain than lose by Scott's intervention. Jeff Johnson told Dave Burgess that the governor's political contacts, his influence with farmers, and the perquisites of his office were too important to abandon.[82]

Eventually, stung by the harsh attacks on him for undue influence on state workers, and because he wanted his nominee to win at all costs, the governor decided to be a more outspoken Graham advocate. Scott hoped that state employees would vote for Graham, but if "they don't it's all right with me." Asked whether he had been pressuring state employees to contribute money to Graham, Scott seized the moment: "From all I've heard they [the Graham campaign] need the money mighty bad. If anyone wants to pass the hat it's okay."[83] Incidentally, he had issued a policy directive informing department heads to see that no state-owned vehicles were used in the transportation of voters to and from the polling places on election day: "I urge all state employees to vote for the candidate of their choice in the party primary. No state official should instruct his employee how to vote."[84] This directive was, as the race would demonstrate, merely cover because Scott intended to at least persuade, if not instruct, state employees to vote for Graham. He was now committed to using all of the power at his command to aid his nominee.

As of late April, Jeff Johnson and other key advisers were intoxicated with visions of an easy victory. Despite inadequate funding and the slow pace of organizing, they simply assumed that Graham could not lose. He was beloved around the state, and the Jewish vote, the labor vote, and the black vote were overwhelmingly for Graham.[85] Even *Newsweek*, in a mid-April prognostication, wrote that the soft-spoken Graham "seemed a sure bet for re-election [sic]."[86]

Scott knew better. He chided the campaign staff for not devising an overall plan to counter and deflect Smith's charges. Nor had any plan emerged, other than Scott's personal intervention, to hold farmers to the Graham standard. Another problem faced by Graham's handlers was the candidate himself, his bid for office hampered by his political inexperience and naïveté. Graham's trust in and kindhearted view of mankind prohibited him from attacking his opponent: "I'm not attacking anybody. If I have to do that to get elected to the Senate, I don't want to go."[87] In addition, he was slow to defend himself. A phenomenon in southern politics, Graham was a candidate fired not by the desire to win at any cost but by the desire to win while doing the right thing as his Christian values guided him.[88] In his mind, his record was clear. Voters could take it or leave it, although he believed they would take it. He thought he would win.

Graham seldom gave campaign strategy a passing thought. When asked in April how the race was going, he replied: "I don't know. They tell me I am doing all right. You know I am no judge."[89] Nonetheless, he was very effective in small groups. He had a phenomenal memory for names and made a good, coherent, if not rousing speech. Finally, he was beloved by people all over the state who recognized that he had spent his life helping others.[90] His campaign advisers continued to believe that his name and character would be enough to carry him to victory.

While Graham might not have been willing to fight back against the Smith onslaught, his friends and advisers had no such reservations. Widely distributed pamphlets emphasized Graham's service in the marines, his Christian faith, and his loyalty to the Democratic Party. Ads admonished voters not to believe the "loose-lipped character assassins" who were traversing the state distributing hate literature: "They cannot lift their little pig-eyes out of the slime long enough to catch a glimpse of the character and stature of a world leader like Frank Graham." These "whispering messengers of defeat" knew Graham was a consistent foe of communism and socialism, and their false charges would not fool the people of North Carolina.[91]

Graham would not attack Smith, but he did begin to defend his own views more vigorously. He defended Truman's decision to build the hydrogen bomb and concluded: "There is no substitute for Americanism."[92] He again denied ever being in any group "knowing it to be a front for Communists" and implied that his detractors were guilty of distortions and misrepresentations. In an attempt to separate himself from Scott and Daniels, he proclaimed: "I take my directions from no groups or no man."[93]

As the first primary approached, the Smith proponents began to realize that the anti-Communist/socialist line of censure would, on its own, not win them the election. They had gained ground, but not fast enough. So they began to focus their attacks more on race. Smith renewed his charges that Graham favored a compulsory FEPC[94] and warned that with the FEPC "one man's job can be claimed by another man just because he is of a different race or color."[95]

As Smith's advisers shifted their emphasis to race, the Graham camp learned firsthand that racism would be the most emotional and divisive issue in the campaign. One of Graham's canvassers, Mary Coker Joslin, approached a white man and asked him to vote for Graham. Her question evoked a violent reaction: "That communist who wants to put Niggers in our schools?" Joslin tried to explain that Graham was not a Communist and did not want to integrate the schools, but the man would not listen: "I ain't voting for no Red and no Nigger lover."[96] Tom Schlesinger, writing in *The Nation,* argued that Graham's future depended on how well he could sell his liberalism. He was "learning the hard way that mill hands in Gastonia much prefer to hear about his labor record than about his success in Indonesia."[97]

Two disparate events in early May changed the focus of the race. Florida voters sent the liberal New Deal senator Claude Pepper into early retirement. Congressman George Smathers had assailed Pepper in a heated battle, condemning his labor support, maligning his popularity among black voters, and ridiculing him as "an apologist for Stalin, an associate for fellow travelers, and a sponsor for Communist Front organizations." Smathers also claimed that "Red" Pepper had championed an FEPC and socialized medicine. He defeated Pepper by more than sixty thousand votes.[98] Willis Smith drew obvious encouragement from Pepper's demise since he was running a similar race. Smith called Smathers's win a "great victory for level headed citizens."[99] Pepper's defeat emboldened the Smith forces. Energized by the news, they seized on the Florida race as proof that Graham could be beaten.

Every political commentator in the state immediately sought possible parallels to the election in Florida in the Smith-Graham contest. The *Charlotte Observer* reasoned that Pepper's rude treatment in Florida was evidence of growing anti-Truman sentiment and signaled a national move to conservatism.[100] *U.S. News and World Report* stressed voters' concerns over federal interference in race relations (i.e., FEPC) and noted that the charge that Senator Pepper used bloc voting by blacks turned many white voters into the Smathers camp.[101] The Pepper debacle naturally alarmed the Graham forces, but Jonathan Daniels put the best face that he could on the Florida primary, writing that, while its results did not help Graham, he would win despite Pepper's loss.[102]

The other circumstance that affected the first primary was that Graham contracted pneumonia and had to miss two weeks of campaigning. It is difficult to assess how his illness might have influenced the outcome of the race, but surely he would have helped his cause more by mingling with voters than by lying in a hotel room. More important, his illness required him to be absent from the Senate during a critical period in the civil rights debate. A cloture motion, designed to cut off a southern filibuster against the bill to create an FEPC, was imminent.[103] Since he could not be on the floor to cast his vote on the cloture motion, his staff developed a clever strategy that would enable him to align himself with other southern senators and blunt the Smith camp's criticism of his civil rights record. When Senator Clyde Hoey went to cast his vote against cloture, which would cut off debate and allow the filibuster to continue, he would say that, if my colleague Senator Graham were here, he would likewise vote nay. Everyone implored Graham to embrace this strategy. Hoey said that the simple act would be worth fifty thousand votes as voters would see that Graham had embraced the position of the white South and, as he had always maintained, opposed a compulsory FEPC.[104]

But Graham balked at the maneuver. His aides implored him to make a stand against cloture; if he did so, it would ensure his victory. The vote against cloture would be consistent with his lifelong advocacy of free speech and would reaffirm his previous stand opposing a compulsory FEPC. Lying on his sickbed, the senator anguished over the decision. He did not want to betray his supporters, nor would he violate his own conscience and principles. Eventually, he decided he could not ask Hoey to speak for him. He explained that he had not been there for the debate over the bill and, thus, was not properly informed. More to the point, he simply could not agree to do anything that reeked of expediency or opportunism even if the decision was philosophically correct and politically sound. Graham could do nothing he viewed as self-serving; conscience and principle were his guiding stars. He simply would not see the world through the eyes of a practical politician.[105] Dr. Frank's decision was inexplicable to experienced politicians and vexed his backers. His unwillingness to allow Hoey to speak for him cost him heavily in the first primary.

While Senator Graham languished in his bed at the Sir Walter Hotel, the state Democratic Party held its annual convention. The Scott-controlled convention lauded President Truman's progressive leadership, endorsed Scott's Go Forward program, and praised the governor for his achievements. Controversial questions—civil rights, an FEPC, federally financed medical insurance—were simply omitted from the platform to protect Graham and avoid a heated floor fight.[106] The Scott administration produced an uneventful meeting, harmonious in appearance and noncontroversial in substance,[107] precisely the result Scott sought.

While Graham was ill, some of his surrogates took up his banner in an attempt to rebut Smith's false canards and to hit back at Smith. Without Graham's approval, George Maurice Hill bluntly told Smith backers that what they were doing to Frank Graham was ugly and vicious and transcended the bounds of partisanship. They had raised the "black banner of bigotry of racial hatred for political gain."[108] D. Hiden Ramsey, the editor of the *Asheville Citizen,* slammed Smith for an entirely negative platform and for appealing to fear with inflammatory statements intended to discredit Graham at any cost. As to the complaint that Graham would be the tool of Governor Scott and Jonathan Daniels, Ramsey declared that anyone who knew Frank Graham realized that no man could boss him or control his vote—he acknowledged only the sovereignty of his conscience.[109]

Now that Graham was incapacitated, Scott decided to enter the contest full bore. Smith's recent attacks had included Scott, and no one had ever assumed the governor would remain above the fray. As the opposition attacks mounted, Scott's advocacy of Graham became more direct and more partisan.[110] Initially, however, he went to great lengths to explain why he appointed Graham, citing his many years of work to improve health care and education in the state. Yet Scott's help did have a negative dimension. It reminded groups opposed to the governor—business interests such as Carolina Power and Light—of the dangerous link now being forged between the maverick governor, his liberal Senate appointee, and the Truman administration.[111]

Scott discounted the risk that he could do more harm than good and plowed ahead, roaming the state defending Graham. He observed that North Carolina had sent corporate lawyers to the Senate for fifty years and that the state should have a liberal layman, a humanitarian, representing it for a change. Graham's election would be, he noted, "a continuation of my program to give the party back to the people."[112]

Scott concentrated his visits on the farming areas of the state, where he was much in favor. In Goldsboro, he showed his approval of Graham's humanitarian activities when he stated that voters need not fear socialism:

"If you call hot lunches for school children socialistic, then I say let it be."[113] His reference to socialism did not help the cause, but Scott simply could not do other than speak his mind, regardless of the consequences.[114] On May 22, he told a radio audience in a set-the-record-straight speech, that the US Senate needed a man who had devoted his life "to the service of others rather than [to] building his own personal fortune and tying his loyalty and support to special interests." He decried Smith's spreading of misinformation about Graham's views and his mocking and demeaning of the Truman administration.[115]

Scott's remarks elicited an immediate and heated reply from Willis Smith. Smith responded that any claims that his charges against Graham were false amounted to slander. He declared that he had been factually accurate in every statement he made about the senator and that Scott was simply trying to divert attention from the facts by crying smear. Graham's leftist record should not be obscured by this smokescreen. Finally, Smith denounced the governor's use of state cars and state employees to elect Graham. "Never before," continued Smith, "has such pressure been brought upon state employees" by the "would-be dictators" of North Carolina.[116]

As was customary, Scott used whatever leverage he had with state employees to get them to vote for his candidate. State workers subject to a gubernatorial appointment knew better than to cross the governor, who viewed disloyalty as an unpardonable sin. Scott probably threatened no one outright, nor would he be foolish enough to give employees time off to campaign, but he did use implied threats of punishment and promises of reward as well as his considerable powers of persuasion to turn out a large state government vote for Graham. For example, the superintendent of state prison camp no. 103 wrote Graham: "Prison Department is one hundred percent for you and stand ready to go down the road for you." And Scott almost certainly used the promise of delivery of state services, especially the new roads he was building, to enlist assistance for Graham.[117]

As voting day approached, the Graham staff became convinced that Scott's assistance had helped their cause. Even if his critics were dismayed by his overt partisanship, Scott would be the key element in Graham's hope for a first-primary victory.[118] The *Durham Morning Herald* gave editorial assent to this view, pointing out that, even though many voters resented Scott's partisanship, his endorsement of Graham meant that rural people would tend to look to Graham with the same confidence they had placed in the governor.[119]

When local soundings indicated that Smith was gaining ground on Graham and might force a second primary, Graham's labor supporters vowed "to throw everything [they could] into the Graham campaign."[120] Dave Burgess focused on voter turnout and the distribution of leaflets to mill workers. He continued to forward advice and money to Graham's Raleigh headquarters.[121]

Labor's effort for Dr. Frank found its complement in the unprecedented mobilization of black voters. James T. Taylor, a key operative in the movement who tried to work as inconspicuously as possible, predicted that Graham would get 99 percent of the black vote.[122] Letters of approval from blacks came into headquarters from all over the state. Willie Jacobs wrote to Graham in a painstaking scrawl, convinced that all the blacks in his county would vote for him: "We feel you are a good and honor[able] man and mean freedom for all people of the world."[123] This virtually unanimous endorsement of Graham's candidacy by the black community would prove to be a double-edged sword and would come back to haunt Graham in the runoff.

Sensing Smith's surge, Johnson and Scott approved a series of ads discrediting Smith. One message asked why the "smear boys" and the "lackeys of greed and privilege" wanted to tear down the state's racial amity. The ad concluded: "They must not crucify North Carolina and its half century of progress in economics and racial amity, on the cross of bigotry, hate and greed." Another ad noted that the US Senate did not need another "knocker and smearer" like Joe McCarthy. North Carolina needed Frank Graham for "cool, considerate, level-headed leadership in world affairs."[124] But citizens in the state did not give a fig about foreign affairs. The issues in 1950 were not about foreign policy; voters were concerned about Graham's views on race and communism.

Convinced in early May that he was gaining ground on Graham, Smith ran with increased fervor and energy. He resumed his attacks on communism and again reproached Scott and Daniels for wanting to be the political dictators of North Carolina.[125] He said that labor endorsed Graham because "he would carry out their program of socialization" in its "full range of horrors": an FEPC and socialized medicine.[126]

While Smith concentrated on ripostes against socialism and the two puppeteers, Scott and Daniels, his supporters went directly for the jugular. In the final days of the first primary, a series of postcards from New York City were sent to hundreds of state residents: "Dear Voter: Your vote and active support of Senator Frank Graham in the North Carolina primary, May 27, will be greatly appreciated. You know, just as we do, that 'Dr. Frank' has done much to advance the place of the Negro in North Carolina. The Negro is a useful tax paying citizen. [signed] W. Wite, Executive Secretary, National Society for the Advancement of Colored People."[127]

Johnson immediately announced that the postcards were "crude frauds" and would not fool anybody. There was a national *association*, not a national *society*, with Walter *White*, not Walter *Wite*, as executive secretary, and the real NAACP was not campaigning for any candidate.[128] Of course, what Johnson did not say was that the NAACP in North Carolina, led by Kelly Alexander, was working overtime for Senator Graham.

The *News and Observer* called the postcards a "scurvy and contemptible fraud" as they had been mailed too late in the race for the poisonous charges to be rebutted: "Any Senator nominated by . . . such tactics would be ashamed along with the state."[129] Indeed, the condemnation of the ploy was nearly unanimous, and Smith forces took pains to disassociate themselves from such activity.

Years later, Smith campaign participants continued to deny having any hand in the racist attacks.[130] Smith's publicity director, Hoover Adams, remembered that the conflict had been the dirtiest and meanest he had ever seen but insisted that Willis Smith bore no responsibility for the baser tactics used against Graham. The Smith campaign simply could not control supporters who were doing such things. Adams recalled that Smith was upset about the postcards and other racist literature and demanded to know whether any of the racial trash came from his headquarters. If so, Adams would be fired, and Smith would withdraw from the race. Smith declared: "I don't want to be senator badly enough to be elected on that issue." Adams assured his boss that this sort of material did not emanate from Smith headquarters.[131]

Nonetheless, not once during the race did Smith publicly denounce the gutter tactics employed against Graham. Nor did he take specific steps to warn supporters to eliminate such reprehensible practices. Admonitions to campaign staffers and denials from Hoover Adams were not enough. If Smith profited from such tactics, and he did, apparently he was willing to accept the benefit. It strains credulity to suppose that Charles Green, Adams, and others in the hierarchy did not have some idea about who was behind the racial slurs. When they complained that they could not control what their supporters did, one should read: "We don't want to control what they are doing." In essence, by refusing to decry the racism, they acquiesced in it.

The NAACP postcard was such a crude fraud that it did Graham little harm. It did, however, mark the beginning of a much more concentrated effort to attack Graham's liberal leanings on race. Far more threatening was the rumor that the senator had appointed a Negro to West Point. In this instance, there was just enough truth to give the story life. Handbills appeared around the state with a photo of a black man, Leroy Jones, with his hair retouched to appear more frizzy. The caption read: "This is what Frank Graham appointed to West Point."[132] Not "who," but "what," as if Leroy Jones were not a person but a thing.

When he became a US senator, Graham decided to make his selections to West Point based on a competitive civil service exam open to all applicants. Leroy Jones, a Negro student at St. Augustine College, took the exam and finished fifth among forty candidates.[133] As a result of his score, Graham made Jones the second alternate for West Point. As it happened, the first choice, William L. Hauser, accepted the nomination and enrolled at West Point. Thus, Jones never attended West Point. Graham, proud that a Negro student made such an excellent score, congratulated Jones and released the names of all six selections to the press.[134]

The Jones handbill circulated statewide, accompanied by the whispers that "Graham appointed a nigger to West Point."[135] Mayne Albright recalled the effect of the Jones circular in the last days of the first primary. Graham's opponents had twisted the facts so effectively that you could not get the phrase "he appointed a nigger" out of the minds of the people.[136]

While Graham and Smith bore in on each other, the forgotten candidate, Bob Reynolds, popped into view. He continued to predict that he would win a huge victory by at least twenty-five thousand votes even though he and everyone else knew he had no chance. The only issue at this point was whether he would get enough votes to force a second primary.[137] Knowing that Reynolds would pull votes away from Graham, some of Graham's advisers tried to persuade him to withdraw, but he refused.[138]

The first primary thus approached its denouement. The candidates, with their hard-hitting campaigns and divisive rhetoric, had aroused voter interest like no political campaign in a generation had. Moreover, the race had captured national attention as a southern referendum on the Truman administration, a litmus test on the status of race relations in the upper South and the effectiveness of Communist bashing. It was, additionally, a critical test of Governor Scott's ability to strengthen his grip on North Carolina politics. Finally, it was a public plebiscite on the career of Frank Graham. In sum, it was a pivotal election that would shape the North Carolina political compass for years to come.

Still hopeful of victory but fearful that his man would not get a majority, Jonathan Daniels penned a final editorial. He wrote that it was time to "Sound the Tocsin," invoking the ancient word for an alarm bell that rang for the protection of the people. He warned about the falsifiers who were trying to destroy a good man and mislead the state's voters. Graham's ouster from the Senate would be nothing short of a tragedy for the state and the nation. Race hatred, he concluded, had no place in the contest. Yet Smith had never repudiated or rebuked these snide tricks nor restrained his staff from the effort to destroy the character of Frank Graham in order to get to the US Senate.[139] In a radio talk, J. O. Talley, a staunch Graham advocate, likewise blasted Smith for the most bitter and unethical race in the state's history: "Where the campaign should have been based on principles, they have attempted to assault personalities. Where the people needed light, they have brought a great darkness. Where they should have debated, they have debased. . . . Where reason was needed, they have goaded emotion. Where they should have invoked inspiration, they have whistled for the hounds of hate."[140]

On voting day, Tar Heels went to the polls in greater numbers than expected, 618,479 voters, the heaviest primary turnout in the state's history. Senator Graham took a commanding lead from the outset and scored a strong victory all over the state, displaying a consistency of appeal that confounded the experts. The final totals showed Graham with 303,605 (48.9 percent) to Smith's 250,222 (40.5 percent). Reynolds had 58,752 ballots cast for him (9.3 percent), and Olla Ray Boyd got 5,900 (1.3 percent).[141] Graham had achieved a resounding victory but, needing 50 percent of the vote, failed to win the first primary outright, falling agonizingly close as he needed only 5,634 additional votes. Reynolds, with his 58,752 votes, had indeed been the spoiler. Magnanimous in his triumph, Graham simply thanked Tar Heel voters for "their faith and loyalty." Willis Smith, election night disappointment chiseled into his face, would respond only with a terse "no comment" when asked if he would call for a second primary.[142] Basking in the warmth of voter approval, Graham and Scott had no idea of the impending disaster that awaited them in the runoff.

7

THE SECOND PRIMARY

North Carolina law provided that if the highest vote getter did not get an absolute majority of all votes cast in the first primary, the second-place finisher was entitled, but not required, to call for a runoff election to be held in four weeks. Amid all sorts of press speculation, Willis Smith agonized over whether to call for a second primary.

The prognosis for a Smith entry into a second contest depended on how experts viewed the first primary. Impressed with the size of Graham's lead, the *Charlotte Observer* thought the victory was a testament to the popularity of both Graham and Scott.[1] The *Greensboro Daily News* agreed, stating that the outcome was the result of Scott's perseverance, particularly in the rural areas of the state.[2] An out-of-town paper, the *Baltimore Sun*, had a different slant. It viewed Graham's vote as impressive evidence of a progressive bent in the state's thinking. It also saw his failure to gain a majority as a sign that North Carolina still retained its traditional attitudes on race and economic individualism. After all, the *Sun* reminded its readers, 51 percent of the votes cast went to Graham's opponents.[3]

Several of Graham's lieutenants concluded that their candidate had been denied a first primary win solely because of the eleventh-hour focus on the race issue by Smith's field people. Mailboxes had been filled with "racial junk." Pictures of Leroy Jones, the "nigger" whom Graham had allegedly appointed to West Point, were prominently displayed at polling places.[4] While some experts simply blamed Reynolds for Graham's failure to win outright, others pointed to race as the decisive issue. The *Fayetteville Observer* came up with a different approach. Rather than blaming the Smith forces' bigoted attacks, it thought that the main issue was the black vote and its massive support for Graham, one reason for his large plurality. Moreover, it correctly predicted that such bloc voting would make blacks a broad political target in a second primary.[5] The columnist Lynn Nisbet concurred, drawing attention to the all-black Hillside precinct in Durham, which cast 1,514 votes for Graham,

7 for Smith, and 6 for Reynolds. This startling result had been repeated in black precincts all over the state.[6] Such huge margins for Graham confirmed some voters' worst fears: black voters might hold the balance not only in a close election but also within the Democratic Party itself.

The most immediate question was whether Smith would call for a run-off. Could he raise the necessary funds? Could he overcome Graham's large lead? Smith remained noncommittal. When asked whether he thought Smith would ask for a second chance, Governor Scott refused to make a public prediction but announced that the first primary results were "very pleasing." When reporters asked Scott whether blacks now held the balance of power in the state, he bailed out, commenting that no more than half the registered blacks had cast ballots on May 27.[7]

Several state newspapers and many of Smith's advocates implored him to call for a runoff; they claimed that he had an obligation to his 250,000 voters. The conservative columnist Nell Battle Lewis wrote to Smith, telling him that he represented the sane side of the campaign. If he saw the slightest chance of winning, she urged, he should stay in the race.[8] The Graham camp tried to convince Smith that his cause was lost and that a second vote would be a needless, expensive, and bitter process that would divide the Democratic Party.[9] Despite all the entreaties and warnings, Smith simply could not make up his mind about a second shot at Graham. When asked about the delay, Scott, candid as ever, said that it might hurt Smith, by weakening his organization, but that it might help him, by giving him time to raise funds.[10]

On June 5, the sweep of national events reached into the state. While Smith deliberated, the US Supreme Court ruled in three critical civil rights cases that promised to alter significantly the state's race relations. As a result of those rulings, statutory segregation in state-supported higher education was all but finished (*Sweatt v. Painter*), railroad dining car segregation in the South was struck down (*Henderson v. U.S.*), and the doctrine of separate but equal had been gravely weakened (*McLaurin v. Oklahoma State Regents*).

The most significant case for North Carolina was *Sweatt v. Painter*. A unanimous court ruled that the all-white University of Texas Law School had to admit the black Houston mail carrier Heman Sweatt. Although the state had established a black law school at Prairie View A&M University, the high court asserted that the black institution was in no way equal to its University of Texas counterpart in terms of the prestige of the school and the reputation of the faculty and administration. This meant that, in practice, no black law school, including the one at North Carolina College for

Negroes in Durham, could meet the test of equality with the established white law schools.[11] The court's ruling heightened the importance of a similar case then pending in federal court in Durham, one brought by black students seeking admission to graduate study at the University of North Carolina at Chapel Hill.

While these cases did not represent a full repudiation of statutory segregation, they did indicate that the assault on legal segregation was gaining momentum. The Court's rulings pushed civil rights news to the front pages of all the dailies and alarmed white politicians and public officials who had been working for years to maintain the separate but equal principle in the courts. The decisions disabused many whites of the belief that segregation was eternal. The *Charlotte News* observed that the *Sweatt* case was "the handwriting on the wall" for the concept of separate but equal.[12] In addition to the court decisions, other factors influenced the runoff. The gradual shift to urbanism and significant population growth threatened the status quo of some traditional rural elements, while the increase in black activism heightened tensions in farm areas.

Smith's backers reacted enthusiastically to the court decisions, certain that the cases would compel Smith to call for a runoff. Despite numerous telegrams and telephone calls, Smith, after much soul searching, decided to withdraw. He thought Graham's lead was insurmountable, and he was out of money and energy. Upset by the lack of active support from people who had promised to rally to his side, he dictated a telegram to Hoover Adams, his publicity director, congratulating Graham on his victory. He asked Adams to send the telegram immediately. Hoping to dissuade Smith from ending his quest, Adams stuck the telegram in his pocket, where it remained, undelivered.[13]

Smith's friends would not let the matter drop. Jesse Helms, Charles Green, and Hoover Adams thought the best approach was an appeal to the people of Raleigh, urging them to gather at Smith's home and show their support for a runoff. Helms, then news director of WRAL radio, sponsored a series of ten-second commercials pleading with Smith to call for a second primary. Fearful that his appeal had fallen flat, he drove over to Smith's house and found a mob scene—the street jammed with cars and a crowd of from two to five hundred people milling about in the yard.[14] Smith addressed the audience three times. He first expressed his appreciation for their interest but said he would not run. When the crowd grew in number and became more vocal, he acknowledged that the demonstration of support might cause him to reconsider. Finally, he asked for some peace and quiet to consider his decision. But, before he retired, he told his partisans: "Don't be surprised if I go with you."[15]

Touched by the evening's display of loyalty and support, and emboldened by the court decisions, on June 7, eleven days after the first ballot, Smith announced that he would call for a runoff. He knew he was the underdog but asked for the support of all who believed in constitutional democracy.[16] If Hoover Adams had obeyed Smith's order to send the telegram, and if Helms had been less persistent, the second primary would never have occurred. The *Charlotte Observer* predicted that Smith would win because he would get the majority of Reynolds's votes. The race would be the "most vigorous and heated" in the state's history, but the paper hoped for a fair and clean contest.[17]

The second primary would last only seventeen days, but it would be one of the most exciting, raucous, and significant periods in the state's political history. The activity began slowly, characterized by the Graham forces' overconfidence and general complacency. Many workers were secure in the belief that, since Smith had wasted eleven days, Graham's huge lead could not be overcome.

Smith started slowly as well, spending much of his time raising funds, planning strategy, and working to get endorsements from Senator Hoey and Bob Reynolds. An open endorsement from Hoey would give Smith a boost no other could provide. Hoey was much closer to Smith in philosophy than he was to Graham, but he rebuffed Smith's overtures. He explained that, when he announced for the Senate, he promised that he would not actively participate in the election of another senator from North Carolina. Most observers knew that, while he did not actively campaign for Smith, he hoped that Smith would triumph. As he wrote Smith: "Still I think you know how delighted I . . . will be to have you as a colleague in the Senate."[18]

Smith had more success with "Our Bob," as Reynolds assured him of his complete support.[19] Smith wrote a letter to all of Reynolds's friends, asking for their vote in the runoff primary.[20] Reynolds's sanction of Smith probably had limited effect on the final outcome.

Although Smith was pleased with Reynolds's blessing, he did not begin active campaigning until eleven days prior to the vote. His themes were generally leftovers from round one. He set the tone for the runoff by excoriating Graham for favoring a fair employment practices commission (FEPC) and socialized medicine and by declaring his steadfast commitment to the principle of separate but equal school facilities for different races. He reminded voters that by calling for a second primary he was simply doing what Kerr Scott had done two years earlier. In a twist on Scott's mantra from that election, he argued that he would have to whip not one but several political machines in order to win—the Scott machine, the national Democratic Truman machine, the Congress of Industrial Organizations Political Action Committee, the NAACP, and those loyal to the University of North Carolina.[21] Pro-Smith newspapers picked up the refrain. It was Smith against the machines, stated the *Rocky Mount Telegram,* and the paper wondered whether he could defeat the machines' money and the huge blocs of votes they commanded.[22]

Some, but not all, of Graham's handlers and supporters realized that he had a tough race against a tough challenger and that they needed to revitalize his followers. President Truman, deeply concerned about the outcome, wrote Jonathan Daniels that he would try to get some help for Graham: "Graham must win—we can't possibly have a loss there."[23] Yet many Graham insiders blithely believed that the issue had already been decided. While visiting Jonathan Daniels, Capus Waynick told him that Graham was going to be defeated. Daniels smiled and assured Waynick that no one could beat Graham—his lead was insurmountable. With such a naive view, Waynick remembered, Dr. Frank's friends were "going to get the hell beat out of him."[24] Throwing off his usual stance of modesty and humility, Graham himself predicted on June 15 that he would win handily.[25]

Graham complicated matters by obstinately refusing to participate in orthodox campaign repartee, saying several times that he would rather be honest than expedient. While refreshing and praiseworthy, his refusal gave comfort to his critics and encouraged rhetorical excesses from the Smith forces. As Terry Sanford has argued, had he defended himself vigorously against Smith's attacks, especially on matters of race, the runoff result might have turned out quite differently.[26] C. A. Upchurch, Graham's publicity director, also bemoaned the senator's unwillingness to make use of practical political expediency. As Upchurch remembered, Dr. Frank would be off "making speeches about Indonesia and world brotherhood when he should have been out talking to the farmers." Graham, he concluded, was "just not a politician" and could have won if he "had not been so stubborn."[27]

Understanding the importance of the farm vote, Kerr Scott asked Lauch Faircloth to drive Graham to several of his campaign appearances. Scott wanted Faircloth, a North Carolina farm boy who could relate to the locals, to ride along because Graham was "out of touch with a lot of rural North Carolina." The senator was a great man, recalled Faircloth, but "he was so naive about country people." He did not understand the lifestyle and values of farmers and did "not think politically"—he was too academic and in another world.[28] Despite the governor's efforts, Graham made little headway with what should have been a natural constituency. Many farmers shared Christian beliefs with Graham, and Dr. Frank had worked his entire life to improve education, living conditions, and health care for rural inhabitants. But, because of the race issue and his inability to relate to their daily lives, they never connected. This failure cost Graham critical votes he needed in the runoff.

Jeff Johnson not only had to work with an unorthodox candidate; he also had to maintain the support of labor and the blacks without Smith's followers finding out what was going on. His attempt to secure a large black turnout without public notice foundered when the state NAACP called for a statewide meeting to urge greater political involvement by the state's black voters. NAACP leaders bragged that they had doubled black voter registration from 50,000 to 100,000.[29] To many whites in the state, the NAACP meeting was confrontational in tone, altogether an outrage, and revived fears that Negroes would take over the Democratic Party.

The NAACP meeting and the Supreme Court decisions had given racial issues a renewed urgency among white voters statewide, especially among eastern North Carolina residents. Smith took advantage of the heightened racial climate in his campaign stops. While a band played his theme song, "Dixie," he would climb on the bed of a truck carrying a sign reading "Save Our South—Get on the Smith Bandwagon" and recite his litany of campaign themes. Upset by Governor Scott's comment that, like Jesus, Graham was being crucified by his opponents, Smith countered that he was not trying to crucify anyone but simply opposing with all his strength "any effort to crucify our country on the cross of socialism."[30]

Although Smith's overall strategy continued to focus on socialism and communism, far more effective were the efforts of local campaign committees, which were now warning voters of an impending racial Armageddon. Local groups employed an endless array of campaign tactics, including rumors, dirty tricks, deception, and fraud. One of the first of many episodes occurred in Washington, North Carolina, when a black man walked into the *Daily News* and paid for a political ad addressed "to the Colored Voters." The ad explained that runoff voting was generally light. Therefore:

"The Colored vote will count more than ever. Go to the polls and support Dr. Frank. WE DID IT BEFORE—WE CAN DO IT AGAIN." A local attorney told Johnson that the ad was a "put-up job" by Smith followers and that black leaders knew nothing about it.[31] On another occasion, well-dressed blacks wearing large hats and conspicuous jewelry rode through small towns in the eastern part of the state in a sedan emblazoned with "Graham for Senate" banners. Local Smith supporters had employed the riders, hoping to create white resentment against the Graham candidacy.[32]

Smith supporters also printed 100,000 copies of the May 27 front page of the black tabloid the *Carolina Times,* which exhorted black people to vote for Graham. The unsigned circular featured two headlines: "Negro Registration over 100,000" and "The Negro Press Endorses Graham."[33] Other circulars appeared in various sections of the state. An incendiary black-and-white snapshot, taken in England during World War II, pictured black soldiers dancing with white women. The ads warned that a desegregated society would lead to the commingling of the races: "Remember these . . . could be your sisters or daughters."[34] An image of Graham's wife, Marian, was allegedly superimposed on the figure of one of the women in the flyer. Such materials were not generally circulated but instead pulled from pockets and flashed to individuals,[35] political pornography as it were. The Marian Graham circular has not survived, but many individuals claim to have seen it. Just as many observers believe it never existed.

One week prior to election day one of the more invidious documents of the campaign appeared around the state. "WHITE PEOPLE WAKE UP!" voters were admonished. "DO YOU WANT," the ad asked, "Negroes working beside you, your wife and daughters in your mills and factories? Negroes eating beside you in all public eating places? Negroes riding beside you, your wife and your daughter in buses, cabs, and trains? . . . Negro children going to white schools and white children going to Negro schools? . . . Negroes as your foremen and overseers in the mills? Negroes using your toilet facilities? If so, vote for Frank Graham. If not, elect Willis Smith, who will uphold the traditions of the South."[36] Another flyer displayed the following headline: "Did you know that over 28% of the population in North Carolina is COLORED?" With an FEPC, in a plant employing 375 people, 105 of the workers would be blacks forced on the plant.[37]

Inexplicably, the Graham camp responded to the racial slurs by reminding voters of their candidate's outstanding personal qualities. They quoted national and state figures, George C. Marshall and others, on the senator's

WHITE PEOPLE
WAKE UP
BEFORE IT'S TOO LATE

YOU MAY NOT HAVE ANOTHER CHANCE

DO YOU WANT?

Negroes working beside you, your wife and daughters in your mills and factories?

Negroes eating beside you in all public eating places?

Negroes riding beside you, your wife and your daughters in buses, cabs and trains?

Negroes sleeping in the same hotels and rooming houses?

Negroes teaching and disciplining your children in school?

Negroes sitting with you and your family at all public meetings?

Negroes Going to white schools and white children going to Negro schools?

Negroes to occupy the same hospital rooms with you and your wife and daughters?

Negroes as your foremen and overseers in the mills?

Negroes using your toilet facilities?

> **Northern political labor leaders have recently ordered that all doors be opened to Negroes on union property. This will lead to whites and Negroes working and living together in the South as they do in the North. Do you want that?**

FRANK GRAHAM FAVORS MINGLING OF THE RACES

HE ADMITS THAT HE FAVORS MIXING NEGROES AND WHITES — HE SAYS SO IN THE REPORT HE SIGNED. (For Proof of This, Read Page 167, Civil Rights Report.)

DO YOU FAVOR THIS — WANT SOME MORE OF IT?
IF YOU DO, VOTE FOR FRANK GRAHAM

BUT IF YOU DON'T

VOTE FOR AND HELP ELECT

WILLIS SMITH for SENATOR
HE WILL UPHOLD THE TRADITIONS OF THE SOUTH

KNOW THE TRUTH COMMITTEE

Perhaps the most widely remembered campaign handout, and arguably the most incendiary, this flyer depicted a society in the throes of an integrationist nightmare. The handbill accused Graham of advocating an end to segregation and was widely disseminated prior to the second primary voting. Daniel A. Powell Papers, Southern Historical Collection, University of North Carolina at Chapel Hill.

loyalty, patriotism, and "Christlike" qualities.[38] A typical ad proclaimed that his hometown of Chapel Hill gave him 91 percent of its votes while Raleigh, Smith's hometown, gave him only 45.8 percent—"By Their Fruits Ye Shall Know Them."[39] In the week before the election, Graham circulars read: "Last Best Chance, June 24, 1950. Today is a Day of Reaffirmation for North Carolina."[40] And on election day there appeared a final plea: "Vote for Graham: Let Your Conscience Be Your Guide."[41] All this was well and good, but the Graham brain trust would have better served its candidate if it had organized a general denunciation of Smith's tactics and fashioned detailed rebuttals to the Leroy Jones–West Point case and the "WHITE PEOPLE WAKE UP!" ad.

One Graham supporter had no fear of controversy. Scott had appointed Graham, thought him the right choice, and in the runoff worked vigorously for him, especially in the eastern part of the state, where he himself had his greatest strength. He told farm audiences that Smith was the corporate candidate, opposed to the welfare of the people,[42] while Graham was "in there right now fighting the battles of the plain people for a more abundant life."[43] He acknowledged that in many places the fight was against Kerr Scott and not Frank Graham. Nonetheless, North Carolina needed a great humanitarian and not a corporation lawyer in the Senate. Smith's proper place, the governor argued, was with the Dixiecrats, not the Democrats.[44] Scott's outdated comments about corporate candidates made little headway, certainly not in a contest where race, not the haves versus the have-nots, had become the dominant issue.

As the racial vilification mounted, Scott did what he could to stifle it, but it was too little, too late. He continued to believe that the people of North Carolina would not be misled by the racist tactics.[45] He contended that Graham's record could not be tarnished by reckless charges and that the recent Supreme Court decisions had no bearing on the Senate race. The injection of the race issue was but an insult to the intelligence of voters and an effort to confuse them. The governor proclaimed that Graham was no socialist, that he opposed an FEPC. He was no one's lackey: "He fights for the rights of labor, but he is not a tool of the unions. I appointed him to the Senate, but he is no tool of mine."[46]

In addition to speaking for and defending his nominee, the governor brought all his political influence to bear. One partisan wrote Scott on June 10, urging him to send the word down "in your usual discreet manner" to all state employees to do all they could to elect Graham on June 24.[47] The governor was only too glad to comply. Predictably, his partisanship continued to create controversy. Some citizens were angered that he used a state car and state telephones to campaign against Smith, a fellow Democrat. Taxpayers should not have to foot the bill for such expenses, they argued.[48]

Three days prior to the second vote, Smith's campaign manager accused Wilbur Clark, the highway commissioner, of using road bond money as a "political football." Armed with an affidavit from a Sampson County farmer, Green tried one last time to discredit Scott. The farmer swore that Clark had told him that, unless he and his friends supported Graham, no new roads would be built in Sampson County and those already under construction would be terminated. Green trumpeted: "This incident is just one of countless instances where Kerr Scott and his appointees have used state employees and state funds on behalf of Frank Graham. Never before in the history of the state has any governor so used the whip to force people to the polls and to require those on the state payroll to campaign actively."[49]

Although irritated by charges that he was a dictator, Scott brushed aside all the charges of using state employees to help Graham. He continued to use whatever persuasion he could muster and damn the complainers. "Naturally, I'm going to stand by my man," he announced as he forecast a Graham victory. He reproached Smith for attacking both state and national administrations: "The Republicans ought not to be allowed to run a candidate in this campaign."[50]

Scott's dismissive attitude toward his critics backfired, and the indictments of Scott, Daniels, and Truman as a Democratic machine out of touch with Tar Heel voters gained traction. The *Henderson Daily Dispatch* blasted the governor for slandering Democrats who bucked the "Scott-Daniels-Truman triumvirate." It was not the middle-of-the-road Smith campaign that had "strayed off the reservation," the paper explained, but those who were advocating socialism.[51] The *Kannapolis Daily Independent* thought Scott was guilty of playing cheap politics by ruling out of the party all those who disagreed with him and Truman. If this were the standard, notable Democrats, like Clyde Hoey, would be forced out of the party.[52]

In the closing days of the contest, charges of machine politics made against Scott were the least of Graham's worries. The strident and often vicious tone of the final push by the Smith backers had induced a full-blown racial panic. Numerous reports from the field by Graham workers pointed out the seriousness of the racial innuendo: "Folks here [Bladen County] are so hot about the Negro question I can't even talk with them about it."[53] Jeff Johnson had expected racial attacks but was not prepared for the anger and cruelty of some of the slurs. Mill workers were told they would be replaced by blacks if Graham won. And, when Graham, a longtime friend of labor, visited the mills, workers often shunned him, refused to shake hands with him, and on one occasion spat in his face. One fifteen-year-old girl in Lumberton received an anonymous phone call warning her that, if her daddy voted for Graham, she would be "sitting by Negroes in school."[54] Most of this activity was local, carried out by rumormongers and frightened people beyond the reach of logic and reason. As far as can be determined, these bigoted tactics were not orchestrated by Smith headquarters. Jesse Helms insisted that Smith was not a racist. He was a kind man with an unassailable character and was not responsible for the bigoted literature passed out around the state.[55]

Graham's advisers decided that the best way to rebut these intolerant assaults was to put the candidate on the stump where he could convince audiences of his integrity, decency, and opposition to integration and an FEPC. Everywhere he went, however, he was dogged by questions about his racial views. He was especially haunted by the specter of Leroy Jones. Repeatedly he explained about the appointment to West Point. He said he had seen pictures all over the state about a Negro boy he was supposed to have sent to West Point. "He is not there." Graham explained that Jones had finished third and that the white boy who had finished first was now a cadet.[56]

So persistent were the questions about Leroy Jones that Allard Lowenstein suggested a bold move: fetch William L. Hauser, the West Point appointee, and have him shadow Graham.[57] Whenever his audience asked about Jones, Graham would proudly display his prize exhibit: "There's the boy who is going to West Point. He was the number one boy. You haven't seen his picture? Well, take a look at him now." Graham repeated his point: Leroy Jones was not going to West Point; Bill Hauser was.[58] Even this ploy did not work. The doubters simply would not believe Graham. After he had introduced Hauser and had concluded his remarks in Beulahville, an angry murmur surged through the crowd: "Why didn't he bring the nigger he appointed? Who was he trying to fool, showing us that white boy?"[59] Others gazed on Hauser and remarked to no one in particular: "He's mighty light, ain't he?"[60] Hauser, for his part, became an enthusiastic campaigner and wanted to speak for Graham. A campaign staffer set him straight: "Look here, boy. We haven't got you out here but for one thing—that's to prove you ain't a nigger."[61]

Far more damaging than Leroy Jones was the charge that blacks were guilty of bloc voting for Graham. In his ads, Smith forces used the results from six well-known Negro precincts to illustrate the point. In Raleigh, precinct 10 had 493 votes for Graham and 9 for Smith. Precinct 16 had 518 votes for Graham and 18 for Smith. In Durham the numbers were even more overwhelming. In Hillside blacks voted for Graham 1,514–7 and in Pearson School 1,187–8. A precinct in Charlotte and one in Greensboro showed similar numbers. Such lopsided vote totals, Smith declaimed, were a menace to democracy and "didn't just happen": "There must be a reason. Did someone make a deal?"[62]

The Graham camp cried foul, but in a bombastic address Smith insisted that he was not the one who had injected race into the contest. Racial feeling had been stirred by the Commission on Civil Rights and its report, which recommended the ultimate end of segregation. Dr. Graham, he reminded listeners, had been a member of that committee. The race issue had been raised when Truman sponsored a bill in Congress providing for an FEPC, and blacks themselves had fanned the flames when they cast almost a solid vote for Graham.[63]

As election day approached, Graham workers from various locations recounted several disturbing incidents that threatened to derail their candidate's hopes for victory. One precinct worker in Wilmington called her manager and hysterically demanded that he come and take back all the Graham literature in her house: "My neighbors won't talk to me." In Raleigh an eight-year-old boy who spoke out for the senator was beaten up by schoolmates as a "nigger lover." When one of Graham's supporters in Durham answered the phone, she was asked: "How would you like a little stewed nigger for breakfast."[64] Jonathan Daniels reported similar harassment, replete with language so vile that his children were not permitted to answer the phone. Some agitators even stoned his house.[65] Such hateful rhetoric cost Graham the votes of intimidated followers, who stayed away from the polls after persuading themselves that Dr. Frank had enough votes to win. "Why should I make enemies of the people I have to live with?" one Graham worker complained.[66]

Smith's adherents flooded the radio stations and newspapers with ads during the last week. According to all reports, Smith headquarters had plenty of money and spent it all.[67] Smith's final full-page ad claimed that the purpose of an FEPC was "to bring about the intermingling of the races by force." Furthermore, blacks would run the FEPC, the Washington, DC, police would enforce the law, and white unions would be forced to accept black members.[68] While that incendiary message was completely untrue, it had a dramatic, last-minute effect. White workers in North Carolina understood that a potential FEPC served as a clear warning that federal interference in race relations was not too far in the future. The best way to stop it was to elect a conservative like Willis Smith.

At his last rally, Graham repeated his opposition to socialism and an FEPC. To those who opposed him he expressed "no ill will but rather an understanding of their rights in our democracy."[69] He made no mention of the personal abuse and insults heaped on him during the last days, nor did he ever display any anger at the indignities directed against him. Perhaps he should have—it would have been the only way to defuse the issue, but that would not have been Frank Graham. Governor Scott, ever the optimist and a Graham loyalist to the end, anticipated a victory margin of thirty-five to fifty thousand, basing his prediction on the belief that Smith had overplayed the race issue and would be undone by a "boomerang" effect.[70]

Election-day temperatures matched the race's intensity, reaching ninety-six degrees in some places, but over 550,000 Tar Heels ignored the sultry day and cast their ballots, a runoff primary record. With the closing of the polls, crowds gathered in courthouses, now thick with cigarette smoke, perspiration, and chalk dust, as the results were tabulated. Precinct workers busied themselves with the laborious task of counting the ballots by hand. This time Smith took an early lead that he never relinquished, and the totals confirmed a monumental shift in voter allegiance. Graham had been defeated, although not by a large margin—only twenty thousand votes—and his brief senatorial career had been brought to a painful close. Smith tallied 281,114 votes to Graham's 261,789.[71] Jubilant Smith adherents shouted, celebrated, sang "Dixie," and in general exulted. "Tell ole Kerr Scott to go to hell," shouted a few diehards, while others sang: "We'll hang Dice Daniels from a sour apple tree, while we go marching on."

Upstairs, on the sixth floor of the Sir Walter, stunned by the defeat, Graham's friends and supporters choked back their bitter disappointment. Defeat was difficult to grasp and painful to accept. Everyone was in tears except Graham, who mingled with and comforted the aggrieved. He then went down to Smith's headquarters and congratulated his rival: "I wish you every success."[72] Once the concession ordeal had ended, young Bill Friday, a campaign aide, drove the Grahams home to Hillsborough. They made the trip in silence—no postmortem, no lamentation, no regrets, no self-pity. Graham did not "utter one word of reaction or outrage." Surely he felt some sense of pained bewilderment at his unexpected loss. The defeat amounted to a rejection of his life and values, and the disappointment would remain with him the rest of his life. Friday praised Graham as "a man at peace with himself, sustained by his great inner spirit," and as such he was "a master of defeat."[73]

Scott and Graham supporters were crushed by an outcome they had not expected. The rejection of Dr. Frank seemed to his followers not only the repudiation of a candidate they cherished but also the acceptance of the race-based politics they loathed. D. Hiden Ramsey lamented: "[The] evil genii of race prejudice are out of the bottle. The chances are that we will not get them back in the bottle in North Carolina for a long time."[74] Seeking to assuage their hurt and to understand the meaning of Smith's victory, Graham's discouraged army filled the mail with letters trying to explain the defeat and offered emotionally charged condolences to each other. John Sanders, a University of North Carolina student, wrote Graham that the primary brought a defeat, "not for you or for the cause which you champion, but for the people of North Carolina who, lacking the confidence of their own conviction, voted against their own best interests and the best interests of the nation."[75] "I weep," Lillian Turner lamented, "for the people of North Carolina . . . because they could be swayed by prejudice, lies, tactics which an intelligent people should . . . see through."[76]

"It was a great fight," scrawled Governor Scott in a message to Graham on June 27. "The Supreme Court decision appearing at the time it did is what turned the tide against you. You did all you could. I'm naturally disappointed because I felt then and do now that N.C. and the U.S. needed your viewpoint."[77] In December, Scott again paid tribute to Graham, expressing his appreciation that he had accepted the position as senator "against [his] desire and preference." However, given neither to self-pity nor to introspection, Scott remained unremorseful. Although Graham had been "politically sacrificed" as a result of the appointment, the governor insisted that, if he had the chance, he "would take no other course than what [he] did." He concluded that history "will record that a distinct gesture was made for representation on behalf of the masses of North Carolina."[78]

Frank Graham replied in kind. He thanked Governor Scott "from the bottom of [his] heart" for his June 27 message: "It is a source of faith and hope that persons defeated become causes that triumph. A sense of comradeship with you in our common cause will be one of the treasures which I shall cherish all my life."[79] And again in August Graham thanked Scott and his staff for their "valiant work" and "for putting up a magnificent fight" during the campaign: "I think everybody did everything they could against, what developed to be, insurmountable odds in the closing days of the campaign." He asserted that it had been "a great joy" to be associated with Scott and continued: "It is my faith that things for which you stand will carry on in the ultimate triumph for the welfare of the people of our state. I am glad to carry on as a soldier in the ranks."[80]

Publicly, the governor congratulated Smith and said that he would do all he could, officially and personally, to help him win a great victory in November. The Democrats had expressed a preference for Smith, and Scott asked all Democrats to rally behind the nominee in the general election.[81] More readily than any other Graham partisan, he brushed off any appearance of postelection depression. "I've been in a lot of scraps," he reminded reporters. "It's not the first time I've been run over."[82] In western North Carolina, he told his audience: "I guess that after what happened to my friend Frank Graham, you think I'm up in these mountains looking for a place to hide, but it's not so. I never miss a chance to enjoy North Carolina's wonderful mountains."[83] A few days later, the irrepressible governor greeted reporters in his shirt sleeves, informing them: "I pulled off my coat just to show you that I had not lost my shirt."[84]

Scott accepted defeat gracefully, but the loss stung. That loss, however, did not dissuade him from his larger goals as governor. He promised that North Carolina would continue to go forward in the Graham-Scott manner. He took credit for the large turnout in both primaries and claimed to have awakened the voters to a heightened interest in their government. He reiterated that he did not regret the choice of Graham: "I still think he is a good man and I still think there's a lot of misunderstanding by good people."[85]

Scott's ebullience did not mask his anger at the tone of the campaign. At the annual August convention of the state labor federation, the governor castigated, in shrill language, the state's white people for their part in the most bitter, racially charged contest North Carolina had seen in modern times. When black delegates applauded his remarks, he turned to them and in a harsh tone said: "I notice you colored brethren clapping pretty hard, but you didn't do your part either. You may be of another color, but in this election you were just as yellow as the other man"—a clear reference to the low black turnout in the second primary. He declared that a nation could never rise to its full height as long as its politics were based on race prejudice.[86]

Scott's somewhat cavalier attitude about a devastating defeat did not hide the embarrassment of his prediction, made to some degree for political purposes, of a Graham victory of thirty-five to fifty thousand votes. Usually a careful observer and one with intimate knowledge of the state's political vibes, the governor had missed the mark by over fifty thousand. How could he have been so wrong? He simply could not imagine that many of his followers could be swayed by such irrational and hateful charges, and he had not anticipated pro-Graham white voters staying away from the polls because of overconfidence and/or intimidation. The low turnout by black voters and the loss of many labor votes also surprised him.

While Scott and others would spend many months on a postmortem evaluation of Graham's defeat, in the end the dominant factor was race. The Supreme Court decisions could not have come at a worse time for Graham. Victor Bryant, a loyal Graham supporter, thought the fight over the FEPC hurt badly.[87] Others stressed the raw emotions the campaign unleashed. One observer noted that, when people became "inflamed and aroused," "it was impossible to head off the stampede": "You could not reach them by appeals to reason because there was no reason in them. You had as well try to beat out a forest fire with a pine bough."[88] Judge W. H. S. Burgwyn regretted the defeat of a good man: "The seed of racial prejudice and hatred has been sown and I fear it will be years before they will be eradicated, if ever."[89] Such observations gave credence to the view that Graham was the victim of an unquenchable and irrational racial hysteria. The Smith loyalists hijacked the emotions of many voters by raising the fear of racial integration and an end to the southern way of life. The Smith ads were effective partly because images—Leroy Jones, black men dancing with white women, "WHITE PEOPLE WAKE UP!"—were more powerful than words and reason.

John Egerton, in *Speak Now against the Day*, summed up the Smith strategy: "Here was the raw nub of Southern demagoguery, the essence of its deceit and venality." The message: "Race mixing, with all the worst sexual and social and economic consequences, is a Communist plot masterminded in Moscow and carried out through the seemingly innocent offices of sympathizers and dupes and traitors like Frank Porter Graham; for the sake of the sovereign South and its traditional way of life, these demons must be cast out and destroyed."[90] Jonathan Daniels, obviously disappointed by Graham's defeat, in a letter to President Truman described the Smith bid as "a Dixiecrat campaign" operated "piously at the top" and "with brass knuckles" and "violence and distortion . . . at the precinct level." Smith's strategy was the "cold-blooded, advertising agency technique employed to arouse prejudices for the purpose of reactionary politics."[91]

Had the same issues shaped the second primary as dominated the first, Graham would have won. But the Supreme Court rulings turned the second primary into a referendum on racial segregation. The Graham campaign leadership paid dearly for their first primary failure. In politics, as in any contest, a moment not seized is a moment lost. Intervening events lent a validity and an urgency to the charges swirling around Graham that did not exist in the first primary. These events convinced many voters that Graham's liberalism, as revealed by his racial views, moderate though they were, could not be forgiven. Poor and rural whites who had voted for Scott felt threatened by black advancement and, in their insecurity, wrapped themselves in the traditional mores of the South, including white supremacy.

Unfortunately for Graham, the black vote probably hurt him more than it helped. Although black turnout in both primaries was overwhelmingly for Graham, it was disappointingly low—much lower than Johnson had expected and black leaders had predicted. In the east, where Graham lost the race, the black vote was negligible. Johnson revealed that more blacks registered than actually entered the polling booth because they were fearful and often intimidated prior to election day.[92]

Willis Smith and his adherents saw a huge benefit in claiming that blacks and Graham, not Smith, had raised the race issue. Bob Thompson, in the *High Point Enterprise,* argued that Johnson had initiated the race issue by registering blacks in "the greatest political organizing of Negroes this state has ever witnessed." He insisted that the Supreme Court rulings and the NAACP convention, where it was claimed that blacks had been the deciding margin in Graham's first primary lead, caused the race issue to backfire on the senator.[93] By harping on the use of bloc voting by blacks, the Smith ads heightened the suspicion that blacks would end up being a powerful force in state politics. Smith himself, in his postelection comments, suggested that bloc voting was an example of controlled voting that North Carolinians resented. He concluded that his victory was due to the recent Supreme Court decisions, a public protest against socialism, and concern on the part of voters about the prospect of a federal FEPC. He also noted that his campaign team had outhustled the Graham organizers.[94]

Samuel Lubell emphasized the effect of the Supreme Court decisions. While they affected only higher education, the fear of radical change permeated the South. Lubell contended that no single issue would "stir as violent an emotional storm in the South as to outlaw segregation in elementary schools."[95] A similar concern could be seen in the furor over Leroy Jones and his attempt to win admission to West Point. The image of a black at West Point triggered grave concern over rapid racial change and the rise of black political power. The issue of race relations became even more menacing when tied to economic issues—demonstrated in the argument over an FEPC and the desegregation of the workplace as pointed out in the ad "WHITE PEOPLE WAKE UP!"

The conclusion that race was the most important factor in Graham's defeat in the second primary can be validated by a close examination of the voting totals in the runoff in the eastern part of the state. In the east, where few blacks voted but where they constituted more than one-third of the population, Graham lost seventeen of the twenty-seven counties he had carried in the first primary. The poor whites and farmers had shifted their allegiance to Smith primarily because of racial tension. Smith carried the east by 21,086 votes, almost precisely his statewide victory margin. Graham went from a lead of 16,605 in May to a deficit of 21,086 in June, a shift of 37,691 votes.[96] The ballot totals in the east were 14 percent less than in the first primary. Owing to complacency and intimidation, many of the senator's early followers did not vote for him in the runoff, and his statewide totals fell from 303,605 to 261,789, a loss of 41,816. Smith advanced his voter appeal by going from 250,222 votes in the first primary to 281,114 in the runoff, an increase of 30,892. In the second primary, Graham did well in the mountains, lost a small percentage in the Piedmont, but fell way behind in the east—which provided the ultimate margin of victory for Smith.

There were, of course, other factors. If Reynolds had not entered the race, surely Graham would have won in the first primary. Although the unions raised considerable funds for the contest, labor could not deliver a vote in North Carolina large enough to offset disapproval of its partisan participation. During the second primary, the Smith forces raised huge sums of cash that enabled them to pay for numerous ads and to turn out the vote. Nonetheless, cash was not the crucial issue as Graham had enough money to win. In addition, the senator had the majority of state newspapers on his side and had a generally effective manager in Jeff Johnson. Still, the overconfidence of Daniels and Johnson after Graham's lead in the first primary cost him votes. The Graham camp could not convince all its loyalists that the contest was in peril even during the frenzied drama of the runoff.

Graham's political inexperience and his unwillingness to act like a politician hurt his cause. Had the senator been a more effective campaigner, he could have sewed up the contest in the first primary. One friend understood his reluctance to fight back. However: "If Frank Graham had, just once, riz up and called Willis Smith a so and so—he would have been nominated."[97] A campaign staffer suggested that Graham's defeat was in large measure a consequence of his charitable character. Smith's attacks required spirited rebuttal and a willingness to rebuke his opponents. Graham should have defended the Truman administration, not apologized for it.[98] John Egerton had a similar view: "Frank Graham was too soft-spoken and self-effacing, too gentlemanly, too repelled by the coarse tactics of hand-to-hand combat in the political trenches; he couldn't bring himself to get down in the mud and slug it out. He turned the other cheek, and went on trying to appeal to the better judgment of North Carolina voters."[99] Of course, many people voted for Graham because they admired those very qualities of character that impeded his political career. Jonathan Daniels praised him for his gracious acknowledgment of defeat "as he accepted the mudslinging against him, without once retaliating in kind or losing his temper." If the campaign had been a referendum on his character, declared Daniels, "then Graham had won the contest."[100] Alas, political races do not usually rise and fall on one's character, and seldom was that more evident than in Frank Graham's defeat.

Certainly, the early problems over Graham's membership in subversive organizations, his support for the Truman administration, and the ever lurking specter of socialism had an effect on the voting. Wilbur Hobby, a labor leader, thought Red-baiting had made the difference.[101] Jesse Helms wrote in his autobiography that Graham had cast votes in the Senate not popular with the homegrown folks and had been a member of groups cited by the attorney general as Communist: "That perhaps naive willingness to be associated with people who may not be loyal to the country was troubling."[102]

The *Charlotte Observer* contended that Senator Graham's defeat served as a rebuke to the Truman administration and to Governor Scott, who gave Graham unlimited support.[103] The *Durham Sun* had a similar view. The vote was a rejection of "the ruthless partisanship and political opportunism of . . . Daniels . . . and was equally a vote of lack of confidence in arrogant Governor Scott."[104] The *News and Observer* agreed that the Scott administration had lost prestige and that Graham's failure would strengthen the hands of conservative legislators in the 1951 General Assembly. However, the Scott administration was not the paramount issue in the contest, and the result could not be construed as a repudiation of the governor's policies.[105] Several fans wrote Scott to allay any fear he might have that the outcome was a slap at his administration. Valerie Nicholson, a reporter for *The Pilot*, wrote:

"You can't appoint a man and then not stand by him with everything you have." Graham's initial approval dissipated owing to "insidious use of lying grapevine propaganda."[106]

Scott's involvement might have hurt Graham in the Piedmont, but his vigorous assistance gave the senator a needed boost in the east. Nonetheless, Scott's and Daniel's visible presence in all stages of the contest fired up Graham's adversaries, who resented what they regarded as an unwarranted intrusion into the Senate race. Voters feared the potential power of a "liberal triumvirate" of Scott, Daniels, and Truman aided by Graham in the US Senate.

The most important outcome of the Graham-Smith clash was the passing of a moment when the liberal-progressive wing of the state Democratic Party could have, at least in the short term, achieved enough influence to change the course of North Carolina politics. While the liberal-progressive strain would be revived by Terry Sanford, Jim Hunt, and others, in 1950 political power had shifted back to the more conservative, traditional wing of the party—not the Gardner/Shelby machine but conservative Democrats. Republicans would be the greatest beneficiaries of the Democratic fratricide in 1950. Economic and racial conservatives in the state began to vote Republican, and Dwight Eisenhower came within 4 percentage points of carrying the state in 1952. Eventually, many of those fighting for Willis Smith, including Jesse Helms, would formally change their allegiance to the Republican Party.

Racial segregation was a strongly held belief in white North Carolina in 1950. The consensus supporting it was deep and powerfully felt. Despite the state's cherished reputation as a beacon of enlightenment in southern race relations, that view had been formulated when there was no serious challenge to the racial status quo. While the state was not obstructionist and its leaders did not stand in the courthouse door, as did other southern politicians, its progressive reputation had been sullied. By 1950 it became clear that no politician could directly question segregation and survive. Any other candidate in the state who held Frank Graham's views on race would have been dismissed in the first primary. Only Graham's stature, popularity, and character enabled him to make such a strong showing.

With Graham's loss, Scott's progressive agenda had received a significant setback. One key to ascertaining the fallout of the 1950 senate race would be how this defeat would influence his relationship with the 1951 General Assembly. Would the governor be in such a weakened state that he would have no influence over the legislative agenda? That remained to be seen.

Governor Scott addressing the crowd at "Singing on the Mountain" gospel festival on Grandfather Mountain after Frank Graham's defeat in 1950. Photograph by Hugh Morton, North Carolina Collection, University of North Carolina at Chapel Hill Library.

Power, Roads, and Phones

When not campaigning for Frank Graham, the governor continued advocating for new roads and for electricity and telephones in every home. On January 6, he outlined his ambitious new goals for the year. He called on the state Highway Commission to complete ten miles of paved roads every day and planned to issue the second $50 million of secondary road bonds to pay for the work. He asked private utilities to extend electrical service to fifty thousand new customers and the telephone companies to install eighty thousand new phones during the coming year. He had discussed the goals with the power and telephone companies and came up with figures they thought they could reach.[107]

Scott let it be known that he would ride herd on the power and telephone companies. He first focused his attention on the phone companies, complaining that less progress had been made putting in phone lines than in either the road or the power programs.[108] In order to speed up the installation of phone lines, he met with the state Utilities Commission and urged its members to bring those companies that had not fulfilled their obligation to Raleigh and have them "show cause" as to why they had delayed the implementation of phone service.[109]

The Utilities Commission did not act as quickly as the impatient Scott demanded, and he accused it of dragging its feet. He wanted to "light a fire under them and see if we can get any action before the next legislature." Although he had appointed all five members of the commission, he noted that, if they did not act, "we may have to reorganize again." Finally tired of the governor's barbs, the five members of the commission complained that every time the governor rapped the telephone companies it became that much harder for the companies to raise money to carry out his program. They diplomatically observed that they were on board with the governor's program and understood that he did not mean anything personal in his remarks—he just wanted to get things done quickly.[110]

The members of the Utilities Commission should have known better. To Scott, it was personal. He kept up the pressure by again reproaching them and telling them to give him phones, not excuses. He noted that any agency that stood in the way of phone service "was just blocking traffic" and that they needed to find some way around the blockage.[111]

Stanley Winborne, the chairman of the Utilities Commission, promised Scott that he would get his telephones, "no alibis." Scott was not appeased. He contended that the commission had done a lot of talking back in recent weeks and that that talk sounded like it was written by the Southern Bell Telephone Company. He told his "friends" on the commission that they could either go to work or resign. He hoped that they would take his challenge in good spirit and stay. However: "[It] just burns my soul to see anybody dragging his feet on a thing like this when thousands of people want it and are waiting for it."[112]

Scott's high-handed, abusive attitude did not sit well with members of the commission or with the general public. Representatives of the seventy-one private phone companies in the state summoned to Raleigh to meet with the state Utilities Commission argued that they were doing all they could to improve service. They insisted that rapid expansion was impossible owing to the need to raise additional funds and hire more personnel.

The governor understood the investment problem but argued that, once the lines were installed, there would be an increase in demand for service. He eased up a little and politely told them he had faith that they could do the job: "It's just a matter of making up your minds."[113] Earlier, while giving one of his fire-breathing speeches complaining about the utilities, the lights went off. After a moment of silence, he drawled: "The telephone probably isn't working either."[114]

Despite public disapproval of his tactics, Scott's persistence began to pay off. The Carolina Telephone Company announced that it would spend $150,000 to increase its service in rural areas, and the Hickory Telephone Company expected to increase spending as well.[115] By April, Scott was praising the same group he had called on the carpet just months ago. He said that the Utilities Commission was "going on with the job." The problem was still big, he reported, but it was gradually being reduced: "They [the phone companies] are stringing wire and cussing me, but they are stringing wire." He even went so far as to congratulate the Carolina Power and Light Company for "filling out its territory."[116] By July, utilities' headquarters reported that some seventy-nine thousand telephones had been installed, including some thirty thousand in rural areas. Scott acknowledged that they were making progress but hoped they would do better since 230,000 farmers still did not have phone service.[117]

The many letters sent to Scott and the Utilities Commission thanking them for the new phones attested to the fact that they were badly needed. Some of the letters, painfully scribbled on cards, school paper, and the backs of magazines, were poignant. Mrs. L. H. Morris wrote Scott: "I shall all ways remember you for what you have done for us country people who really needed the telephone service."[118] Tom McClure also appreciated Scott's assistance in getting him a phone: "I am sorry that I haven't rote [sic] you befor [sic] now, but I now have time to do so."[119]

After facing some resistance from the phone companies, Scott fared better with the electric companies, despite his ongoing feud with L. V. Sutton of Carolina Power and Light. He asserted that there was a dearth of cheap, available power in North Carolina and kept prodding the electric companies on to greater production. He believed that the state's greatest need was additional electric power and that that would give greater encouragement to industrial development than anything else. Sutton insisted that there was no power shortage in the state and complained to his good friend Senator Clyde Hoey about the various groups that were trying to "socialize all business and particularly the power business." Hoey agreed with Sutton and vowed to continue the fight against government encroachment on private enterprise.[120] The *Raleigh News and Observer* supported Scott's contention that in an expanding economy there was no such thing as a surplus of energy. The government agencies needed to join with private utilities to support projects that provided power by damming rivers and helping with flood control.[121]

Scott admitted that power-producing facilities had been expanding at a commendable rate, but he also noted that private companies lacked the vision to produce the required amount of power. Convinced that surplus power produced demand by attracting new industries,[122] he reinforced this point when he welcomed the Riegel Paper Company, which was building a $13 million pulp mill in Acme, to North Carolina. He declared that the state was now on "the threshold of tremendous industrial development" and that new capital was going into new types of diverse manufacturing that would enable the economy to grow.[123]

Although Scott had chastised private industry for its failure to live up to electricity demands, he tried to mollify utility officials: "I'm not blaming anybody. I'm just saying the services are not there." L. V. Sutton was not fooled. He knew that he was the target of the attack and angrily insisted that "the utilities produced enough power."[124] As in all his other endeavors, Scott kept up the pressure until he got what he wanted.

The governor had much greater success with his pet project, building new roads. By the spring of 1950, work had begun once again, and the state accepted bids on 456 miles of projects, primarily rural roads, and discovered that the work would cost half a million less than expected.[125] In May, the governor proudly dedicated 16.2 miles of blacktop road from Johnston County to the Wilson County line, noting that his Go Forward program was a "close to the people program" and benefited "65 percent of our people who live in rural areas."[126] He indicated his long-term commitment to better roads by using $1.5 million from the highway fund surplus to complete the erection of a new building in Raleigh to house the expanded state Highway Commission.[127]

With more roads and more cars on the highways, Scott knew that highway safety would be a major issue and appointed a special committee to deal with that problem. The idea was to reduce highway accidents and get unsafe drivers and vehicles off the roads.[128] By the end of the year, the committee came forward with fourteen recommendations. These suggestions included the reenactment of the motor vehicle inspection law, a mandatory five-day jail sentence for drunken drivers, better enforcement of existing laws, and an interesting idea, in a state where NASCAR was born, "that stock car races be banned over the state."[129] Scott had already proposed increasing the size of the Highway Patrol since accidents had increased and "the death toll was out of bounds." The governor knew that the patrol was vital to the safety of citizens of the state by keeping drunks off the road and by effectively controlling other problems.[130] He also considered building heavy-duty turnpikes for large trucks and buses traveling between major cities. The turnpikes would reduce traffic accidents, speed up traffic flow, and be paid for by tolls. He set up a study committee,[131] but this idea was way ahead of its time, and nothing was done for many years.

Scott's hopes for a more effective Highway Patrol came undone with a scandal featuring Tony Tolar, his controversial appointee to head the patrol. Tolar, a big, friendly, youthful ex-car dealer and farmer, had supported Scott in 1948, and, against the advice of several friends, Scott had rewarded him with the job as commander. In March 1950, Commander Tolar had been indicted on charges of reckless driving and improper use of a siren at a funeral, and, in April, he was cited in Fayetteville for speeding: he had been going sixty miles per hour in a thirty-five-mile-per-hour zone.[132] Scott was furious as this was not the behavior citizens expected from the head of the Highway Patrol. He met with Tolar, who expressed a willingness to resign "if his actions had embarrassed the administration in any way."[133]

While deliberating on whether to accept Tolar's resignation, Scott received some harsh criticism of the original appointment. One correspondent wrote: "[The] appointment was never popular and [Tolar's] increasing indiscretions continue to give your enemies opportunity to belittle your administration and lower the prestige of the patrol."[134] Several letters urged him to curtail Tolar's tenure as commander immediately: "You cannot make all appointments with 100% success and a jackass trying to become a racehorse is not helping your average."[135]

Scott quickly cut his losses and cast Tolar out. He informed Tolar in a letter of April 15 that "for the best interest of the state" he would accept his resignation.[136] Just minutes after Scott's announcement, the former commander told the press that he had been "crucified by the Scott administration" and complained that the governor had initially told him that his resignation would not be accepted and "to stay away from reporters to let this thing cool down." Scott then selected Major James R. Smith as the new commander. Press reports indicated that the governor had on this occasion

chosen a competent and experienced man, eliminating any political consideration for the position.[137]

As is the case with almost all job appointments by a chief executive at
any level, some of Scott's choices for key positions proved to be embarrass-
ingly inadequate, and the governor regretted several of them. He, like many
other politicians, tended to seek out loyal supporters and friends rather
than find the most competent person for the job. Scott felt an obligation to
reward support of and service to his campaigns. He candidly confessed that
some of his appointments had proved disappointing but that overall he was
satisfied since "perfection was not permitted in this world."[138]

One of those who failed to live up to Scott's expectations was J. B.
Moore, the director of prisons. He had been tried on two criminal charges
of embezzlement. One charge read: "[Moore] with force of arms, being a
person of fraudulent mind and evil disposition, unlawfully and willfully,
fraudulently, feloniously and deceitfully did . . . cheat and defraud the state
of North Carolina of the sum of $578.82." Eventually, Moore relinquished his
position, was found guilty in superior court, and was fined $1,000.[139] None
of these embarrassing episodes helped Scott's frame of mind, but they did
cause him to look more carefully at his future appointments and to rely less
on cronyism and more on qualifications.

On a more positive note, Scott once again cited great progress in road
building. In October, he reported that in the three previous months the state
set a record by constructing 2,282.7 miles of hardtop roads. He announced
that the bids for construction had come in under estimate and that the state
would be able to build more roads than originally promised. He also noted
that, owing to the increase in car mileage and gasoline usage, the one-cent gas
tax had almost been sufficient to pay off the bond debt when it came due.[140]

Scott also applauded his administration's progress in the field of public
health, a cornerstone of his Go Forward plan. While North Carolina was
considered progressive in some circles, it was still a very poor state, with a
1948 per capita income of $930, far behind the national average of $1,410.
The state had made some progress by spending more funds on those in
need (the 1949–1950 appropriation was three times that allocated in the
1944–1945 budget), especially on aid to dependent children and old-age
assistance. Nonetheless, Scott realized that, although the recent legislative
largesse did more for the general health program than had been done in
the past, the state had to do more in the field of public health. With the new
health program he helped launch in the public schools, he believed that in

four years no child would have to attend school with correctable physical defects. He predicted that increased funding would lead to complete control of tuberculosis in the near future. He praised the current health construction program, which provided new buildings for the school for the deaf and the state mental hospital in Morganton.[141]

Schools were the third pillar of the Go Forward program. In March, the governor notified citizens that the money set aside for modern schoolhouse construction was being effectively used and that building was under way across the state.[142] Understanding that teachers were the key to educational progress, he worked hard to get the state's teachers the pay raises promised to them by the 1949–1950 legislature. Initially, the Advisory Budget Commission informed teachers that they would have to wait another year to see whether there would be enough state surplus to pay the increases. Education leaders in the state appealed to the governor to use his influence to overturn the commission's decision. Scott persuaded the Advisory Budget Commission to award $7 million to the state's twenty-six thousand teachers to fund the pay hikes promised in 1949.[143] He wrote several teachers indicating that the state had a definite obligation to pay the raises and that he was pleased that the teachers had been rewarded. Several teachers, including the president of the Charlotte Classroom Teachers Association, wrote him thanking him for his support.[144]

Despite the racist nature of the Senate campaign and the distinct possibility of negative political fallout, throughout 1950 Scott pursued his goal of better conditions for minorities. In a speech at A&T Negro College in Greensboro, he forcefully affirmed that "the time for opportunity for advancement for minorities in N.C. was now." He reminded his listeners that the last legislature had given a much larger proportion of funds to Negro colleges than it had in previous years. Negro public schools would also receive a higher percentage of state money than they would have had their allocations been based on the actual Negro percentage of the population. Scott then revealed a startling statistic—some 350 schools in the state had no electricity. Most of these were the small one- and two-room school buildings in which Negroes were taught, and this inequity needed to be resolved immediately.[145]

At a news conference in March, a Negro reporter asked the governor to comment about a charge that Negroes were discriminated against when they tried to register and vote in the state. The *Asheville Citizen* had reported that, although the number of Negro voters had increased each year, some were still being denied the right to register. The governor commented that discrimination did exist, but he thought that there was no need for new legislation to stop the discrimination: "You have all the laws you need." He observed that a change in local sentiment and attitudes would be needed before Negroes would be permitted to register and vote freely.[146]

Scott was not as aggressive or as effective in dealing with voting discrimination as he had been with improved education for minorities. Citizens in general saw the need for improved schooling for Negroes, but, when it came to voting, there was still serious opposition from racist whites. The governor's comments smacked of the old southern paternalistic view of Negro voters. Eventually, men of goodwill would decide that minorities should have the right to vote. Until then, wait.

The context in which he made these remarks might provide a clue as to why Scott was reluctant to be more outspoken in regard to voting discrimination. At the time he made those remarks, March 11, he was heavily involved in getting Frank Graham elected to the Senate. The race issue had already flared up, and he did not want to antagonize white voters by demanding the registration of more Negroes. After the Smith-Graham race ended, he expressed his renewed commitment to more equal opportunities for minorities in a speech to some four thousand listeners in Rich Square. He denounced racial and religious intolerance and in particular condemned the injection of the race issue into the recent senatorial campaign.

Scott also decried religious prejudice, primarily anti-Catholicism. "I used to think when I was a boy," he said, "that only a Presbyterian, a Democrat or a man who raised Jersey cows, could get into heaven. That was religious prejudice." Warming to his task, Scott ended his peroration with a fervent appeal: "A nation can never rise to its full height when it works against the rights of individuals. . . . As long as we base our state-wide action in politics on race prejudice or religious prejudice—as long as we work against the rights of the human—how in the world can we convince Russia that the American way of life is right—when we fight each other right here in this state."[147]

The *Greensboro Daily News* and the *Carolina Times* lauded Scott for his remarks. The *Daily News* commented that the governor had "too often been charged with demagoguery when he was merely speaking out about what was on his mind, perhaps with an undue disregard for fact and finesse." In the final analysis, as reflected in his Rich Square speech, he "demonstrated courage more than any other trait."[148] As one of his critics noted: "You have got to give him credit, he meant everything he said when he was running for office." Most candidates disregarded their campaign promises. In fact, most governors would be going up and down the state making speeches about things that everybody wanted to hear. Not Scott: "He is different."[149]

Scott had always been a hard worker, and his time in the governor's office was no different. He kept a busy and at times brutal schedule. His staff estimated that he traveled some 58,107 miles during 1950. He loved pressing the flesh and greeting constituents. However, he complained: "[It is] physically impossible for me to see everyone who wants to see me. If we had a 48 hour day, maybe we could get around to everybody." He knew that some visitors went away disappointed and thought they were being given the runaround, but that was not the case: "There just isn't enough time." However, when Scott did take a few days off, he came back to work looking fresh and frisky. His staff could tell he was relaxed when he settled back in his big leather chair, took an extra big chew of tobacco, and announced that he was ready to go to work.[150]

An astute politician with an eye to the future, the governor pushed aside his disappointment at Graham's defeat and advocated party unity for the November elections. He joined with Willis Smith, party chairman B. Everett Jordan, and various other Democratic officials and officeholders and led a caravan around the state to urge support for Democratic candidates. He told one audience: "Let's elect a full Democratic ticket. And let's give Senator Smith one of the biggest votes you have ever given here."[151] He even went so far as to contribute $100 to the party's fall campaign fund. B. Everett Jordan wrote and thanked him for his "generous help and . . . loyalty to the party."[152] The November election was a clean sweep for the Democratic Party. Smith won by a four-to-one margin over his Republican opponent, while voters returned Clyde R. Hoey to the Senate, and all twelve incumbent Democratic congressmen won reelection.[153]

It must have been particularly galling and difficult for Scott to drive around the state in the company of Willis Smith and urge voters to support a man he obviously disliked. Scott, a pragmatist and a realist, knew that he had to work within the Democratic Party if he ever wanted another shot at elective office. So he swallowed his pride and marched gamely alongside Smith and Jordan in the name of party unity. Senator Frank Graham also graciously appeared on the same stage with Smith and asked the people to vote for his former opponent. The political interaction with Smith in the senatorial contest apparently did not upset the kindly, forgiving Graham, but Kerr Scott was another matter.

There was a bitter residue left from the crippling defeat of Frank Graham, and Scott could not forget his anger and resentment at the bigoted nature of the Smith attacks. He began planning his revenge the day the Senate contest ended. He hoped to challenge Smith, who would be up for reelection in 1954, in what would be called the "third primary." Senator Smith died in office on June 26, 1953, so the anticipated contest never took place. Nonetheless, the Senate race of 1954 would see the same forces that backed Smith in 1950 once again arrayed against Scott.

The rambunctious Scott became embroiled in another controversial appointment when A. A. F. Seawell, an associate justice of the North Carolina Supreme Court, died on October 16, 1950, at age eighty-five. Seawell's successor, and how he would be chosen, was to be decided by the remaining members of the court. The court advised Scott that he could make an interim appointment and that that person would serve until the general election in November, when the voters would make the ultimate selection. The interim choice would be subject to the approval or disapproval of the state Democratic Executive Committee.

The list of possible nominees included Jeff Johnson, William B. Umstead, Hubert Olive, Susie Sharp, Senator Frank Graham, I. T. Valentine, and several others.[154] Scott's pick, if approved, would have a significant advantage in the election on November 7. The governor, who had drawn criticism for taking seventeen days to persuade Frank Graham to accept the nomination to the Senate, now acted with alacrity and made his choice in three days. Once again he did the unexpected. "As casually as a man firing a shotgun in a parlor," he named as the new justice Murray A. James, a Wilmington lawyer, an old friend of Scott's and a man completely unknown in state politics. Scott explained that there was a good list of candidates, and that they all had splendid endorsements, but that James was a courageous man and a gentleman who would maintain the dignity of the high court. He did not list any other qualifications that James had for the post.

James's name had not appeared on any of the lists bandied about by the press. Journalists and politicians scurried about trying to glean any information on the improbable nominee. Furthermore, Scott had not bothered to consult the Democratic Executive Committee about his pick and apparently did not discuss the matter with anyone else. In the process of choosing James, he managed to bypass a group of twenty-two distinguished North Carolinians and, by choosing an outsider, ended up angering the backers of all twenty-two pretenders. B. Everett Jordan, trying to be supportive of the governor, said: "I think it is a good appointment. I never heard of him."

Initially, everyone assumed that this would be just an interim appointment and that Scott would not ask the Democratic Executive Committee to approve James. The pundits once again misread the governor. Although he had ignored the Executive Committee and made a choice that was not only inexplicable but anathema to many backers of Johnson, Olive, and others, he decided to use his clout to force the Executive Committee to recommend James as the Democratic nominee for the November 7 election.

The governor and James never had a chance. Miffed by Scott's imperious actions, the committee voted, by secret ballot, for Jeff Johnson as the Democratic nominee for the November election. There were only two candidates, Johnson and James, and it was obvious from the outset that James had very few backers. Even Jonathan Daniels voted for Johnson. The decisive rejection of his nominee was yet another blow to Scott's sagging prestige and power. The governor confessed that he was not surprised at the result and said that he was thoroughly behind Johnson and had no hard feelings. Johnson was elected overwhelmingly in the November election, and, in one of the more bizarre incidents in the history of the North Carolina Supreme Court, Justice Murray James served only one month, from October 30 until November 30, 1950.[155]

Why had Scott chosen James in the first place? One rumor had it that, when both were students at North Carolina State, Scott had promised James that, if he ever became governor, he would pick him for the supreme court. Anyone who knew how Scott operated dismissed that suggestion out of hand. Why not select Jeff Johnson in the first place? Johnson, a man of integrity and ability, had strong backing around the state, had managed Graham's 1950 campaign, and had earned Scott's appreciation for his hard work. His selection would have been approved easily by the Executive Committee. By pushing James's candidacy, Scott picked a fight he could not win. Here, he again demonstrated his stubborn and unpredictable behavior. He chose a man no one had ever heard of, one who would never be approved by the Executive Committee. He did so because James was his choice—no one else's. By choosing James he could demonstrate his political authority and indulge in another of his surprise selections. He made a huge mistake and paid the price, much to the delight of his enemies. Even more puzzling, why would he subject his so-called lifelong friend to such humiliation and ridicule? Citizens began to worry about the governor's judgment, and this incident bode ill for him as he began preparations for the 1951 legislative session.

As the end of 1950 approached, Scott appeared to be in a weakened position politically owing to several personnel scandals and the defeats of Frank Graham and Murray James. He was, however, in a better position than one might imagine. In the legislative races in June 1950, his supporters did quite well despite Graham's loss. The *Raleigh News and Observer* thought that, in the Senate, Scott would command a nucleus of eighteen to twenty legislators while fifteen or so would oppose him on most issues and another fifteen to seventeen whose views were not known would be flexible in their voting patterns. In the House, Scott would have around thirty-five to thirty-seven members who would be inclined to vote with him, while the anti-Scott forces would command some eighteen to twenty legislators. The governor gained one advantage with the election of his brother Ralph Scott to the state Senate, but Kerr Craige Ramsey and Frank Taylor, two of his biggest critics, won reelection to the House. The *News and Observer* pointed out that Scott's success in the 1951 legislative session "depends to a large extent upon the amount of tact the customarily blunt governor uses in his dealings with the legislators before they come to Raleigh and in the first few weeks of the session."[156]

With his usual bravado, Scott said that he was not worried about the upcoming 1951 legislative session. "I always have loved 'em," commented a beaming Scott. "I got practically everything I wanted from 'em the last time. I think we did rather well by them—and still got a balanced budget. I go on the assumption that it couldn't be any worse than last year and expect the best." Nor, the governor allowed, was he worried about what might happen after the adjournment of the 1951 assembly. "After the second legislature," he grinned, "the governor doesn't amount to very much anyway." Scott admitted that he would be a lame duck, but, whatever happened with the 1951 legislature, the work would go on—lots of people would still want "roads and paroles, and telephones and power and favors."

When asked whether he had any definite plans for his political future—specifically, whether he had his eye on another office—Scott coyly replied: "I have no plans to that effect." A reporter mentioned that, if he did decide to run for another political office, the goal might be to take on Willis Smith. Scott remained noncommittal.[157] Although running against Smith was exactly what he had in mind, he had to deal with the 1951 legislature and complete the last two years of his term before he could settle on his political future.

8

TRIALS AND TRIBULATION

The Last Two Years, 1951–1953

From day one of the 1951 legislative session, Governor Scott knew that he would face a contentious and conservative legislature determined to thwart as much of his agenda as possible. Scott understood, as previously noted, that he was a lame duck and would have less influence and control over legislative matters than in 1949, when he enjoyed a public mandate for change. Unable to succeed himself, with no veto power and most of his appointments already made, he was limited in influence and at the mercy of a hostile legislature. In addition, his prestige had been battered by the defeat of Frank Graham, some strange decisions on appointments (e.g., Murray James), and a series of embarrassing scandals.

In 1950–1951, the United States was engaged in a conflict against communism in Korea. It faced a war economy with shortages of materials and federal funds being allocated primarily to the military rather than to social problems. The cost of the nation's commitment to winning in Korea discouraged new domestic initiatives, and, with wage and price controls initiated by Truman, the future economic outlook was uncertain.

By 1951, North Carolina no longer had the surplus of funds that had enabled it to expand social services in 1949. The state had a large debt, and demands for appropriations far exceeded projected revenue. The six members of the Advisory Budget Commission included the four most powerful and influential members of the legislature, and all four were considered anti-Scott. In its 1951 budget proposals, the commission adopted a very conservative outlook, indicating that the state would have no extra money for new or expanded programs. Given the uncertain economic times, North Carolina would have to operate on a pay-as-you-go basis. The commission refused to recommend funding for some of Scott's pet programs—increased teachers' salaries and reduction of the teaching load, merit pay increases for state workers, and money for permanent improvements, including completing the rural hospital program.[1]

As the legislators assembled in Raleigh for their biennial session, the House chose W. Frank Taylor of Goldsboro, a conservative and an outspoken critic of Scott, as speaker. In the Senate, John W. Larkins, another strong fiscal conservative, became chair of the Appropriations Committee. He and other reactionaries formed a group that dubbed themselves the "Hold-the-Liners." They met regularly to plan strategy to curb the thrust of Governor Scott's programs.[2]

Undaunted by this opposition, Scott decided to propose some new initiatives in his biennial address to the legislature. He wanted to consolidate the achievements of the 1949 session and revive some issues that had been rejected. He began his January 4, 1951, address by assuring his listeners that he favored a balanced budget and did not anticipate any new taxes. He added that he also believed "that it is as important to balance the state's budget of social and economic needs as it is to balance its income and expense account." Although he understood that the present world crisis was dangerous and that the state would be affected by the general emergency, he called on legislators to "be firm in our purpose to continue improvements of public service . . . that both people and material resources are worthy of great investment."

At the outset, Scott discussed his stewardship and brought legislators up to date on the progress made during the past two years. He reported completion of 45 percent of the secondary road paving program. The state had nearly six thousand miles of new hard-surfaced roads—more work done in the past two years than in any other like period in the state's road-building history. The work had come in under cost, and quality had been emphasized. Since most of the secondary roads had been completed, the administration's emphasis would now be focused on primary roads. The governor endorsed a proposal by the Municipal Roads Commission recommending that, if funding was available, the state take over construction and maintenance of city streets.

Scott urged assemblymen to make the contingent teachers' salary of $2,200–$3,100 permanent and enforce the compulsory school attendance law, citing the fact that a large percentage of North Carolinians had failed to pass selective service mental tests in World War II. In health care, progress had been made, but there were still too many deficiencies. The governor asked for completion of the Medical Care Commission's program since seventeen counties still had no hospital facilities. He advocated "sensible" prison reforms.

Scott did not pass up the opportunity to revive his concern about the service provided by public utilities. He lamented that too many people still lacked electricity and telephone service and suggested that, in order to "justify their position of privilege and freedom from competition," public utilities "should provide the services to which the people are entitled" and at a reasonable cost. He recommended legislation requiring utility companies to apply for franchise certificates from the state Utilities Commission, a procedure that would allow for better regulation and more equitable distribution of services. He acknowledged that he had been charged with a socialistic attack on private enterprise, but he asserted that he remained a firm believer in free enterprise. He argued that, in the development of utilities and the conservation of natural resources, the people should not leave all the responsibility to private enterprise. There should be interaction and cooperation between the state bureaucracy and private companies.

The remainder of the talk included some previous proposals not enacted into law by the 1949 legislature. Scott called for a state minimum wage law and the repeal of the 1947 Anti–Closed Shop Act, lowering the voting age to eighteen, a statewide referendum on liquor sales, reinstatement of a motor vehicle inspection law, increased highway safety and an addition of 105 men to the Highway Patrol, and abolishing a law that limited campaign expenditures. He renewed his call for the conservation of natural resources and stream pollution control. He concluded with his often-expressed view that future generations of Tar Heels deserved more and better services.[3]

The reaction to Scott's speech was more favorable than many had anticipated. John Umstead, a staunch backer, liked the talk and remarked that the governor "has a damn sight more sense than a lot of those who are criticizing him." Kerr Craige Ramsey, a former speaker of the house, thought that it was a good statement of general objectives but that "financing these services is the problem." Many of the legislators seemed pleasantly surprised about how much they could agree with the governor's words, "a clear chart for future progress," but many wanted to defer comment until they heard his budget message.

State newspapers responded positively to the governor's comments. The *Raleigh News and Observer* viewed the message as sound and constructive. Those who believed with the governor that the people's welfare came first would support his plans, but those who thought that the state had already had its growth and that it was folly to plan for an expanded future would oppose them.[4] The *High Point Enterprise,* a conservative paper, found the biennial talk solid: "Even his most caustic critics admit that he made many good recommendations."[5] Lieutenant Governor Pat Taylor congratulated Scott on his "State of the State" address and called it a "ten strike." He particularly liked the optimistic and courageous statement of future goals.[6]

The governor's budget address on January 8 also produced positive responses from legislators and daily papers. Scott began by again commenting on the grave national emergency and opposed any new bonds, any new taxes, or any increase in the tax rate. He did, however, request $38 million more than the Advisory Budget Committee had recommended to meet essential services left unfunded. He asked for the reinstatement of merit raises for state employees, $6 million to complete the hospital building program, and $10 million for authorized permanent improvements. He offered three options for raising the necessary revenue to pay for these items. One would be to eliminate some or all of the exemptions from the state sales tax. Scott did not consider that as a new tax. A second option would be to improve the collection of taxes by hiring more employees, and a third would be to restore a 3 percent sales tax on moving picture admissions.[7]

The state's legislators seemed surprised that Scott did not ask for more than he did. John Larkins Jr. thought the governor was conservative in his proposals. While many voiced approval of Scott's recommendations, most warned that they would reject any tax increases.[8] The latter comments did not bode well for the elimination of any tax exemptions, as most legislators saw that as a new tax. The *Charlotte News* agreed with Scott that the state could move forward if "the legislature had the political courage to revamp the sales tax and crack down on income tax collections."[9]

The governor had been thoughtful and shrewd in presenting his agenda and budget to the state. He understood that his best option was to consolidate previous gains, especially in health and education, while urging the state to continue his Go Forward program without any new taxes and with a balanced budget. He hoped that the idea of ending some tax exemptions would be a possible alternative that the General Assembly might be willing to accept.

Prior to the opening of the legislative session, the governor was uncommonly polite to the legislators. In a press conference, he expressed the hope that he and the legislators would get along more harmoniously than they had two years ago: "I just have a general feeling that they're going to find some of the things we fought so hard for the last time are proving all right. I think, too, they'll find my horns are not quite so long as they thought they were."[10]

Scott's unrealistic hopes for a positive relationship with legislators quickly faded as the hold-the-line anti-Scott forces took control of both chambers and the administration's bills bogged down in committees. Scott began to lose patience as the legislative logjam worsened, and by mid-February he vented his anger at the recalcitrant legislators. In a speech to the state Farm Bureau convention, always a safe haven for him, he lashed out at the powerful bloc that would draw the line on the progress and future well-being of the state for the sake of what it called *economy*. He warned that, because of the "defeatist" attitude of the assembly, teachers and public employees would never get pay raises and the people would never get proper hospital facilities. He did not believe that the citizens of North Carolina were "so morally, spiritually and financially bankrupt" that they would want education, hospital care, and state services to "slip backward." He deplored the "short-sighted vision" of the legislators. "I have no patience with this philosophy—call it conservatism, hold the line, or what you may."[11]

Scott quickly abandoned his peaceful overtures and took to the airways to renew his broadside against the General Assembly. He accused legislators of holding secret "executive sessions" from which the public and press were barred. It had become clear to him that the hold-the-line philosophy was as much political as economic. Legislation was judged not on its merits but on "whether it is pro-Scott or anti-Scott." The economy bloc was committed to "a policy of stop-gap, piecemeal legislation," and it disregarded the work of study groups and simply railroaded its legislation "through on well-greased skids in order to win its political goal." Noting, "I tell you tonight that it is seeking to obtain that goal at any cost and at the expense of your welfare," he asked whether any group could be so callous "as to hold the line on education and hospital care for the aged, infirm and mentally ill?"[12]

Scott surely purged some of his pent-up disappointment through this assault, but the brusque and brash way he made his points forced the legislators into an even more inflexible and unbending stance. Several of them, angered by his speech, constantly castigated him and ignored his legislative requests.[13] Scott responded vigorously to their attacks and their unwillingness to consider his agenda. It was simply not his nature to give in without a fight, and their arrogance and close-minded views angered him. He frequently referred to the Senate Appropriations Committee as the "Do Nothing for Nobody Club."[14] Later, he reminded listeners that the attitude of the assembly was simply to embarrass him and to not let this administration do anything.[15]

John Marshall wrote Capus Waynick that the 1951 legislature had "but one objective"—"to embarrass and discredit Kerr Scott"—and was "endeavoring to stack the cards against anyone who might run [for governor in 1952] on a similar ticket." He believed that the conservative bloc had overplayed its hand and would continue to do so. The hold-the-line gang had gone so far in opposition to Scott that even B. Everett Jordan and Bob Thompson of the *High Point Enterprise* tried to talk the conservatives into abandoning some of "their bitter and vicious tactics." Marshall reported that the Scott administration had started out with a conciliatory attitude and had met frequently with the speaker and committee chairmen but that all were "hell-bent on discrediting this administration." Scott finally realized that he had to reproach the legislature with public speeches if he were ever to get any of his bills approved. Despite all the difficulties getting bills passed, Marshall revealed that the governor's mail indicated "widespread discontent at the high-handed methods being used in the General Assembly."[16]

From the beginning, one of the main bones of contention between the legislature and Kerr Scott would be his recommendation that the state take over responsibility for paving and maintaining city streets. John Marshall called it "the No. 1 fight." Since the cities had been largely ignored by Scott's 1949 road program, they expected the legislature to tend to their needs in 1951. To address this issue, Scott established the Municipal Roads Commission to study possible solutions. The commission determined that it would take $8–$9 million above and beyond the current allocation to pay for the state takeover of city streets. Scott, the League of Municipalities (representing city governments), the Municipal Roads Commission, and the state Highway Commission together came up with a plan to raise the necessary $9 million by increasing annual auto license fees $5 and raising the gas tax one-half cent per gallon.

As soon as the Scott bill appeared on the floor, Junius Powell, the chairman of the Senate Roads Committee, introduced a countermeasure. The so-called Powell Bill eliminated any gas tax or license fee increase and determined that the money to care for city roads would be taken from the current highway fund.[17] Scott immediately called the Powell Bill "ill-considered" and reminded the assembly that the three commissions that had studied the bill all favored Scott's proposal. The Powell Bill, he complained, was an outstanding example of the hard-liners' "shenanigans." The bill had been introduced for political purposes because it was the opposite of what Scott wanted.[18]

The conservative bloc answered by putting the Powell Bill on the fast track, and it quickly cleared several committees despite aggressive pressure from the Scott forces. When the governor saw that the bill would be "steam-rollered through the Senate," he took action. In his considered opinion, Senate Bill 120, the Powell Bill, would seriously impair the state's primary highway system by removing $5 million per year to pay for the upkeep of city streets at a time when these "lifelines of our economic life" needed significant work. Not only that, but the plan would result in a few large cities getting most of the money and smaller towns getting less than they were now receiving.[19]

In an attempt to rally public opinion to his cause, the governor went on the radio, continuing his tirade against this "confusing legislation."[20] He instructed the Highway Commission to delineate what influence the Powell Bill would have on primary roads in each county. The commission reported that some favorite projects in Mecklenburg and Guilford Counties would have to be stopped for lack of funds and that people would be "gypped" when some bridges would not be built in eastern North Carolina. When proponents of the Powell Bill accused him of applying unfair pressure, the governor grinned and explained that it was not pressure: "It's merely telling 'em what's gonna happen. You can't take $10 million away from something without hurting something. It's just common sense." He then laid down the gauntlet: "If you want to call it pressure, put it on me."[21]

In spite of his fervent pleas, Scott lost the battle. The General Assembly passed the Powell Bill on March 15. The final act took $5 million from the state highway fund to be directed to the cities for the building and maintenance of city streets. The bill did not provide any new tax money, but it did siphon off one-half cent of the current state gasoline tax to be allotted to the cities on the basis of population and street mileage.[22]

In retrospect it is difficult to fathom why Scott put his prestige on the line and fought so hard to defeat the Powell Bill. It was abundantly clear from the beginning of the session that the General Assembly would not authorize any new taxes and, thus, that part of his request for state funding for city streets had no chance of passage. He wanted the state to take over support for city streets, and, to a large degree, the Powell Bill accomplished what he had requested. He just disagreed with the legislature about how to pay for it. Everyone knew the bill would pass, and, since the governor had no veto power, why not accept the inevitable and withdraw from the field of battle?

Scott viewed the Powell Bill as a personal affront. He knew that the legislature was anti-Scott and thought that it was trying to embarrass him and his administration in any way possible. He was correct in that assessment, but his reaction was too emotional and irrational. He still resented those in the assembly who had favored Charlie Johnson in 1948, and they returned his animosity. Always a battler, Scott liked the give and take of political debate, but in this case he should have withdrawn his opposition. The fight—not one of his priorities—was not worth the effort. His defeat in the major battle of the 1951 legislative session badly undermined his rapidly dwindling influence and prestige.

The Powell Bill illustrated the problem with a progressive administration trying to improve social conditions and public services in the South in 1950. The groups that had supported Scott's reform package in 1949—newly enfranchised blacks, farmers, returning veterans, and disaffected whites—had been co-opted by the vicious racial and antilabor rhetoric and virulent anticommunism of the day. The brief period after the war that allowed liberal politicians in the South to transcend racism had ended. Now the hard-line reactionaries used anticommunism, racism, socialism, smaller government, no new taxes, and states' rights to create a seminal realignment in southern politics. By 1950 any politician tainted with integration or liberalism stood little chance of winning elective office. Throughout the South, from 1948 on, conservative Democrats slowly moved into the Republican Party. In 1964 Strom Thurmond of South Carolina became the first southern Republican US senator since Reconstruction, and Jesse Helms joined him in 1972.[23] Thus, in 1951 Scott faced a rebellious conservative coalition fearful of its political future and hell-bent on wresting control of the state from those wild-eyed liberals Daniels, Scott, and Graham. When conservatives banded together to quell any so-called liberal legislation, Scott's bills had no chance of passage. Much of the opposition was to big government and liberal legislation, but in North Carolina the conflict between Scott and the legislators was personal.

The governor was acutely aware of the animosity emanating from many members of the 1951 General Assembly and their overarching anti-Scott bent. The hard-liners wanted to denigrate Scott at every opportunity and went so far as to try to undermine his power by transferring the authority to name special judges from the governor to the General Assembly. Another proposal would have given the Advisory Budget Commission (four of its six members were legislators, and those four were Scott opponents) control over the highway surplus fund. If the governor lost control of this fund, his highway program would be taken over by the legislature, and his executive authority would be diminished. Legislators also considered a bill to abolish the current Highway Commission, appointed by Scott, and replace it with members elected by the House and Senate.

None of these bills, which would have given the legislature unprecedented power, came to fruition as Scott resisted any attempt to reduce his authority. He said that the anti-Scott bills undermined the state constitution and the powers specifically delegated to the governor and, thus, violated the principle of separation of powers. He pointed out that the long-term effect of these bills would be that legislative committees would control the executive branch for years to come. He predicted that these blatant attempts to undermine his authority had gone too far and would backfire. When several legislators rallied in his support, antiadministration leaders backed down and did not push the bills. Their effort, however, demonstrated how much conservative legislators disliked Scott and how determined they were to punish him. One legislator even passed out "SOS"—"Sick of Scott"— buttons.[24]

In other legislative matters, Scott got some of what he had requested in his initial speech,[25] but in many cases the legislature shut him out. He sponsored a bill to establish a state turnpike authority to build and regulate toll roads. The bill failed because the assembly once again rejected a Scott proposal out of hand and because of opposition from the driving public, which did not like the idea of paying to use state roads. The General Assembly refused to reinstate motor vehicle inspection and ignored Scott's plan to improve highway safety. In a minor concession, it added the 105 highway patrolmen he had requested.[26]

Education did not fare well in a session dominated by the economy-minded faction. The North Carolina Education Association (NCEA) lauded Scott for being "resolute in his support for education," despite constant attempts to weaken his influence or discredit his judgment.[27] The governor addressed NCEA members, asking for help in completing the school construction program, and deploring the fact that without adequate pay many teachers would leave the profession: "Let us keep the lights burning as far as education is concerned . . . for a steadily increasing population with a steadily increasing income."[28]

Scott was bombarded with letters, editorials, and suggestions as to how to raise the necessary revenue to achieve superior schools in the state. One mother proposed a tax on soft drinks that would raise $5 million and urged "tax[ing] where the money is"—beer, whiskey, wine, soft drinks, and tobacco products.[29] Mrs. Dewey Kirstein Sr. expressed the general view of most of the governor's correspondents: "We need better paid teachers, a reduction in teaching load, better buildings and better equipment, in fact, everything the NCEA is asking for."[30] The *Asheville Citizen* expressed anger at the dominant conservative bloc for striking a hard blow to public education. It chastised the legislature for its failure to address teachers' pay, classroom hours, new school buildings, and, most importantly, libraries, "which are perhaps the sole means of broadening the base of adult education, especially in the remote rural areas."[31]

When the legislature adjourned, it had refused to give teachers a cost-of-living increase.[32] The *Charlotte Observer* noted that, despite the demands of education organizations, thoughtful citizens, and newspapers, it had failed the schools: "Nothing else the legislature did or failed to do brought so much disappointment to so many people."[33] Near the end of the session, Scott appointed Miss Margery Alexander and Dr. Roma Cheek to the state Board of Education because there were no women on it and he believed that women should be represented. Education experts hailed the selections as both were well qualified. One woman complimented Scott's vision and wrote that she was "proud to have such a smart governor."[34] Unfortunately for the smart governor, the legislature refused to seat the nominees.

Scott managed to gain some success in the health field. The Medical Care Commission had requested $6 million to finish the local hospital program, but the legislature allocated only $2 million. The psychiatric wing at the University of North Carolina hospital, a major emphasis of the governor's, became a reality through a transfer of unused state funds.[35] Perhaps the most significant development in the health field was the laying of the cornerstone of the university's new teaching hospital. The facility would supply some four hundred new beds, and the four-year medical school would train enough doctors to give better care to the sick. At the opening ceremony Scott stressed that the new facilities "actually and symbolically mark a new era in the Good Health Program for the State and nation."[36]

The recalcitrant lawmakers refused to enact any prison reform, nor did they make any substantial commitment to public welfare despite North Carolina's 1950 ranking of forty-third out of forty-eight states in per capita income.[37] There were still many pockets of poverty throughout the state, especially in some mountain counties and down east. Many elderly and poor families found it difficult to earn enough to meet living expenses and medical bills. The 1951 General Assembly ignored this issue as economy in government trumped human considerations. Although the legislators also rejected his request to issue franchise certificates to public utilities, Scott continued to prod the private companies to increase their output.

The governor announced his plan for conservation of water and natural resources by proposing a water management program that would serve irrigation needs, lessen pollution, halt soil erosion, guarantee adequate water supplies, prevent floods, and provide recreational facilities. He conceded that private companies could not be expected to finance river basin development even though they benefited from such projects. The state government was responsible for managing and conserving water. Scott did not care who distributed the electricity—the private sector, the Rural Electrification Administration, or the government—just as long as the state's water resources were developed.[38]

While the legislature had no interest in power and basin development, it was, surprisingly, concerned about stream pollution. Perhaps because many of the legislators were fisherman, they passed a bill setting up the Stream Sanitation Committee under the state Board of Health to supervise and control waste disposal in rivers. Owing to complaints from several manufacturers about government intrusion, the committee had limited power, but it could survey the water resources and issue orders to stop contamination. For the first time the state had the authority to regulate and protect its streams from pollution. It was not what the conservationists, including Scott, wanted, but it was a beginning.[39]

Once again labor got shut out in the 1951 session because of cries of socialism.[40] The legislators bypassed Scott's request for a cost-of-living wage increase for state employees. His suggestions for election reform met with some success as the assemblymen voted to abolish the often-violated limitations on campaign expenditures. North Carolina became the thirty-fourth state to ratify the Twenty-Second Amendment to the US Constitution, limiting the tenure of future American presidents to two terms.[41]

As the 1951 General Assembly began to wind up its business, it passed a $506 million appropriations act—more money allocated than at any time in the state's history and $40 million over what the Budget Commission recommended. Since Scott asked for $38 million extra, this could be considered a victory for him, except that the legislature rejected his demand that some tax exemptions be ended and ruled that the $40 million would have to come from increased revenues. This put the problem squarely on Scott's shoulders. If the state coffers were not full, the $40 million would not be available to spend, and he would have to call another legislative session to deal with the problem.[42]

The 1951 session was not as contentious, as momentous, as long, or as controversial as the 1949 session. With a lame-duck governor, the Korean War, economic uncertainty, and a hold-the-line legislature, the 1951 session was an afterthought with little significant legislation passed. The *News and Observer* concluded that the conservatives were completely in control from start to finish, as independent of the governor as any legislature in modern times. The governor, as the principal advocate of progressive ideas, had most of his agenda ignored or rejected.[43] The *Charlotte Observer* noticed that, although the majority of the members of the assembly were members of the same party as Scott, there was less harmony between the legislature and the executive than if they had belonged to different parties. In fact, in ideological terms they did belong to different parties. Most of the conservative bloc would later join the Republican Party. The legislators were so heavily anti-Scott and opposed him on so many issues that some observers thought the best way to kill a bill was for the governor to support it.[44]

As one might expect, Scott expressed displeasure with the 1951 assembly and described it as the most negative he had ever seen. He thought more should have been done for the needs of state hospitals, teachers and state employees, schoolhouse construction, and highway safety.[45] The *Greensboro Daily News* had a pragmatic view of the situation. In uncertain times, and with an antitax group in charge, the General Assembly "went about as far as any realistic observers thought it would go," and, "despite the admittedly low ebb of Governor Scott's influence," the session did not do too badly.[46]

Because of the hold-the-line economy faction in the General Assembly, Scott did not achieve many of his goals in the 1951 session. Embarrassed by his comeuppance over the Powell Bill, he managed to achieve some good but only limited results in health care, pollution control, and election reform. He held off the legislators who tried to undermine his constitutional power as governor, but those bills were more of a threat than a real possibility.

The governor was limited to one term, and he did not have a mandate for the bold, popular programs he had championed in 1949. Conservative Democrats were determined to wipe out the influence of the Scott machine and replace Scott in the 1952 governor's race with one of their own. Any opportunity to embarrass him aided their chances to return power to the conservative wing of the party. Ever the pugnacious politician, Scott did not help his cause with epithets hurled at legislators. Still, while his Go Forward program was not enhanced, it had not been derailed, and his major programs—roads, electricity and phones, education, local hospitals—continued. And, while determined to undermine his authority, many legislators recognized that his Go Forward legislation had improved the economy and the lives of the people of the state and were reluctant to cut back on these popular programs.

The road program continued to make significant progress with new bridges and more paved mileage every day.[47] At the dedication of a new $1.25 million highway bridge across the Neuse River in New Bern, Scott proclaimed that the state had finally become more transportation conscious. He thought that there was now general agreement around the state that the extensive road programs were badly needed.[48] Some of his critics, with an eye on 1952, observed that the roads had been built too fast and were crumbling and derisively referred to them as "Scott tissue." They predicted that they would last only as long as Scott's tenure in office and that his failure to build efficient, permanent highways would be a good reason to wipe him off the political map for good.[49]

One of Scott's most difficult problems in 1951 was how to tackle a revival of the Ku Klux Klan that had been responsible for random acts of violence in the state. Thomas L. Hamilton, a South Carolina Klan leader, made several forays across the North Carolina state line, starting klaverns in Gastonia, Greensboro, Wilmington, Tabor City, and other sites in the eastern part of the state. In January, a group of forty to fifty Klansmen from South Carolina stormed the house of a Negro woman in Whiteville and beat her severely.

Scott, who disliked the Klan intensely, was determined to stop its depredations in his state.[50] He met with Attorney General Harry McMullan and the director of the state Bureau of Investigation to discuss how to "control a hoodlum element which calls itself the Ku Klux Klan."[51] He also wrote to those who had opposed the Klan, congratulating them on their strong stand against this radical group. He stated emphatically: "North Carolina is no place for the Klan." And he vowed to use the state Bureau of Investigation, the Highway Patrol, and all law enforcement agencies in the state to prevent future mayhem by the Klan.[52]

Incidents of violence in Whiteville escalated in November with a Klan flogging of two white men. One citizen wrote the governor warning of the "encroaching menace of the subversive, hooded KKK into southeastern

North Carolina" and wanted him to take action: "How long must we hear the rantings of the 'rabble rousers'?"[53] The mayor of Whiteville also asked Scott for help in curbing the lawlessness.[54] The *Wilmington Star News* sent notice to him that the beatings in Whiteville and a public meeting of the Klan in Brunswick County created a problem that southeastern North Carolina could not ignore. The paper urged decent-thinking people to shun this group as if it were the plague.[55]

At the Klan's meeting in Brunswick, before a crowd of some fifteen hundred, the grand dragon denounced Jews, boasted that the Klan was "growing from Boone to the coast," and claimed that the Klan stood for what was "good and just in America."[56] Scott once again pledged his support in assisting law enforcement agencies in combating Klan violence,[57] and by March 1952 the governor could report that North Carolina was beginning to win the battle. The Klan had finally learned that local prosecutors, the state Bureau of Investigation, the FBI, sheriffs, and local authorities were determined to stamp out its activity. In fact, sixty-three Klansmen were convicted of illegal violence, and the state legislature passed an antimasking law.[58] Fortunately for Scott, the Klan's meetings did not attract many new followers, and the threat of renewed violence faded away, but the revival of the KKK signaled a growing anxiety among whites about race relations in the South. Scott, who despised irrational violence against innocent parties, understood that increased nativism and racial unrest would further undermine his populist agenda and personal popularity.

Having dealt with the Klan, the governor hoped that the state could avoid any additional serious racial incidents. That hope, forlorn in the contentious 1950s, was quickly dashed when both the NAACP and the Communist Party became more aggressive in demanding the integration of the University of North Carolina and more heavily involved in trying to prevent police brutality against minorities.

Scott could brush off court challenges from the Communist Party, but he had some difficulty dealing with a more aggressive NAACP. Kelly Alexander of Charlotte, who became the state organization's chief spokesman in 1948, developed a more outspoken style of leadership. In 1951 he denounced the "so-called liberal North Carolina" and announced that his movement planned to eliminate racial segregation in the field of education by challenging segregated schools in the courts. His dramatic and aggressive stances led to an outburst of white anger and death threats from the KKK.[59]

Fearing an outbreak of racial violence, Scott responded immediately to

Alexander's comments. While he was a moderate on race in many instances, his comments placed him squarely in the camp of the segregationists. Never an integrationist, he asserted: "[Alexander does not] speak the sentiment of the majority of the Negro leaders in the state. I do not believe that segregation will ever be abandoned on the grammar and high school level." Scott thought that most Negroes preferred to associate with members of their own race, but he could understand their desire to gain access to graduate institutions that offered courses not otherwise available to them. He admitted that the courts might end segregation on the public school level, but he thought that such a court decision would not have the support of most Negro leaders.[60]

Scott received numerous letters and was the subject of many editorials in support of his views. Galt Braxton, the editor of the *Kinston Daily Free Press,* observed that the integration of schools on an elementary and high school level would be "disastrous." Braxton believed that responsible Negro leaders would agree with his assessment. No white parent would consent to have their children taught by Negro teachers.[61] While there were a few black leaders opposed to blacks entering white schools,[62] other blacks had different views. Otis L. Hairston, the editor of the *Baptist Informer,* wrote Scott to tell him that, while Alexander did not express the sentiments of some Negro leaders, the governor "would be surprised . . . to know that he does speak the honest sentiments of a more vital and important segment of the Negro—and that group represents the new Negro." The new Negro would not be frightened into a belief that segregation was his best course and to his advantage. Hairston wanted the immediate end to segregation as the "only way to end discrimination and to establish equality."[63] Scott held his ground.

The appeals of the NAACP for integrating grammar and high schools in the state would not be resolved for another three years with *Brown v. Board of Education,* but the legal challenge to graduate and higher education in the state paid immediate dividends. In March 1951, the US Court of Appeals for the Fourth Circuit ruled that the University of North Carolina must admit Negroes to its law school. The state had contended that it had met legal requirements by establishing an accredited law school for Negroes at North Carolina College in Durham. The court disagreed, writing that the University of North Carolina Law School had superior prestige and that it was a "definite handicap for the Negro student to confine his association in the law school to people of his own class."

The university reacted swiftly to the ruling. President Gordon Gray asked the Board of Trustees to appeal the decision to the US Supreme Court, and it did so. Gray explained that the Board of Trustees had already agreed to admit Negroes to the Medical School as there was no comparable institution for them to attend but that they did have the option of the law school in Durham. Outraged at the court's ruling, legislators threatened to cut off funding for the Negro law school in Durham and to cut off appropriations for any schools that broke down racial barriers.

Scott disagreed with the legislators' threat to cut off funding as it was a "negative approach." He praised the Board of Trustees for taking a positive approach and agreeing to admit qualified Negroes to the Medical School before it was mandated by the courts. He expected the university not to dodge any racial matters and to "meet the issue squarely."[64] Three weeks later, as promised, the Board of Trustees formally admitted a Negro to the university medical school and, thus, became the first white southern university to do so without a court order.[65]

In June, the US Supreme Court refused to grant certiorari on the petition to hear an appeal of the Fourth Circuit ruling admitting Negroes to the University of North Carolina Law School. The high court's decision closed the case. The university had no further legal recourse, and, in June, four Negro students were admitted to the Law School. Gratified by the result of his court challenge, Kelly Alexander observed: "[The] winning of the University of North Carolina Law School case is only the beginning of a series of suits that will be filed in the entire field of education seeking the rights of Negroes to receive equal educational opportunities on both the graduate and professional levels and also elementary and secondary levels."[66]

Scott tried to stay above the fray and did not make many public comments about the court decision. He did, however, receive a large number of complaints from citizens who feared some sort of racial upheaval and worried that primary and secondary schools would be integrated next. O. M. Powers had lost faith in Scott as he seemed to be very much in favor of President Truman's civil rights program. Powers told Scott: "We Southern folks are not going to allow Negroes to come into our schools . . . to mingle with and influence and lower the standards of the Caucasian Race." This social interaction, he insisted, would eventually lead to intermarriage and the destruction of the white race.[67] Scott responded by explaining that he had "never advocated the elimination of segregation in schools" and thought the state's best response was to establish equal school facilities for both races.[68] Mrs. T. S. Norman wanted Scott to find some way to prevent mixing of the races as Negroes should realize that they could never be accepted as social equals. Scott waffled, making a noncontroversial reply by promising a solution in the best interests of both races. He reiterated his view that he could not believe that the majority of Negroes wanted to eliminate the current school system and "bring about unpleasantness that could otherwise be avoided."[69]

Scott's views on race were slowly evolving. He had always opposed integration of the primary and secondary schools, but he had favored admission of Negroes to state graduate schools when they had no other option. He had been willing to speak with Negro leaders, appoint Negroes to important state commissions and boards, and chose a highly visible racial liberal to fill a US Senate vacancy. He favored funneling more money to Negro colleges and wanted to improve Negro schools at all levels. By 1951, however, he had hardened his stance against integration and, by 1957, would be a virulent opponent of the Civil Rights Act. His view that most blacks did not want integrated schools was bothersome to his liberal adherents, and his carefully crafted replies to those outraged by integration at the university indicated his sensitivity to the political aspects of the issue.

What had changed? Partly Scott was reacting to the flood of emotional letters protesting the court decisions and opposing integration at all levels. Perhaps he was put off by the aggressive moves of the NAACP. He probably was thinking about running against Willis Smith for the US Senate and knew that Smith and his adherents would use the race issue in much the same way they had used it against Graham in 1950. In reality he had always opposed forced integration, and, as the challenges to the traditional system became more partisan and effective and the federal government became more involved, he became more of a defender of the status quo. A search of his papers does not give any insight into the motivation for his changing attitudes about race. Never very introspective at best, Scott bluntly defended the decisions he made but seldom explained the deliberative process whereby he arrived at them.

The governor's next appointment to the state Supreme Court was, in some ways, almost as difficult to explain as his choice of Murray James. On October 13, Chief Justice Walter Stacy, who had been on the court for more than thirty years, passed away. After deliberating only four days, Scott moved Justice William A. Devin, aged eighty, to the post of chief justice and once again fooled the prognosticators by selecting his old friend Itimous Valentine to take Devin's position as associate justice. The interim appointment was good through the election of 1952, at which point Valentine would have to defend his seat. Scott had received numerous letters supporting other candidates, including Judges Allen Gwyn, Leo Carr, and William H. Bobbitt, all of whom had more judicial experience than Valentine, who had never been a judge. In explaining his choice he told the press that he had considered appointing a woman, almost certainly Susie Sharp, but had placed emphasis on the amount of support received by the eight to ten candidates he had considered. All had strong recommendations from various groups, but Valentine had the strongest.[70] Valentine had been one of the few attorneys to campaign for Scott in the 1948 race and had now been rewarded for his loyalty.

Scott had, for the second time, chosen a supporter and friend for the high court rather than someone with more relevant experience and judicial ability. The number of letters from backers should not have been a primary criterion for selecting a supreme court justice. Scott valued fealty to his cause above all else. He apparently did not appreciate the judicial experience or the intellect necessary to serve effectively as an associate justice.

During his time on the bench, some experts thought Valentine an inferior justice and considered him vulnerable in his bid for election in 1952. By November 1951, five candidates, including the superior court judges passed over by Scott, had announced for the seat. Judges Gwyn, Bobbitt, and R. Hunt Parker entered the contest, creating the highly unusual situation of several prominent Democratic jurists vying for a place on the high court. In the Democratic primary runoff in May 1952, R. Hunt Parker defeated William Bobbitt. Valentine finished third.[71] Valentine's loss was yet another rejection of one of Scott's appointments and a rebuke to his judgment. The governor, who twice had chosen friends and political supporters for the high court, had a dismal record of success in his selections as both of his nominees had been rejected—once by the Democratic Executive Committee and once by the people.

Newspapers in 1951 were fixated on the deadly war in Korea, Supreme Court decisions, and the activities of celebrities. There were huge headlines in state papers when the crooner Frank Sinatra left his wife for the gorgeous, sultry Ava Gardner, a Smithfield, North Carolina, native. Despite the crises in the state and around the world, Scott plodded along on his mundane duties as governor—attending a North Carolina State basketball game, speaking to the Grange, greeting various visitors and dignitaries at the governor's office, meeting with highway officials, and writing letters attacking the private power companies whenever the mood struck him.

On one occasion the governor received a note from a friend who wanted him to go hunting with him. The note read: "Please assure him that this is a genuine man-to-man invitation to hunt, with no strings attached. I don't know of anyone I want hired or fired, don't want to get nobody in or out of prison, not asking for no roads, bridges, telephones or power lines or school buildings, white or colored. And last but not least, we will try to put up with the Tidewater Power rates a little longer."[72] Another time Scott found in his daily mail bag a missive from a constituent, Fred Flagler, who was ashamed that he had voted for him. The writer despised him because of the persons and the ideals he had betrayed. In an interesting rejoinder, Scott said he thought that Flagler did not really mean that he despised anyone: "I think I can truthfully say that there is no man living or dead that I have hated or anything of the . . . plant kingdom unless it is Johnson grass; but I soon learned that if you work with nature, even Johnson grass is one of the best grasses for livestock that I know." He invited Flagler to come down to Raleigh and "get acquainted."[73]

As Scott neared the end of his third year in office, the press speculated about his future political plans. Initially, he said he was not running for anything: "[I am] saving my candidacy for the Kingdom of Heaven. And I'm having a lot of opposition on that."[74] He next kidded reporters that he was thinking of running for lieutenant governor, and that his campaign was making some progress, but that it was too early for an announcement. When asked whether he really was running for lieutenant governor, he replied: "Well, I ain't said no yet."[75] All this chitchat was a ploy to keep reporters off his back and have a little joke at their expense. In their wildest dreams, none of them could imagine a former governor, especially Scott, running for lieutenant governor.

On a national level, Scott continued his strong and vocal support for President Truman. In October he told the press that his first three choices for the Democratic nomination in 1952 were Truman, Truman, and Truman. He predicted that Truman would be stronger than ever in 1952 and would defeat Eisenhower if the general were the nominee of the Republican Party.[76] He renewed his correspondence with Truman, who at the time had come under fire from all sides for his civil rights views and the stalled war in Korea, writing: "Don't let them get you down. Remember, the best horse gets the most currying."[77] In October the president came to Winston-Salem to dedicate the new campus of Wake Forest University. Scott greeted him at the airport, and the two chatted and laughed for several minutes. Scott then climbed into the presidential limousine for the ride to the dedication.

He thanked Truman for his visit to the state, and Truman replied that it had been a "great pleasure" to see him and renew an old acquaintance.[78] In February 1952 Governor Scott, accompanied by Henry Jordan, paid a visit to President Truman to request funds for the completion of the Blue Ridge Parkway. Truman did not respond favorably to the governor's entreaties, but Scott's main purpose was apparently to encourage the president to run for another term in office. When asked whether he would, Scott responded that the president had not yet decided.[79] He expressed disappointment when the president ultimately decided against running again.

1952—The Final Year

Except for the 1952 gubernatorial and presidential races and some very controversial firings, Scott's last year in office was somewhat anticlimactic after the turmoil of the three previous years.[80] In February the governor announced that tax receipts had increased and that the state had a budget surplus of $17 million, primarily attributable to increased tax revenues in a growing economy and economy measures. That amount would be sufficient to take care of all the items in the budget. Scott would not have to call a special session of the legislature to deal with any financial shortfall.[81]

Although pleased that the state could boast of a sound financial situation, Scott remained displeased with what he viewed as slow progress by the power companies in expanding their output. He had never wavered in his demand for increased electric power and insisted that the state was still short of what was needed. The Duke Power Company bolstered Scott's case in its annual report. When asking for a rate increase, it had to admit that it needed 10–15 percent more power than its current peak output in order to bring its reserve up to accepted engineering standards. Scott, now vindicated, reminded his critics that they had accused him of talking through his hat when he had reached similar conclusions. He admitted that everyone, including governors, "needs a little kick occasionally to keep us up to snuff," and he confessed that he was "just naturally" the kind of man who planted an occasional kick.[82]

As Scott neared the end of his term, the last thing he wanted was to turn state government back to the conservatives and the remnants of the Shelby machine. He had been fighting the conservative bloc for over three years and had no intention of letting it dismantle his hard-won Go Forward program. He began planning for a worthy successor as early as March 1951, fourteen months before the 1952 Democratic gubernatorial primary. He knew he would need a formidable candidate as there were clear indications that the conservatives would back William B. Umstead, a former congressman and US senator and a machine favorite. Moderate possibilities included Judge Hubert Olive, Dr. Henry Jordan, and Capus Waynick. Early on Scott professed his preference for Waynick.[83] Surely he felt some guilt for not having chosen Waynick for the US Senate seat in 1949, and he certainly owed him a great debt for his work in the 1948 campaign, but mainly he believed that he would be a successful candidate. On May 2, Scott publicly indicated that, if Waynick ran, he would have his support, although he did "not want to take too much part"[84] in the 1952 race.

One could never imagine Scott staying out of the 1952 campaign for long. Sure enough, before anyone could stop him, he fetched up in Cartagena, Colombia, where Waynick served as the US ambassador. As told by Waynick, the governor spent most of one day trying to persuade him to return to North Carolina and run for governor. He said: "If you don't do it, we will have to run Hubert Olive, and I'm afraid we can't win with him."[85] Eventually, Waynick opted to stay in his diplomatic post and decided not to run.[86]

Scott then switched his allegiance to Dr. Henry Jordan, the chairman of the state Highway Commission. After praising his outstanding performance as chairman, Scott told people that, if Jordan ran, he would support him.[87] Jordan hemmed and hawed and kept putting off a decision. The newspapers reported, correctly, that B. Everett Jordan, chairman of the state Democratic Executive Committee, favored Bill Umstead for governor over his brother Henry. When asked whether he would stay on the sidelines or throw his support to Umstead, B. Everett laughed and said: "Bill and I are mighty good friends." B. Everett Jordan apparently discouraged his brother from running against Umstead, and Henry Jordan decided not to enter the race.[88]

On September 11, the lean, bespectacled William B. Umstead let it be known that he was a candidate for the office of governor in the Democratic primary of 1952. The announcement was an open secret as his backers had been quietly building support across the state for months. Umstead finally sought the office he had long desired. He would have run in 1948 had not Governor Cherry appointed him to the US Senate in 1947.[89] The conservatives and machine regulars who backed him in 1952 knew that he had the necessary credentials and had excellent name recognition across the state. An added plus was that he "hated anything that touched Scott." The machine wanted someone who would rid it of the corrosive influence of "the wild bull of Alamance."

Unfortunately for his supporters, Umstead had heart problems and was a sick man when he announced. Bob Hanes, who would put a lot of money into Umstead's candidacy, thought he might not last a full four years and opted for a contingency plan. He got Luther Hodges, formerly an executive at Fieldcrest Mills, to run for lieutenant governor.[90] In the end, it proved a wise decision for Hanes and the industrialists in the state as Umstead died during his second year in office, to be succeeded by Hodges.

Since Umstead was the only announced candidate and Waynick and Jordan were out of the picture, reporters asked Scott whether he would support Umstead, unaware of the intense animosity the two had for each other. One reporter even asked whether he planned to make speeches for Umstead. With a deadpan gaze, Scott dryly explained that he did not have his schedule worked out yet. Later there were rumors that he would support Umstead for governor if Umstead would return the favor when Scott ran for the US Senate. Scott had no comment except to say that no one had contacted him about any "horse-trading."[91]

Scott could have accepted the inevitable and avoided yet another political setback if he had chosen not to challenge Umstead, the odds-on favorite to win the Democratic nomination. He simply could not avoid a clash with a candidate he disliked intensely, and he could not resist battling the conservative wing of the party that might undo his achievements as governor. At that point, Superior Court judge Hubert Olive, a handsome man who looked like a governor ought to look and was well-known around the state, announced his candidacy. Scott initially was somewhat lukewarm about the candidacy because, as he had confided to Capus Waynick, he did not think Olive could win. He thought that it would be best if he relaxed on the sidelines. "Of course," he drawled, "I might from time to time take the opportunity to point up what I think ought to be pointed up."

The very next day, after an hour-long visit from Judge Olive, the governor changed his mind and announced his support as the judge would be the best man to keep the Go Forward program alive. He reiterated his desire not to get on the stump or make any speeches, but, if anyone asked, he would tell them where he stood. He wrote Capus Waynick and explained that he had come out "flat-footed" for Olive since his platform closely paralleled his own views.[92] In late May, when he made a few forays around the state to encourage folks to cast their lot with Olive, he laughed as he explained that he was not involved in a political campaign: "I'm just waving the olive branch of peace."[93]

As the contest between Umstead and Olive captured the headlines and the attention of the state, Scott had to face a problem of his own making that would plague him for the remainder of his time in office. He already knew that Assistant Budget Director David Coltrane, Landon Rosser, the motor vehicle commissioner, and George Ross, the head of Conservation and Development, among others, had committed to Bill Umstead. The outspoken governor felt strongly that the members of his administration owed their jobs to him and should stick with his chosen candidate. He said that he had appointed these public servants to carry out his program and that "they ought to carry it through." Constantly using the words *duty* and *loyalty,* he allowed that it did not look good for any of his key advisers to get on any other team. He then turned around and said that key personnel could vote as they pleased and that he would not put any pressure on them or the workers they supervised.[94] The not-so-subtle message that was sent meant that, if any key employees backed Umstead, they would be searching for a new position. Despite his statement that he would not put any pressure on government employees, by demanding loyalty Scott tried to intimidate any state official who valued his or her job.

Umstead and Olive, two decent and capable candidates, ran a subdued race for chief executive. Umstead, who always looked wan and sickly, appeared to observers as a colorless, taciturn man. Not a scintillating stump speaker, he nonetheless had the advantage over his opponent as he had the money and the organization of the machine behind him. Olive, despite his upbeat persona, began the race far behind, and Scott's backing did not lead to a rush of support. The race never generated the intense interest of the 1948 Scott-Johnson race or the 1950 Smith-Graham campaign. The *New York Times* said that there were no clear-cut liberal versus conservative lines drawn between the contestants. It conjectured that most of Graham's supporters favored Olive while Umstead attracted those who worked for Smith in 1950. The race revived some of the factional bitterness that marked the 1950 campaign, but it was not nearly as heated as those in 1948 and 1950.[95]

The race issue did surface during the contest, although it had little discernible influence on the outcome. Some Umstead supporters put out propaganda leaflets on the eve of the vote, warning that, if elected, Olive planned to appoint a Negro paroles commissioner and, in so doing, was attempting to break down segregation. A photo in the ad pictured Olive with Robert

Hendrick, a Negro dentist: "Is this kowtowing to the Negro vote merely a desperate effort by Candidate Olive or is it a deliberate attempt to end segregation? Do you want a Negro paroles commissioner? Do you want your children to go to school with Negroes?" Scott denounced the tactic, saying that it might help a candidate in the short run but that it was not good for North Carolina and helped keep the KKK inflamed in the state.[96] Umstead, unlike Smith in 1950, emphatically stated that the leaflets may have been passed around on his behalf, but not with his knowledge or consent: "I am absolutely opposed to such tactics."[97]

Umstead directed his campaign largely against Scott and charged that, as governor, he had been trying to set up his own permanent political machine.[98] Umstead's advocates castigated the governor for his hypocritical and "high-handed" tactics in attacking Umstead as a machine candidate. One supporter claimed that Scott had unfairly pressured state employees to vote for Olive and that, if Olive were elected, Scott's "dominant personality will continue to exert itself." He thought that machine rule was no more desirable in 1952 than it was in 1948.[99]

In a sworn statement, a prison camp superintendent revealed that the head of the state Prison Department had come to him and announced that Scott was backing Olive and that the employees should go along.[100] Umstead repeated his frequent accusation that the governor was using the powers of his office to assist Olive: "Despite all the hurried telephone calls from Capitol Hill, all the automobile trips in state cars, all the stakes driven for promised roads, all the propaganda sent out by tip sheets marked 'confidential,' all the whispered insinuations and all the other evidence of desperation which have been resorted to—it will avail them nothing. The people will not be deceived."[101] Scott's harsh condemnation of machine politics in 1948 had now been co-opted by the Umstead forces, much to Scott's dismay.

Just prior to the gubernatorial vote on May 31, the state Democratic Party held its annual convention in Raleigh. Much of the discussion prior to the convention centered on the candidates for president. Harry Truman had disappointed Scott by announcing that he would not run, but B. Everett Jordan, pleased by the decision, said it would lead to greater party unity.[102] Without Truman, the contest for the national Democratic Party nomination was wide open. The progressive wing of the party seemed to favor Governor Adlai Stevenson of Illinois. Southerners thought that Stevenson was too liberal and that his candidacy would be a disaster, especially since General Dwight Eisenhower seemed the likely Republican nominee. Many southerners sought a more conservative candidate who would protect states' rights. In an attempt to head off the nomination of Stevenson, the Dixiecrats began rallying to the banner of Senator Richard Russell of Georgia. Scott, a firm supporter of Stevenson, acknowledged that Russell had been well received in the state and would get some Tar Heel votes at the national convention.[103]

As the delegates began arriving in Raleigh for the state convention, most took up residence at the Sir Walter Hotel, a four-hundred-room edifice conveniently located only a few blocks from Capitol Square. For many years the Sir Walter had been the major meeting place for legislators, hangers-on, onlookers, supplicants, lobbyists, and newspaper reporters. Numerous legislators had rooms at the hotel for the sessions of the General Assembly, and politicians worked out many deals and compromises in the lobby. The hotel usually served as the headquarters for the Democratic Party candidates, so large numbers of colorful political signs and banners for Olive and Umstead were draped over the railing around the lobby mezzanine.[104] As the party faithful trooped in, most realized not only that there would be a showdown between the forces of Olive and Umstead but also that the party was split as to which candidate, Russell or Stevenson, should be endorsed for president.

As the convention began, it became evident to the assemblage that Scott had become angry with and estranged from his longtime friend and supporter B. Everett Jordan. The Jordan family had helped Scott tremendously in the 1948 race, and the governor had, as we have seen, appointed B. Everett Jordan as chairman of the Democratic Executive Committee and selected his brother, Henry Jordan, as head of the state Highway Commission. The rift probably began in 1949 when B. Everett harbored some resentment against Scott for not appointing him to the US Senate seat after Broughton's death. Jordan believed that Frank Graham was too liberal and refused to go along with Scott's pick in 1950, backing Willis Smith with both money and contacts.[105] To compound the problem, in 1952 both Jordans worked assiduously for Umstead instead of Scott's choice, Olive. Scott considered Everett's defection in 1950 and his aid to Umstead in 1952 disloyalty of the highest order.

The two men, by now enemies, clashed at the opening of the Democratic convention. Although Jordan had extended Scott a personal invitation to sit on the platform,[106] when the delegates assembled, the governor's chair on the dais remained vacant. Scott had, unannounced, taken a seat with the delegates from Alamance County, in effect boycotting the proceedings. When Jordan noticed that the governor's seat was unoccupied, he dispatched an

Governor Scott conferring with Jonathan W. Daniels (behind Scott), the publisher of the *Raleigh News and Observer*, a close adviser to Scott and the Democratic national committeeman, and B. Everett Jordan, chairman of the state Democratic Executive Committee (on Scott's left). Ca. 1952. Courtesy of the State Archives of North Carolina, Raleigh.

aide to persuade Scott to take his seat on the podium. Scott angrily refused and sent word back to Jordan: "No. I am not going. I'm going to sit out here and you know why."

The immediate cause of the ire was that, without consulting Scott, the titular head of the party, Jordan had decided to remove four of Scott's selections as national convention delegates. He ousted two of the four female delegates as well as Bill Staton, the president of the state Young Democratic Club. They had been replaced by conservative supporters of Bill Umstead. Scott thought that he and Jordan had agreed on the makeup of the delegation the night before, and he learned of the changes only when he arrived at the convention, too late to make a floor fight. He was incensed that the

Young Democrats now had no representation and that the number of women representing the state had been cut in half.

Scott's choice not to sit on the dais embarrassed Jordan and upset some party leaders, especially Umstead backers. When Everett Jordan and Scott crossed paths one week after the convention, Jordan came up to Scott and asked the governor whether he was still mad. Scott looked Jordan in the eye and said: "Everett, you double-crossed me." Jordan said he did not and could explain the circumstances. The governor icily responded: "Make it sometime when you have a lot of time because it'll take a lot of explaining why you didn't give me the giant double-cross."[107]

The conservative wing of the party—mainly those who favored Umstead—controlled the machinery of the state convention. In an aggressive attempt to wipe out the influence of the Scott faction, it not only stacked the national convention delegation with Umstead admirers but also made Scott a delegate-at-large with only half a vote. While they were at it, the conservatives decided to make a clean sweep and "fire" Jonathan Daniels as national committeeman. Faced with implacable opposition, and knowing that the conservatives had the votes to oust him, Daniels stated that he would not be a candidate. These decisions by the anti-Scott forces amounted to a serious rebuff of the governor and his adherents. The conservatives now held power in the party, and, after three and one half years of anger and frustration with Scott and his controversial leadership, his enemies had taken full advantage of an opportunity to bushwhack him.

Scott, no neophyte in politics, realized that his days were numbered and that his influence had dwindled. No longer able to control state politics, he became angry and frustrated by his weakened status. Although Jordan's disloyalty and changes to the delegation list stung, his decision to vacate the governor's chair and sit with the Alamance delegation was unwarranted. Here was Scott at his worst—stubborn, churlish, and petulant. His demand for loyalty was obsessive and unrealistic. He could not command his followers to agree with him on every issue—they had a right to think and act for themselves. When he did not get his way, like a spoiled child he sat in the corner and pouted.

The main issue at the state convention was a decision on the Democratic candidates for president. After much discussion, the party endorsed the candidacy of Russell but declined to specifically instruct the delegates to vote for him. The majority of the conventioneers favored him, the closest thing to a Dixiecrat on the national scene, and by the June 25 convention's end twenty-one of the thirty-two delegates had announced for him. Among the undecided was Kerr Scott, despite indications that he favored his fellow governor Adlai Stevenson.[108]

Once the convention concluded, Olive and Umstead resumed their electioneering. Scott encouraged folks to vote for Olive but did not make a serious effort on his behalf. On election day, Scott suffered yet another defeat as Umstead outdistanced Olive by a vote of 260,612–236,427.[109] The total was relatively close, but a dispirited Scott, who had lost significant prestige over the previous year, simply could not transfer his influence to another candidate. The machine and conservatives had regrouped and had exacted a measure of revenge for Johnson's defeat in 1948. Since Umstead and Olive had similar platforms, neither candidate posed a real threat to the Go Forward program. Still, Scott wanted Olive in the governor's office partly because he wanted to continue to have a say in North Carolina politics. He also backed Olive because he thoroughly disliked Umstead, machine politics, and the conservatives he had been fighting for four years. Even faced with a losing proposition, he simply could not stay out of a battle with his arch adversaries. Once again, his ego and passion got the better of him.

As the campaign drew to a close, with Umstead almost certainly the victor, Scott vented his anger at key employees such as T. C. Johnson, the paroles commissioner, and Dave Coltrane, the assistant budget director, who were openly supporting Umstead. He called those disloyal to his cause "deviationists" and repeated his view that they should be faithful to his choice or remain neutral. By April he said that, if they were disloyal, they should be honor bound to resign. He had particularly harsh words for Coltrane, accusing him of delaying state projects and holding up money in order to build up a surplus for the next governor—Bill Umstead. He also charged him with raising money for Umstead's race.[110]

Coltrane reacted swiftly to Scott's attacks. He said that anyone could examine the state books and see that he was not holding up any projects. Some projects had been delayed, but that was because there was a war on and a shortage of some materials. Coltrane supported Umstead but had not raised a cent on his behalf and had done little campaigning. He thought he was doing a good job as assistant budget director and had no intention of resigning.[111] He invited the Advisory Budget Commission to come to the Budget Bureau to examine the state's building program. The commission, no friend to Scott, concluded that 94 percent of the projects had been handled satisfactorily and were either complete, under construction, or definitely committed.[112]

Once the Democratic primary ended, an angry governor began wielding the ax. The first to fall was T. C. Johnson, the commissioner of paroles. Scott accused him of running out on his team and joining forces with Umstead. The *Raleigh News and Observer* agreed with Scott's decision because Johnson had garnered much criticism for his performance as commissioner and probably should have been fired earlier.[113] Johnson's ouster was just the beginning. The next day Landon Rosser, the commissioner of motor vehicles, lost his job. The Rosser removal set off tremors in many offices around Capitol Square as those who had backed Umstead feared for their jobs. Observers had hoped Scott would end with Johnson and Rosser, but now it appeared that there would be a general housecleaning.[114]

An anonymous letter to the governor chastised him for trying to dominate state politics and for failing "so miserably in getting along with other public officials." The writer asked Scott to take it easy for the remainder of his term, try not to find fault with his appointees, and try not to fire anyone else.[115] Scott received other letters in the same vein. Mrs. Jerry Grimes noted that she had voted for him because she thought he was a broad-minded person but that public employees should have the freedom to exercise their personal beliefs, even if they did not agree with him: "Why fire him just because you dislike the way he thinks? There are a lot of people who do not agree with you." Scott's reply was tepid and unpersuasive. He wrote that, if Mrs. Grimes had all the facts, she would be critical of him for not having taken action sooner.[116] He did not provide any facts.

Undismayed by the protests, the governor continued his vindictive rampage. He could not fire his next target, Dave Coltrane, since Coltrane had a four-year appointment, not due to expire until June 1953. Thus, his only alternative was to ask for Coltrane's immediate resignation, explaining that his usefulness in administering the affairs of his office had been hampered by his disloyalty. Coltrane declared that he had tried to be a loyal, conscientious, and cooperative employee and argued that Scott's dissatisfaction was based solely on the fact that he had supported Umstead instead of Olive.[117] The two former friends would now engage in a brutal battle of wills that would besmirch the reputations of both.

In a public letter, Coltrane formally refused the governor's request to resign and mentioned that he had the unwavering support of friends and state officials who had urged him to stay on and fight back. He reported numerous phone calls and telegrams imploring him to "stick to [his] guns" and not yield "to a poltroon or a demagogic blatherskite even though he be parading as governor." Others referred to Scott as a dictator and said there was no room for "Kingfishism" in North Carolina. Thirteen members of the General Assembly promised Coltrane that, if the governor cut his pay, the legislature would restore it in full during the next session. Coltrane also had promises to finance any legal expenses incurred "in bucking the man with the cigar and the swinging axe."[118] The conservatives had tired of Scott's high-handed behavior, and they would take a stand on the Coltrane affair. Enough was enough.

The *Raleigh News and Observer* rushed to Scott's defense. Although Scott's choices in the beginning were not wise and it might seem to be petty politics for the governor to purge his own appointees, the chief executive had to have subordinates on whom he could depend if he were to do his job. Scott may have made mistakes in "both method and timing" in connection with the dismissals, but he had the right to do so.[119] The *Asheville Citizen* agreed. It recalled that the governor had been guilty of some rash and intemperate acts during his term that the paper had criticized vigorously, but this was not one of them. He was legally responsible for the budget, and an assistant who did not enjoy his confidence was "like a vermiform appendix" and should be removed.[120]

On June 11, Coltrane raised the stakes, categorically refusing to leave his post and informing Scott that he had no power to fire him and that he had no legal ground to cut his pay.[121] Angry and annoyed at how the duel with Coltrane was unfolding, Scott allowed his temper to overrun his good judgment. Since he could not fire Coltrane, he should have let the matter rest. But he wanted his revenge—no one dared be disloyal to Kerr Scott. He lanced the boil two days later when he stripped Coltrane of his role in state fiscal affairs and reduced him to the status of a payroll clerk. Coltrane would maintain his desk, his title, and his salary, but the bulk of his work would be taken up by a temporary assistant director of the budget.

Coltrane backed down but did not resign. He meekly stated that he did not intend to challenge the governor's latest ruling. He would come to work and do the best he could to see that the state spent its money judiciously. He announced that he would not accept any state pay until "the normal functions of my office are restored." He understood that the legislature would reimburse him for his lost income in the next session. Also, he knew that, as soon as Scott left office in six months, he could resume his official duties and would hold his title at least until June 1953.[122] The 1953 legislature did reimburse him for the loss of income, and Governor Umstead reappointed him as assistant director of the budget.[123]

In his reply to numerous letters of criticism in regard to the firings, Scott defended his right to fire Rosser, Johnson, and Coltrane. In regard to Coltrane, his only regret was that he did not do it sooner, and he denounced Coltrane for staying in office on a technicality: "If you knew all the facts I really believe that you would take the same position I did." In answer to the charge that he fired people willy-nilly, Scott claimed that out of some sixty thousand employees he had asked for only six resignations.[124] That, of course, was a misrepresentation of the first order. He dismissed entire state boards when he first took office and collected the scalps of state workers at a significant rate throughout his term as governor. Bodies were scattered all over the state capital. He fired all seven members of the state Highway Commission and replaced them with cronies and supporters and dismissed as many of Johnson's 1948 supporters as he could.

Although Scott stated emphatically on June 18 that he was through with firings, the imbroglio hurt him. Any way one looks at it—and T. C. Johnson probably should have been dismissed for cause—the firings were political, and Scott came across as vindictive and arbitrary, a tyrant to his opponents. However, even his critics concluded that Coltrane hurt his own reputation by staying on in his post and not resigning.

While struggling with the Coltrane controversy, the governor took yet another massive hit when the *Greensboro Daily News* revealed that he had personally benefited from his roads program. The paper reported that the state built some fifteen miles of paved roads around and through his Haw River farm and paid him $12,000 for crop losses and in damages for thirty-nine acres taken from him in the building of Highway 70. When asked about the situation, Scott admitted that he had profited by the new roads because he could now get his milk to market. He told the press: "If I have stolen a nickel, it was for the church." What he meant was that, with the new highways, church attendance at Hawfields Presbyterian was up 25 percent. Scott observed that Alamance County and the Fifth Highway Division were behind the rest of the state in road building and that, if he had not gotten his roads while governor, he might never have gotten them. He confessed that he got the roads because he "persuaded" the highway engineers to take care of them first: "[I] rode herd on 'em." He told Jim Barnwell, the local engineer: "I want this neighborhood fixed up." Barnwell replied: "Well, you're the boss." Scott: "That's how I got 'em."

The governor made no apologies for getting his roads, but there was a problem. Chairman Henry Jordan had not approved the construction, noting that the roads were lightly traveled and that there was already an "undue concentration" of highways around Scott's property. As he usually did when facing criticism, Scott brushed off the paper's exposé. With a big smile on his face, he said that he was merely doing what he promised in his platform, building roads: "I have just started here at home." When asked about the specific charges in the *Greensboro Daily News,* which had supported Umstead in the gubernatorial race, he called them just another attack on him: "It is part of a propaganda campaign to destroy my influence. They's [*sic*] so darn scared that I am going to run for the Senate against Willis Smith they don't know what to do. And they're using this and other things to discredit me."[125]

Two months later, as the furor over his Hawfields roads had subsided, Scott dropped a political bomb by announcing that he had found $750,000 in surplus highway funds and had personally allocated all the money to county roads in Alamance County. His action was unprecedented, the first time that surplus road funds had been devoted to a single county. With extraordinary arrogance, Scott blithely justified this move because, as he had said before, road building in Alamance had been neglected for many years. The public outrage at this announcement was immediate and vocal. Critics saw the addition of a $750,000 allocation, after the state had already built fifteen miles of roads on his farm, as adding insult to injury. The *News and Observer* thought it "bad judgment" for the governor to assign those funds to Alamance County after the outcry over the excessive road building in his home neighborhood: "The governor has made a serious governmental and political mistake."[126]

Scott initially ignored the carping. Two weeks later, however, buffeted from all sides by bitter and unending disapproval, he rescinded the allocation. He still believed that Alamance needed the money but realized that "such an allocation would create other inequities and therefore would not be in the public interest."[127] He admitted his mistake and rectified his error, but only under intense scrutiny and censure from both friends and opponents. He clearly overstepped the bounds of good judgment and arbitrarily and unwisely exercised his gubernatorial powers. For a man who prided himself on his political acumen, Scott self-destructed during his last year in office with the Dave Coltrane incident and by feathering his own nest at state expense. Like many people in power, he had begun to believe he could do anything and get away with it. He once again interpreted these attacks on his integrity as an attempt to poison what would surely be his bid for Willis Smith's Senate seat. He coyly commented that he was uncertain about future plans: "I am not running for anything yet."[128] Everyone knew differently.

When not firing associates or building roads in his neighborhood, Scott turned his attention to national affairs. As a delegate to the Democratic national convention and a sitting governor, he received numerous letters from the various presidential candidates, including Adlai Stevenson, Estes Kefauver, and Dick Russell, seeking his vote. He assured Russell that he did not "feel unkindly toward [him] and [his] campaign,"[129] but he went to the convention uncommitted.[130] He thought Russell too close to the Dixiecrats, believed Kefauver could not win, and pinned his hopes on Adlai Stevenson.

Scott arrived in Chicago for the national Democratic convention on July 20. That night he attended the caucus of the North Carolina delegation[131] and sat by helplessly as the delegates approved a slate backed by Governor-Elect Umstead. The anti-Scott faction dealt the governor a calculated and deliberate insult when the party denied him the position as head of the delegation, choosing instead former governor Cam Morrison.[132] By tradition, the sitting governor had been designated as chairman of the state's delegation, and the decision to snub Scott was nothing more than petty politics. By so doing, the conservatives had brashly notified Scott that his time was over. Scott did not forget the rebuke and would get his revenge in the Senate election of 1954.

On the first ballot for president, the Tar Heel delegation cast twenty-six votes for Russell and five and a half for Stevenson, including the governor's half vote. On the second ballot, the delegates made a big move to Stevenson, and the convention, including North Carolina, made the nomination of Stevenson unanimous. After the Democrats picked John Sparkman of Alabama as the vice-presidential nominee, Scott said: "We've got a mighty fine team. I'm mighty pleased."

Despite the unpleasantness in the caucus, Scott claimed to have enjoyed the experience in Chicago. When asked about all the pointless demonstrations for the various candidates, he explained that they made little sense to the observer but that, after you had been sitting for hours, you are glad to get up and move around: "You'd demonstrate for anybody. It was a good thing that near the end of the ordeal that somebody didn't nominate a Republican; the delegates probably would have put on a demonstration for him."[133]

Despite the rude treatment he received from the conservative wing of the party, Scott campaigned for Umstead and the entire Democratic ticket in the fall. He predicted that the Republican nominee for governor, the irrepressible H. F. "Chub" Seawell, would run well behind Umstead and did not think much of Eisenhower's chances in the general election against Stevenson: "I have heard of other generals fading away [a reference to Douglas MacArthur's farewell address to Congress]. I think this one will too." He demonstrated his ability to poke fun at himself while making a political speech for the Democrats. When he was introduced as an honest man, he said he appreciated the sentiment but noted, "I tried to steal some money for roads in Alamance County awhile ago and couldn't get away with it." The audience roared with laughter.[134]

The governor joined Bill Umstead and other Democratic Party stalwarts in visits to congressional districts and worked strenuously for the ticket right up to the general election.[135] The *New York Times* predicted that Stevenson would win the state's fourteen electoral votes but reported that Republican sentiment had been on the upswing in rural areas because of race and some economic issues.[136]

The *Times* had it right. Conservatives in the state were slowly abandoning the Democratic Party owing to the liberal racial policies of Truman. Fear of a fair employment practices commission and integration of the schools fueled the Republican surge. Although Chub Seawell did not win, he benefited from the gradual shift from Democrats to Republicans by garnering more votes than any other Republican gubernatorial candidate in the state's history to that date. In his campaign, Seawell laid some of the groundwork for the rise of Republicanism in the state by preaching family values, lower taxes, economy in government, and the reduction of government influence in individual lives—standard fare for later Republican platforms.

"Cousin Chub," in many ways a lightweight candidate, proved to be the most colorful Republican politician in memory and became a statewide sensation. He denounced the state legislature, saying that the last one laid taxes on everybody and everything "except air and water." He constantly railed against the evils of liberalism and reckoned that America had become an "atheistic, intellectual, bureaucratic, socialist dictatorship." He cried out that the state was first in ignorance and crime and last in health and per capita income and that those failures were due to one-party Democratic rule. He even took a swing at the governor: "Scott promised to raise a few windows and let in a little fresh air, but what he let in wasn't exactly fresh. It looks like the only purpose of raising the windows was to throw someone out."

As voting day approached, B. Everett Jordan predicted that Stevenson would get over 600,000 votes and would win by a margin of 250,000. He got the first figure right but underestimated Republican strength. Stevenson carried the state's fourteen electoral votes by 652,803 (53.9 percent) to Ike's 558,107 (46.1 percent): a winning margin of 94,696, not the 250,000 advantage that Jordan expected. Eisenhower had done extremely well in the state and ran far ahead of all the other Republican office seekers. Umstead defeated Seawell 796,306 (67.5 percent) to 383,329 (32.5 percent). On the national level Eisenhower and Richard Nixon won a smashing triumph, 442 electoral votes to 89 for Stevenson.[137]

Although North Carolina had cast more electoral votes for Stevenson than did any other state and the Democrats won all the state races except for one congressional seat, the closeness of the contest dismayed some party leaders. Not Scott. Although the national election was not to his choosing, there was some pride to be taken in carrying the state for Stevenson, despite the close vote.[138] Scott told the press that he did not see that the outcome indicated any real resurgence of Republican strength in the South. It was just one election and had no significance for the future. Nor did he see the possibility of a two-party system in the South.[139]

As his final days in office approached, Scott generously offered to work with and help Governor-Elect Umstead in any way possible and cooperated with him on the new budget.[140] He also invited Lieutenant Governor–Elect Luther Hodges to sit in and observe the activities of the Advisory Budget Commission.[141] Scott's foes, naturally, were thrilled to see him go and as a parting gift crafted an "objective view" of his administration. The article had just enough flattering references to make it seem credible, but the purpose of the effort was to convince the public that, as governor, Scott did far more harm than good. The main focus of the evaluation was to discredit Scott and perhaps knock him out of any consideration as a potential candidate for the US Senate against Willis Smith.[142]

The governor fought back by issuing a small pamphlet summarizing his accomplishments. He admitted that from time to time the administration had made mistakes but that prompt action had been taken to correct them. And those mistakes were little ones, "no major ones." His biggest accomplishments were roads, schools, telephones, and electricity. He said that he did not intend to continue to defend his Go Forward program as the results spoke for themselves: "Critics may attempt to distort it and depict it in a false light in furtherance of selfish interests or even with well-meaning motives. That is their privilege."[143] The *News and Observer* agreed that Scott had made little mistakes, but no big ones. It reminded readers that the die-hard critics who opposed him in 1948 continued to do so, seeing his time in office as a personal affront.[144]

Scott vigorously defended his four years in office with an emotional farewell speech from the governor's office broadcast over statewide radio on December 30, 1952. In his "final report to the people," he discussed his achievements in detail. More than $10 million had been earned in interest after the investment of previously idle state funds. More than $331 million had been spent on permanent improvements—"greatly needed schools, hospitals and administration buildings." A school building program had been responsible for the addition of 8,000 new classrooms, 175 gymnasiums, and 350 new lunchrooms. His proudest achievement was the investment of over $430 million in highway construction and improvement and maintenance of the highway system and city streets, including more than twelve thousand miles of newly paved farm-to-city roads—"more roads [paved] in the last four years than any other state ever has in a like period." In addition, there were fourteen thousand miles of roads stabilized for all-weather use.

Scott cited unprecedented progress in the medical field—seventy-seven new and improved hospitals with 4,406 beds in seventy-three of the state's one hundred counties. He also announced that the state had improved care for the mentally ill, the elderly, and the physically handicapped. Industrial development resulted in 401 new plants, giving employment to forty-one thousand workers. He was also pleased with the increase in electricity and telephone availability around the state. He insisted that his program could not be measured by a dollar-and-cents yardstick. The Go Forward program, he said, "was conceived and built upon a foundation of human needs. Its mortar was the longing of human hearts for better things of life for themselves and their children."

Prior to the completion of his fifteen-minute talk, the governor struck back one last time at his adversaries. He recalled that, when he took office, there were fears that the state would embark on a spending spree that would bankrupt it. He had, however, proved "the falseness of these fears" by the fact that his successor would inherit a surplus in excess of $40 million and that all these accomplishments had been done with only one tax increase—

the one-cent gas tax voted in by the people. He praised all who helped him in his quest: public servants, his staff, the people who voted him into office, and, finally, the industrial leaders of the state, especially the telephone and electric companies.

At the end of his talk, his voice faltered and broke when Scott mentioned that he was nearing the "end of the row we have been plowing together for the past four years." After several moments he collected himself and wished everyone a happy new year.[145] The *News and Observer* said that both Governor Scott and the people of the state had a right to be proud of his achievements: "Together, they certainly have not got behind in their hauling."[146]

Scott devoted his last days in office to clearing out his desk and preparing to move back to Haw River. At Umstead's inauguration on January 8, 1953, he accompanied the governor-elect to Memorial Auditorium for his address. As the two men alighted from the car, Umstead looked wan, somber, and nervous, while Scott grinned and waved to onlookers. Umstead's speech, which seemed fairly conservative to most legislators, called for bond issues to expand public school building and improve mental hospitals. Scott thought it was a good speech: "He's got a good program. They ought to back him up on it."[147]

After an exhausting inaugural day, Governor Umstead reported to his office on January 9, 1953, but the chaos of organizing the office was so great that he got little accomplished. Tired and feeling ill, he retired early to the governor's mansion. That night he suffered a severe heart attack. Thus, on his very first day in office, he fell gravely ill, and that unexpected turn of events left the state in shock. After six weeks of convalescence, Umstead returned to his office for limited work, but he never fully recovered his health. He would die in office on November 7, 1954.[148]

Once the inaugural ceremony had ended, Scott was eager to return home. After receiving profuse thanks from the Umsteads for his courtesies during the transition, he and Miss Mary jumped into a new tan Ford given to him by friends and employees. A state trooper led them as far as the Wake County line. They continued on to Hawfields, happy to be home. Scott kidded that he would now "milk cows instead of the public." Shortly after arriving, the ex-governor was in his hunting clothes and out chasing rabbits: "I'm on relief now and I've got to get us some meat to eat."[149]

The departing governor, who had traveled 245,000 miles and given over nine hundred speeches during his four years in Raleigh, faced reporters one more time to discuss his tenure in office. When asked what his biggest

The inauguration of Scott's successor, William B. Umstead, January 8, 1953. Photograph by Edward J. McCauley, North Carolina Collection, University of North Carolina at Chapel Hill Library.

disappointment was, Scott remarked that many assumed it was the defeat of Frank Graham. It was not. He would choose Graham again if he had it to do over: "I gave the folks a chance. If they turned it down, I felt like I had done my part." His greatest disappointment—and frustration—was the number of folks who were in a position to help the Go Forward program and instead tried to block it. Still, the naysayers were now coming around and admitting that they were in error.

Scott's most important accomplishment was not just the new roads but the effect they had in strengthening rural church life. Reporters wanted to know the most important event of his four years in office: "Election night [in 1949] when the returns came in showing that the people of North Carolina saw eye to eye with me on the question of better schools and roads. That was the night the Go Forward program became a reality." His most unpleasant task was deciding the fate of men on Death Row. Another question concerned what criticism cut him the deepest. Scott said that in general criticism did not bother him but that the press "really did get under [his] skin" with complaints about the "resignations" of Rosser, Johnson, and Coltrane. Those resignations, he explained, whether voluntary or requested, had nothing to do with the 1952 political campaign and were long overdue. Scott's attempt to soften the harsh dissent over the firings was unconvincing. None of the resignations had been voluntary. Anyone who presumed that loyalty and politics did not figure into the decisions did not know Kerr Scott.

When asked what he would miss the most, the Squire of Haw River declared that he would miss the crowds: "I love people individually and collectively." However, he acknowledged that being away from them for a while would be a relief and would give him a chance to "shake the cobwebs out of [his] head and plan for the future." This statement and others indicated that he was out of office but not out of politics. He had made it perfectly clear that he did not plan to rust in retirement.[150]

The state's press had varied opinions about Kerr Scott's achievements as governor. Most newspapers praised his courage and his determination to serve the needs of the people but often complained about his methods and judgment. The *Durham Morning Herald* noted that he had presided over "four of the most remembered, stormy and unpredictable years this state had ever seen" and pointed out that there certainly was no lukewarm feeling about the man—it was either red hot or icy cold. The paper praised his work with schools, roads, and health care but thought he had

Ex-governor Scott and Miss Mary stopped to have lunch on the way out of town after four years in Raleigh. January 8, 1953. Photograph by Edward J. McCauley, North Carolina Collection, University of North Carolina at Chapel Hill Library.

been too stubborn and tactless in achieving his goals. His strong adherence to loyalty led him to take ruthless action against those who stepped out of line, actions that cost him precious prestige and increased opposition to his programs.[151] The *Progressive Farmer,* which heaped praise on Scott for his great improvements in the rural areas of the state, also took him to task for too often acting on his own impulses and consulting too few advisers—he simply decided to go ahead and get the job done, and to hell with the critics.[152]

The *Raleigh Times,* like many papers, gave a mixed review. It applauded the unprecedented progress in the state but chastised him for his rough, intemperate approach to individuals and for driving a wedge between urban and rural areas.[153] The *Raleigh News and Observer,* an advocate and stalwart defender of Scott for most of his term in office, lauded him for providing wider representation on state boards for blacks, women, and farmers. It welcomed his "refreshing candor" and "frankness in speech" as many citizens had become weary of political platitudes.[154] Down east, the *Southport Pilot* believed that Scott left behind a record that would stamp him "as one of our great leaders" and concluded that, if the state had been governed by a stand-pat conservative over the past four years instead of the aggressive Scott, it would have been "well-nigh fatal."[155] The most effusive praise came from the *Winston-Salem Journal.* While admitting that Scott was stormy, tactless, and impulsive, the daily declaimed that those faults attested "to the warm, human qualities of the man" and that "some of them in a sense were virtues": "Above all his mistakes, Kerr Scott stands out as a man of sincerity, stout courage and strong . . . patriotism." He also left a record of four full years of remarkable state accomplishments.[156] John Marshall, who served as Scott's private secretary and knew him as well as anyone, acknowledged that his unorthodox methods and manners made him one of the most controversial figures in state history, but he thought that historians "would record what he did, not how he did it."[157]

To be sure, Scott did not accomplish all he hoped for as governor. He never obtained all he wanted for labor and the environment, but, considering the adamant and hard-fought opposition to his programs, he achieved more than anyone thought possible. Very few observers thought a farmer from Hawfields could change the history of the state.

After Scott returned to his farm, speculation swirled about his political future. When he hinted that he would focus not on the past but on the future, most pundits took that to mean a challenge to Senator Willis Smith.

Capus Waynick knew him well: "No one knows how long you will resist the lure of further campaigning. I am not sure you will be content to stay out of public service."[158] Waynick was prescient. Kerr Scott could not endure life out of the political arena for long. One year later he announced his candidacy for the US Senate.

9

The Third Primary, 1954

For the first six months after leaving office, Scott the private citizen worked on his dairy farm and tried to catch up on farm work that had been delayed while he presided over the state's business. He generally stayed out of the public eye except for one press conference on January 24, 1953. Clad in overalls, a work shirt, and brogans, the ex-governor talked mainly about racial issues. He considered broadened racial representation on state boards as part of his mandate when elected in 1948 and thought his appointment of Dr. Harold Trigg and his selection of Negroes to serve on the boards of the five colleges an important milestone.[1]

Scott kept a low profile, but according to Lauch Faircloth and others he had already decided to run against Willis Smith in 1954. Still bitter over Graham's defeat in 1950, he wanted to beat the man who had beaten Graham.[2] In the meantime, he wanted to maintain some contact with his constituency. Therefore, beginning in February 1953, he arranged to have his own radio show, which was to be carried by fifty-five North Carolina stations. Broadcasting from his home in Hawfields, he was on the air three times a week. In a typical broadcast on March 1, 1953, he discussed foreign affairs and national news and talked about the effect his Go Forward programs, especially roads, had on the state. He spent time telling stories, jokes, and homilies to a mostly rural audience.[3] He continued these broadcasts until January 1954.

On June 26, 1953, citizens of the state learned of the sudden death of Senator Willis Smith—the third US senator from North Carolina to pass away in the past ten years. Senator Smith had been on an exhausting three-week speaking tour, making twenty-four talks in twenty days. On returning to Washington, he suffered a severe heart attack. Taken to Bethesda Naval Hospital in Maryland, he passed away after a second heart attack two days later. Vice-President Richard Nixon attended Smith's funeral, as did the ever gracious Frank Graham.

After leaving office, Scott returned to his Haw River farm, put up his tuxedo, and dressed to go hunting. He claimed that he was happy to be out of the public eye, but his political career was not over as he was already planning to run for the US Senate in 1954. Photograph by Edward J. McCauley, North Carolina Collection, University of North Carolina at Chapel Hill, Library.

Governor Umstead, who had only recently returned to work following his heart attack, now faced the grave responsibility of choosing a successor to Smith. Ed Rankin, Umstead's secretary, said that the selection of a replacement for a deceased US senator "was about as important a decision as a governor will ever make." Rankin recalled that the governor had to consider not only politics but also the future of the country.[4] As soon as Smith's funeral concluded, vigorous campaigns were mounted on behalf of several hopefuls—L. Y. "Stag" Ballentine, John D. Larkins, Fred Royster, Congressman Harold Cooley, and others. Letters, telegrams, phone calls, and delegations flooded into the governor's office. Umstead ignored the tumult and went quietly and thoroughly about the process of selecting Smith's replacement.

Umstead conferred daily with many of his friends and associates, but he confided in no one. He faced a difficult choice as his appointee would have to defend his seat in less than a year, and, if he picked someone the voters rejected, it would diminish his prestige and influence for the remainder of his term. Since Senator Clyde Hoey was from the west, Umstead promised to name an easterner to the post. While the governor deliberated, much of the press speculation was not so much about the possible appointee as about the candidates who would oppose him. Heading the list of potential challengers was Kerr Scott, who had been regarded "as an almost certain opponent of Smith."

Umstead astonished everyone when he picked Alton Lennon, an obscure two-term state senator from Wilmington. Lennon's name had never surfaced as a serious candidate, nor had he promoted his own candidacy. Some of the local cognoscenti conjectured that Royster, Cooley, and Larkins had consumed each other in the fierceness of their campaigns. Tired of all the politicking, like Scott with Graham, Umstead chose someone from outside the inner circle of North Carolina politics. He probably chose Lennon because he was an unknown, had no record to defend, and, thus, would have few enemies. Although Lennon had no statewide name recognition, Umstead, who had just won office with the help of the machine, believed that he had sufficient popularity and political strength to carry a dark horse like Lennon across the finish line. His key consideration was to choose someone who could keep Kerr Scott out of the US Senate.

In many ways Lennon was a sound pick. He was young (forty-six), handsome, personable, and willing to mount a vigorous campaign. He was close to the governor, having worked on Umstead's 1948 US Senate campaign, had aided Umstead when he ran for governor in 1952, and had toiled for

Willis Smith in 1950. He had been one of the "hold-the-line" group in the state legislature and earned Umstead's approval by helping stymie much of Scott's legislative program. The governor confided that he selected Lennon because he knew that he would make a good senator and was pleased that "a young man with youth and vigor" would represent the state: "I am proud of my appointee."[5] Terry Sanford thought that the choice of Lennon was a clever move. With such a total unknown, the contest would, in reality, be Umstead and the machine versus Kerr Scott.[6]

In the election of 1954, Lennon would have the advantage of incumbency, but he would also have to overcome the historic record of previous gubernatorial appointees to the Senate. Cameron Morrison lost to Bob Reynolds in 1932, Mel Broughton defeated Umstead in 1948, and Willis Smith edged out Frank Graham in 1950. Some observers thought the choice of Lennon misguided and would open the way for Scott to win the Democratic primary. The Raleigh Times believed that Lennon would be a far less formidable candidate than Willis Smith would have been.[7] The Transylvania Times concluded that Lennon was a good choice and that, while Scott might be a candidate, he would not be successful. He no longer had a machine, had lost when backing Graham and Olive, and had "made a lot of folks mad with uncalled for statements."[8] B. Everett Jordan, still estranged from Scott, chimed in that he did not know whether Scott would run but that Lennon "would be a good, hard campaigner."[9]

Not long after Lennon took office, Scott began to take soundings around the state as to whether he should run. He wrote Capus Waynick: "Am toying with the idea of running for the Senate. . . . It would be a hard race." Waynick was not surprised: "I fancy you are under considerable pressure to run from those in the party who hope for a real contest over this nomination." As he did in 1948, Scott still vacillated: "I am receiving much encouragement for running for the Senate, but have made no definite decision so far."[10]

One of those urging Scott to run was Terry Sanford, who suggested that he set up a campaign committee in the fall to accept contributions. That decision, continued Sanford, would not require him to make a formal announcement of his candidacy, but it would allow him to raise some funds while sampling sentiment around the state.[11] Encouraged by Ralph Scott, Sanford dropped by Haw River to discuss politics with the Squire and encouraged him to run.

Kerr Scott wanted to meet with Sanford because his brother Ralph, as well as Capus Waynick and Frank Graham, had suggested that Sanford would be a good campaign manager. Sanford, an ambitious, intelligent young politician, had been president of the Young Democrats, had close ties with the Jaycees around the state, and had good contacts with graduates of the University of North Carolina. As a younger man, he could give Scott access to young professionals in the urban areas of the state—a distinct Scott weakness. The two men were unlikely bedfellows, but Scott imagined that his rough-hewn Branchhead Boys could ally with Sanford's urban professionals on behalf of the same kind of progressive reforms that he had championed as governor. If the merger took place, it might be formidable enough to defeat the machine one more time.

Initially, Scott was somewhat reluctant to trust his fortunes to a man inexperienced in running a political campaign. If offered the job, Sanford would have to think long and hard about taking it. He knew about Scott's propensity to be his own man, to speak his mind regardless of the circumstances, and wondered whether he would be able to control such a loose cannon. He knew that to join Scott would be to buck the dominant faction in state politics and that, if Scott lost, it might undermine Sanford's own political future.

Terry Sanford, however, wanted to be governor one day and knew that taking the post would give him a great opportunity to meet people all over the state and learn how to run a statewide campaign. He finally accepted the post, but on the condition that Scott agree to curb his tongue and speak from material written by Sanford. Scott agreed, and, knowing that taking on a US Senate campaign was a reckless step, Sanford accepted the challenge: "Sometimes it is good for the soul to be reckless and I wanted to see Kerr Scott representing North Carolina in Washington."[12] It turned out to be a wise choice for both men.

Before making a final determination about entering the race, Scott decided to conduct a survey of state voters, much as he had done in 1948. The ex-governor wanted to see whether there would be enough support, chiefly financial, from around the state. He wrote countless cards and letters to potential donors, and this effort paid off—as early as August 1953 Scott reported contributions coming in from all sections of the state.[13]

Some of Scott's entreaties, however, fell on deaf ears. He wrote former governor R. Gregg Cherry and asked for his help in the campaign. However, even though Cherry "felt kindly" toward anything Scott did, he would not be able to help in the race because of his "personal relations and obligations to Governor Umstead."[14] A letter to state senator John D. Larkins, who had fought Scott in the legislature, resulted in a similar response.[15] One letter did get a favorable reply. Scott penned an epistle to Harry Truman announcing that "things look very encouraging toward my getting in the Senate race, with the exception of finances," and requested Truman's help. Truman informed Scott that he would do anything in the world to help Scott in his race. However: "It will have to be done on the quiet because it will not be proper for me to take any part in a primary fight in any of the states but there are a lot of things I can do that will be helpful to you."[16] In similar letters to friends throughout the state, the ex-governor indicated that the outlook seemed favorable for his entering the contest.[17]

At Terry Sanford's suggestion, Scott took several exploratory trips to key counties, sixty-eight in all, in order to determine his level of support. He sent Sanford a detailed report on each visit. In Mt. Airy Scott divulged that, while in 1948 75 percent of the Democrats were against him, now 60 percent were for him. In Alamance he reported that some 150 people urged him to get into the race and that they were "more enthusiastic than in 1948."[18]

As word spread about his potential candidacy, Scott began to pick up backers. Writing to the editor of the *Southport Pilot,* one admirer observed that, if Scott did run, "he will get strong support from the people of southeastern North Carolina."[19] Another backer notified Scott that, if he committed to the race, he could "carry Avery County by a big majority."[20] A county agent in Burnsville said that Scott would get great support there as his "efforts to improve the state, especially the schools, health, and local programs are still fresh in the minds of the public."[21]

Scott had decided to take on Lennon but stayed below the radar as he did not want to announce too soon. Nonetheless, political experts knew that he was already running hard. The columnist Lynn Nisbet concluded that Scott's surveys had ended and the race was on. He revealed that Scott had gotten such gratifying support and so many pledges of money "that he cannot afford not to run."[22] Scott told one audience that, if he did run, he would run "like a rabbit with six hounds on his tail."[23]

Nisbet surmised that the Scott-Lennon race would be interesting in several ways. For the first time, Scott would be running "for" something rather than against "something"—that is, the machine. Nisbet reckoned that Lennon started out at a disadvantage as he had no experience in statewide campaigning, was not well-known, and would have to spend much of his time in Washington, DC, attending to Senate business. On the other hand, he had the support of Governor Umstead, the remnants of the Shelby dynasty, and the business community and had no record for Scott to attack. Scott, of course, did have a record, a very controversial one at that, and he would have to defend his time in the governor's mansion. Nisbet saw Scott as the "liberal" candidate who would gain traction with the followers of Frank Graham and Jonathan Daniels. Lennon was the "conservative" candidate, the darling of the right wing.[24]

Scott had promised a decision on entering the race by February, and, as that date approached, it became obvious to the general public that he would announce. Some voters who had opposed him in the past did not want to be left out this time. One old-timer said: "I let the critter get by me twice, but this time around I'm latching on early and riding him clear to the barn." Lennon tried to stem Scott's momentum by choosing John Rodman, a distinguished and influential former legislator, as his campaign manager. Governor Umstead chimed in by promising that he would not pressure state employees to back Lennon. However: "Don't be surprised if they do, in wholesale, all-out fashion."[25]

The state now waited for Scott's pronouncement. Scott ended his radio show, "the last ringing of the old farm bell for this series of broadcasts from my Hawfields farm house," by telling his audience that he would run for the US Senate. He reminded his listeners that when he left the governor's office, he told the public that he would not hibernate and would continue to be interested in critical issues. His travels throughout the state and numerous letters convinced him that he should take up the responsibility of public office once again. He revealed that in his peregrinations he found unrest in the state—housewives worried about rising prices, farmers concerned over falling prices for their goods, laboring people fearful of layoffs, and small business owners unsure about the future. He assured his listeners that his convictions and experience would serve them well in Washington, and he promised to carry his quest into all sections of the state.[26] Ben Roney, who knew the political Scott better than anyone, said that Scott chose to run because of the outpouring of support, because he had always been against the machine, and because he feared that Umstead and the conservatives would weaken his programs. He was still very angry about Graham's defeat and wanted revenge.[27]

The official announcement came on February 6, 1954, six years to the day after Scott signified that he would be a candidate for governor. In the sitting room of his farmhouse the former governor began by commenting: "The people of North Carolina are well aware of the fact that I do not know how to act coy, or disinterested." He asked the citizens of the state to support him on the basis of his record and his desire to help people achieve a more wholesome life. He proclaimed that the state had become richer and more productive under his leadership. Still: "We must not lose ground we have gained. We have barely scratched the surface of our tremendous natural resources and our Tar Heel common sense." He promised, as if anyone doubted it, that he would speak his convictions freely. In the press conference that followed the announcement, he chewed on his ever-present cigar and joyfully responded to every query from the press. He realized that this would be a difficult race and that he had not yet raised sufficient funds, but he had to have faith that people would provide as the campaign progressed. Not wanting to get into a controversy at the outset, he pointedly refused to explain his position on any national or international issue he might face as a senator.[28]

The following day, newspaper editorials weighed in on the significance of the race. The *Greensboro Daily News* saw the contest as being fought along classic liberal-conservative lines and felt that the battle would determine which faction would control the Democratic Party in North Carolina. It saw a resurgent conservative tide in the nation and state since 1950, but Scott entered the contest as the favorite because his "relentless energy, his sense of humor, his candor and homespun qualities give him a tremendous appeal to the average voter." Nonetheless, Lennon would give him a real race.[29] The *Newton Observer*, a small-town paper, asserted that Scott was the better bet because of his impressive record as governor and because he had made more friends in the state than any other state executive.[30] Most state newspaper editors believed that Scott would win because of his popularity with the little man and the fact that the state had never elected an appointed senator. Those who backed Lennon concluded that Scott had 90 percent of his vote at the start but that the youthful, energetic Lennon would gain votes as the campaign progressed and raise more money than Scott.[31]

On February 9, Scott made Sanford's selection as his campaign manager official. Sanford began his job by promising that the Senate race would be "one of the cleanest campaigns ever conducted in North Carolina": "We intend to be frank and candid all the way through this campaign." He explained that Scott would run his race on the code adopted by the Young Democratic Club, which made it unethical to appeal "to racial, religious or other prejudice."[32] As Sanford well knew, a clean fight would benefit Scott as the ex-governor had a most controversial record to defend. Committing

Terry Sanford, Scott's campaign manager and a future governor of North Caro-lina, introduces Scott at a campaign rally in 1954. Courtesy of the State Archives of North Carolina, Raleigh.

to a nondisputatious conflict might help him restrain his temper. If Sanford could persuade him to ignore some of the charges that would be forthcom-ing, it would improve his chances of winning.

The conflict began on a light note. The *Raleigh News and Observer* described the contest as between Lennon, the "promising political Gala-had," and the grizzled veteran of numerous political wars.[33] Although both sides had promised no back-biting and Scott had specifically said that he "would not trade rabbit punches," the truce did not last long. Less than a week after Scott's commitment to the race, Lennon's supporters were cir-culating rumors that Scott had heart problems. Scott's handlers reminded the voters that he was "as chipper as any bull yearling snorting about an Alamance dairy farm."[34] Lennon next trashed Scott's record as governor, especially his ruthless firing of those who refused to back Judge Olive. As planned, Scott did not respond.[35] When asked by a young reporter whether he expected Lennon to use the race-baiting that had helped defeat Graham in 1950, Scott smiled and responded: "I'll take care of it son. I'm not as good a Christian as Frank Graham."[36]

An experienced campaigner, Scott knew that the contest "would be a tough fight"[37] and immediately tasked Sanford with arranging a speaking schedule and organizing the key workers in the campaign.[38] He trusted Sanford's judgment and generally followed his instructions: "He gave me a program and I would go." While Scott was a good off-the-cuff speaker, in the 1954 race Sanford and Ben Roney wrote almost all his formal speeches in an attempt to control what he would say. Roy Wilder recalled that, although Scott's staff tried to make him stick to a script, he would slip the reins now and then.[39]

Sanford recognized that during Scott's time as governor there had been too much antiurban rhetoric and that that had to change. The party conservatives that Scott routed in 1948 were determined to thwart him in 1954 and would take advantage of the animosity many urban leaders harbored against him for favoring rural interests. As Bill Friday recalled, the remainder of the old Shelby machine had reorganized with new leadership and new money and had begun working hard for Lennon. Sanford suspected that Scott's "rag-tag branch head organization, while forceful, was in the minority" and that the campaign had to appeal to businessmen and younger voters in order to win.[40]

Lennon's headquarters, momentarily ignoring Scott, concentrated on fund-raising, with some success. Although he was the state party chairman, B. Everett Jordan worked behind the scenes for Lennon and supplied $5,000 in cash. Lennon also received $5,000 from Leroy Martin, the president of Wachovia Bank and a longtime Scott opponent. J. Spencer Love, the head of Burlington Industries, thought it was in Burlington's and the state's best interests to have Lennon continue in office: "I see Scott as another Cole Blease or Tom Heflin if he ever gets in the Senate."[41]

Scott loved being back on the stump, pressing the flesh and kissing babies. He focused on his base, spending much of his time jawing with "good ole boys" in small-town courthouses, in local diners, on farms, and in country stores. He was a good listener, enjoyed telling stories, and exuded charm and good fellowship. He had a good instinct for people and still thought that the poor in the state continued to be oppressed. He made very few formal speeches, and those presentations he did make were tightly scripted and closely monitored. In his travels he concentrated on raising money and encouraging the local workers to get out the vote. Sanford advised him to avoid any "high falluting language," to keep things on a North Carolina level and not worry too much about foreign affairs.[42]

Always on the lookout for good publicity, Scott regaled an audience in Kinston about the time he walked twenty-one miles over an unpaved road from Kinston to Hargett's store to attend a cattle sale. He bragged that he had made the trip in six hours. The story evoked quite a favorable response, so he impetuously volunteered to give a registered bull calf to anyone who could beat his time. His staff set up a walking date for anyone who accepted the challenge. W. M. Pence, a retired seventy-one-year-old mail carrier, wrote Scott that he "would walk twenty-one miles in five hours and vote for you to boot."[43]

On the designated day, thirty-six walkers made the trip in under six hours.[44] A cartoon appeared the next day in the *Greensboro Daily News* with Scott standing next to a bull festooned with two signs: "Trot with Scott" and "Go Far with Kerr." A bystander, holding a newspaper with the headline that Scott was giving away thirty-six young bulls, asked: "Any danger of running out of bull, Squire?" The paper did not know how much the bull calves cost Scott. Nevertheless: "The publicity they garnered couldn't be purchased for ten times that amount." The *News* thought that the gimmick was a lot of bull but that it had that down-home touch.[45] Scott's willingness to take part in such a hokey stunt underscored his need to retain his rural followers. He was trying to find that sweet spot between his populist constituents and the growing modern, urban, middle class in the state.

In early May, milking the event for all it was worth, Scott presented official certificates to all who participated in the walk, making them associate members of the Athletic Order of the Survivors of the Great Bull Calf Walk. The certificates noted that the participants had demonstrated "certain admirable qualities, those including good humor, alertness, and ability to stay in the fight": "This then certifies that the bearer henceforth will be known as one who has caught up on his hauling and doesn't drag his feet."[46] While the walk garnered some attention in rural circles and might have helped Scott with farmers, it did not affect the race.

Scott made his campaign headquarters at the Carolina Hotel, a bit run down and several blocks from the Sir Walter, the more upscale hotel used by Lennon. By electing to use the Carolina, he expressed his estrangement from the established Democratic machine that was organizing Lennon's race.[47]

As soon as Sanford established headquarters, he homed in on his major goal for the next three months—fund-raising. His efforts never ceased. He wrote everyone he could think of, making it clear that the campaign was "in urgent need of funds."[48]

Remembering the importance of the women's vote in 1948, Sanford set up the Women's Division of the Scott campaign. He told a gathering of the group that their efforts would be important because Scott worked for those aspects of progress in which women were interested, that is, schools and health care. He asked them to help raise money, to be vigilant in squelching false rumors, and to get people to the polls.[49]

Sanford also began distributing flyers and a booklet, "Kerr Scott: Tar Heel Builder," to county managers. The booklet asserted that people knew what Scott could do for them in the Senate because "they REMEMBERED what he did as governor." Scott would be "the fighting friend" needed by independent businesses. The booklet listed the achievements of the Go Forward program and reminded voters that Governor Scott appointed the first woman judge and would continue to recognize women on a national level.

Much of the "Tar Heel Builder" covered Scott's early life, his work for the church, his family, and his public service. The propaganda bulletin ended with a reminder that under his leadership the state became better educated and more prosperous and that Scott would continue to be a "builder of better things."[50] As March ended, the ex-governor claimed that reports from various parts of the state were most favorable to his chances. He added a word of caution: "It sometimes sounds too good and we are constantly reminding our friends to be on guard. You know, it doesn't do to take chances in a race like this."[51]

His advisers thought Scott should make some comments on national affairs, so he launched into an attack on "certain committees" in the legislative branch of the federal government for "unwise, unwarranted and unfair" assaults on American freedom. He never mentioned Joe McCarthy by name, but he referred to the investigative subcommittee chaired by the senator from Wisconsin. McCarthy, noted for his arrogance, false accusations, and lack of facts, bludgeoned and intimidated anyone who questioned his motives or methods.[52] Scott emphasized that "these committees" had, in a vicious and unbridled way, abused the legitimate investigative functions of Congress. A one-man bully committee did not have "a right to brow-beat and debase witnesses." The country was moving in the direction of a police state that violated individual freedoms. If this disease were to go unchecked, Scott feared, America would "crumble in a chaos of fear, suspicion and distrust."[53] Scott mailed a copy of the speech to Harry Truman. Truman liked it and reminded Scott that he was in his corner come hell or high water: "But be sure not to let me cost you any votes."[54]

Well aware that he had started the contest far behind Scott, Lennon made a series of allegations in an attempt to undermine Scott's integrity and credibility. John Rodman, Lennon's campaign manager, cited Scott for paying only $100 in federal income taxes in 1952 owing to a reported operating loss on his farm of $15,000–$16,000. Rodman did not have the actual tax returns but knew the figures were accurate. He did not accuse Scott of doing anything dishonest but noted that the $12,685 the state paid Scott for road right-of-way was income and should have been reported. Scott's tax lawyers concluded that the money was not income and not reportable. Scott, in one of the few times he reacted to his opponent, said that, if his tax returns were in error, then the Internal Revenue Service could challenge them. They had not done so. He refused to give out his tax returns, saying it was nobody's business. The issue backfired on Lennon when he made his tax returns public and revealed that he had earned only $6,000 during the previous year. A radio personality commented that, if Lennon had earned only $6,000, he could not be much of a lawyer.[55]

Lennon tossed out a few more accusations, hoping one of them would stick. He upbraided Scott for allocating $750,000 in road money to Alamance County even though Scott had rescinded that order. He also criticized him for accepting an honorarium while making speeches at state institutions and using political pressure to raise the appraisal on the right-of-way on his farm. A Winston-Salem reporter checked and determined that the charges were unproven except for Scott's accepting $75 to speak at East Carolina Teacher's College.[56] If this was the best that Lennon had to offer, he would make no inroads on Scott's lead. Lennon's failure to gain much traction with these accusations may have led his campaign staff to resort to more drastic measures in the waning days of the contest.

Sanford never took his focus off the main issue—more money. In a letter to a labor leader, he complained that Scott could "lose this campaign for a lack of funds."[57] As in 1948, Scott received political support and funds from the North Carolina State Federation of Labor[58] but kept these contacts and contributions from the public. Sanford and Scott had a similar clandestine plan regarding minorities. They worked hard to get the black vote but did not want that information leaked. A close look at Sanford's list of workers in various counties included, for example, fifty-nine black workers in Pitt County and thirteen Lumbee supporters in Robeson County.[59] Thomas Kluttz, a black funeral director in Wadesboro, assured Scott of his admiration and promised him "the support of the colored voters of Anson County."[60]

When local donations began to fall off, Sanford pursued major donors outside the state. He asked Kenneth C. Royall to contact wealthy Democrats in New York. Royall managed to gain funds from several wealthy contributors, but Scott wrote Royall in May citing a "great need" for additional contributions.[61] Sanford also enlisted Jonathan Daniels to use his numerous contacts to increase giving, and Daniels had some success with wealthy benefactors in New York.[62] Frank Graham, who was then making a good salary at the United Nations, sent Terry Sanford two checks for $300 each and then mailed in more checks later. Deciding that Dr. Graham had done enough, Sanford tore up four or five of the checks.[63]

Financial problems plagued the Scott campaign to the end. Just days before the vote, Scott complained about the ongoing struggle to get enough money to run the race properly: "And we are in a very shaky condition for the last few days."[64] One reason the Scott camp needed cash was because, in a buying spree over the period May 17–28, it had purchased extensive radio and television time. The cost was $17,396.25, and Sanford had to pay the bills, or the programs would not be aired.[65]

Although their candidate was well-known throughout the state, Scott's handlers continued to run a grassroots crusade. They distributed a newspaper, "The Tar Heel Senator," advancing the view that, as senator, Scott would help the whole nation go forward and would "stand straight" with no mudslinging or McCarthyism. To attract new voters, the campaign sponsored "The Man from Haw River," a fifteen-minute documentary on Scott's life. The brain trust wanted to expound on his record as governor but also to let the people know just what kind of man he was. The film used vignettes of Scott at home, with his family, and at work. The publicity director recalled: "[There] was no fancy oratory, no damning of the opposition, no pledges of this vote or that promise. It was simply the man as he was and is. As a result, it was a drastic departure from the usual campaign pitch and we feel it was as successful as it was different."[66]

Scott had, in early April, been getting "mighty good reports" about campaign progress,[67] but some of his scouts had discovered "entirely too much Lennon support to please them."[68] Several benefactors worried that Scott's failure to attack Lennon was costing him votes, enabling Lennon to gain ground. W. A. Aldridge, a loyal supporter, advised Sanford and Scott "to take the white gloves off" and "start smacking this boy around a little"; otherwise, Scott might lose.[69] Scott and Sanford understood that Lennon had indeed closed the gap but decided not to change their strategy.

Sensing a popular surge to his banner, Lennon increased newspaper ads and stepped up his harassment of Scott. One ad wanted to "Ban Scottism from North Carolina." The message defined *Scottism* as "using public service for personal gain." The ad listed newspaper articles from Scott's time as governor when he attacked urban dwellers, civic clubs, and the Chamber of Commerce for not helping farmers enough or for not living up to their responsibilities: "It is wrong to put town against country, country against town and class against class." North Carolina needed unity, not prejudice, and Lennon wanted to "weld the people together, not divide them."[70] Other ads continued to blast Scott for feathering his own nest and getting "$312,500 worth of secondary roads for his 2,300 acre plantation": "Lennon Believes Public Office is a Public Trust."[71]

When reporters asked about the status of the Korean War, Scott deferred the question, admitting that he had not had time to keep up with foreign policy issues, venturing the view that Korea "was a long way from Haw River." Lennon jumped all over the ex-governor for that statement, expressing shock at Scott's indifference to and lack of knowledge about foreign affairs. Another ad presented Lennon as a statesman who could see beyond his own neighborhood and warned Scott that Korea "was nearer than you think."[72]

In an attempt to humanize Lennon, his headquarters printed up several leaflets showing him with his wife and children, emphasizing his success as a lawyer, his public service, and his commitment to the church. The ad presented him as a man who "keeps his feet on the ground, [and] is known for his level thinking."[73]

The month of May would see a relatively peaceful contest evolve into a hard-fought, cutthroat fight, loser leave town. Numerous significant events, such as the death of Senator Hoey and the *Brown v. Board of Education* decision, would change the focus of the contest and ratchet the political rhetoric to full volume. What began as a mild-mannered contest now became an emotional conflict.

Trying to undermine "the myth of Scott inevitability," Lennon continued to snipe at the ex-governor on a variety of issues. He again questioned his personal integrity, accusing him of working more for himself than for his constituents. He pictured Scott as a dangerous free spender and alleged

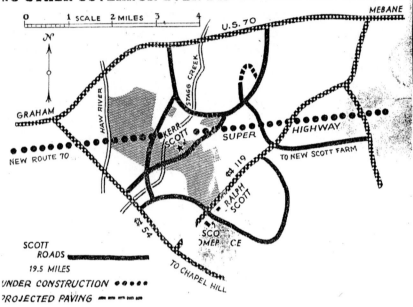

SCOTTISM: USING PUBLIC OFFICE FOR PERSONAL GAIN

NO OTHER GOVERNOR EVER DID SO WELL FOR HIMSELF

Map of Kerr Scott Plantation (shaded areas) and 19½ Mile Network of Paved Roads.

$312,500 WORTH OF SECONDARY ROADS

Based on average cost of $16,023 per mile on five nearby Alamance road projects.

This authentic map shows the new paved roads serving the "model" Kerr Scott plantation and its 17 tenant families, plus some relatives. . . . Dotted line going through 2,300-acre plantation is route of new super highway for which Scott got $12,658 in right-of-way money. . . . This he used to buy a new 480-acre farm in Orange County and---by golly---he's even got a paved road headed out to his new estate!

LENNON BELIEVES PUBLIC OFFICE IS A PUBLIC TRUST

PLEASE HAND THIS LEAFLET TO A FRIEND WHEN YOU HAVE FINISHED WITH IT.

(over)

Ad paid for by the Alton Lennon forces in the 1954 Senate race warning voters about "Scottism." Lennon accused Scott of using his office for personal gain. John Harden Papers, Southern Historical Collection, University of North Carolina at Chapel Hill.

that his road program showed signs of "wasteful haste" as some of the roads had been poorly built and were already crumbling.[74] Circulars incessantly reminded voters that, when governor, Scott received $312,500 worth of secondary roads on his "plantation." The ad helpfully provided a map to delineate exactly where the new roads had been built.[75]

A follow-up ad featured a cartoon with the headline: "Folks are getting tired of no answer to why Scott got all the extra roads while many of us are still in the mud." The cartoon had Scott replying: "Tell 'em nothing. What they don't know won't hurt them. After all, we can't deny most of it so why rock the boat? By the way, keep that sleek Cadillac under the shed until after May 28."[76] Yet another shot at Scott combined the charges on the roads with his lack of knowledge of foreign affairs. The cartoon had him smoking a cigar sitting on a bag of money worth $12,658 and saying that Korea was a long way from Haw River. A citizen said: "Ain't Washington a long way from Haw River?" Lennon commented that peace or destruction in the world depended on decisions made in the Senate and that he, implying that Scott did not, hoped to have the wisdom to "chart the proper course for our country and all mankind."[77]

Scott refused to bite. The *Durham Morning Herald* described "the former buzz saw of North Carolina politics" as having had his teeth honed. The man who had always applied the needle relentlessly and effectively was no longer the blunt, bare-knuckle fighter people expected. Scott, reported the paper, had been controlled by careful planning and had generally refused to get into a dogfight with Lennon. Sanford and other advisers thought that the state had had enough of the political brawling that characterized the 1950 Smith-Graham race.

Scott shrugged off Lennon's public demands that he take a position on certain issues or provide copies of his tax returns with an abrupt "no comment." He simply ignored the charges, "leaving Lennon punching vigorously at thin air." For the most part, Scott kept to his promise to run a fair, clean campaign. He got angry when "the other side" violated the code of ethics by sending an intern to Duke Hospital to check his medical records, but he did not attack Lennon. He tried to stay away from the controversial issues in the state by subtly focusing on a few national issues: advocating 90 percent parity for farmers and a more liberal farm loan program and attacking congressional witch hunts in Washington.[78] The *Greensboro Daily News* pointed out Lennon's dilemma with a cartoon showing Lennon as a bullfighter with a red flag trying to coax Scott into reacting to his charges. The ad pictured

Scott had faltered badly in a discussion of foreign policy and had dismissed the war in Korea and problems in Indo-China as a "long way from Haw River." An observer noted: "Ain't Washington sorta far from Haw River, too?" At the bottom of the ad, Senator Lennon explained that he was deeply concerned about the international situation and that the future of the world would depend on wise decisions made by the US Senate. Note that Scott sits in the middle of various paved roads near his Haw River home with a bag of money worth $12,658—the money paid to him for the right-of-way to his property. John Harden Papers, Southern Historical Collection, University of North Carolina at Chapel Hill.

"Aw, Come On Bull—Be Reasonable!"

Cartoon from the 1954 Senate race shows Scott as a reluctant bull who adheres to his strategy in the race and refuses to get into any arguments with Alton Lennon. John Harden Papers, Southern Historical Collection, University of North Carolina at Chapel Hill.

the relaxed ex-governor as a bull smoking a cigar and smelling a flower while in repose. Lennon pleaded: "Aw, come on bull—be reasonable."[79]

Constantly chomping at the bit, the former governor finally hit back in a radio speech the day before the vote. He asserted that he had been the target of a "vicious and desperate attack" of the McCarthy type by a "little group of selfish men" who "not only have made false charges" but "have carefully hidden facts." He answered charges of income tax impropriety by saying that his tax returns had been "gone over with a fine tooth comb" by the government and found in order.[80] Scott told other audiences that he had run a positive race and was outraged by attacks "that are out of the realm of politics and political campaigns."[81] Lennon's accusations had been mild compared with previous state campaigns. That was about to change.

During the final month of the race, Scott's handlers tried to accentuate the positive: "He was a great fighting governor—he'll be an even greater fighting Senator!" The testimonials praised Scott as a man of courage and vision who knew how to make the right decisions. Over and over they listed Scott's accomplishments as governor, all achieved without any tax increase.[82] In an attempt to preclude a potential racist attack, Scott reaffirmed his belief that the best school system for North Carolina was the equal, but separate, system, and he opposed white and Negro children going to school together.[83]

Perhaps the best way to understand the Lennon headquarters thinking and strategy was by examining a series of confidential memos prepared by C. A. Upchurch Jr. and sent out to all Lennon county managers and campaign workers. Upchurch used the May 10 letter to keep followers updated on events and provide talking points. Upchurch enthusiastically reported a decided swing to Lennon and predicted victory on May 28. Upchurch, who had worked for Graham in the 1950 campaign, now turned on Scott and called him a "selfish, grasping politician" who had used a machine built on "political favors and road deals" to line his own pockets. He urged workers to make a fuss about Scott's unwillingness to release his tax returns. Scott had said his record was an "open book," but he ducked the issue because "THERE ARE THINGS IN THE BOOK THAT KERR SCOTT WOULDN'T DARE LET THE PEOPLE SEE."

Upchurch also decided to take Scott to task about his military record. In a recent speech, Scott said that "he fought" in World War I and that he therefore knew something about the horrors of war. Lennon headquarters used official documents to demonstrate that Scott was inducted into the army on September 7, 1918, and discharged on November 30, 1918, after "a grand total of eighty-four days in service"—all of the time spent at Camp Taylor, Louisville, Kentucky, "where he learned about the horrors of war": "If he earned any battle stars he must have got mixed up in a Kentucky feud." In one respect, continued Upchurch, "he was a veteran. A veteran of thirty years at the public trough. It was time for him to fade away like other old soldiers."[84] The World War I accusation did not help Lennon as he was forced to explain his own World War II 2-A classification, which enabled him to escape the draft. Lennon denied avoiding service, stating that he had registered but had not been called.[85] Scott did not let this explanation pass unremarked since Lennon had questioned Scott's patriotism. He pointed out that, while he had worn a military uniform, Lennon never had. He accused his opponent of cravenly using several strategies to avoid having to take a Draft Board physical exam.[86]

The Lennon team received some help trashing Scott from a negative editorial in the *Dunn Daily Record*. The paper printed a long list of charges against Scott, ridiculing the ex-governor for cussing and criticizing various civic clubs, causing dissension and strife between city and rural dwellers, using state funds for improvement of his private property, and pressuring state workers to vote for Graham and Olive—basically the official attack line of the Lennon camp. The *Daily Record* made it clear that Scott loved to cuss out opponents but that he could not stand "being cussed himself so he hides behind the false claims of smear and mudslinging."[87]

On May 15, on a statewide radio hookup, Lennon, Scott, and the other candidates answered questions put to them at a meeting of the League of Women Voters. Scott performed badly. He fumbled some questions, hemming and hawing with his answers, and had to admit that he simply did not know the answer to others. Lennon made an excellent impression with his knowledge of foreign affairs. The *Durham Sun* called Scott "shockingly uninformed and woefully inarticulate" about foreign affairs and "lamentably ignorant of national affairs." It praised Lennon for discussing the issues intelligently and coherently.[88] In Confidential Memo no. 2, Upchurch wrote that he blamed Scott not for being ignorant about national issues but for trying to win an office "that is far above his head" and trying to unseat "an able, well-informed man who is head and shoulders above him in dealing with the complex issues in the Senate.[89]

Lennon's strategists had hit Scott in a vulnerable area. While Sanford thought the best way to win was to focus on local issues and ignore most national and international issues, Scott's embarrassing lack of knowledge in those areas hurt him badly. Had Scott been running for governor, it would have been acceptable to avoid international issues, but in a race for the US Senate such ignorance was a liability. Fortunately for Scott, foreign affairs did not constitute an important factor in determining citizens' votes in 1954. Nonetheless, his lack of sophistication and disinterest in such matters undercut the support he received from his middle-class constituency and gave Lennon a significant boost. Tar Heel voters did not want an ignorant rube representing them in the august environs of Washington, DC. Would Scott be up to the task when it came to foreign affairs?

With Lennon gaining ground on Scott each day, his strategists in the Sir Walter rapped the ex-governor on his relationships with labor. In a letter to "Fellow North Carolinians," Lennon repeated his stance on major issues. He favored an increase in personal exemptions from federal income tax, 90 percent parity for farmers, and honesty in government. He opposed giving the federal government any control over public schools, and denounced communism as a threat to Christian institutions and world peace.[90]

Lennon's May 22 Confidential Memo no. 3 crowed that Scott had run out of money and was losing votes because he had never explained his tax problems. Upchurch warned his managers to continue to work hard because, if Scott were elected, it would be a grab for long-term political power in the state and he would then attempt to pick the next governor.[91]

Heartened by Lennon's climb in the polls, his headquarters made a critical mistake. Knowing that one more significant issue was needed to put Lennon over the top, the campaign resorted to racial prejudice. Under the headline "Scott is trying to get Negroes to go to bed with him again," the third memo pointed out that a Negro Congress of Industrial Organizations (CIO) labor organizer and two representatives from the NAACP were working for Scott. Upchurch also divulged two secret meetings Scott held with Negroes in Winston-Salem: "Oxford Negroes got the word from the NAACP last week: bloc-voting for Scott."[92] These sleazy tactics worked in 1950, but this was 1954, and Scott backers hoped that voters were tiring of racially motivated politics. The Lennon brain trust pulled back from this initial attempt at fearmongering, but the campaign saved its biggest blunder for last.

As the contestants entered the last two weeks in their quests for office, two events, one expected and one unexpected, changed the political landscape. On May 12, the seventy-six-year-old Clyde Hoey died suddenly of a stroke in his Senate office. The long-haired Hoey, a legend in his home state, had been elected to Congress, served as governor from 1937 to 1941, and had been elected to the US Senate in 1944.

Hoey's passing complicated matters for both campaigns. On the stump when he learned of it, Scott praised Hoey and called off his electioneering in deference to his memory.[93] Lennon also ended his active campaigning. The state now had only one US senator, and Lennon informed the press that it was his duty to return to Washington to protect the interests of North Carolina. He was "keenly disappointed" in having to curtail his travel in the state, but he urged his campaign manager and supporters to "redouble and revitalize [their] efforts on [his] behalf."[94] When Lennon's handlers announced the memorial service for Hoey, they implied that, if Hoey had lived, he would have voted for Lennon as he "was very fond of his young colleague."[95]

One cannot be certain how Hoey would have voted since he was officially neutral in the race, but he clearly favored Lennon. He was more conservative than Scott and still resented the blow Scott had given to the machine in 1948. It is also not clear how Lennon's necessary absence from the state affected his campaign. He had to be in Washington more than he had anticipated as senators were grappling with many important issues—Dien Bien Phu had fallen on May 17, the Army-McCarthy hearings were in full swing, and the Supreme Court issued its decision in *Brown v. Board of Education*, also on May 17. His reduced time on the circuit might not have hurt him, but it certainly did not help his chances in a very close race since he did not have Scott's name recognition.

For the first time in the state's history, a governor would be making a second selection for a vacant US Senate seat. While Umstead pondered his choices, political activity in the state reached a fever pitch as hopeful candidates and their supporters jostled each other in vying for the governor's attention. Umstead received recommendations and expressions of interest on behalf of some fifty potential candidates. Before choosing the next senator, he had another difficult decision to make. Should he wait until after the primary to choose, or should he make an immediate appointment?[96]

While Umstead contemplated his choice, a second major event occurred. On May 17, just five days after Hoey's demise, the US Supreme Court handed down the landmark *Brown v. Board of Education* decision, ruling unanimously: "In the field of public education the doctrine of 'separate but equal' has no place. Separate educational facilities are inherently unequal." Segregated public schools should be integrated. The Court understood that its verdict would have major consequences on the nation and, thus, proceeded slowly, initially avoiding the issue of compliance. One year later, in what is known as *Brown v. Board of Education II,* the Court advised that the public schools were to be integrated "with all deliberate speed."[97]

The state exploded in a firestorm of protest. Umstead announced that he was "terribly disappointed" with *Brown v. Board of Education* and thought the Court opinion "a clear and serious invasion of the rights of the sovereign states." But he recognized that the Court had spoken and did not plan to call a special session of the legislature to deal with the issue since enforcement of the edict had been delayed for one year. His reasoned response was in the state's tradition of moderation. He knew that the complex problem of school integration needed a wise solution, one that would require careful and thoughtful study from everyone.[98]

The Court's ruling certainly influenced Umstead's thinking in his selection for the vacant Senate seat. Under pressure from all sides to make a quick decision, the governor was buttonholed by supporters of Samuel J. Ervin, associate justice of the state supreme court. Ervin's backers convinced the governor that the selection of a conservative like Ervin would meet with near unanimous public approval and would allay some of the fears resulting from the *Brown* ruling. While the *Brown* ruling had some influence on the governor's selection, there were other considerations. Umstead wanted someone capable and popular enough to triumph in the special election in November 1954 and win a full six-year term in 1956. Ervin fit that bill.[99] Ed Rankin Jr. pointed out that Umstead and Ervin were World War I buddies and were close personal friends[100] and that Justice Ervin's selection did not, therefore, surprise many people.

The Scott and Lennon camps now had to deal with the tumultuous uproar caused by the *Brown* ruling. Sanford and others feared that the racial hatred of the 1950 campaign would be revived on the part of many outraged citizens of the state. As Richard Kluger put it in his magisterial book on *Brown v. Board of Education:* "Probably no case ever to come before the nation's highest tribunal affected more directly the minds, hearts and daily lives of so many Americans. . . . The decision marked the turning point in America's willingness to face the consequences of centuries of racial discrimination."[101]

Sanford knew how important Scott's first public reaction to the *Brown* ruling would be, so he skipped Hoey's funeral and spent several hours preparing a statement for Scott to read. He and other observers remembered that the Supreme Court decisions in 1950 had come down while Willis Smith pondered a call for a second primary and played a large part in his final decision. Sanford wanted to tamp down the racial fires that were certain to erupt. He knew that in 1954 it would be a disaster for Scott to come out in favor of integration—a political death sentence for a southern politician. Even a moderate response to the verdict could prove costly.

Despite his previous overtures to blacks and his desire to improve race relations, Scott knew that his election was in jeopardy and in his prepared statement took a hard line on integration. He had never used race as a propaganda tool, for he was no Cole Blease or Strom Thurmond. However, in a statement issued on May 17, he made it abundantly clear, as he had many times before, where he stood on segregated schools. He insisted: "I have always been opposed, and I still am opposed, to Negro and white children going to school together." He hoped that, since no candidate favored the end of segregation, the *Brown* decision "would not become a controversy in the present senatorial campaign." The contestants should avoid stirring up fear and bad feeling between the races. He asked both blacks and whites to remain calm and promised that he would do all he could to preserve the state's historic principles and traditions.[102] He did not talk about interposition, nor did he make any defiant statements about opposing *Brown*. He still thought that the best way forward was to improve the Negro schools. Years later, Bob Scott recalled his father's comments about the *Brown* ruling: "Well, it took them one hundred years to decide we were wrong. They ought to give us fifty years to get it worked out."[103]

Shocked and dismayed by *Brown*, Lennon immediately sought to make school segregation a bigger issue in the race. He maintained that Scott and some of his advisers "have encouraged the abolition of segregation in our public schools for years" and insinuated that there were "agitators" from minority groups who were trying to influence Scott's election by use of bloc voting. Since the federal government was about to dictate a solution to school segregation, voters should elect Lennon to fight for "constitutional state sovereignty."[104]

Many newspapers in the state chastised Lennon for his remarks. The *Charlotte News* wrote that, whether it helped or hurt Lennon, the injection of race into the campaign could "only harm the state in whose service he enlisted."[105] The *Durham Morning Herald* likewise found his remarks regrettable and an example of "rather sordid politicking." This was "a pretty sorry way for a politician to get votes," and it indicated that Lennon was losing and that "desperate measures were needed to win."[106] Lennon did not repeat the charges. The outcry from state newspapers and even some of his advocates made him realize that he had overreached in resorting to tactics that had been successful in 1950.

The high court's ruling was front and center when Democrats gathered in Raleigh for their annual convention. Most delegates did not anticipate a shrill denunciation of the *Brown* ruling as North Carolina did not traditionally respond with demagoguery or irresponsible statements. North Carolina would not close its schools, as Virginia had done, nor would it turn public schools into private schools to resist integration. It was not the Deep South. The calm reaction by Governor Umstead and other leaders was in the best North Carolina tradition of reasoned moderation. Scott, Lennon, and Umstead, however, remained adamant about maintaining separate but equal schools.

As the Senate race drew to a close, Lennon's last confidential memo claimed that Scott was desperate: "They know they are licked." Scott would lose so badly, it predicted, that he would wonder why he entered the race in the first place. Lennon gave a final radio speech and aired a fifteen-minute talk on seven television stations. He expected to win as his support had increased in the last three weeks.[107] All this was mere bluster as C. A. Upchuch and Lennon's advisers had determined that they would lose unless there was a dramatic shift to Lennon. They decided they had to use a racial smear in a last-ditch effort to win.

Expecting an appeal to racial issues after the *Brown* ruling, Sanford and Ben Roney had alerted all workers to inform headquarters as soon as any leaflets showed up.[108] Sure enough, Lennon's final, desperate ad first appeared in the *Winston-Salem Journal* on May 26. At first glance it appeared to be a legitimate ad for Scott. It featured a photo of Dr. Harold L. Trigg with the following text: "Member of the state Board of Education. . . . The first and only member of our race to serve. . . . Kerr Scott increased Negro appointments to official state boards by more than 300 percent. He has demonstrated his interest in our race and has aided our cause of non-segregation. Vote for W. Kerr Scott for United States Senate, a friend of the Negro." It was signed by J. H. R. Gleaves, president of the Progressive Civic League.[109]

The ad, which "shook up the Scott campaign," prompted an immediate response from Sanford. He knew that the fallout from the ad had to be contained in order to save the election as racial enmity could sweep through the eastern part of the state and "turn the thing around." In chasing down the source of the ad, Sanford discovered that Marshall Kurfees, the mayor of Winston-Salem and a Lennon backer, had prepared and paid for it. At

The controversial, last-minute attempt by the Lennon strategists to win the 1954 Senate race. The ad raised the race issue by touting the support that Scott had given the Negro. The ad was a fake, and the ploy failed. John Harden Papers, Southern Historical Collection, University of North Carolina at Chapel Hill.

the same time, he received a call reporting that the state purchasing agent, David Holton, had left two packages of leaflets featuring a reprint of the Trigg ad at a gas station in Columbia, North Carolina.[110]

Faced with disclosure, Mayor Kurfees took full responsibility for the controversial ad, branded by the Scott forces as a "falsehood." The mayor said he wrote and paid for the ad, then persuaded Gleaves, a Negro leader, to sign it. He emphasized that neither Lennon nor his headquarters knew about the ad, and Lennon headquarters categorically denied having any knowledge of the leaflets. Trying to stem any negative publicity, Sanford persuaded Gleaves to sign a statement saying that he had been tricked into approving the ad. Gleaves insisted that he did not pay for the ad, that he did not take it to the paper, and that he "was shocked beyond words" when he saw it printed.[111]

Sanford did not want a repeat of the 1950 Graham race, during which Graham refused to respond to racial charges. He wanted to put the Lennon group on the defensive, and the only way he could do that would be to prove that Lennon's organization was the source of the illegal leaflets. His counterattack was not without risk as it would call added attention to the ad and leaflets, but he realized that he had to react immediately.

In an attempt to catch the Lennon campaign in a lie, Sanford sent a trusted "spy" to see Abie Upchurch to ask him for some leaflets to distribute. Upchurch provided Sanford's informant with the location of the print shop where he could get the leaflets and instructed him that they should be put on the porches of houses in mill towns and in the mailboxes of rural homes: "That's where we think they will be most effective." Sanford's agent learned that Upchurch had gotten the idea from the 1950 Graham race: "They [Smith backers] beat me with this and it ought to be good enough to try it again." Sanford also learned that Lennon headquarters sent four thousand of the leaflets to Greene County and another forty thousand to Salisbury. With this inside information, he had caught the Lennon camp red-handed.

Sanford took his agent's statement, had it notarized,[112] and hid him away from the press in a hotel room. He then took the information to Jonathan Daniels at the *News and Observer*. Daniels held the presses for one hour in order to get the exposé in the paper. The headlines the next day, May 28, told the story: "Alton Lennon Forces Flood State with 'Phony' Race Issue Leaflets."[113]

Sanford called the distribution of race literature a "last minute effort of desperate, panicky men who know their cause is lost." Furthermore: "It is dirty politics and the people who printed it know it is dirty politics." Sanford next called on the state attorney general, the state Bureau of Investigation, the FBI, and the US district attorney for an investigation of the illegal documents. He named Abie Upchurch and David Holton as the main culprits. In a telegram to J. Edgar Hoover, he accused Upchurch of the distribution of unsigned campaign literature that appeared to be in violation of federal law (specifically, Title 18, USCA, Section 612). The Trigg flyers, he argued, were intended to adversely influence the candidacy of Kerr Scott.[114]

At the same time, Sanford wired all Lennon's county managers, threatening prosecution if they distributed the material. This threat had a favorable outcome as a few Lennon managers burned the leaflets even though others continued to distribute them. The FBI helped the cause by responding to Sanford's letter and indicating that it would begin an investigation. On Saturday morning, May 29, voting day, some eastern papers carried the headline "FBI Investigating Lennon Headquarters." If that were not enough, the Scott forces aired a thirty-minute, paid political radio program the afternoon before the vote. There were disclaimers before and after the broadcast, but the presentation, in the form of a news story, was "very realistic." The "reporters" in the broadcast told of Upchuch's playing racial politics and the FBI investigation while mentioning the possibility that those involved might be prosecuted. Sanford remembered: "We put that prairie fire out. We might have gotten our hands burned a little by doing it but we damned well put it out in two days' time." In a later interview, he recalled that, if they had not discovered the ads and reacted quickly, "Alton Lennon would still be the United States Senator."[115]

After the election was over, Terry Sanford sent a confidential letter to all of Scott's county managers. He asked them whether the "Winston-Salem Negro" leaflets had been distributed in their area. Very few were found in the larger counties like Guilford or Forsyth; most were located in the eastern part of the state and in mill towns. W. H. Pitt, from Perquimans County, sent word that the leaflets had been distributed the last two days of the race and had a "very decided effect" in favor of Lennon. J. F. Fisher reported that Scott lost Cabarrus County "by a considerable margin as a direct result of the distribution of these leaflets." There was a large distribution in Gates County with "a loss of over 100 votes" for Scott.[116] After gathering all the information he could, Sanford concluded that, while there were indications that the Trigg brochures helped Lennon and damaged Scott, by using biased and intolerant material "the type of campaign the opposition used hurt them more than it helped": "For our part, we are doubly glad to have won with honor."[117]

After denying having anything to do with the Trigg leaflets, the Lennon hierarchy decided that it could still take advantage of the situation. Unaware of Sanford's activities in uncovering its duplicity, the Lennon camp, with a large dose of chutzpah, ran a new, full-page newspaper ad that defended the Trigg leaflet as legitimate. It even reprinted parts of the original leaflet and denounced Sanford for claiming that it was "planted," "just another cry of desperation" from Scott. And, on election day, another testimonial trumpeted "Nothing Phony About This," insisting that the leaflet was not a fake but had been signed by the Scott supporter Gleaves in an attempt to help his candidate. The ad ended with: "Judge Where the Truth Lies. Vote for Integrity, Vote for Honesty, VOTE FOR LENNON."[118] On election day, under fire from newspapers and some Lennon advocates, Upchurch finally admitted that his headquarters had the circulars printed and delivered throughout the state. Unrepentant to the end, he contended that there was nothing illegal about the leaflets even if they were unsigned.

Lennon closed his campaign with a final speech and fired one last shot at Scott, declaring a need for leadership "that puts the good of all the people above private and personal gain." Scott ended his race in Haw River, saying: "Although it has not been easy, I have waged a clean campaign." Both sides were confident of victory.[119]

As citizens flocked to the voting booths, observers were unable to assess what implications the furious activity of the previous two days would have on the outcome. As the returns trickled in, Scott showed well in the east and rural sections of the state, as expected, and Lennon got good margins in some of the larger cities. Lennon trailed throughout the night and finally dropped by the Carolina Hotel headquarters to greet Scott. Since the final tallies had not been completed and there was a remote possibility of a runoff, he did not immediately concede. He promised that, if the results stayed as they were, he would support Scott in November.[120]

The final results were closer than Scott and Sanford had expected, but the ex-governor won by a respectable 25,323 votes—312,053 to Lennon's 286,730. The overall turnout was much larger than anticipated. Scott received the largest vote ever given for a Democratic senatorial nomination. Lennon gained the largest vote ever given to a losing candidate. The total vote of the other five candidates was not enough to create a runoff, and Scott avoided a second primary by 9,448 votes.

Terry Sanford, the successful manager of the 1954 campaign, and Kerr Scott celebrate their victory over Alton Lennon and the conservative forces in the state. *Raleigh News and Observer*, May 30, 1954. Courtesy of the State Archives of North Carolina, Raleigh.

Lennon captured forty-three counties, mostly in the Piedmont and mountain areas, where he won twice as many counties as Scott. Scott won fifty-seven counties, excelling in the Coastal Plain, and prevailing in most of the eastern counties with large margins in Alamance, Wake, and Orange Counties. Lennon had a huge win in his native county of New Hanover by 12,155–2,576 and was victorious in Mecklenburg by a two-to-one margin.[121] His defeat preserved a state tradition that no US senator chosen by a governor since 1930 (Morrison, Umstead, Graham, and Lennon) had managed to win the voters' approval.

After the contest ended, Scott sat under a tree in his front yard, sipping a cool drink, and acknowledging congratulations on his victory. When asked how he felt, he replied "almost tolerable" and acknowledged that this race was "a little rougher" than his run for governor.[122] Having won both the short term (to January 1955) and the long term (1955–1961), in his first press conference as the Democratic nominee he predicted that he would get along well with Senator Ervin since they were not too far apart on issues. On how the state should respond to *Brown v. Board of Education,* he reasoned that such decisions should not be rushed and that North Carolina ought to get the wisdom of thoughtful people: "I still think we can work this out."[123] Umstead congratulated Scott on his victory. He was sorry Lennon did not win but proud of the fine vote his appointee received.[124]

In the aftermath of the contest, state pundits pontificated on the whys and wherefores of Scott's triumph. Jonathan Daniels exulted at Scott's vindication and started his editorial in the *News and Observer:* "There is retribution in history." The election, he crowed, was "a rebuke given to those who tried for a second time to injure a progressive North Carolina leader by false and underhanded race smears." By conducting a race free of venom and based on the issues, Scott got revenge on those conservatives who had tried to humiliate him at the 1952 Democratic national convention. He also avenged Frank Graham's defeat in 1950.[125] In his private correspondence, Daniels vented his anger at Lennon's tactics. He wrote Mrs. Max Ascoli, thanking her for her help in "one of the really great campaigns for freedom in this country": "It is tragic to have to go through it again, but this campaign in the aftermath of the recent Supreme Court decision, is really and clearly the fight between the people of good will and the people of evil intent in the South today."[126] He wrote Gerald W. Johnson, telling him that he enjoyed "the spanking we gave the people who assassinated Frank Graham in 1950. It was wonderful to catch them in the same old underhanded 'nigger' issue trick and see it backfire on them."[127]

As for why Scott won, the opinions varied. Most papers pointed out that he was better known, had more administrative experience, and started the race with a big lead. Lennon had the backing of the anti-Scott, old Shelby machine faction, but the conservatives did not work for him as hard as they would have for Willis Smith, who certainly would have been a better candidate and might well have beaten Scott. Lennon ran hard and, except for the racial issue, acquitted himself well.

Did the racial invective by the Lennon camp provide the winning margin for Scott? Most papers judged the racial literature as un-American, false, and malicious. Lynn Nisbet called the distribution of the leaflets unethical and politically unwise but did not conclude that it cost Lennon the race.

Terry Sanford repeated his opinion on a number of occasions that, although Lennon gained some votes because of the ads, the revulsion occasioned by the propaganda outraged many citizens, turned many votes to Scott, and saved the campaign.[128] The *Greensboro Daily Record* doubted that the racist literature affected the outcome in any way. It maintained that Scott won because of "his vote-getting personality," his wide acquaintance across the state, and his experienced political techniques.[129] The *Northhampton News* agreed with Sanford. In its county, the voters had been "sickened and infuriated by the bombardment of illegal race issue circulars," and, even though Lennon had been gaining strength, in the end they turned to Scott.[130] The *Shelby Star* had a different, if misinformed, interpretation. It concluded that the phony circular was not phony at all but a legitimate appeal for votes by Mr. Gleaves, an ardent Negro supporter of Kerr Scott. Thus, Scott, not Lennon, had been responsible for raising the race issue.[131]

The election had national significance, and the controversial ending caught the attention of key newspapers throughout the nation. Referring to Scott as one of "the foremost liberals in the South," the *New York Times* saw his victory as significant because of his strong support for farm and labor interests and because he would be at odds with the southern conservative faction in Washington. It declared that this was the fourth victory for political liberals in the South in May, as John Sparkman of Alabama had won reelection to the Senate, Estes Kefauver had retained his Senate seat in Tennessee, and James E. Folsom had won the gubernatorial nod in Alabama.[132] *U.S. News and World Report* agreed that Senator-Elect Scott had broken with the southern conservatives and would bring a "New Deal attitude to many issues in Congress."[133] The *Washington Post* hailed the "unmistakable victory for a progressive-minded candidate" as the voters did not succumb, as they had done in 1950, to those who whipped up racial fears.[134] Lynn Nisbet disagreed that there was a trend toward liberalism in the South and North Carolina. He perspicaciously argued that the only trend in North Carolina was a consistent record of narrow margins between conservative and liberal elements in the Democratic Party.[135]

Although he still had to face the Republican candidate in the November race, Scott received congratulations from all over the country since the Democratic nomination was tantamount to election. Harry Truman sent a telegram,[136] as did Walter Reuther of the CIO. Reuther proclaimed that working men and farmers had reason to rejoice with Scott's win: "We in the CIO are sure that you wil [sic] make a great contribution in statesmanship and service to our nation."[137] Several correspondents praised Scott for "staying above the mud-slinging which the opposition injected into the campaign,"[138] and others congratulated him for "the clean campaign [he] waged against all the slur and slander of the opposing forces."[139] Scott answered everyone with a form letter expressing his deep gratitude for their time and effort in getting him elected: "Because of your participation in my campaign, we won a great victory."[140] Terry Sanford, the architect of Scott's success, received several letters lauding his performance, one calling it "a magnificent job."[141] H. Pat Taylor Sr. was convinced that Sanford was "responsible for his [Scott's] victory and that a campaign conducted any differently would have resulted in his defeat."[142]

Scott won because he was well-known in the state and an experienced campaigner who effectively used remnants of his 1948 organization, particularly the county farm agents, to get out the vote. He had strong support from labor, almost all the Negro vote, and the Branchhead Boys came through for him. Sanford restricted the confrontational Scott's tendency to make outrageous statements and offend people, and this blueprint paid off. He constantly reminded Scott that the object was to win, not to entertain the public.[143] By any standard, he did a superb job in managing the campaign. By connecting Scott with the younger element of the party and with businessmen in the state, he helped Scott win twenty-two counties he had lost in 1948.

John Rodman thought that Scott's failure to answer questions about his tax returns and the building of roads on his personal property hurt him as voters thought he had something to hide. His disastrous performance at the League of Women Voters' debate indicated that his knowledge of and interest in foreign affairs was sadly lacking. Because of Scott's failures, Lennon turned out to be more formidable than the Scott camp had anticipated despite his limited experience and his lack of name recognition. He was the incumbent, had the backing of Umstead and the machine, and had plenty of money. Certainly, the timing of the *Brown v. Board of Education* ruling helped Lennon, but it is difficult to assess how much.

The wild card was the Trigg leaflets. Sanford remained convinced that his swift reaction to the leaflets tamped down the potential firestorm of racism and saved Scott from defeat. Upchurch and Lennon's advisers hoped that, coming so soon after the *Brown* decision, the leaflets would be enough to carry Lennon to victory. Some of the electorate disliked the sleazy politics of race-baiting, but Scott's victory did not demonstrate that North Carolinians were less disposed to defend segregation than in 1950.

Because of *Brown v. Board of Education*, the race issue was potentially more potent in 1954 than it was in 1950. This was certainly true for the other southern states' vociferous outrage and unrepentant resistance to the court decision. There was a qualitative difference between the more moderate North Carolina and the other southern states in how they approached racial problems and in their reaction to *Brown*. Nonetheless, Scott won partly because both he and Sanford understood what a powerful and emotional issue race was and prepared accordingly. Scott's repeated insistence that he opposed integration and a fair employment practices commission (FEPC) quieted the waters considerably. If the Trigg leaflets had been distributed earlier and in greater numbers, the result might have been different. If Willis Smith had been Scott's opponent in 1954, the race card would have probably swept Smith back into office. Racism had not died down in 1954, but Sanford had handled the issue adroitly, and that enabled Scott to hold on to a twenty-five-thousand-vote victory. In the end, voters chose Scott to a large degree because of his success with the Go Forward program. Many voters had new roads to market, better schools and health care, and telephones and electricity, and, when they entered the voting booth, they turned to Scott as a known quantity. Kerr Scott now sported a record of 5–0 in statewide elections, a testament to his skill as a campaigner.

Scott would not officially become a US senator until he won the general election on November 2 and that vote was certified on November 3. Scott would finish out the unexpired term to which J. Melville Broughton had been elected in 1948. The same Senate seat had now been occupied by Mel Broughton, Frank Graham, Willis Smith, Alton Lennon, and Kerr Scott— the first time in the history of the state that five different senators served during one six-year term.

Scott was heavily favored in November to defeat the Republican nominee, Paul West, who was not even well-known among Republicans.[144] Scott, this time as the standard bearer, joined the state Democratic Party's fall caravan and attended a meeting in each of the congressional districts.[145] When he appeared at a barbeque rally at Griffin's restaurant in Goldsboro, the local paper described the event. He arrived and shook hands with all present, "missing no one." The reporter did not view Scott as a robust, back-slapping politician; rather, he thought that he had a more modest, informal approach—just one of the boys—and that this low-key attitude was part of his charm. His speech lacked polish, but he conveyed "sincerity and service." People trusted him. The paper noticed that, while mining for votes, he did not use flattery or try to cajole anyone into supporting him: "He is not overly influenced by or subservient to any man, any group of men or any philosophy of government."[146]

Scott trounced West in the fall election by almost 2–1, 408,312 votes to 211,322.[147] The death of Bill Umstead of congestive heart failure on November 7, 1954, cast a pall on the campaign.[148] Umstead and Scott were never friends, had different philosophies of government, and had gone against each other on several occasions, but Scott had respect for the office and for Umstead's honesty and hard work and paid proper homage to his memory.

There was much speculation about what kind of senator Scott would make. Ralph Howland, a political writer for the *Charlotte Observer*, maintained that, while some called him a liberal, he would not favor racial integration or an FEPC and would not join the liberal bloc in the Senate. On the other hand, he would not side with the southern conservatives. He would probably be a moderate and would vote differently than Willis Smith and Clyde Hoey would have. However he voted, the paper urged him not to make snap statements without thinking. He was now on a world stage, and embarrassing controversies would damage his reputation. If he behaved himself, Howland thought that Scott had the capacity to become "a most important figure in Washington."[149] Burdened by high expectations, and concerned about his new responsibilities, the Haw River farm boy was now ready to take up his duties as a US senator. Always upbeat, he looked forward to his new challenge.

10

THE SENATE YEARS, 1954–1958

W. Kerr Scott's tenure as a member of the US Senate began on an auspicious note as more than one thousand Tar Heels journeyed to Washington on November 29, 1954, to see Scott and Senator Sam Ervin take the oath of office. Included in the official party were Governor Luther Hodges and other state dignitaries. When the Senate formally convened shortly after noon, Ervin and Scott walked down the aisle accompanied by Minority Leader Lyndon Johnson. The oath was then administered to both men. Scott and Ervin signed the Senate register to a thunderous round of applause from the spectators in the gallery. Scott's oath was for the short term, and he would later be sworn in for the six-year term in January 1955. He surely savored the moment, and he must have felt great pleasure at having vanquished his enemies in the third primary. Frank Graham stated that he was inspired to see so many people from all over the state: "It brings to mind the inauguration of Andrew Jackson. Senator Scott will make a great senator and serve all the people."[1]

Scott held his first press conference just four hours after taking the oath. He had enjoyed the give and take of his frequent press conferences in Raleigh, but now he faced a more informed, experienced, and formidable press corps. Thus, during his first outing in Washington, he was cagey and very circumspect. He informed those present that he had not decided how he would vote on a pending resolution to censure Senator Joe McCarthy. He also refused to take any position on any key issues since he had not had time to study all the details. When asked whether he were a left-winger or a right-winger, he replied with another farm analogy: "When I am farming, I always go down the left side and throw the dirt on the right side."[2]

Prior to coming to Washington, Scott had spent a considerable amount of time organizing his Senate staff. He selected Ben Roney as his administrative assistant. Roney had worked with Scott since the 1949 bond campaign and had proved invaluable to him in state matters. Bob Scott remembered that Roney had a "unique sense of politics" and "a shrewd political mind" with a keen sense of timing.[3] Roney also had an uncanny memory for those who had opposed Scott and those to whom Scott owed favors. Bill Whitley became the press secretary, Robert Redwine served as the speech writer, and Roy Wilder Jr. also worked in the office.

Scott made a wise decision in hiring Bill Cochrane as his executive secretary. Cochrane, who held an A.B. and an LL.B. from the University of North Carolina and a master's of law from Yale University, had been working in the North Carolina Institute of Government since 1945. Scott said he "was mighty glad to get his services" because Cochrane was "well-acquainted with many problems facing municipalities" and because his background "gives him a non-political approach to some of the state's most pressing problems."[4] Cochrane gave Scott the sophistication and academic credentials that the former governor lacked and so desperately needed at the national level. The press hailed Scott's choice. A friend wrote Cochrane that his "excellent knowledge of government should be of immense help to Senator Scott in his discharge of his duties."[5] The *Chapel Hill Weekly* lauded Scott, who was not an attorney, for picking Cochrane, a student of law and government rather than the usual political hack. It also commented that it had been a long time "since the men with the sweaty shirts and knotty hands have had a representative and spokesman in Washington" and that "Scott's presence will add something to the effort to restore a balance in a Senate that too often has been overweighted on the side of wealth and power."[6]

Scott had assembled an excellent group of advisers who proved to be worthy of his trust. Immediately after taking office, he was assigned by the Senate leadership to the committees he most desired—the Agriculture Committee, his first choice, and Public Works as well as Interior and Insular Affairs and the Post Office Committee.[7] His initial goals as senator included his desire to get as much federal money for his state as possible and to improve the living conditions of farmers through federal subsidies. He restated his interest in water and soil conservation, irrigation, pollution control, and flood control. He continued to favor the expansion of the state's port facilities and a comprehensive program of water power development while renewing his commitment to expanding the nation's highways. He also worked hard on behalf of the state's tobacco interests, handing out tobacco products to visitors, and advertising the products with his ever-present cigar or plug of tobacco.[8]

Senator Scott's first vote was the pending censure of Joe McCarthy. Still feared by many senators, McCarthy had taken a blow to his prestige and power during the Army-McCarthy hearings in April 1954.[9] After being chastised on public television, he lost most of his public support, making it easier for the US Senate to prepare a motion of censure against him. He was nonetheless a formidable opponent with strong backing from the Republican Party. One day prior to the vote, despite his attacks on McCarthy during the 1954 Senate race, Scott seemed unsure as to how to cast his ballot. He said he would "read and listen a lot before voting."[10] After all, he had been sworn in only two days before, and this would be a momentous vote. In the history of the Senate members had rarely been censured. Although censure carried no penalties such as loss of vote or committee assignments, it was the harshest punishment the Senate could apply short of expulsion.

The final Senate resolution accused McCarthy of "obstructing the constitutional processes of the Senate" and of acting contrary to Senate ethics and thus bringing the Senate into "dishonor and disrepute." The vote to censure one of the most powerful senators in living memory was overwhelming, 67–22. Forty-four Democrats, one independent, and, in a show of courage, twenty-two Republicans voted yes. Scott and Ervin both voted in favor of the resolution.[11] Most papers in the state applauded the vote of censure. The *Asheville Citizen* approved of the blow to "this sly, malevolent and divisive force."[12]

For the most part, during his early years in Washington Kerr Scott kept a low profile and observed how the Senate operated. He knew he was not a great orator, so he seldom spoke on the floor. He did most of his work behind the scenes, on committees and in conferences with other senators.[13] While he might have come into this august body with something of an inferiority complex (after all, Washington *was* a long way from Haw River), he could have taken solace from advice given to Harry Truman when he first came to the nation's capital: "Don't you go to the Senate with an inferiority complex. You'll sit there about six months and wonder how you got there. But after that you'll wonder how the rest of them got there."[14]

When Scott took office, southerners controlled the Senate. The southern representatives had enormous influence over legislation because of their long tenure and the seniority rule, where long-serving chairmen maintained autocratic control over key committees. Southern senators also had the added weapon of the filibuster and used this tactic to block any legislation they deemed unfair to the interests of the South. The southerners' main focus was to defend the region against civil rights legislation and to prevent the intrusion of the federal government into their states' affairs.[15] The question Scott pondered as he settled into his duties was how he would line up with his fellow southerners. Would he join the conservative, anti–civil rights group led by Senator Dick Russell, or would he go his own way as a more progressive, liberal legislator?

Scott's maiden speech on the floor of the Senate featured a strong attack on Eisenhower and the Republican Party. Paul Butler, chairman of the national Democratic Party had, in a critique of the Eisenhower administration, stated that a military background was obviously not an adequate preparation to be president. It was not surprising that a Democratic senator agreed with Butler, but Scott seemed especially eager to attack Ike and the Republican Party: "There have been times when I questioned whether Eisenhower measured up."[16] The newly minted senator characterized the Republican Party as "a circus of selfish interests, complete with sideshows of despair and confusion," and called on the president to foster a more bipartisan foreign policy while using the talents of the Democratic leaders to create a more "effective policy."[17]

As might be expected, during his first full year in the Senate Scott focused his main attention on agricultural problems.[18] Noting that the state's major crop, tobacco, was in an economic downturn created by a drop in tobacco exports and reduced consumption, he feared a significant loss of income by farmers. He referred to tobacco as "the life blood of N.C." and hailed the crop as one of the most important commodities in agriculture and in federal tax revenues. He pointed out that tobacco farming had become a more dangerous financial undertaking in recent years owing to diseases and "a lot of scare headlines and some loose talk about the possibility that smoking causes cancer." He therefore proposed a greatly expanded special research program to determine the chemical components of tobacco and tobacco smoke and, thus, whether smoking caused cancer.[19]

Scott, an inveterate cigar smoker and user of chewing tobacco, was not particularly interested in improving public health. He wanted to demonstrate that tobacco did not cause cancer in order to shore up tobacco sales in the state. He used a memo from the National Association of Tobacco Distributors to bolster his case: "There is not one iota, not one scintilla of proof from any laboratory anywhere, conclusively linking smoking with harmful effects on the human anatomy."[20] Scott wanted to believe that there was no link between smoking and cancer, but he did not get the opportunity to prove it. Congress voted for tobacco research but did not include

Scott's $1 million for determining the relationship between smoking and personal health.[21]

Scott also worked hard to increase farm subsidies and favored 90 percent parity support for major commodities. In several speeches he explained that small farms nationwide had suffered a drop in income and predicted that the farm recession would grow and "gnaw the backbone out of our entire economy."[22] He defended farm subsidies, arguing that farmers were not the only people profiting from government largesse. He listed government subsidies to business and to railroads, mail subsidies, and tax write-offs. He had lost patience with those who yelled for a free economy and opposed farm tariffs while at the same time clutching "to their bosom their own particular type of subsidy."[23]

On a tour of farms in the Midwest, Scott lashed out at Secretary of Agriculture Ezra Taft Benson and the Eisenhower administration for assuring everyone that things were fine when farm income had gone down 10 percent in the last year. He told an Iowa audience in Council Bluffs that the administration was "willing to sit back and let the family size farms of this country be forced out of existence."[24] He repeatedly went after Benson for his failure to aid farmers. The farm economy was sick, and Benson "cannot convince farmers everything is rosy with his double-talk about prosperity."[25] He called on the president "to swallow his pride and sign" the measure granting 90 percent parity for price supports. Eisenhower, he contended, cared less about the farmers than about "the needs of the White House."[26] Scott had very little success with his criticisms of the Eisenhower administration, but Harry Truman thought the Council Bluffs speech a "crackerjack," and he wanted to borrow some of Scott's ideas for a farm speech he was to make.[27]

Perhaps Scott's most important contribution as a senator came with his proposal for a world food bank. He understood the importance of foreign aid to less fortunate democracies whose friendship was essential to American security and developed a businesslike proposal to help the poorer countries economically and at the same time earn their gratitude. The food bank would be operated through the United Nations and patterned after the International Bank for Reconstruction and Development. In time of famine and other disasters, member nations could borrow food from the bank and repay it when they were able to do so. America had excess stocks of food, and this surplus could go to fill the stomachs of millions of hungry people around the world. Scott saw this concept as an effective weapon in the battle against communism as that evil ideology flourished best where poverty existed. It was high time, he thundered, to put surplus foodstuffs to use for peaceful and humanitarian purposes without loss to the American taxpayer.[28]

State newspapers applauded Scott's effort. The *Charlotte News* asserted that the food bank "could become an effective, doubled-edged weapon against the problems of terrible hunger abroad and mounting stockpiles at home."[29] The *Greensboro Daily News* saw this as a typical achievement for Scott: "This is the Squire of Haw River in character, seeing something that needs doing and pitching in to do something about it. Sounds sensible to us branchhead folks."[30] Senator Scott received numerous personal letters commending his idea, one, for example, noting: "This is the soundest approach I have heard of to deal with surplus agricultural commodities."[31] When there was no positive response from the White House, Scott slammed Eisenhower for ignoring his proposal but promised not to let the "lack of interest in the American farmer and underfed people of the world . . . stop this resolution."[32]

In May 1955, Scott fulfilled his campaign promise to work for the development of the Cape Fear River basin. He believed that no problem facing the nation was more important than water conservation and flood control. He touted the importance of the Cape Fear River basin as it was the largest in the state and one-third of the state's population lived in its watershed. The area had been plagued by severe flooding in the past, so the river needed to be harnessed and tamed by modern technology for the benefit of the people. The building of three dams would lead to better flood control, an increase in public water supplies, better irrigation for farmers, and public recreation. The Cape Fear project should be part of a sound and dynamic water development and conservation program at the local, state, and national levels.[33] The *Greensboro Daily News* lauded Scott for trying to ensure the state's continued growth with the construction of dams and control of flooding: "As an advocate of Tar Heel water development Senator W. Kerr Scott has no peer."[34]

The senator also demanded that the federal government support public water power. In an irate attack, he condemned the Eisenhower administration's policy toward electric power and water resources. The administration had awarded a contract to a private company, the Idaho Power Company, to build three small hydroelectric dams in the Columbia River basin in the Pacific Northwest. Scott viewed the contract as a reward for political support. He wanted the federal government, not a private company, to build a dam at Hell's Canyon as part of an overall development of the Columbia River basin. When the private companies protested that federal interference would impede free enterprise, he announced that "nothing could be farther from the truth." In this case, he contended, the private company would exploit the project without fully developing its resources, "a clear case of selfish interests trying to snatch away something that belongs to all of the people of this country."[35] Scott cosponsored a bill calling for a federal dam for power, flood control, and irrigation to be built at Hell's Canyon. Owing to pressure from the Eisenhower administration, the Senate defeated the bill 51–41. Scott accused the administration of once again giving away natural resources.[36] Eventually (by 1967), the Idaho Power Company built three dams on the Snake River, making it the largest privately owned hydroelectric power company in the nation.

While Scott focused on farm policy and water resources, several crises in foreign policy demanded his attention. Throughout the 1950s, the primary focus of America's foreign policy continued to be the Cold War. The United States wanted to blunt the spread of the Red Tide of communism everywhere in the world. As the Cold War conflict accelerated, there was a grave emergency almost every year—Vietnam and the Geneva Conference in 1954, Quemoy and Matsu in 1955, the Suez Crisis in 1956, Sputnik in 1957, Lebanon in 1958. As a rule, Scott did not dabble much in foreign affairs. He understood that he lacked the depth of knowledge necessary to analyze America's defense policies in any meaningful way, so he listened to the experts and usually took their advice about how to vote. Aware of the threat posed by the Soviet Union, he voted yes on the Senate resolution to recognize the Communist Party as part of an international conspiracy against the United States.[37] He also voted in favor of the Southeast Asia Treaty Organization, a collective defense treaty against Communist activity in Asia.[38] He joined the majority of his colleagues, who voted 76–2 in favor of rearming the Federal Republic of Germany and making it a sovereign member of NATO, the European defense pact against Russia.[39] He opposed the admission of Red China to the United Nations as "unwise" under the present circumstances.[40]

The most dangerous crisis during 1954–1955 came when Red China demanded the return of two islands in the Formosa Straits, Quemoy and Matsu. The islands were controlled and occupied by the Nationalist Chinese in Formosa (later Taiwan) under the leadership of Chiang Kai-shek. When Nationalist China refused to comply, Red China began bombarding the islands. The United States had a commitment to defend militarily the Nationalist forces on Formosa, and to back down would be a blow to America's credibility. The best way to defend the islands would be to send

American troops, but Eisenhower did not want a war with China over islands of such little strategic value.[41] As the crisis worsened and tensions mounted, Eisenhower and Secretary of State John Foster Dulles informed the American people that defense of the islands might "require the use of atomic missiles" against Communist aggression. Eventually the Chinese backed down, defusing the situation. Several historians credit Eisenhower for ending the standoff by threatening the use of nuclear weapons.[42]

While generally supportive of the president's Cold War policy, Scott broke ranks over the Quemoy-Matsu imbroglio. In his first substantial Senate speech on foreign policy, he accused the administration of "drift and confusion . . . over Quemoy and Matsu that has now carried us dangerously close to the brink of war." Eisenhower was "the master architect of confusion" as the White House floundered with contradictory and confused orders.[43] The state papers cheered Scott's speech, saying he was "reminiscent of his old self, talking straight and talking strong."[44] Senator Scott, said the *Greensboro Daily News,* had been lying low as expected of a freshman, but his comments on the Eisenhower administration's confusing responses to the crisis were justified.[45]

On the domestic front, from 1951 to 1955, Scott voted overwhelmingly with the Democrats. Out of ninety-four key votes, the conscientious Scott missed only eight. He resumed his longtime interest in roads and schools and pushed for more national park development and additional federal funds for roads in North Carolina. The state eventually received $216 million for roads, and the National Park Service responded with $2.2 million for the Blue Ridge Parkway. Scott cosponsored a two-year emergency school construction bill for $75 million, "with no strings attached." The federal government would pay two-thirds of the cost, and the states would pick up the other third.[46] Eventually, the government provided part, but not all, of the money requested.

Scott continued his advocacy of aid to the poor and elderly by casting a yes vote on the Housing Act of 1955, which approved construction of 135,000 new housing units and 10,000 public housing units for the elderly.[47] He endorsed a bill that would reduce taxes for families making under $5,000 per year. Secretary of the Treasury George Humphrey opposed the bill because it would lead to inflation. Scott, already incensed by what he viewed as Republican policies favoring the wealthy, flayed Humphrey for "pure hog wash" in trying to confuse the issue. The poor already lacked purchasing power, and the measly tax cut would have little effect on inflation. Ever the populist, Scott said that taxpayers were not as gullible as "the Republican magicians" think they are. They know of the large handouts to the rich— "big fat checks on a silver platter."[48] Senator Hubert Humphrey of Minnesota hailed Scott's assault on the Eisenhower administration and wrote Scott that he was "mighty proud that you are in our ranks."[49]

Scott closely observed political activities in his home state and noted that in 1955 Luther Hodges was gearing up to run for a full term as governor in 1956. Some experts thought Scott might create some opposition to Hodges's candidacy as Scott loyalists feared Hodges might run for Scott's Senate seat in 1960. Scott saw Hodges as a potential threat at some point down the road, but he did not push anyone to run against Hodges in 1956.[50] In another strategic political move, Scott endorsed his colleague Sam Ervin, who was up for election in 1956.[51] Although the two men differed ideologically, he came out for Ervin partly because he admired his character. He also did not desire to create a political breach in the state by ignoring Ervin and his adherents since he himself intended to run for retention of his own seat in 1960.

Scott received many more letters as a senator than he did as governor. The letters from constituents were, as in Raleigh, on subjects important, obscure, and irrelevant. November 13–19, 1955, a typical week, gave an indication of the varied responses required of Scott's Senate staff. One writer thought that the Carolina Power and Light Company charged his sister too much for electricity; another correspondent proposed a new forty-eight-member Supreme Court, with one justice from each state. There were numerous applications for admission to the service academies, requests for assistance with welfare and social security and government publications, invitations to speak, questions about tax relief and tax refunds, veterans' pensions, disability checks, army transfers, leaking basements, tickets to the Army-Navy football game, relief from hurricane damage, jobs, and passports, requests for autographed pictures, and a complaint about the closing of the rural postal route in Climax, North Carolina.[52] Scott took great pride in helping his constituents and asked his staffers to answer queries as soon as possible.

After one year in office, Scott found the biggest difficulty was adjusting his thinking from the state to the national level. He described his work in the Senate as hard, with long hours, but not as punishing, stressful, and time consuming as being governor. And therein lay the problem. The energetic Scott did not like the Senate. He had always been a mover and shaker and had gotten things done on his own. He chafed over the inability of any one senator to get anything accomplished, decried the often partisan bickering, and disliked the frequent violations of Senate etiquette. In the Senate he was out of his element and, like many former governors, never quite felt comfortable as a lowly senator without any real power. As he wrote his brother Ralph: "It is a hard matter, as you know, to get any fire set under anybody up here."[53]

During his early years in the Senate, Scott worked constantly to improve his health and reduce his weight. He walked to his office almost every day from his apartment, approximately five miles away, cut out salt, and reduced his caloric intake. Even though he came from a family that "liked to eat," he managed to reduce his weight from 250 pounds to 180 partly by telling the workers in the Senate cafeteria: "Just give me some of the stuff that doesn't taste good." He refused, however, to cut back on chewing tobacco, Peach and Honey snuff, and numerous cigars each day. He realized that his smoking threatened his health and worried about how it might affect his heart. His doctors told him over and over again to lose weight and cease smoking or he could die at an early age. He usually ignored them and joked about death. He once said that, when he died, there would be three different crowds at his funeral: one little group that was really sorry he was gone, a much larger crowd of those who were glad he was gone, and, finally, "those afraid to take a stand one way or the other," by far the largest crowd.[54]

Far and away the most pressing and divisive issue for the remainder of Scott's time in the Senate was civil rights. While North Carolina was moderate in its response to *Brown v. Board of Education,* it never considered full compliance with the high court's decision as a viable option. On the surface, it appeared to be agreeable to integration, but support for segregation was strong throughout the state, and state officials intended to prevent integration of the schools by any legal means available. In August 1954, Governor William Umstead announced the formation of a nineteen-member biracial committee, the Governor's Special Advisory Committee on Education. The committee, which included women and three Negroes, would study the school situation in the state and make recommendations to the state legislature about how to respond to *Brown.* Umstead selected Tom Pearsall, a former speaker of the House with a good reputation as an arbiter, as chairman. Unfortunately, Umstead died on November 7, 1954, before the Pearsall Committee had completed its work.

Lieutenant Governor Luther Hodges succeeded Umstead as governor and immediately had to face the conundrum of devising a viable racial policy. Although Hodges, a retired textile executive, had no prior political experience, he evolved into a shrewd, effective politician. Since he did not want to accept the *Brown* decision, he tried to devise a pragmatic response to the court and save the state from closing its schools.

In late December 1954, the Pearsall Committee submitted its initial report to Governor Hodges. Pearsall thought the state could not ignore *Brown* but did not want to take the drastic step of privatizing the schools, as other southern states had done. On the other hand, he opposed speedy compliance, and his committee's report noted that immediate mixing of the races would threaten the peace and alienate public support of the schools and should not be attempted.

The Pearsall Plan was a clever attempt to circumvent the Supreme Court. Rather than open defiance of the Court, the Pearsall Committee tried to avoid the more drastic options of closing the schools or utilizing private school tuition grants. The 1955 legislature incorporated the Pearsall Committee's recommendations into the Pupil Assignment Act, which gave control of education decisions to local school boards. This tactic effectively limited blacks from entering white schools since qualified minorities could be denied admission by local school boards on vague, nonracial grounds, such as "the best interests of all students."[55]

The state initially appeared to have stemmed the tide of integration, but, on May 31, 1955, in *Brown v. Board of Education II,* the US Supreme Court changed the game. The Court ordered that segregated school systems should be eliminated "with all deliberate speed." Implementation and enforcement of the order had to be carried out by the local school boards under the supervision of the federal courts. The Court's language indicated that it did not expect swift compliance, but everyone knew that desegregation was the ultimate goal.

In response, Hodges appointed a second advisory commission and again chose Pearsall as chair. This time the committee had only seven members, all white, prosegregation legislators. After "careful and prayerful discussion," Hodges and Pearsall had decided that African Americans would be deliberately excluded from the commission on the premise that they would "have to work under almost impossible conditions because of outside pressure" from the NAACP and, thus, could not be objective.

On August 8, Governor Hodges's hard-line stance became apparent when, in a statewide radio and television address, he proposed a plan of "voluntary segregation." He argued that the Supreme Court's edict did not forbid a dual system of schools and did not require integration; it merely forbade discrimination. If the concept of voluntary segregation did not work, the state would be forced either to integrate or to close the public schools. Thus, voluntary segregation was the only alternative to two equally unacceptable extremes.[56] As expected, no school volunteered.

It is noteworthy that Scott made no public comment on the state's reaction and policy decisions made in regard to *Brown v. Board of Education* in 1955. Perhaps he was still trying to sort out the political ramifications of his civil rights stance, or maybe he decided it was good policy to avoid comment for the time being. That option, however, soon evaporated.

Infuriated by the *Brown* decision and what they perceived as a real threat to their way of life, southern leaders in the Senate decided that a more unified effort was needed to defy the Supreme Court. With black plaintiffs in court demanding that local schools comply with *Brown* and southern states working frantically to pass a series of anti-desegregation bills, Senate leaders wanted a statement of support for those states lawfully resisting forced integration. The key organizers of what would be known as the Southern Manifesto were Strom Thurmond of South Carolina, Harry F. Byrd of Virginia, and Richard Russell of Georgia.

The initial draft of the manifesto contained a harsh denunciation of the Supreme Court and called for interposition and massive resistance. A revision committee emphasized reasonable and logical legal arguments and excised the more intemperate phrases from the original draft. The more moderate document was written to appeal to several senators who refused to admit that the *Brown* decision was unconstitutional. Russell and others wanted to force those wavering senators to go on record either for or against the decision, knowing that many would have to sign or face defeat in the next election. Another purpose of the manifesto was to persuade northern politicians and the courts that imposing desegregation on the South was a futile proposition.

On March 11, 1956, Senator Walter George read the entire text of the Declaration of Constitutional Principles, now known as the Southern Manifesto, into the *Congressional Record*. The manifesto called the *Brown* decision a "clear abuse of judicial power" and lambasted the Supreme Court for taking over the powers of Congress, for legislating social change, and for encroaching on "the reserved rights of the states and the people." It firmly defended the concept of separate but equal, an established legal principle then in effect for half a century. The *Brown* decision had already produced negative social consequences by destroying friendly relationships between the races and had created "hatred and suspicion" in place of "friendship and understanding." The document ended with the pledge that the South would use "all legal means" to reverse the decision and would work to "prevent the use of force in its implementation."

Nineteen southern senators, including Ervin and Scott, along with eighty-one members of the House of Representatives signed the document. The only southern senators not signing were Albert Gore Sr. and Estes Kefauver of Tennessee and Lyndon Johnson of Texas.[57] Gore courageously refused to sign a document he considered "utterly incomprehensible and unsupportable" because it bordered on an act of secession that would encourage southerners to defy the government and disobey its laws.[58]

Scott was in a quandary over whether to sign the manifesto. He had been a member of the southern caucus that had discussed a response to *Brown v. Board of Education* at length, but he had not taken a public stand on the issue. The day that Walter George was to read the manifesto on the floor of the Senate, Scott called Bill Cochrane and asked: "Is there any way you can get my name off that thing?" Cochrane knew that George would read the manifesto in one hour and that advance copies had already been released. Although it hurt Cochrane to say so, he replied: "There's no way to withdraw your name now. You'd call more attention to yourself that way than if you left it on there." Scott agreed, "I guess you are right," and hung up. Later, Cochrane thought it was sad that he could not get Scott's name off the manifesto: "Senator Scott never had any problem with black people and he never went in for that kind of strong stuff."[59]

There is no corroborating evidence for Cochrane's account of the event, but Bill Cochrane was a man of integrity, and there is no reason to assume he made up the story, even to protect his boss's reputation. Scott probably bowed to pressure from Ervin and the southern caucus and understood that if he did not sign, he would be hounded in his reelection campaign in 1960 with rhetoric and attacks similar to those directed at Graham in 1950. He chose the pragmatic course despite his previously moderate views on race. As Tony Badger has demonstrated, moderates like Scott understood that *Brown* was the law of the land but feared that southern white conservatives were so fired up about integration that making their true position known would imperil their reelection chances. So they became "closet moderates" or gradualists. While accepting segregation and token compliance with

Brown, they hoped that men and women of goodwill in both races would eventually resolve the issue.[60]

Scott's position on civil rights became even more difficult on April 5, 1956, with the report of the second Pearsall Committee. The second report took a much stronger stance than previously and called for a state constitutional amendment that would permit local communities by majority vote to end the operation of public schools if conditions became "intolerable" as a result of forced integration. The amendment would provide for the payment of private school tuition grants from state or local funds for parents whose children had been assigned against their wishes to a desegregated school.

Governor Hodges called a special session of the legislature to consider the Pearsall Plan. He told the state that the plan had been designed to avoid a complete shutdown of the state's schools but that both he and Pearsall hoped that the plan would not have to be implemented. The House of Representatives approved the Pearsall Plan by a vote of 118–2. In the Senate the vote was unanimous. The people of North Carolina would have the opportunity to approve or disapprove the constitutional amendment in a September 8 statewide referendum.[61]

There had been some speculation that the Scott forces might oppose the Pearsall amendment. Scott feared that Hodges, a possible opponent in his reelection bid in 1960, could gain significant political support with his fight against integration. After initially deciding not to get involved, Scott and Sanford agreed to support Henry Jordan against Hodges in 1956 as a way to head off Hodges and "prevent him from using another four years as governor as a launching pad for a contest with Scott in 1960." Sanford visited Hodges to ascertain his future political intentions. Hodges replied that he would not rule out a race against Scott but that he had no real desire to enter the US Senate. Scott's plan to thwart Hodges went awry when, as in 1952, Henry Jordan suddenly withdrew from the race.[62] When Hodges announced his plan to run for the four-year term as governor, Scott did not comment, nor did he endorse him.[63]

Scott knew that the constitutional amendment would pass overwhelmingly and that it would be political suicide to oppose it, so he went on record as favoring the plan. He explained that, although he would not be at home to cast his vote, he would vote an absentee ballot in favor of the amendment. Terry Sanford also approved the Pearsall Plan, but both Scott and Sanford indicated that they hoped it would never be needed.[64] The *Raleigh News and Observer* opposed the amendment because it would not "save the schools" as touted but would permit the closing of the schools and lead to the abandonment of public education.[65]

On September 8, the state's voters approved the constitutional amendment by a four-to-one vote: 471,657–101,424. All one hundred counties voted in favor. Hodges expressed pleasure at the overwhelming approval of a moderate approach.[66] Fortunately, the Pearsall Plan was never implemented—no school was ever closed in North Carolina, and no state tuition grant was provided for private school students. It worked, however, even though it was declared unconstitutional by federal courts in 1966, because it allowed the state to resist integration while appearing to comply with *Brown*. The Pearsall option postponed meaningful integration for almost ten years. The result was "token integration" as a handful of black students were accepted in public schools in Greensboro and other districts. Blacks, however, were not yet welcome in white public schools, and by 1960 fewer than 1 percent of the state's schoolchildren studied in integrated classrooms.[67]

Although North Carolina did not adopt some of the more extreme measures of other southern states and did not insist on interposition, its so-called moderate response was questioned by the historian William Chafe, who called the plan a "subtle and insidious form of racism." In the end, the Pearsall Plan was a brilliant political move for Hodges. Both he and the state now had the reputation, or at least the self-perception, of being moderate and enlightened on racial matters, having found a peaceful way to deal with school integration.[68]

In the Senate, Scott concentrated on issues of interest to North Carolina, especially tobacco, water power, and coastal harbor projects. He worked hard at his committee assignments but rarely sponsored a bill himself. As the *Winston-Salem Journal* commented, he operated most effectively in the cloakroom and in committee conferences.[69] In 1956 he voted with the Democratic Party on twelve of fifteen key issues. He opposed the Bricker Amendment, which would have limited the president's power by preventing him from making executive agreements without the consent of Congress. Ike vigorously fought the amendment because it would limit the president's power to act quickly and would undermine America's influence during the Cold War. Scott characterized the amendment as a "very dangerous thing,"[70] and, despite several attempts, the amendment failed.

By the end of 1956, Scott was again complaining about the difficulty of getting things done and about some of the frustrations of being a US senator. His son Bob recalled that as time went on his father became more and more disillusioned:

> He never did like it up there. People who have been in the executive branch of government don't do well in the legislative branch. The reason is, of course, when you are in the executive branch, you are responsible for getting things done and within reason you can get things done. When you are in the Congress of the United States . . . you are just one of many unless you have been there long enough to be a powerful [committee] chairman. When you introduce legislation by the time it comes out you may be voting against it. It's just a different ball game, a different environment, a different culture. My Dad was too impatient to get things done. It just irritated him to death to have to sit through those committee meetings. . . . He said they could talk all day.[71]

Despite his disappointment with his life as a senator, Scott apparently liked it well enough. In November 1956, he announced that he would run for reelection in 1960. Notoriously a late starter, he said that he wanted all his friends to know of his intentions "well ahead of time" so that they would not commit to another candidate,[72] obviously referring to Luther Hodges. Calling him a "Democrat of the hardfisted, harsh-tongued Harry Truman School," *Time* magazine reported that Scott said that he would rather be safe than sorry by proclaiming the opening of his reelection campaign.[73] Why did he decide to run again for an office and a job he did not enjoy? He hoped that by his second term his seniority would give him more influence, and he wanted to try to discourage Luther Hodges's followers by announcing four years early. He was not certain in 1956 that he would want to run for another six years, but he wanted to make his path as easy as possible in case he eventually decided he wanted to spend more time in Washington.

In the national election of 1956, Scott once again came out strongly for Adlai Stevenson. Stevenson thanked Scott for his endorsement and predicted that it would be a "long and weary road" to win the presidency.[74] Prior to the Democratic national convention in June 1956, the governor of South Carolina, John Bell Timmerman, sent a letter to Scott asking him to consider a third-party movement if he were unhappy with the Democratic nominee for 1956. Scott issued a sharp reply: "I have no patience with anything that suggests a third party. The resolution is nothing but Dixiecrat sugar coating.

1956 Democratic national convention. Scott with Senator Sam Ervin (left) and North Carolina governor Luther Hodges (in the middle). At the time, Scott worried that Hodges might be a candidate for his Senate seat in 1960. Photograph by Hugh Morton, North Carolina Collection, University of North Carolina at Chapel Hill Library.

It is tailor made for the Republicans. They are doing everything they know how to split us [the Democratic Party]. . . . I am a Southern Democrat, a North Carolina Democrat and I refuse to get split." Most southern Democrats, who more or less agreed with Timmerman on the race issue, nonetheless decided to stay within the Democratic fold and fight out the race issue there. They agreed with Scott that there was no real chance for a third party movement and that, if one did materialize, it would give the Republicans a decisive edge in the election.[75] Here again Scott showed his willingness to distance himself from the typical, demagogic southern politician. In 1956 his motivation was more about electing Stevenson than about race, but at this point he still held himself aloof from the more radical southern leaders such as Governor Timmerman.

Pleased when Stevenson won the 1956 Democratic Party nomination on the first ballot, Scott went on the offensive and castigated Eisenhower. He noticed that voters ate up Ike's smile and hand waving, but still, he declared, "behind the Eisenhower smile is a man who represents big business." He felt that the president will find it hard to "laugh away the farm problems that now confront us after four years of his administration." Although Stevenson was much better known by 1956, he had no chance against the popular Eisenhower and lost by a bigger margin than he had in 1952. Eisenhower got 457 electoral votes and 57.7 percent of the vote to 73 electoral votes for Stevenson. The Democratic nominee carried only seven states, including North Carolina, where Eisenhower made a surprisingly good showing. Stevenson narrowly won the state by a vote of 590,530 to Ike's 575,062.[76]

When not struggling with his stance on civil rights, Scott concentrated on the areas with which he felt most comfortable—agriculture and public works. He continued his plea for a world food bank to help block the Communist drive to recruit millions of hungry people around the globe. When a subcommittee of the Senate Foreign Relations Committee held hearings on the two resolutions that would establish the bank, the US Department of State raised Scott's ire by trashing the idea, saying that such a program was not needed. On June 13, 1956, Scott spoke on the Senate floor, asking his colleagues and President Eisenhower to use good common sense and revive the idea of a world food bank.[77] Despite support from several other senators, the idea never made much progress. The final blow came in a meeting of the Economic and Social Council of the United Nations when US representatives said that a world food bank would be too difficult to administer and in conflict with normal world trade.[78]

Conscious of the difficulties facing farmers in lean economic times, Scott became enraged with Eisenhower's veto of the 1956 Farm Bill. He remarked that, time and again, Secretary of Agriculture Ezra Taft Benson had demonstrated that he never intended to do anything about farm problems despite a crisis in the farm economy.[79] In a speech to the annual Mule Day Festival in Benson, North Carolina, the Tar Heel senator reminded listeners that, when campaigning for office, Eisenhower had promised that he would resolve all the farm problems and that farmers would become more prosperous. He told his audience that, every year since Eisenhower had been in office, farm income had gone down and surpluses had increased until the farm economy was at one of its lowest ebbs in history.[80] The old dairy farmer was overheard telling a constituent: "Eisenhower's as interested in farmers' welfare as farmers are in his golf course."[81]

Another area of concern for Senator Scott was federal disaster relief for his state. North Carolina had been badly damaged by four hurricanes in 1954 and 1955. It had suffered over $100 million in damages from the flooding and $30 million in crop losses. Scott sent President Eisenhower and Secretary Benson a telegram asking for $1 million in emergency funds to aid those farmers in desperate need. Later, he joined with Governor Hodges in testifying before a Senate appropriations committee seeking some $5.4 million for draining North Carolina canals, streams, and ditches of trees and other debris deposited by the hurricanes.

Scott described the grave damage inflicted by these storms—twenty-five thousand farm homes and buildings destroyed, four thousand urban homes destroyed, nineteen people killed, and property damage of more than $193 million. Torrential rains from the 1955 storms flooded 25 percent of the total land area in twenty-two coastal counties and destroyed many acres of crops. Both Scott and Hodges indicated that state resources had not been sufficient to repair the damage and that insurance coverage had been inadequate. Eisenhower had declared the area a major disaster area and allocated $4 million for the cleanup, but the state needed still more federal help. Scott spoke out in favor of federal flood insurance as insurance companies were reluctant to write wind or storm insurance. He believed that the federal government had a "very real responsibility" to bridge the gap.[82]

Scott's work on the Interior Committee consumed much of his time during 1955 and 1956. As chair of a joint Senate-House committee, he became involved in the investigation of an alleged boondoggle that gained national attention and later became known as the Al Serena case. The Democrats charged the Eisenhower Interior Department with "a frantic scheme" to pass $500,000 worth of publicly owned timber land to Al Serena, a private mining corporation in Oregon, on the basis of questionable mining claims.

Scott and the Democrats called this another "giveaway" of public lands to private interests by the Eisenhower administration. Scott said that the Department of the Interior was "determined to hand over many thousands of dollars' worth of national forest timber to private interests on a silver platter." Never one to mince words, he concluded: "As a result of high-level interference in the Department of the Interior, weasel-word legal opinions and questionable mineral sampling have been substituted for the dedicated judgment of government experts."

Scott promised to conduct the investigation of the Al Serena deal in a thorough and fair manner. The Republicans argued that the investigation was politically inspired and a veiled assault on the Eisenhower administration. Representative Claire Hoffman charged the Democrats with "bias and cowardly tactics, inflammatory and prejudicial statements, abusing the Constitution, maligning a private company's reputation," "relying on New Deal smear artists," and abandoning civil liberties and ordinary courtesies. Scott brushed off the negative comments and said that he would get to the bottom of the matter. He never did. Because of the partisan conflict, the hearings ended on February 7 without coming to any final conclusion.[83]

Every paper in North Carolina and most national periodicals supported Scott's investigation. R. C. Rome, a constituent, approved of his action in "protesting this give-away of valuable forest timber,"[84] while the *Rocky Mount Evening Telegram* thought that there were "smelly and suspicious" aspects of the deal and concluded that the Republicans were guilty of a "sell out of the public interest on a monumental scale": "Senator Scott seems to have hit pay dirt. . . . More power to him."[85] The *Washington Post* ran a series of eight articles examining the practices of the Interior Department, and its research demonstrated that the department had been "playing fast and loose with timber resources, . . . with dam sites and grazing lands." The result of this activity could "leave a larger black mark on the Eisenhower Administration than the stain given to the Truman administration by mink coats and deep freezers."[86]

The Eisenhower administration was simply doing what political parties had done for eons, rewarding its backers and contributors. The Democrats had been guilty of the same practices. The difference for Scott was that the Republican Party wanted to shift power away from government agencies and increase participation by private corporations. The Republicans hoped to eliminate what they called *creeping socialism* in the federal government and to restrain an ever larger, more intrusive government. Scott, always looking out for the people's interests over those of big business, had caught the Republicans in the act and had called them out.

After Scott announced in November that he would run for reelection in 1960, he kept a wary eye on Governor Luther Hodges. Hodges said he was interested only in state legislative matters, but Scott knew from several sources that he was considering the possibility of running for the Senate. Senator Clinton Anderson informed Scott that Bob Hanes had told him that Hodges was after Scott's Senate seat. When these rumors surfaced, Bob Reynolds, of all people, wrote Scott: "Don't worry about the opposition. If Hodges leaps from his pond to your bank, he is a dead frog. We are all for you." Reynolds's letter was accompanied by a cartoon showing Hodges squatting on a lily pad surrounded by all sorts of targets for which to jump, including Scott's Senate seat.[87] Harry Stokely, an old friend, told Scott that, regardless of what he said in public, Hodges "wants to be senator." Stokely cautioned that, while 1960 was a long way off, "let's not sleep."[88]

The *Charlotte Observer* speculated that Scott's supporters considered Hodges an almost certain challenger in 1960 but had wisely refrained from any early criticism of him. By early February 1957, when it appeared that Hodges was serious about running for Scott's seat, Terry Sanford signaled a shift in strategy. He dismissed Hodges's legislative program as "dangerously wrong" and too much in favor of big business. The *Charlotte Observer* called the comment "the opening gun in the 1960 campaign."[89]

At any rate, Scott was not taking any chances with a potential challenge by Hodges and decided to solicit the approbation of the state Bankers Association, a cornerstone of Hodges's support. To the astonishment of many, he lauded the bankers: "The entire population is indebted to the bankers for the foresight and leadership you have shown. . . . The North Carolina Bankers Association is widely recognized as a leader in farmer-banker relationships throughout the country." The *Charlotte Observer* could not believe that the man who stomped around the state in 1948 and 1954 cussing the moneychangers would now praise them. The next thing you know, it opined, he would talk sweet to a civic club and would be flattering the public utility companies.[90] Always an astute politician, and always in campaign mode, Scott was merely courting support from a key constituency in preparation for 1960.

By the end of 1957 Hodges had apparently given up the idea of running for Scott's seat, having concluded that Scott was unbeatable.[91] By November there were rumors that, instead of mounting a Senate bid, Hodges might want to be considered a possible candidate for vice-president on the Democratic ticket in the 1960 campaign.[92] Scott immediately signed on: "I'm for Governor Hodges as long as he wants to run for vice president and doesn't get the idea of running for the Senate, which I think would be a mistake."[93]

By 1957 Scott had developed a unwavering daily routine. After his brisk five-mile walk from his apartment in the Westchester, he tended to his correspondence and then spent much of his day in committee meetings and conferences with constituents and public officials and worked on the current legislative agenda. He concentrated on four subcommittees, all areas of professed interest: Flood Control and Water Conservation, Highways and Roads, Rural Electrification Administration and Farm Credit, and Postal Policy.[94] By 1957 he had become somewhat more conservative in some areas, primarily in the reduction in the size of government and proposed substantial cuts to the federal budget.[95] He had always been a fiscal conservative, as reflected by his frugal term as governor, but now he was witness to extraordinarily wasteful spending at the federal level and wanted to reign it in.

In the Eighty-fifth Congress, Scott voted in favor of small business tax relief and an 11 percent pay raise for federal employees and missed only 13 of 104 recorded votes during the first session.[96] In early January, he won bipartisan support for his resolution urging a Senate investigation of recent price increases in gasoline and fuel oil. His views on oil companies had not changed since he took office as governor. The recent one-cent increase in gasoline prices, he announced, "strongly indicates the possibility that the large oil companies are taking advantage of the public." The *Charlotte Observer* approved of Scott's probe as the inflationary spiral had to be stopped.[97] The *Greensboro Daily News* ran a cartoon showing Scott as a raging bull about to gore the wealthy oil companies.[98]

Scott worked assiduously for the comprehensive water plan for North Carolina that he had promoted since entering the Senate. His proposal envisioned $350 million for several projects: flood control, municipal sewage treatment, irrigation, improvement in city water supplies, and soil conservation. The plan would assure the state abundant and clean water, better soil protection, and immunity from the ravages of floods. Scott said that he wanted "to do for the waters of North Carolina what I have done for the roads of the state."[99]

Foreign policy issues held very little interest for Scott except for his fervent dislike of the new Eisenhower Doctrine. In 1956 Eisenhower persuaded Congress to pass a resolution to authorize the president to use military force and economic aid to stop aggression in any country in the Middle East that might be invaded by Communists. Eisenhower would act only with an invitation of the country under attack and would seek the approval of Congress in advance.

In a fiery speech on the Senate floor, Scott again accused Eisenhower of creating a chaotic foreign policy. Scott favored diplomacy and appeals to the United Nations rather than an impetuous military intervention, and he recalled that in October the president promised that he would not use American armed forces in the Suez crisis but, instead, seek a settlement through the United Nations. Now he appeared committed to a policy of go-it-alone intervention. Would he shoot first "and then consult Congress . . . before employing the armed forces?"

Scott saw the Eisenhower Doctrine as an "undated declaration of war" and called on Secretary of State John Foster Dulles to resign. Not for the first time, he insisted: "Dulles has got to go. All along we have been led to believe that we were on the verge of lasting peace. After many months of lulling us to sleep, the President now tells us bluntly that we are hanging on the brink of war." Dulles should resign because America needed a secretary of state who generated confidence, not confusion. Scott wanted to stop communism at all costs, but he "would feel a lot better . . . if Mr. Dulles was not calling the signals."[100]

As during Scott's previous three years in the Senate, civil rights issues dominated the domestic agenda in 1957. Responding to demands from northern liberals and blacks that there needed to be greater federal protection of voting rights in America, Eisenhower came up with the Civil Rights Act of 1957. The bill provided federal district courts with more authority to guarantee individual access to voting and gave the US attorney general the authority to file suit when voting rights had been violated. It also created a civil rights division in the Justice Department to be headed by an assistant attorney general and authorized the establishment of a nonpartisan civil rights commission that would study black-white relations and offer recommendations.

As expected, southern opposition to the bill was fierce and prolonged. Senator Harry Byrd said that it was "the most vicious legislation" he had seen in his career as the bill sought to "humiliate and destroy the South" for the sake of "collecting Negro votes." Fearful of impending integration, southern senators now began an organized and hard-nosed fight to prevent the civil rights legislation from passing.

Southern senators, led by Richard Russell, understood that in order to succeed they needed to tone down their rhetoric, deemphasize the question of race, and concentrate on constitutional issues, mainly states' rights. They had to placate their constituents, the great majority of whom opposed *Brown v. Board of Education,* but also try to persuade the North and moderates in Congress of the constitutional validity of their defense of states' rights. Since many southerners were powerful chairmen of key committees, they simply refused to hold hearings or used time-consuming procedural methods to prevent civil rights legislation from even being considered. These tactics, plus the filibuster, had worked effectively in the past. The southern caucus in the Senate realized that it probably could not prevent the legislation from passing, but it could, it felt, compromise and water it down with numerous amendments to the point where the bill would have little effect.

Senator Dick Russell's main problem with the civil rights act was Title II, which to his mind gave the US attorney general the power to use any means, even military force, to compel compliance with any civil rights order. This power, insisted Russell, would lead to the mingling of the races and bloodshed. However, when he convened the southern caucus, including Kerr Scott, he preached compromise, not filibuster. He and his team inserted into the civil rights bill a much debated amendment guaranteeing a jury trial in cases involving voting rights violations. This addition seemed democratic on the surface, and the southerners presented it in that light, arguing that the right to a trial by jury was guaranteed by the Constitution. The reality was that, in the segregated courts in the South, the all-white juries would seldom sustain the complaints of black litigants.[101]

From the outset, Scott was in the forefront of the fight against the civil rights bill. On January 3, 1957, he accused Eisenhower of turning "the dogs loose on the South" and chastised him for a "determined effort to shove a political civil rights bill down our throats." He hoped that the current administration would "just leave us alone in the South": "We can work out our own problems. . . . Somehow, we have got to make those people who have a warped conception of the South understand what we are up against."[102] Leave it to Scott to have a reference to dogs during a diatribe against impending civil rights legislation.

Scott had been inundated by letters from North Carolinians pleading with him to do everything possible to defeat any civil rights legislation. A Burlington native feared a "Hitlerite state" and wanted Scott's ongoing opposition to the "Civil rights monster."[103] Scott replied in a similar vein to most of the letters. To one correspondent he wrote: "You may count on me to oppose these proposals all the way down the line." To another: "We have really been whacking away at the civil rights legislation until the last tooth has been ground out."[104]

In March, never timid when facing an unreceptive audience, Scott spoke to a predominantly Negro audience in Roxboro. He began by announcing that he favored segregation and blasted the proposed civil rights bill as it would "pave the way for legal lynching of some of our most cherished existing rights." He condemned "demagogues of both races" and then praised the cooperation between whites and Negroes in Roxboro in winning a Rural Progress Award. He called the effort a fine example of good race relations in difficult times. North Carolinians had to show that "we can solve our own problems": "Any court decision that destroys the good will of people who have got to live and work together is worthless."[105] The *Norfolk Journal and Guide,* a black newspaper in Norfolk, Virginia, lauded Scott for having the courage to speak to a Negro audience and for trying to keep open the channels of communication between the races.[106]

In his stubborn defense of segregation and his outmoded concept of black goals, Scott missed the point of civil rights legislation. Negroes in North Carolina were not satisfied with the limited progress the state had made toward equality. Many blacks in the state could not vote, could not serve on juries, had a separate, vastly inferior education system, and constantly faced discrimination. Surely Scott knew that this discrimination existed, so why did he try to prevent federal intervention to improve the rights of minorities? He believed that many of the problems between the races could be worked out by North Carolinians of good faith without federal intrusion. As a southern gradualist, he was of the opinion that "legislation cannot be passed that will change the hearts and minds of human beings."[107]

However, in his speech on the Senate floor against the Civil Rights Act of 1957, Scott sounded less like a moderate on race and more like the southern demagogues he had recently condemned. Prior to his peroration, he admitted that he could not be elected to office in North Carolina unless he supported the southern position on civil rights and segregation. He told listeners that he thought he could help the white race. However: "I can help the colored man far more in the years to come by being re-elected to the United States Senate." He called the hypocritical supporters of the civil rights bill "self-styled, righteous civil righters and the buzzards of inequity." They were do-gooders, "the uninformed and misinformed politicians who spend their time slobbering about how cruel the South is to the Negro." These do-gooders were concerned not about the Negroes' right to vote but about how they voted. Civil rights legislation was really a battle for black votes in the big cities: "Political expediency and success at their home polling places where bias and prejudice are the rule rather than the exception, meant more to those who would press the bitter cup of integration to the lips of the Southland."

Scott's remarks were, for the most part, more about the constitutional rights of the states and the right to a trial by jury than a virulent attack on the Negro race. His greatest fear was that the bill would allow the president to send federal soldiers, armed with bayonets, into the South to force integration. This "new generation of carpetbaggers" would "enforce upon a peaceable people a way of life which a majority of neither wants." He also worried that the Civil Rights Commission would go around the South checking on election officials, a "sort of roving election year Gestapo."

He insisted that the state of North Carolina had made tremendous progress in the last few years, with better schools for Negroes and some twenty thousand new Negro voters. He reminded listeners that as governor he had appointed Dr. Trigg, a Negro, to the state Board of Education because he felt that Negro children should be represented on the board. Federal force would not work in his state: "I made this decision of my own free will and I have never regretted it. But I would have resigned as governor before I would have made that appointment under a court order."[108] In a later speech, he admitted that some Negroes had been denied the vote, but he assured his audience that discrimination in voting was not as serious as the public had been led to believe.[109]

Discrimination in voting existed in North Carolina, and, while not significant to Scott, it was important to black voters. Denial of the right to vote was unconstitutional and made a mockery of the concept of democracy. Scott persisted in his belief that blacks were perfectly happy with things as they were and convinced himself that his previous efforts to aid the Negro race were sufficient. His patronizing attitude smacked of racism, although he never personally expressed antagonism or prejudice against blacks. His views were typical for the time. He had always been for a segregated society, but he was more willing than most to work to improve the well-being of blacks and to encourage dialogue between the races. He believed in states' rights, although he was not a Dixiecrat, and he sincerely feared that federal intervention would lead to a race war. He was now on a different stage as a senator than he had been as governor and had been, to some degree, influenced by his fellow southern senators.

In the end, the southerners emasculated the civil rights legislation and got what they wanted—the right to a trial by jury and a significant reduction in federal enforcement authority. The Civil Rights Act of 1957, the first since Reconstruction, did establish some enforcement procedures and set up the nonpartisan Civil Rights Commission and the Civil Rights Division in the Department of Justice, but it had little effect on segregation in the South. Scott thought that the final bill was much improved over "the shrewdly contrived, vicious" one initially presented to the Senate. Southerners in the

Senate hoped that the passage of the bill would satisfy the liberals and curtail some of the civil rights activism in the country.[110]

An event that frightened southerners more than the civil rights act occurred in the fall of 1957. A federal district court had ordered the integration of the all-white Central High School in Little Rock, Arkansas, to commence in September. Bowing to the rabid segregationists in the state, Governor Orval Faubus tried to block integration of the school by declaring a state of emergency. When the federal court denied the governor's appeal to postpone the court's order, Faubus called out the Arkansas National Guard and ordered it to prevent blacks from entering Central High.

Faubus had blatantly disobeyed a federal court order and created the most significant crisis of the civil rights struggle to date. On September 23 and 24, 1957, Little Rock erupted into violence as a mob of over one thousand protestors gathered at the school to prevent the Negro students from attending. The demonstrators beat up four Negro journalists and threatened mayhem if the black students tried to attend classes. The mayor of Little Rock wired Eisenhower that the situation was out of his control and pleaded for federal troops. The president had earlier indicated that he could not imagine any set of circumstances "that would ever induce [him] to send Federal troops . . . into any area to enforce the orders of a federal court, because [he] believe[d] [that the] common sense of America will never require it." Aware of his fondness for the South and his dislike of the *Brown* decision, diehard defenders of states' rights never expected him to intervene in Little Rock.

The southerners misread the president's commitment to the rule of law. Appalled by the mob action at Central High, Eisenhower warned that he would use whatever force was necessary to uphold the court order, although he feared that such a decision would lead to more violence. Since Governor Faubus brazenly continued to flout federal law, on September 24 the president ordered one thousand troops from the 101st Airborne Division to Little Rock and federalized the Arkansas National Guard under his command. The troops quickly restored order, but photos of armed troops with fixed bayonets patrolling in Little Rock caused consternation all over the country, particularly in the South. Although he once again refused to endorse the *Brown* ruling, Eisenhower said that he sent in troops because of his "inescapable" responsibility and a strong sense of duty to enforce the law at all costs. He blamed the crisis on disorderly mobs led by "demagogic extremists" who tried to substitute force for the rule of law.

Stunned by the turn of events, southerners responded with obvious bitterness over what they perceived as Eisenhower's betrayal. Some compared the intervention to Hitler's use of storm troopers, and Faubus claimed that his state was now "occupied territory." Others referred to the destruction of the social fabric of the South.[111] Scott thought that the president had acted unwisely in sending troops into Little Rock in what he called "the carpetbagger invasion." Eisenhower moved with such vengeance, Scott declaimed, that it made matters worse. Not only did he not have the constitutional right to send in troops; no federal judge had the right to come in and tell the governor of Arkansas what to do—it violated the sovereignty of states. The greatest mistake, concluded Scott, was when Federal District Judge Ronald Davies refused to give Faubus more time to work out the problem on his own. He reminded Eisenhower of his July statement that he could not imagine sending in federal troops: "He's going back on his word."[112]

Scott had now moved from a moderate position on civil rights to a more forceful denunciation of federal intervention. Nonetheless, either from sincere conviction or from a need to protect his political viability, he stood shoulder to shoulder with the Thurmonds and the Russells of the world in condemning federal intervention in Little Rock. His states' rights bombast and an increasingly tin ear for the rights of minorities disappointed his progressive supporters both in the Senate and back home. Jonathan Daniels castigated Faubus for defying the law and for disarming "the decent South."[113] He did not specifically refer to Scott, but clearly he was unhappy with his longtime friend's descent into demagoguery.

As Scott began what would prove to be his last year serving the people of North Carolina, his main interests were as they had been for the duration of his political career. He had made it a practice early in each session of Congress to write his constituents to inform them of his thinking on vital problems facing the country and elicit their ideas and comments. In his 1958 letter, he announced a concern about the economic recession and President Eisenhower's indifferent attitude toward the problem. His key proposals for legislation that year included reduction of individual income taxes, an increase in small watershed projects and water conservation, a more realistic farm program, a program for school construction and scholarships without surrendering state control of school policies, and a step up in the federal highway building program.[114]

Scott had always been a hard worker, and his wife and advisers continued to have some concern about the state of his health. He had a yearly checkup at Duke University, and on every occasion the doctors reported an increase in hypertension and recommended a significant weight loss, more rest, and an end to the use of tobacco products. In 1953 Dr. Nicholson at Duke had reported the onset of hypertensive vascular disease with evidence of myocardio ischemia. In his yearly checkup on September 16, 1957, however, there were no warnings of any potential heart problems.[115]

On April 9, 1958, Senator Scott was on the way to have his driver's license renewed when he became ill. His wife, Mary, noticed that he was perspiring heavily and having trouble breathing. He was rushed to Alamance County Hospital in Burlington, and doctors determined that he had suffered a moderate heart attack.[116] Scott managed to survive the first critical twenty-four-hour period, and his doctor told reporters that his condition had improved. Resting in an oxygen tent, he was alert, talking and joking with family and staff. Dr. Blair said that Scott mainly complained about not getting enough to eat and reported that he had not taken "too kindly" to the doctor's decision to cut off all tobacco. By April 12 the prognosis was good for a full recovery, although Scott would need three months of rest before returning to work. One doctor assured friends that he should be able to run for reelection in 1960. After the doctor's visit on April 16, Scott was in good spirits and looked forward to his birthday on April 17.[117]

Assuming that the senator was on the road to recovery, the state and the nation were surprised to learn of his sudden passing. Scott died without warning on the eve of his sixty-second birthday. Dr. Blair later reported the cause of death as a sudden extension of the original heart attack with a rupture of the part of the heart damaged by the previous attack. Oxygen, artificial stimulants, and artificial respiration were used in an effort to revive the senator, without success.[118]

Senator Sam Ervin announced Scott's death in the Senate chamber: "It is with profound shock and sorrow that I convey to the Senate the sad tidings that my able and distinguished colleague, Senator W. Kerr Scott, died tonight at Alamance Hospital."[119] In Room 462 of the Senate Office Building, Scott's office workers wept unashamedly when they heard the news. One staff member recalled: "It's a funny thing you know, the last thing he voted for in the Senate was roads."[120]

Praise for Scott flooded in from all over the country. Governor Hodges said: "North Carolina has lost a great and distinguished citizen and public servant. . . . He was a man of strong conviction, a staunch friend of the people of North Carolina who served them well." Congressman Harold Cooley recalled: "He performed every public task magnificently during a long and distinguished career." Most encomiums referred to his strong, emotional tie to the little people of his state. Senator Lyndon Johnson noted: "His long and colorful career endeared him to the people of his state and all who knew him. He talked straight." State representative John Umstead pointed out his effect on North Carolina politics: "His death is a great loss to the liberal forces in North Carolina and in this country." His colleague Senator Sam Ervin said: "He has plowed to the end of the row; his furrow is deep; time will not erode his indelible imprint upon our great state for which he so unceasingly labored and gave his full measure."[121] Calling Scott "one of the foremost liberals in the South," the *New York Times* reported that as governor he had spoken out for Negro rights and had cracked down on the Ku Klux Klan. At the same time, he was unwilling to break down the barriers of segregation in his state and thought that most Negroes did not want integration.[122]

Scott was survived by his wife, Mary, two sons, Robert and Osborne, one daughter, Mary Kerr Loudermilk, and four brothers, Ralph, S. Floyd, Henry A., and A. Hughes Scott. The family planned the funeral for a Friday afternoon at the Hawfields Presbyterian Church, where Scott had been an elder, and where his family had worshiped for many years.

On a golden April day, under warm spring sunshine in plowing time, Kerr Scott was laid to rest. Services were at the simple brick church built in 1852. The pastor, the Reverend Ralph Buchanan, paid tribute to Scott for spending his life "in service to his fellow man" and for centering his life around "home, church and community": "This is the combination of loyalties that produces great men." Buchanan noted: "As long as men read history, the life of Senator Scott will be an inspiration."

Both state and national dignitaries attended the funeral. One motorcade included Senator Sam Ervin and seventeen fellow US senators. Governor Luther Hodges led another motorcade of the state's top officials. The dignitaries were men of power and position, but the vast majority of the crowd, estimated at seventy-five hundred, were Scott's neighbors and the Branchhead Boys, who were with him until the end—wet-eyed, gnarled old men hobbling on canes who had come in battered pickup trucks over "Scott-top" roads to pay their respects. Prior to the ceremony, a steady stream of common folk filed by Scott's open casket to view his rugged countenance one last time. Scott, of course, had always predicted that there would be a big crowd at his funeral: "A lot of my friends will come and a lot of curious folks will turn up. And there'll be a lot who want to know if the s.o.b. is really dead."

Although they had mechanical means available, a dozen of his friends

A crowd of mourners at Kerr Scott's funeral on April 18, 1958, at the Hawfields church in Haw River. Courtesy of the State Archives of North Carolina, Raleigh.

had risen before dawn to dig his grave, honoring a Haw River tradition that friends see to a man's final resting place. Bob Scott, his son, said that act had always impressed him because it reminded him that his neighbors considered Kerr Scott as "one of their own." Many of the plain country folk who attended the funeral had been directly affected by Scott's labor for better roads, schools, and medical care and were grateful for his work in getting phones and electricity for the rural areas of the state. One close friend said that the country was losing "a friend of the farmer": "I always thought he was a good, clean statesman who said what he thought and fought for what he thought was right."[123] Many of those who had been helped by Scott were deeply saddened by his death. Some said they had not seen such an outpouring of grief for a public man since the train bearing Franklin Roosevelt's body passed through the state. Scott's pastor, Ralph Buchanan, remembered that, on the day of his funeral, he had gone to the church early and noticed a car parked adjacent to the cemetery. Its occupant, Mr. Coble, had delivered Scott's mail for thirty years. Coble was watching his neighbors dig Scott's grave and, with tears running down his cheeks, told Buchanan: "The poor people of North Carolina have lost the best friend they ever had."[124] A Franklin County farmer summarized the feelings of many of Scott's supporters: "It hurts so bad I didn't know what to do. He was one of the finest men we ever had in Raleigh and up there in Washington. There just ain't nobody to take his place. They just don't have the heart in 'em he had. I just don't know what we are going to do without him."[125]

Scott was laid to rest in the century-old cemetery next to the Hawfields church, near his ancestors, covered with the soil he loved so well. He would never again be far from Haw River. Miss Mary believed that his time in the Senate, away from Hawfields, had hastened his death. In Washington he could not get home as often to the nurturing and relaxing home place that he missed so much and that had sustained him over the years. His tombstone read:

> William Kerr Scott, April 17, 1896–April 16, 1958
> Son of Walter and Elizabeth Hughes Scott
> Elder in Hawfields Presbyterian Church, 1933–1958
> Commissioner of Agriculture, 1937–1948
> Governor of North Carolina, 1949–1953
> U.S. Senator, 1954–1958
> "I have fought a good fight, I have kept the faith." Timothy 4:7

Editorial comments from around the state and nation were uniformly positive. Most recounted his Go Forward program and what good roads and schools and better health care had done for the state. The *Charlotte News,* never a fan, thought of him as an "uncommon common man who had a sure knowledge of the sources of power in a democracy and who brought new strength and unity to the state": "His courageous and candid spirit would remain a moving force in the state for years."[126] The *Wilmington Star,* a frequent foe, grudgingly admitted that, although Scott was controversial and a disturber of the status quo, he was a resourceful, determined man and one of the state's most progressive leaders.[127] The *Morganton Citizen* said: "We think North Carolina is a better place to live because Kerr walked this way."[128] The *Asheville Citizen* commented on his personality: "[His rugged exterior] failed to hide another side of his character. He was gentle, loyal, affectionate, qualities that endeared him to family and friends." The outpouring of genuine grief from persons in all walks of life testified to that esteem.[129]

On August 11, 1958, the US Senate held a memorial service for its departed colleague. There were two remarkable things about the proceedings. It was practically the only time that people got together to talk about Scott "without a word of criticism being uttered," and praise for the North Carolinian came from a remarkably diverse group. Wayne Morse of Oregon called him "a great southern liberal," while Herman Talmadge of Georgia, at the opposite end of the political spectrum from Morse, acknowledged his work "in the interests of the little people." Accolades came from Strom Thurmond and John Stennis from the South but also from New Englanders like George Aiken of Vermont and westerners like Frank Church of Idaho. They recognized that Scott understood that "democracy is essentially the accommodation of the conflicting interests of the people."[130]

One other, unresolved event had an immense significance for the Scott family and friends. After Scott's death, Governor Luther Hodges had to select his successor to the Senate. Hodges, who later claimed to have been under tremendous pressure from conservatives in the state, paid his respects to Mrs. Scott on April 17, one day prior to the funeral. After delivering his condolences to the widow, he immediately departed to visit B. Everett Jordan at his office in Saxapahaw. On April 19, 1958, just twenty-four hours after Scott's burial, Hodges called his aide, Harold Makepeace, to inform him that he had selected B. Everett Jordan to serve the remaining two years of Scott's term. When Hodges made the announcement to the press, he revealed that he had carefully studied a list of thirty-three names before making his selection.[131] Since he made his choice in forty-eight hours, it would have been impossible to study the list carefully. Hodges usually made decisions quickly, and on this occasion he wanted to avoid pressure from the press and constituents. It was Jordan from the outset.

Hodges picked Jordan partly because they were friends. Both worked in the textile business and had shared time in the Rotary Club. Much more conservative than Scott, Jordan was acceptable to the old guard in the state and would work closely with Senator Ervin. Hodges appreciated that the sixty-one-year-old Jordan was a skilled political operative, having served as chairman of the state Democratic Executive Committee and then as the state's Democratic national committeeman.[132]

Many newspapers assumed that Jordan would be a seat-warmer for Hodges, who would run for the Senate in 1960,[133] but Harold Makepeace

US Senate appointee B. Everett Jordan and his wife shortly before he was sworn in as a US senator. Angered by the choice of one of Scott's bitter enemies, his supporters thought Jordan's selection was a personal insult to Scott's memory. Photograph by Edward J. McCauley, North Carolina Collection, University of North Carolina at Chapel Hill Library.

insisted that there was no deal for Jordan to sit in for Hodges until 1960.[134] Mrs. B. Everett Jordan said that, when Hodges made the offer to her husband, she never heard Hodges say that he wanted the seat or that Jordan was a temporary appointee.[135] The *Raleigh News and Observer,* as expected, excoriated the choice and chastised Jordan as an extreme conservative. The paper accused him of breaking with Scott and opposing his Go Forward program. By his actions Jordan had "callously betrayed" Scott.[136] The *Scotland Neck Commonwealth* defended Hodges's choice, saying that Jordan was a man of considerable ability with both business and political experience. It denounced the *News and Observer* for expecting Hodges to name someone with the same political philosophy as Kerr Scott. It thought it entirely proper for a conservative governor to select someone who fit his philosophy, just as Scott had done with Frank Graham. And since when, argued the paper, did a difference of political views become betrayal?[137] Several of Scott's enemies chortled over the demise of the Scott organization: "The collectivist, left-wing group that attached themselves to Senator Scott is now boiled down to a small, hard core in whose center are sitting Terry Sanford and Jonathan Daniels."[138]

Angered and "deeply offended" by Hodges's choice of Jordan, Scott supporters considered the selection a personal insult to the memory of Kerr Scott. Although Hodges tried to soften the blow by pointing out that Scott and Jordan were neighbors and Scott's wife Mary and B. Everett were first cousins, such posturing did not help. Terry Sanford said that the choice was "outrageous" as Jordan was a political foe of Scott and far removed from his political philosophy.[139] Ben Roney and Roy Wilder Jr. refused to work for Jordan and resigned immediately. Roney explained why: "He betrayed Kerr Scott and Kerr Scott considered him more concerned with special interests than with the good of the people."[140]

Whatever people's view of the Jordan appointment, the Kerr Scott era had ended in North Carolina. He was gone, but his spirit and his legacy would live on. He would be remembered as one who truly cared about the forgotten people in the state. He spoke their language and shared their faith and their hopes. The people understood him and believed in him, and he came through for them. His goal as a public servant was to labor for their advancement. He built roads, schools, and hospitals in order to improve their future and give rural people greater opportunity. He took his strength from these plain, strong, and unpretentious people and never forget from whence he came.

11

LEGACY

The greatest contribution Kerr Scott made to his state came during his term as governor. His time in the US Senate was limited owing to his untimely death, and, as a junior senator, he never had the influence and power to promote significant legislation. A doer and a mover, he had been frustrated at the slowness and complexity of the congressional legislative process and frequently complained that it was difficult to get anything done. He devoted most of his time and energy in the Senate to his committee responsibilities.

His goals in the Senate never wavered: the protection of agricultural subsidies, especially for tobacco; the improvement of the living conditions of farmers; water and soil conservation; pollution control and flood control; and the development of water power and the nation's highways. His proposal for a comprehensive and coherent water plan for North Carolina served as a blueprint for later improvements.

Scott remained a populist during his days in the Senate, often excoriating big business, investigating what he considered unwarranted increases in gas prices, and voting for projects to assist the poor and the elderly, such as better public housing, federal aid to education, and a form of national health insurance. He cast some significant votes during his time in the Senate: in favor of the censure of Joe McCarthy, for the National Defense Education Act, against the Bricker Amendment, and against the Civil Rights Act of 1957. He rained criticism on Ezra Taft Benson, the secretary of agriculture, for his failure to aid the farmer.

Civil rights consumed much of Scott's time in the Senate. His speeches on *Brown v. Board of Education* and his support of the Pearsall Amendment reflected his opposition to integration. He signed the Southern Manifesto and vigorously fought the Civil Rights Act of 1957. In denouncing *Brown,* he used harsh rhetoric uncharacteristic of his past pronouncements. He referred to the decision as a "legal lynching" and called Eisenhower's use of troops in Little Rock "a carpetbagger invasion" and a violation of states' rights.

In foreign policy, Scott usually followed the line of the Democratic Party and listened to policy experts before casting his vote. He voted in favor of the Southeast Asia Treaty Organization and approved rearming West Germany and its admission to NATO. While usually a strong supporter of the administration's Cold War strategy, he sharply criticized Eisenhower for taking the nation close to war in both the Quemoy-Matsu crisis and the Middle East conflict in 1956.

Scott remained a strong Democrat throughout his time in Washington, voting with the party approximately 80 percent of the time. He supported liberal candidates on the national level, campaigning for Truman in 1948, and endorsing Stevenson in 1952 and 1956. Perhaps his greatest contribution in the Senate came with his proposal to establish a world food bank to feed the poor, reduce farm surpluses, and fight communism. Although the idea never took hold during his lifetime, it perfectly captured his commonsense approach to politics and his ongoing concern for the downtrodden in the world.

While Scott made numerous contributions to the farm community in North Carolina while commissioner of agriculture, he made his chief mark as governor. A recap of his major accomplishments in that office and the effect of his Go Forward program is essential in evaluating his legacy. As he remarked when beginning his gubernatorial campaign, rural North Carolina was the land of forgotten people, and what was bad for two-thirds of the state was bad for the entire state.

During his term in office, Scott made great inroads in correcting those inequities. He proposed and helped pass a $200 million bond issue for roads and a $50 million bond issue for schools. Those funds resulted in 14,810 miles of newly paved roads and thousands more miles of upgraded and improved byways. Farmers could get their products to market more easily and visit larger cities for the goods and services available there. Buses now carried students to school over much-improved roads.

Education was dear to Scott, and he knew, as well as anyone, that in 1948 a state with a significant rate of illiteracy and an average of only 7.9 years of schooling for whites and 5.3 years for Negroes needed major improvements in its education system. The problem was especially acute in rural areas, where there were not enough classrooms or qualified teachers. By 1952, 8,000 new classrooms, 175 gymnasiums, and 350 lunchrooms had been constructed. Scott could boast of $330 million worth of permanent improvements in institutions of higher learning during his four years in Raleigh. He insisted on pay raises for teachers, and he got them. Understanding that the state's richest possession was the great army of children who would be the citizens of the future, he knew that children needed inspiration from teachers and that teachers needed to be honored and their work valued.

Owing partly to Scott's constant prodding of electric and telephone companies, some 31,000 rural phones were installed and 150,000 additional rural electric service connections were made. These technological improvements ended the crippling isolation of rural communities. Electric power improved productivity, and telephones enabled RFD residents to communicate with customers, doctors, and neighbors. Scott also demanded more electric power from the private power companies, and they responded. His proposals for dams and hydroelectric power in the Cape Fear River basin served as the basis for future industrial development in the state.

Scott's concern for bettering the health of the citizens of North Carolina resulted in a $550,000 annual appropriation for a statewide school health program. This program helped children afflicted by the diseases of poverty—pellagra, rickets, and hookworm. Permanent improvements were provided at mental hospitals at a time when very few government officials were concerned with mental health. Governor Scott pushed for the building of the new dental school and the new teaching hospital and medical school in Chapel Hill, a huge boost to improved health care in the state. He presided over the construction of new hospitals, nursing homes, and community health care centers, in many instances in areas where there had been no previous facilities. Additional monies were allocated for public health programs and the treatment of tuberculosis. Old-age assistance and aid to dependent children increased significantly during his time in Raleigh.

Under the Scott administration, agricultural programs achieved unprecedented goals. The governor began a modernization of the prison system and curbed excessive punishment by corrections officers. In an effort to rehabilitate prisoners, Scott proposed a prison psychologist, an education director, vocational training, and a first offender training center.

Scott was the first governor to be concerned about the great significance of water and water conservation for the future of the state. He produced the first real comprehensive plan in North Carolina for the development and conservation of water and natural resources. His goals were to improve the amount and quality of water for irrigation, to get better sewage treatment, and lessen pollution, halt soil erosion, and prevent flooding.

Kerr Scott, the most prolabor governor of his era, changed the relationship between state government and labor unions by protecting workers' rights to bargain collectively. Rather than automatically backing business owners, he worked as a neutral arbiter in management/labor conflicts such as the Hart Mill strike. He also expressed his concern for the working man by trying to repeal the anti–closed shop law and by promoting a minimum wage.

A devout Presbyterian, Scott spoke out against religious prejudice, in particular anti-Catholicism. He fought for diversity in thought and belief, arguing that a nation could not achieve its full promise when it used racial or religious prejudice to work against the rights of individuals. He was awarded the *Carolina Israelite* Gold Medal in 1950 as the North Carolinian "who made the most outstanding contribution to human rights." When Jonathan Daniels presented the award to Scott, he declared: "I don't believe there has been any man in my lifetime more worthy to wear this medal."[1]

Although not always interested in details, Scott became an effective manager of the state's affairs. He presided over balanced budgets (in conjunction with a conservative legislature), worked hard to cut down government waste, and had only one tax increase during his four years in office—the one-cent tax on gasoline. He also earned more than $10 million for the state by investing surplus, previously idle funds. He ran his Go Forward program on a foundation of human needs. In his biennial address in 1951, he reminded Tar Heels that it was as important to balance the state budget on the social and economic needs of the people as it was to balance its income and expense accounts.

Under Scott, the state achieved the centuries-old dream of deep water port facilities and outlets on the coast with the construction of modern facilities in Morehead City and Wilmington. While Scott frequently pounded on civic clubs and big business for their one-sided view of the world, he eagerly promoted industrial development in the state. He did not cater only to farmers as some 398 new industrial plants were brought into the state and several new power plants came on line. These new industries provided employment for an estimated thirty-nine thousand North Carolinians. Dr. Frank Graham expressed the views of many North Carolinians in 1963 when he honored Scott "for the enduring things he did to move our state forward on so many fronts": "North Carolina is a stronger democracy and a wider servant to people in agriculture, business, roads, schools, colleges, hospitals, medical centers and better health facilities . . . because of his valiant and forward leadership."[2]

These statistics constitute the physical and measurable effect that Scott had on the state. As a visionary, forward-looking governor, he provided citizens with a positive attitude toward new beginnings and the commitment to ensure that all elements of society were represented in government. He changed the political landscape in 1948 by besting the old guard and the Gardner machine that had controlled state politics for a quarter of a century. The election of 1948 shifted priorities and altered the focus of state government to a more progressive, all-inclusive agenda.

A skilled, pragmatic politician, Scott never lost an election. He was elected three times as commissioner of agriculture and won one term as governor and one term as a US senator. He triumphed in his only bond election by setting up a citizens' committee to organize the successful vote. He understood the needs and yearnings of the average people in the state and turned that insight into a huge political advantage. The Squire's relentless energy, his sense of humor, his candor, and his homespun qualities appealed to the average voter. He pushed an astounding array of game-changing bills through the 1949 legislative session after conservative legislators pulled out all the stops to impede his programs. He achieved the goals of his Go Forward program when the experts said that he lacked the vision and the courage to be successful. While often tactless and impulsive, Kerr Scott succeeded largely *because* he was a man of integrity and demonstrated courage, vision, constancy, and practical good sense.

Scott presided over one of the most open and accessible gubernatorial terms in modern history. He held press conferences on a weekly or biweekly basis when in residence and, almost without fail, answered questions from the press in a straightforward manner. There was never much doubt about where he stood on any issue.

Perhaps as important as any of Scott's legislative successes were his appointments to key state positions. The selection of Susie Sharp as the first female superior court judge improved the status of women in the state and struck a blow for women's equality. As Judge Sharp mentioned in her response to Governor Scott on her selection: "I know that when you honored me, you also honored the women of the state." Convinced that women could serve as well as or better than men in public office, Scott provided the opportunity for other women to serve their fellow citizens by selecting many women for state boards. He appointed the first two women to the state Board of Education, the first woman to the state Board of Conservation and Development, and the first female assistant commissioner of paroles. Fifteen percent of his gubernatorial appointments went to women—over twice the number of his predecessor. He had a woman as his assistant campaign manager in 1948, and as a US senator he sponsored a bill giving women more rights.

The bold choice of Dr. Harold Trigg to be the first black member of the state Board of Education took fortitude and a belief that this opportunity would improve education for Negroes in the state. Scott appointed other blacks to state boards, primarily the governing boards of black public institutions of higher education in the state. He consistently argued for making Negro schools equal to white schools. He made certain some of the $50 million school bond money went to repair existing schools and build new schools for minorities and determined that Negro public schools would receive a higher percentage of state money than they would have had the allocation been based on their percentage of the population.

Scott's willingness to begin a dialogue with Negroes in the state and to listen to their grievances marked a step forward in race relations. In 1950, without fear of a political backlash, the governor said that the time for advancement for minorities in the state was now. He frequently spoke to Negro audiences and talked openly and honestly about his views. He never went so far as to push for expanded voting rights or for integrated schools, but he kept his promise and increased funding to black schools and colleges.

There were, of course, significant political defeats. The most prominent, and perhaps the most disappointing, was Dr. Frank Graham's loss to Willis Smith in 1950 in the second primary. Scott loved to do the unexpected and had the audacity to appoint the state's foremost liberal to an open US Senate seat, choosing a nonlawyer and a university president instead of a typical politician. He did lose some prestige and power because of that defeat, but it did not deter his Go Forward program. The 1950 senate campaign, with its racial bigotry and callous charges, was a blow to the integrity of the political process and to the prestige of North Carolina as a progressive state. Scott gained a measure of retribution over his 1950 tormenters when he won the race for the US Senate in 1954 in what became known as "the third primary."

Scott got credit from some political observers for making a bold and uncompromising choice in Graham, but giving his seal of approval to Hubert Olive in the 1952 gubernatorial race proved to be an unwise decision. Scott thought Olive would be a good governor, but he mainly wanted to defeat William Umstead and the conservatives to prevent them from undoing his Go Forward program. He put his prestige on the line for a candidate who was a decided underdog, and Olive's loss by a substantial margin embarrassed him. He could not transfer his popularity to other candidates. In

1950 Graham had been done in by racial invective Scott could not control, and in 1952 Olive lost because he was a weaker candidate than Umstead.

Scott took on too many lost causes. His battle against the Powell Bill was doomed to failure, but his ego was involved, and he could not admit defeat. He was too combative and made everything personal. For him, however, it became personal when opponents tried to derail his programs. If he had stepped back on occasion or agreed to compromises, he might have been more successful with the legislature, but that was not how he operated. He liked to stir things up. The 1951 legislature defeated virtually all his key proposals, and those same conservatives dealt him perhaps his most humiliating setback when they denied him the traditional position as head of the state delegation at the 1952 Democratic national convention.

As governor, Scott made some very good appointments to state offices, but too often he selected cronies and political friends instead of the best-qualified candidates. His choice of Tony Tolar as head of the Highway Patrol proved to be a disastrous decision, and his stubborn attempt to have his former friend David Coltrane forcibly removed from office showed his petty, vindictive side. He dismissed many good public servants because of what he perceived to be disloyalty to him or his cause. These wholesale firings undermined the morale of state workers and led to charges that Scott was a tyrant who would not brook any disagreement.

Scott's choices for the state supreme court bordered on the unfathomable. Scott did not like or understand lawyers, but, even so, the selection of his old friend Murray James was simply inexplicable. He should have picked Jeff Johnson, who was better qualified. In an unprecedented move, the state Democratic Executive Committee ended up selecting Johnson anyway, thus negating Scott's choice of James. Scott acted out of friendship, but his judgment in this case caused him a humbling defeat that could have been avoided. When he picked I. T. Valentine for the North Carolina Supreme Court, the Democratic Party once again turned against him and defeated Valentine at the polls. Perhaps his most egregious mistake as governor came when he elected to set aside $485,000 of surplus highway funds for Alamance County. He had already profited by having the state pave all the roads around his farm, and this unwise and regrettable move was too much for most North Carolinians. He should have been reimbursed $12,000 by the state for his land and loss of crops, but he clearly took advantage of his position as governor to get all his roads paved at once. He arrogantly admitted directing the engineer to build the roads, much to the distaste of the many state citizens who had to wait for their roads. There was no hint of scandal surrounding Scott during his time in office, but this money grab smacked of an excessive use of power and led to charges of a Scott dictatorship. At least he had the good sense to cancel the grant.

Scott's place of birth and the strong influence of his Scotch Presbyterian ancestors to a large degree determined his personality—his tenacity, his faith, his conscience, and his great desire to help people help themselves. Always a man of the soil, Scott reflected the basic common sense of the farmer and lived his life buttressed by his unbending belief in family, God, and public service. His personality, a major factor in his political success, was, to say the least, controversial. His speech was native and salty, as apt to sting as to delight. His actions were direct and unpredictable, and his blunt, outspoken approach to issues and to individuals offended many of his foes. He said in his early years that, if he ever had a conviction about something, he would come out with it. Some critics saw his certainty about issues as self-righteous and stubborn, and often it was. His friends admired his candid, sincere, straight talk and preferred to view his steadfast views as loyalty to an idea and a cause.

Scott could be alternately gruff, brusque, and aggressive and then humorous and charming. The Scott grin, as ubiquitous as his cigar, often reflected his amusement at a subject and frequently disarmed his adversaries. An artful, crafty politician, Scott usually had a purpose for his brash comments. He loved a fight and hated to lose. He believed that the best way to get people to accomplish what he wanted was to push and prod them. Complacency and acceptance of the status quo rankled him. He wanted change, and he worked constantly to achieve his goals.

While Scott accomplished much of what he wanted and the end results were beneficial to the state's citizens, there were problems with his autocratic leadership and win-at-all-costs attitude. Despite his many successes, the cult of personality had its drawbacks. His harsh criticism of his foes increased the growing rift between the progressive and the conservative wings in the Democratic Party. His arbitrary and vindictive firing of those he considered disloyal restricted their democratic right to advocate for the politicians of their choice. Letters to the governor's office constantly complained about his highhanded tactics and his willingness to insult foes and run roughshod over any delaying tactics. Scott remained convinced that there were no other options. He knew that he had a limited amount of time to accomplish his goals, and he believed that the only way to achieve results was to bulldoze his way past conservatives who had denied equal rights to citizens for too long. He knew that he had antagonized and upset many citizens in the state, but he always believed his work was for a good and noble cause.

In many cases Scott succeeded in goading people into desired behavior. Surely he would not have been as effective in getting the power companies to put in new electric lines and the phones companies to install new phones without his constant complaints that they were not living up to their responsibilities as good citizens of the state. He probably overdid it by sniping at civic clubs, and his job as governor would have been easier if he had not continually insulted the state legislature. The resourceful Scott understood that he could often bypass the legislature and get his way if he could manipulate public opinion in favor of his cause or call public attention to a problem that needed fixing. He knew that his foes would dislike him whatever he said or did and that his hard-core advocates would stand by him under most circumstances. He thought that he had little to lose, and he took it on himself to influence those who were undecided.

Scott's philosophy of government had been strongly influenced by his early Populist views, FDR's New Deal, and Harry Truman's Fair Deal. Scott believed that government should supply important services to the people such as social security, a minimum wage, and public housing. As governor, he helped get the have-nots some of the long-overdue public services denied them by conservatives in state government. To his mind, government, both state and federal, had the additional responsibility of securing the future of all its citizens through protection of the environment, rural electrification, health care, better education facilities, and farm subsidies—all of which would reduce the gap between rich and poor and promote economic growth. He did not favor helping the poor with low-wage jobs; instead, he wanted new industries in the state that offered better-paying jobs to increase mass purchasing power. He realized that poverty was a serious issue in the state and would restrain the state's progress unless resolved with strong, across-the-board economic development. He desired frugality in government and opposed high taxes, but he was adamant that citizens needed to pay their fair share for necessary services.

How, then, does one characterize this political philosophy? Was Scott a populist? A progressive? An agrarian liberal? If a populist is defined as one who represents and concerns himself with the interests of the ordinary people, particularly farmers and industrial workers, then Kerr Scott qualified. Throughout his career, he devoted his time and energy to improving the lives of those who were physically isolated or who fell into the lower income bracket—the common man. When asked why he wanted to run for governor, he replied that he wanted to represent those who did not have a lobbyist in Raleigh. When asked about the most important event in his four years as governor, he said that it was when on election night in 1949 the state approved the bond issues and agreed with him on the importance of better roads and schools. He never relented in his unwavering commitment to the underprivileged of society.

Perhaps most telling for a populist, Scott feared the increasing influence of the private corporations that were coming to dominate the economic scene and wielding immense political power. He frequently denounced the "big money boys" because he feared that, if these irresponsible capitalists were allowed to operate unchecked, they would overwhelm the public good and undermine democracy. That is why, in his inimical way, he argued with bankers over interest on state deposits and fought the oil companies over increased gas prices. He had a naive view of the business world and thought that big business had only one goal, corporate profit. He tended to overlook business leaders' significant contributions to the state economy in investments, support for education and health care, and supplying jobs.[3]

Scott certainly did not fit into V. O. Key Jr.'s description of North Carolina's "progressive plutocracy." Key recognized that an aristocracy or oligarchy of bankers and industrialists dominated the state's political and economic decision making. He saw the Gardner machine as progressive because it moved the state forward in many areas. Scott viewed machine politics as undemocratic and always favoring the upper classes at the expense of the poor. He was certainly more progressive than Charlie Johnson. If Johnson had won in 1948, the state would have had slower growth, limited advances for women and Negroes, only slight achievement in schools and public health care, and only $100 million in road improvements—in short, the status quo.

Paul Luebke, in his book *Tar Heel Politics,* generally agreed with Key's definition of *progressivism.* He used the terms *traditionalists* and *modernizers* to define the competing philosophies of the development of North Carolina. The traditionalists by and large were conservatives committed to economic change that would benefit the state's business community and preserve the old guard. They opposed social change, they were antitax and anti–big government, and their beliefs were often based on fundamentalist Protestantism. The modernizers wanted to build a New South and focused on individual economic development, the diversification of the economy, a commitment to improve education, the accommodation of blacks, women, and union members, and a belief in an active government. Luebke argued that they were not real liberals on either social or economic issues and that at best the modernizers were "moderate-conservatives." He concluded that the Scott progressives got short-circuited in Graham's 1950 defeat and then became moderates.[4] He did not, however, allow for the possibility of a modernizer-progressive blend, which would be the most appropriate way to describe the administrations of Kerr Scott, Terry Sanford, and Jim Hunt. He believed that the populists and the liberals had little influence in North Carolina, but he underestimated Scott's dramatic effect on the state and his work to give greater political equality to citizens along racial and gender lines, thus setting the stage for Sanford and Hunt. Scott's progressive reform agenda was not promoted by Governors Umstead and Hodges, and the state quickly reverted to its more conservative ways. In the 1950s South, long-term progressive changes were difficult to achieve and hard to maintain. The race issue dominated much of the political activity during that period, and southern conservatives held firm sway except for an occasional J. W. Fulbright or Albert Gore Sr.

How does one define Scott in terms of his views on race? Although he favored racial segregation in society, for his day he was a moderate, not a radical. He repeatedly noted that he had never advocated the elimination of segregation in the schools. He believed that forced integration would bring on conflict that could otherwise be avoided. Despite some incendiary oratorical flourishes in the Senate, he did not preach hatred or violent and illegal action to maintain segregation. He was not a demagogue on race and never used racial epithets to gain office—he denounced such tactics. He fought the Klan and opposed the Dixiecrats, favoring state responsibility, not states' rights. He respected the rule of law; he simply disagreed with the *Brown* decision. He remained convinced that whites and Negroes could work out their own problems if the federal government would stay out of their affairs. He wrongly assumed that Negroes were happy with the status quo and that they too opposed integration.

Scott began to move away from his more moderate positions on race with the *Brown* decision, the Civil Rights Act of 1957, and his censure of Eisenhower's decision to send troops to Little Rock. He was closer to the positions of Senator Lister Hill and other more moderate southern senators than to the views of Senators Richard Russell and Eugene Talmadge. To some degree, he compromised his views on race for what he believed was the good of the country. He knew that he could aid the farmers and the poor only if he kept his seat, so he accepted the southern position on civil rights.

These tenets of gradualism and paternalism became part of the accepted tradition of southern white liberals. Despite his overtures to Negroes and his earlier moderate position on race, Scott failed to promote the one thing that would have enhanced southern progress—greater equality for Negroes. Numan Bartley maintained that, when former liberals became moderates on race, they explained their retreat by citing the certainty of a violent reaction from lower-income whites. Expecting that economic development and education would eventually resolve the problem, former liberals rejected northern and federal intervention in southern affairs. They never got around to soliciting local support for a policy of gradualism.[5] Ralph McGill concurred with Bartley's view. He argued that the ideology of moderation was mostly myth and that racial liberals ended up standing on the sidelines urging both parties to be calm but proposing no constructive plan of action to tamp down the animosity.[6] When Kerr Scott failed to build up support for gradual change in race relations, the conservatives and racists won by default. In this way, he was like many other "closet moderates," who believed that they simply could not change the southern view on race without seriously damaging their own political careers. When he moved away from his progressive stance on race after 1954, he became just another southern politician.

If Kerr Scott could have been magically transported into North Carolina in 2012, he would have been both astonished and pleased with what he had helped put in motion. The state had been transformed from an introspective, backwater, segregated society that depended economically on textiles, tobacco, furniture manufacturing, and agriculture into a vibrant, diversified global economy. It had developed excellent state university and community college systems and featured superior statewide medical facilities. It had become a center of the industrial, banking, and information revolutions in the South. The birth of the Research Triangle helped make it a leader in technology and pharmaceuticals. Population growth made North Carolina the ninth largest state in the nation, and it now boasted of a more diverse group of inhabitants owing to an influx of foreign nationals. Scott surely would have been gratified with the state's superior road system and with the significant improvement in universities originally built for blacks.[7]

Kerr Scott's accomplishments as governor rank him as one of the most influential governors in twentieth-century North Carolina political history. Scott was an enlightened, responsible leader who recognized the needs of the people for more and better state services and was willing to put the taxable resources of the state to that end. His main goal was always to improve the living standards of the rural, forgotten segment of the state's population—the bottom layer overturning the top.

Testimony from two of North Carolina's most progressive and successful governors, Terry Sanford and Jim Hunt, validate this assessment. Speaking before a joint session of the General Assembly at the unveiling of a portrait of Kerr Scott in 1959, Sanford paid tribute to a man who, during forty years of public service, "gave unstintingly of his time, his great energy and his unique talents to the building of a better way of life for the people he loved—the people of North Carolina." Few people in the state, continued Sanford, could match Scott in "the deep personal affection accorded him by the people he sought to serve."

Sanford contended that the state's history would record "the many achievements of the Scott administration, undiminished in importance": "They are engraved on the face of the land in many forms and they will not soon be forgotten by our people. The roads he helped pave, the schools he helped build, the medical programs he established or expanded, the principles of government he lived by—all stand as solid evidence of his dedication and ability." Sanford admitted that Scott could be unpredictable, stubborn, and unyielding, but, he asserted, he was also understanding, gentle, practical, and sentimental. Through his vision and perseverance he "got things done," and, thus, North Carolina was and would remain a better place to live because of his contributions.[8] In his inaugural address as governor, Sanford again acknowledged "the tough-minded, warm-hearted unbeatable drive of the Great Agrarian, Kerr Scott, bodily lifting up the rural segment of our economy, putting a new pulse beat into the progressive heart of North Carolina."[9]

Governor Jim Hunt was also influenced and motivated by Kerr Scott's achievements. In an address to a Youth Advisory Council meeting in 1977, he said: "I first learned what state government was all about when I was a young boy living on my family's farm in Wilson County. I remember when Kerr Scott paved the dirt road that ran in front of our house. It showed me that government can do something for people. It can have an impact on our lives, it can make this a better world."[10] The paving of that road taught Hunt the vital importance of roads for his family and business: "Governor Kerr Scott changed the lives of thousands of rural citizens. When I became governor, I wanted to continue that commitment to good transportation."[11]

In many ways, Scott was Hunt's hero: "Kerr Scott was our political savior—that's the way we looked at him. There was a fervor and a passion about Kerr Scott and the change he would make in our lives that is very unusual in politics." Rob Christensen, an astute, longtime observer of North Carolina politics, referred to Kerr Scott as the father of the post–World War II progressive wing of the Democratic Party that "helped produce Terry Sanford, Bob Scott, Jim Hunt, Mike Easley, Kay Hagan and Beverly Perdue."[12]

The best commentary on Kerr Scott's life and contributions to his state came from an unlikely source, the *Daily Tar Heel*. In an editorial a week after Scott's death, the paper began by expressing the view that the students of the university mourned his loss with the "special sorrow of a favored friend": "He was the champion of the unbossed spirit and the forgotten cause, the great rumpler of fine feathers and of mental cobwebs. Our generation has it better for his having lived and we are heavy losers in his untimely death." The *Tar Heel* asserted:

His petty failings fade and the stature of his good works dwarfs his critics. He dared to think fresh and breathe free and of his courage came great things: roads and schools for the people, hope and leadership for bypassed humanity in the state. Scott lit lights on farms and in the minds of people. This improbable and refreshing man is of that tiny band of human beings who are more sorely missed the week after their death than the day after, who will be even more sorely missed a year after than a week after, and whose legacy endures and grows and triumphs despite defeats and beyond death.[13]

ACKNOWLEDGMENTS

As with any historical work, this book would not have been possible without the support, encouragement, and advice of many people. I thank Dr. H. G. Jones for his advice to go ahead with a study of Scott. Robert Anthony has been a godsend with information about valuable sources, help in finding those sources, and general encouragement throughout the process of writing. My companions in the Thursday lunch group, D. G. Martin, Ferrel Guillory, Jim Peacock, John Shelton Reed, Otis Graham, Bob Anthony, Lynn Blanchard, Bob Ashley, and several others, willingly gave of their time and expert knowledge. The curators at the North Carolina Collection, the State Archives, and the Southern Historical Collection have provided service and counsel above and beyond the call of duty. William A. Link graciously shared some oral history interviews he had done. Rob Christensen, an astute observer of North Carolina politics over the decades, allowed me use of several of his oral history interviews and other research he has done on the Scott family. He has an encyclopedic knowledge of North Carolina politics, and his general advice on how to interpret Kerr Scott's political career proved extremely valuable.

Two of North Carolina's most distinguished public servants, Willis P. Whichard and John L. Sanders, gave an extraordinary close reading of an early draft of the manuscript and saved me from numerous errors of both fact and interpretation. John Sanders is the recipient of numerous awards for his remarkable service to the state and worked as the director of the Institute of Government from 1962 to 1973 and from 1979 to 1992. Willis Whichard, who also has many honors and accolades, is the only person in the history of the state to serve in the state House of Representatives, in the North Carolina Senate, and on the North Carolina Court of Appeals and the North Carolina Supreme Court.

Much of the material in the chapter on the election of 1950 came from Julian M. Pleasants and Augustus M. Burns, *Frank Porter Graham and the 1950 Senate Race in North Carolina* (Chapel Hill: University of North Carolina Press, 1990). I have added some important new material, unavailable at the time.

I am grateful to the staff members of the University Press of Kentucky for all of their valuable advice, courteous responses, and professional expertise. In particular, Anne Dean Dotson and Bailey Johnson were present at the inception of this project and guided the manuscript through its developmental stage with encouragement, helpful observations, and wise counsel. Joseph Brown and David Cobb provided invaluable input on the editing of the manuscript, and their skillful work saved me from numerous errors. Blair Thomas assisted with the marketing materials.

The staff members at the North Carolina Collection at the University of North Carolina, the State Archives in Raleigh, and the Southern Historical Collection at Chapel Hill performed admirably in directing me to the right sources and helping clarify some abstruse issues. They should all get significant pay raises.

NOTES

The abbreviation SOHP refers to the Southern Oral History Program, Center for the Study of the American South, University of North Carolina at Chapel Hill.

Introduction

1. *Raleigh News and Observer,* January 4, 1953.

2. V. O. Key Jr., *Southern Politics in State and Nation* (New York: Knopf, 1949), 205–6.

3. I have chosen to use the terms *black* and *Negro* when referring to African Americans. These were the terms that were in standard use in the 1940s. The great majority of times they are used in direct quotations or in the paraphrasing of newspapers or letters to Scott. Almost all the African Americans who wrote to Scott used the word *Negro* to describe their race. During this time period, that word reflected respect for blacks' culture and history.

4. *Greensboro Daily News,* April 18, 1958.

1. The Early Years

1. *Raleigh News and Observer,* January 4, 1953.

2. Stephen E. Massengill, *Biographical Directory of the General Assembly of North Carolina* (Raleigh: Department of Cultural Resources, 1982); William D. Snider, "The Scotts of Haw River," in *North Carolina Century: Tar Heels Who Made a Difference, 1900–2000,* ed. Howard E. Covington Jr. and Marion A. Ellis (Charlotte: Levine Museum of the New South, 2002), 518–19; Herbert S. Turner, comp., *The Scott Family of Hawfields* (Durham: Seeman, 1971), 122–30; Scott, interview by Christensen.

3. Robert Redwine, "The Life of Kerr Scott," n.d., 1–7, Kerr Scott Senatorial Papers, North Carolina Department of Archives and History, Raleigh; Terry Sanford, "Remarks Accepting a Portrait of Former Governor Kerr Scott," May 7, 1959, unedited version, 3–7, Scott Senatorial Papers.

4. *Raleigh News and Observer,* April 24, 1944, November 14, 1948; *Durham Morning Herald,* April 10, 1949; *Winston-Salem Journal,* April 28, 1972.

5. Bob Scott, December 18, 1998, interview by Rob Christensen, SOHP.

6. Hugh Morton, *Making a Difference in North Carolina* (Raleigh: North Carolina Light Works, 1988), 86.

7. Sanford, "Remarks," 17.

8. *Raleigh News and Observer,* April 14, 1948; Redwine, "Life of Kerr Scott," 8–10.

9. David L. Corbitt, ed., *Public Addresses, Letters and Papers of William Kerr Scott, Governor of North Carolina, 1949-1953* (Raleigh: Council of State, 1957), xvi; Redwine, "Life of Kerr Scott," 11. Henry M. London, ed., *North Carolina Manual, 1937* (Raleigh: Capital Printers, 1937), 120–23.

10. Thad Eure, ed., *North Carolina Manual, 1941* (Raleigh: Edwards & Broughton, 1941), 196–97, and *North Carolina Manual, 1945* (Chapel Hill: Orange Print Shop, 1945), 204.

11. *Raleigh News and Observer,* June 7, 1936; *Greensboro Daily News,* April 16, 1978; Bob Scott, September 18, 1986, interview by Karl Campbell, 20, SOHP.

2. The Election of 1948

1. V. O. Key Jr., *Southern Politics in State and Nation* (New York: Knopf, 1949), 205–14; George Tindall, personal communication, n.d.

2. William A. Link, *North Carolina: Change and Tradition in a Southern State* (Chapel Hill: University of North Carolina Press, 2009), 342–44; Key, *Southern Politics,* 205–15; Rob Christensen, *The Paradox of Tar Heel Politics* (Chapel Hill: University of North Carolina Press, 2008), 76–78; Jack Fleer, *North Carolina Politics: An Introduction* (Chapel Hill: University of North Carolina Press, 1968), 115–21; R. Mayne Albright, "O. Max Gardner and the Shelby Dynasty," *The State* 51, no. 3 (August 1983): 8–11.

3. Link, *North Carolina,* 258–74; George B. Tindall and David Shi, *America,* brief 3rd ed., 2 vols. (New York: Norton, 1993), 2:573–86.

4. Howard G. Brunsman, preparer, *Census of Population, 1950,* pt. 33, *North Carolina* (Washington, DC: US Government Printing Office, 1952), 33–49; Link, *North Carolina,* 369–78; James C. Cobb, "World War II and the Mind of the Modern South," in *Remaking Dixie: The Impact of World War II on the American South,* ed. Neil R. McMillen (Jackson: University of Mississippi Press, 1997), 10–20; Clarence L. Mohr, "World War II and the Transformation of Higher Education," in ibid., 52–55. Cobb was referring to W. J. Cash, *Mind of the South* (New York: Knopf, 1941).

5. Tim S. R. Boyd, *Georgia Democrats, the Civil Rights Movement and the Shaping of the New South* (Gainesville: University Press of Florida, 2012), 24–33.

6. Thomas F. Eamon, "The Seeds of Modern North Carolina Politics," in *The New Politics of North Carolina,* ed. Christopher A. Cooper and H. Gibbs Knott (Chapel Hill: University of North Carolina Press, 2008), 15–24.

7. Judy Barrett Litoff, "Southern Women in a World at War," in McMillen, ed., *Remaking Dixie,* 67–69.

8. Sarah M. Lemmon, *North Carolina's Role in World War II* (Raleigh: Office of Archives and History, 1964), 11–67; Link, *North Carolina,* 356–58.

9. Jennifer E. Brooks, *Defining the Peace: World War II Veterans, Race and the*

Remaking of the Southern Political Tradition (Chapel Hill: University of North Carolina Press, 2004), 4–11, 169–71.

10. Ralph Scott, December 20, 1973, interview by Jack Bass, 9, SOHP.

11. Robert W. Scott, December 18, 1998, interview by Rob Christensen, 7, SOHP.

12. Ibid.

13. *Raleigh News and Observer,* January 4, 1953.

14. *Raleigh News and Observer,* January 10, 1948.

15. Lexie R. Ray, "The Scott Clan," June 10, 1981, 1, typed manuscript, Roy Wilder Jr. Papers, Southern Historical Collection, University of North Carolina, Chapel Hill.

16. *Durham Morning Herald,* January 11, 1948.

17. E. B. Jeffress, "Scott, the Devil Chaser," n.d., 8–11, North Carolina Collection, University of North Carolina, Chapel Hill.

18. *Raleigh News and Observer,* January 13, 1948.

19. Scott, interview by Christensen; Lauch Faircloth, September 26, 2001, interview by Rob Christensen, in possession of the interviewer.

20. Faircloth, interview by Christensen.

21. Capus Waynick, February 4, 1974, interview by Bill Finger, SOHP.

22. Albright, "O. Max Gardner and the Shelby Dynasty," 8–11; *Raleigh News and Observer,* January 7, 1948.

23. *Raleigh News and Observer,* June 27, 28, 1948; William S. Powell, ed., *Dictionary of North Carolina Biography,* 6 vols. (Chapel Hill: University of North Carolina Press, 1979–1996), 3:288.

24. *Raleigh News and Observer,* June 27, 1948.

25. *Raleigh News and Observer,* February 7, 1948.

26. Ray, "The Scott Clan," 2.

27. Capus Waynick, April 1, September 17, 1979, interview by Bill Finger, 21, Joyner Library, East Carolina University.

28. *Burlington Daily Times News,* February 5, 1948.

29. *Raleigh News and Observer,* January 21, 1948.

30. *Raleigh News and Observer,* January 22, 1948.

31. Ray, "The Scott Clan," 3.

32. *Burlington Daily Times News,* February 6, 1948; *Raleigh News and Observer,* February 7, 1948.

33. Albright, "O. Max Gardner and the Shelby Dynasty," 9.

34. *Durham Morning Herald,* February 8, 1948; *Raleigh News and Observer,* February 7, 1948; *Burlington Daily Times News,* February 7, 1948.

35. *Raleigh News and Observer,* February 7, 1948.

36. *Durham Morning Herald,* February 8, 1948.

37. *Burlington Daily Times News,* February 7, 1948.

38. Typewritten note, n.d., Wilder Papers.

39. Roy Wilder Jr., *You All Spoken Here* (New York: Viking Penguin, 1984), xv.

40. *Raleigh News and Observer,* February 7, 1948; *Burlington Daily Times News,* February 7, 1948.

41. *Burlington Daily Times News,* February 9, 1948; *Raleigh News and Observer,* February 10, 1948.

42. *Raleigh News and Observer,* February 12, 1948.

43. *Raleigh News and Observer,* February 13, 14, 1948.

44. *Burlington Daily Times News,* February 17, 1948.

45. *Raleigh News and Observer,* February 17, 23, 1948.

46. *Raleigh News and Observer,* March 1, 2, 1948.

47. *Raleigh News and Observer,* February 19, 1948.

48. Ralph Scott to Staley Cook, February 16, 1948, Ralph Scott Papers, North Carolina Department of Archives and History, Raleigh.

49. Ralph Scott to J. A. Doggett, February 25, 1948, and Ralph Scott to John R. Church, February 25, 1948, Ralph Scott Papers.

50. *Raleigh News and Observer,* February 24, 1948.

51. Albright, "O. Max Gardner and the Shelby Dynasty," 10–11; *Burlington Daily Times News,* February 23, 1948.

52. *Elizabeth City Independent,* March 8, 1948.

53. *Elizabeth City Independent,* February 25, 1948.

54. *Burlington Daily Times News,* March 6, 1948; *Raleigh News and Observer,* March 2, 3, 1948.

55. *Raleigh News and Observer,* March 9, 10, 13, 1948.

56. Albright, "O. Max Gardner and the Shelby Dynasty," 10; *Raleigh News and Observer,* March 6, 16, 1948; *Burlington Daily Times News,* March 16, 1948.

57. *Raleigh News and Observer,* March 15, 16, 1948.

58. *Raleigh News and Observer,* March 24, 1948.

59. Waynick, February 4, 1974, interview by Finger.

60. Capus Waynick to W. Kerr Scott, February 20, 1955, Capus Waynick Papers, Joyner Library; Waynick, February 4, 1974, interview by Finger, 1–3.

61. W. Kerr Scott to Capus Waynick, February 25, 1955, Waynick Papers.

62. Lauch Faircloth, December 14, 2006, interview by William A. Link, in possession of the interviewer; Faircloth, interview by Christensen.

63. *Burlington Daily Times News,* March 27, 1948.

64. *Burlington Daily Times News,* March 27, 1948.

65. Postcard from Scott Headquarters, March 28, 1948, H. Patrick Taylor Jr. Papers, Joyner Library.

66. Ralph Scott to T. J. Hamme, February 11, 1948, T. J. Hamme to Ralph Scott, February 11, 1948, and T. J. Hamme to Ralph Scott, March 15, 1948, Ralph Scott Papers.

67. *Raleigh News and Observer,* March 31, 1948.

68. *Burlington Daily Times News,* March 31, 1948.

69. Albert Coates, "East Is East and West Is West—but Which Is Which?" *Popular*

Government 14, no. 8 (August 1948): 7, 16; Jack D. Fleer, *North Carolina Government and Politics* (Lincoln: University of Nebraska Press, 1994), 29–32; Charles Prysby, "The Reshaping of the Political Party System in North Carolina," in Cooper and Knott, eds., *The New Politics of North Carolina,* 69–71.

70. *Raleigh News and Observer,* March 31, 1948; *Burlington Daily Times News,* March 30, 1948.

71. Coates, "East Is East and West Is West," 7.

72. *Burlington Daily Times News,* March 31, 1948.

73. *Burlington Daily Times News,* March 30, 31, 1948.

74. *Burlington Daily Times News,* April 8, 1948; *Raleigh News and Observer,* April 8, 1948.

75. Julian M. Pleasants, "Many Campaigns of the Pinetown Pig Breeder," *The State* 53, no. 10 (March 1986): 10–11; *Raleigh News and Observer,* April 4, 1948.

76. Roy H. Park to Stewart Underwood, April 6, 1948, Ralph Scott Papers.

77. Charles Parker, Publicity Director, to Ralph Scott, April 6, 1948, Ralph Scott Papers.

78. Ralph Scott, March 13, 1981, interview by Ben Bella, in possession of the interviewer.

79. *Raleigh News and Observer,* April 5, 1948.

80. *Raleigh News and Observer,* April 16, 1948.

81. Confidential Bulletin no. 2, April 10, 1948, Ralph Scott Papers; *Charlotte Observer,* April 7, 1948; *Raleigh News and Observer,* April 7, 1948.

82. Capus Waynick, February 4, 1974, interview by Finger, 4, 8.

83. *Burlington Daily Times News,* April 10, 1948.

84. Confidential Bulletin no. 2, April 10, 1948, Ralph Scott Papers.

85. *North Carolina Legion News,* April 1948, 16.

86. *Raleigh News and Observer,* April 10, 1948; Coates, "East Is East and West Is West," 7.

87. *Raleigh News and Observer,* April 11, 1948.

88. Charles Johnson to H. Patrick Taylor Jr., April 7, 1948, Taylor Sr. Papers, Joyner Library.

89. Don L. Spence to Charles Johnson, April 5, 1948, and B. B. Sapp to Friend, April 5, 1948, Waynick Papers.

90. *Raleigh News and Observer,* April 10, 1948.

91. *Burlington Daily Times News,* April 12, 1948.

92. *Burlington Daily Times News,* April 13, 1948.

93. W. Kerr Scott to Dear Friends, April 8, 1948, State Headquarters, Scott for Governor, Kerr Scott Private Papers, North Carolina Department of Archives and History.

94. *Raleigh News and Observer,* April 29, 1948.

95. *Raleigh News and Observer,* April 30, 1948.

96. Weekly Schedule, n.d., typed transcript, Wilder Papers.

97. *Raleigh News and Observer,* April 20, 1948.

98. *Charlotte Observer,* April 20, 1948.

99. Capus Waynick to Mrs. Sarah L. Avery, April 27, 1948, Waynick Papers.

100. Anna R. Hayes, *The Life of Susie Marshall Sharp* (Chapel Hill: University of North Carolina Press, 2008), 115.

101. Terry Sanford, May 14, 1976, interview by Brent Glass, 46, SOHP.

102. *Burlington Daily Times News,* April 22, 1948.

103. Bob Scott, September 22, 2005, interview by Rob Christensen and Jack Betts, in possession of the interviewers.

104. *Raleigh News and Observer,* April 19, 1948.

105. *Raleigh News and Observer,* April 21, 1948.

106. *Raleigh News and Observer,* April 22, 1948.

107. *Raleigh News and Observer,* April 27, 1948.

108. *Raleigh News and Observer,* April 29, 1948.

109. *Raleigh News and Observer,* April 16, 1948.

110. *Durham Morning Herald,* April 25, 1948; *Daily Tar Heel,* April 25, 1948.

111. *Laurinburg Exchange,* April 29, 1948; *Warren Record,* April 23, 1948.

112. *Raleigh News and Observer,* April 22, 1948.

113. *Burlington Daily Times News,* April 30, 1948; *Raleigh News and Observer,* April 30, 1948.

114. *Durham Morning Herald,* May 1, 1948.

115. *Wilmington Morning Star,* May 1, 1948.

116. *Elizabeth City Independent,* April 18, 1948.

117. *Washington Daily News,* May 4, 1948.

118. *Raleigh News and Observer,* May 2, 1948.

119. *Raleigh News and Observer,* May 1, 1948.

120. Capus Waynick to Friends of the Schools, May 5, 1948, and J. Y. Joyner to Capus Waynick, April 23, 1948, Waynick Papers; *Raleigh News and Observer,* May 5, 6, 1948.

121. Grace Furman, May 30, 2009, interview by Rob Christensen, 3, in possession of the interviewer.

122. "Kerr Scott Faces Facts," n.d., Folder on Education, Kerr Scott Private Papers.

123. *Burlington Daily Times News,* May 7, 1948; *Raleigh News and Observer,* May 7, 1948.

124. *Dunn Dispatch,* May 10, 1948; *Columbus County News,* May 12, 1948.

125. *Burlington Daily Times News,* May 6, 1948; *Raleigh News and Observer,* May 6, 1948.

126. *Raleigh News and Observer,* May 4, 1948.

127. *Burlington Daily Times News,* May 11, 1948; *Raleigh News and Observer,* May 11, 1948.

128. "Kerr Scott on State Reserve Funds," Kerr Scott Private Papers; Typed Address,

May 11, 1948, Wilder Papers; *The Robesonian* (Lumberton, NC), May 12, 1948; Raleigh *News and Observer,* May 12, 1948; *Burlington Daily Times News,* May 12, 1948.

129. *Duplin Citizen,* May 18, 1948.

130. Estelle T. Smith to Dear Scott Worker, May 12, 1948, Ralph Scott Papers.

131. *Pamlico County Herald* (Bayboro, NC), May 14, 1948.

132. *Raleigh News and Observer,* May 16, 1948.

133. Campaign Bulletin no. 5, May 18, 1948, Ralph Scott Papers.

134. *Raleigh News and Observer,* May 14, 1948.

135. *Raleigh News and Observer,* May 15, 1948.

136. *Laurinburg Exchange,* May 20, 1948.

137. *Raleigh News and Observer,* May 20, 21, 22, 1948; *Burlington Daily Times News,* May 19, 20, 21, 1948.

138. *Raleigh News and Observer,* May 24, 1948.

139. *Raleigh News and Observer,* May 24, 1948; Roy Wilder, Typed Note, n.d., Wilder Papers.

140. *Sampson Independent,* May 20, 1948.

141. *Charlotte Observer,* May 28, 1948; *Raleigh News and Observer,* May 22, 25, 1948; *Burlington Daily Times News,* May 25, 1948.

142. Albright, "O. Max Gardner and the Shelby Dynasty," 8–11.

143. *Raleigh News and Observer,* May 22, 1948; *Burlington Daily Times News,* May 24, 1948.

144. "Expenses and Contributions," n.d., Waynick Papers.

145. *Raleigh News and Observer,* June 18, 19, 1948; *Wilson Times,* May 25, 1954.

146. Campaign Bulletin no. 6, n.d., Ralph Scott Papers.

147. *Raleigh News and Observer,* May 26, 1948.

148. *Raleigh News and Observer,* May 28, 1948.

149. *Raleigh News and Observer,* May 26, 1948.

150. *Winston-Salem Journal,* May 26, 1948; *Greensboro Daily News,* May 26, 1948.

151. *Raleigh News and Observer,* May 28, 1948.

152. *Charlotte News,* May 27, 1948.

153. *Raleigh News and Observer,* May 29, 1948.

154. *Burlington Daily Times News,* May 29, 1948; *Raleigh News and Observer,* May 29, 1948.

155. *North Carolina Manual, 1949* (Raleigh: Office of the Secretary of State, 1949), 199–201; John William Coon, "The Go Forward Governor" (M.A. thesis, University of North Carolina, Chapel Hill, 1968), 23–25; *New York Times,* May 31, 1948; *Raleigh News and Observer,* May 30, 31, 1948.

156. *Raleigh News and Observer,* May 31, 1948; *Burlington Daily Times News,* May 31, 1948.

157. *Burlington Daily Times News,* May 30, 1948; *Raleigh News and Observer,* May 30, 1948.

158. *Durham Morning Herald,* May 31, 1948; *Burlington Daily Times News,* May 31, 1948; *Raleigh News and Observer,* May 30, 1948.

3. The Second Primary, 1948

1. *Winston-Salem Journal,* June 2, 1948; *Burlington Daily Times News,* June 1, 2, 4, 5, 9, 1948; *Raleigh News and Observer,* June 2, 4, 5, 7, 1948.

2. William Smith to Capus Waynick, June 4, 1948, and William Smith to Dear Brother, June 4, 1948, Capus Waynick Papers, Joyner Library, East Carolina University.

3. Ralph Scott, December 30, 1973, interview by Jack Bass, 16, SOHP.

4. *Raleigh News and Observer,* June 15, 1948.

5. Typed Paper, n.d., Roy Wilder Jr. Papers, Southern Historical Collection, University of North Carolina, Chapel Hill.

6. Campaign Bulletin no. 7, June 4, 1948, Ralph Scott Papers, North Carolina Department of Archives and History.

7. *Coastland Times* (Manteo, NC), June 4, 1948.

8. *Burlington Daily Times News,* June 9, 1948; *Raleigh News and Observer,* June 9, 1948.

9. *Zebulon Record,* June 11, 1948.

10. *Raleigh News and Observer,* June 10, 1948.

11. *Elizabeth City Independent,* June 14, 1948.

12. H. H. Baxter to Dear Mr. Mayor, June 18, 1948, Waynick Papers.

13. Charles M. Johnson to Rex O. Wilson, June 18, 1948, Waynick Papers.

14. *Burlington Daily Times News,* June 15, 1948.

15. *Durham Morning Herald,* June 19, 1948.

16. *Raleigh News and Observer,* June 12, 1948.

17. *Raleigh News and Observer,* June 18, 1948.

18. *Greensboro Daily News,* June 17, 1948; *Zebulon Record,* June 18, 1948; *Raleigh News and Observer,* June 17, 1948.

19. *Durham Morning Herald,* June 19, 1948.

20. *Zebulon Record,* June 4, 18, 1948.

21. *Raleigh Times,* June 10, 1948; *Burlington Daily Times News,* June 10, 1948; *Raleigh News and Observer,* June 10, 1948.

22. *Raleigh News and Observer,* June 21, 1948.

23. *Raleigh News and Observer,* June 23, 1948.

24. *Fuquay Springs Independent,* June 24, 1948.

25. *Raleigh News and Observer,* June 21, 1948.

26. *Charlotte Observer,* June 22, 1948; *Charlotte News,* June 22, 1948; *Greensboro Daily News,* June 25, 1948; *Raleigh News and Observer,* June 25, 1948.

27. *Raleigh News and Observer,* June 23, 1948.

28. *Raleigh News and Observer,* June 22, 24, 1948.

29. *Burlington Daily Times News,* June 25, 1948; *Raleigh News and Observer,* June 25, 1948.

30. Capus Waynick to Estelle T. Smith, June 24, 1948, Waynick Papers.

31. *North Carolina Manual, 1949* (Raleigh: Office of the Secretary of State, 1949), 212.

32. *Winston-Salem Journal,* June 27, 1948.

33. Excelle Rozzelle to Capus Waynick, June 27, 1948, Waynick Papers.

34. John A. Lang to Capus Waynick, June 28, 1948, Waynick Papers.

35. J. Walter Lambeth to Capus Waynick, June 28, 1948, Waynick Papers.

36. Luther Hamilton to Capus Waynick, June 29, 1948, Waynick Papers.

37. *Burlington Daily Times News,* June 28, 1948; *Raleigh News and Observer,* June 28, 1948.

38. John L. Cheney, ed., *North Carolina Government, 1585–1979* (Raleigh: Secretary of State, 1981), 1380–81; *North Carolina Manual, 1949,* 199–201.

39. *Raleigh News and Observer,* June 28, 1948.

40. *Charlotte News,* June 28, 1948.

41. *Asheville Citizen,* June 28, 1948.

42. *Henderson Daily Dispatch,* June 28, 1948.

43. *Greensboro Daily News,* June 28, 1948.

44. Numan V. Bartley, *The New South* (Baton Rouge: Louisiana State University Press, 1995), 70; Numan V. Bartley and Hugh Davis Graham, *Southern Politics and the Second Reconstruction* (Baltimore: Johns Hopkins University Press, 1975), 25, 30.

45. *Raleigh News and Observer,* June 10, 1948.

46. G. S. Steele to Capus Waynick, December 31, 1948, Waynick Papers.

47. *Greensboro Daily News,* June 25, 1948.

48. Thad Eure, December 12, 1973, interview by Jack Bass and Walter DeVries, 14, SOHP.

49. *Raleigh News and Observer,* June 28, 1948.

50. Terry Sanford, n.d., interview by Jack Bass and Walter DeVries, 31, SOHP.

51. Capus Waynick to Paul Whitaker, January 4, 1949, Waynick Papers.

52. Clipping, *Textile Labor,* July 3, 1948, n.p., Waynick Papers.

53. *North Carolina Almanac of 1950–1951* (Raleigh: Almanac Publishing Co., 1950), 171–73, 321–25, 351.

54. Bill Friday, June 28, 2010, interview by Julian Pleasants, in possession of the interviewer.

55. *Greensboro Daily News,* July 13, 1948.

56. Kerr Scott to H. Patrick Taylor Sr., July 1, 1948, H. Patrick Taylor Sr. Papers, Joyner Library.

57. David McCullough, *Truman* (New York: Simon & Schuster, 1992), 638–41; Robert J. Donovan, *Conflict and Crisis: The Presidency of Harry S Truman, 1945–1948* (New York: Norton, 1977), 406; Rob Christensen, *The Paradox of Tar Heel Politics* (Chapel Hill:

University of North Carolina Press, 2008), 129; Thad Stem Jr., *PTA Impact: Fifty Years in North Carolina, 1919–1969* (Raleigh: Congress of Parents and Teachers, 1969), 148–49.

58. Capus Waynick, February 4, 1974, interview by Bill Finger, 22, SOHP.

59. Howard E. Covington and Marion A. Ellis, *Terry Sanford* (Durham, NC: Duke University Press, 1999), 96–97.

60. Clyde R. Hoey to J. E. Sentelle, August 17, 1948, and Clyde R. Hoey to Arthur C. Smith Sr., October 26, 1948, Clyde R. Hoey Papers, Perkins Library, Duke University.

61. *Raleigh News and Observer*, October 6, 7, 1948; Kari Frederickson, *The Dixiecrat Revolt and the End of the Solid South, 1932–1968* (Chapel Hill: University of North Carolina Press, 2001), 146; Christensen, *The Paradox of Tar Heel Politics*, 129; Covington and Ellis, *Terry Sanford*, 97.

62. *Raleigh News and Observer*, October 8, 18, 1948.

63. *Raleigh News and Observer*, October 7, 12, 1948.

64. *Raleigh News and Observer*, October 19, 20, 1948.

65. *Raleigh News and Observer*, October 20, 1948.

66. *Raleigh News and Observer*, November 2, 1948.

67. McCullough, *Truman*, 708–11.

68. *North Carolina Manual, 1949*, 193, 198–200, 202, 204, 211; Julian M. Pleasants, "Claude Pepper, Strom Thurmond and the 1948 Presidential Election in Florida," *Florida Historical Quarterly* 76, no. 4 (Spring 1998): 439–73.

69. *New York Times*, October 27, 31, November 4, 1948.

70. *Raleigh News and Observer*, November 4, 6, 1948.

71. Clyde R. Hoey to Kerr Scott, November 5, 1948, Hoey Papers.

72. *Raleigh News and Observer*, November 5, 1948.

4. Roads and Schools, 1949

1. *Asheville Citizen*, December 6, 7, 1948; *Raleigh News and Observer*, December 6, 7, 1948.

2. *Asheville Citizen*, December 8, 1948.

3. *Durham Morning Herald*, December 7, 1948.

4. *Raleigh News and Observer*, December 10, 1948.

5. *Raleigh News and Observer*, December 16, 1948.

6. *Raleigh News and Observer*, December 17, 1948.

7. *Raleigh News and Observer*, November 19, 1948.

8. *Raleigh News and Observer*, December 18, 1948.

9. *Raleigh News and Observer*, November 18, December 19, 1948.

10. Capus Waynick, Memoirs, n.d., chap. 10, pp. 4–5, Joyner Library, East Carolina University.

11. Bill Friday, June 28, 2010, interview by Julian Pleasants, 4, in possession of the author; *Raleigh News and Observer*, November 14, 1948.

12. *Raleigh News and Observer,* January 1, 1949.

13. Roy Wilder, Typed Note, n.d., Roy Wilder Jr. Papers, Southern Historical Collection, University of North Carolina, Chapel Hill; Carroll Leggett, "Roy Wilder Remembers Tar Heel Characters," *Metro Magazine* (Raleigh), April 2008, 1; Bob Scott, September 22, 2005, interview by Rob Christensen and Jack Betts, in possession of the interviewers.

14. *Raleigh News and Observer,* January 2, 5, 6, 1949.

15. *Raleigh News and Observer,* June 4, 6, 1948.

16. *Raleigh News and Observer,* January 7, 1949.

17. *Raleigh News and Observer,* January 7, 1949.

18. Inaugural Address, January 6, 1949, in David L. Corbitt, ed., *Public Addresses, Letters and Papers of William Kerr Scott, Governor of North Carolina, 1949–1953* (Raleigh: Council of State, 1957), 3–15; *Burlington Daily Times News,* January 7, 1949; *Raleigh News and Observer,* January 7, 1949.

19. *Raleigh News and Observer,* January 7, 1949.

20. *Durham Morning Herald,* January 7, 1949.

21. *Raleigh News and Observer,* January 7, 1949.

22. *Raleigh News and Observer,* January 2, 8, 1949; *Charlotte Observer,* January 1, 1949; *Shelby Star,* January 4, 1949; John William Coon, "The Go Forward Governor" (M.A. thesis, University of North Carolina, 1968), 31–32.

23. Frances Lee Reesman, November 15, 2009, interview by Julian Pleasants, in possession of the author.

24. Ibid., Terry Sanford, May 14, 1976, interview by Brent Glass, 49, SOHP.

25. Reesman, interview by Pleasants.

26. Bob Scott, September 18, 1986, interview by Karl Campbell, 8, SOHP.

27. Jack D. Fleer, *The New Politics of North Carolina* (Chapel Hill: University of North Carolina Press, 1968), 132–49; Robert Rankin, *The Government and Administration of North Carolina* (New York: Thomas Crowell, 1955), 84–97.

28. *Raleigh News and Observer,* January 8, 1949.

29. *Raleigh News and Observer,* January 9, 1949.

30. *Raleigh News and Observer,* January 12, 1949.

31. *Raleigh News and Observer,* January 14, 1949.

32. *New York Times,* January 15, 1949; *Hartford Courant,* January 17, 1949; *Raleigh News and Observer,* January 15, 1949.

33. *Raleigh News and Observer,* January 18, 1949.

34. *Charlotte Observer,* January 8, 1949; *Asheville Citizen-Times,* January 2, 1949.

35. *Raleigh News and Observer,* January 18, 1949.

36. *Raleigh News and Observer,* January 19, 20, 21, 1949.

37. Reesman, interview by Pleasants; document written by Mrs. Reesman following her employment as secretary to Governor Scott, in possession of the author; *Raleigh News and Observer,* January 13, 23, 28, 29, 1949; Rankin, *The Government and*

Administration of North Carolina, 88–89. James Creech died at 10:13 A.M. in the state gas chamber overcome by deadly cyanide pellets dropped into the acid under his chair.

38. *Raleigh News and Observer,* January 28, 1949; J. W. Hassell to Kerr Scott, February 2, 1949, Kerr Scott Gubernatorial Papers, North Carolina Department of Archives and History.

39. W. C. Pou to Kerr Scott, February 13, 1949, Kerr Scott Gubernatorial Papers.

40. Kerr Scott to D. M. Tyner, February 1, 1949, Kerr Scott Gubernatorial Papers.

41. Kerr Scott to Jonathan Daniels, January 24, 1949, and Ira T. Johnson to C. L. Shuping, January 31, 1949, Jonathan Daniels Papers, Southern Historical Collection; Jonathan Daniels to Capus Waynick, February 10, 1949, Capus Waynick Papers, Joyner Library; *Raleigh News and Observer,* January 27, 1949.

42. *New York Times,* February 27, 1949.

43. Governor's Office, Press Release, January 28, 1949, Kerr Scott Gubernatorial Papers; *Raleigh News and Observer,* January 29, February 2, 1949.

44. *Raleigh News and Observer,* February 3, 1949.

45. *Raleigh News and Observer,* January 27, 1949.

46. Robert A. Johnson to Kerr Scott, January 28, 1949, Kerr Scott Private Papers, North Carolina Department of Archives and History.

47. Mrs. R. L. Welsh to Kerr Scott, January 28, 1949, and Kerr Scott to Mrs. R. L. Welsh, January 31, 1949, Kerr Scott Gubernatorial Papers.

48. T. F. Young to Kerr Scott, January 31, 1949, and Charles Parker to T. F. Young, February 5, 1949, Kerr Scott Gubernatorial Papers.

49. Brooks Hays to Kerr Scott, February 11, 1949, and Kerr Scott to Brooks Hays, February 21, 1949, Kerr Scott Gubernatorial Papers.

50. *Raleigh News and Observer,* February 5, 1949.

51. *Raleigh News and Observer,* February 3, 5, 1949.

52. Kerr Scott to H. A. Greene, March 17, 1949, Kerr Scott Gubernatorial Papers; *Raleigh News and Observer,* March 18, April 2, 1949.

53. *Raleigh News and Observer,* March 3, 1949.

54. Corbitt, ed., *Public Addresses,* 26–30; *Raleigh News and Observer,* February 5, 11, 1949.

55. *Raleigh News and Observer,* February 12, 1949.

56. *Raleigh News and Observer,* February 23, 1949.

57. John D. Larkins Jr., *Politics, Bar and Bench: A Memoir of John Davis Larkins, Jr.: Fifty Years,* ed. Donald R. Lennon and Fred D. Ragan (New Bern, NC: Owen G. Dunn, 1980), 35.

58. *Raleigh News and Observer,* February 5, 23, 1949.

59. *Raleigh News and Observer,* February 7, 8, 1949.

60. *Raleigh News and Observer,* February 10, 1949.

61. *Raleigh News and Observer,* February 15, 17, 1949.

62. *Raleigh News and Observer,* February 13, 1949.

63. *Raleigh News and Observer*, February 20, 24, 1949.

64. *Raleigh News and Observer*, February 19, 25, 1949.

65. L. H. Fountain to Samuel W. Johnson, February 25, 1949, in Samuel W. Johnson, "Kerr Scott and His Fight for Improvement of N.C. Roads" (M.A. thesis, University of North Carolina, 1969), 22–23, Wilder Papers.

66. *Raleigh News and Observer*, March 2, 5, 1949.

67. *Raleigh News and Observer*, February 26, 28, 1949.

68. *Raleigh News and Observer*, March 9, 1949.

69. *Charlotte Observer*, March 7, 1949; *Raleigh News and Observer*, March 7, 1949.

70. *Raleigh News and Observer*, March 8, 1949.

71. *Greensboro Daily News*, March 8, 1949.

72. Jonathan Daniels to Jo Rosenthal, March 9, 1949, Daniels Papers; *Raleigh News and Observer*, March 8, 1949; *Charlotte Observer*, March 7, 1949.

73. *Charlotte Observer*, March 9, 1949.

74. *Wilmington Star-News*, March 8, 1949; *Charlotte Observer*, March 9, 10, 1949.

75. Jonathan Daniels to Arthur Simmons, March 10, 1949, Daniels Papers; *Norfolk Journal and Guide*, March 12, 1949.

76. Helen Heatherly to Kerr Scott, March 12, 1949, Kerr Scott Gubernatorial Papers.

77. *Asheville Citizen*, March 22, 1949 (quoting the *Gastonia Gazette*).

78. T. Boggs Dellinger to Kerr Scott, March 12, 1949, Kerr Scott Gubernatorial Papers.

79. E. D. Craven to Kerr Scott, March 10, 1949, Kerr Scott Gubernatorial Papers.

80. Kerr Scott to E. D. Craven, March 16, 1949, Kerr Scott Gubernatorial Papers.

81. Ormond Fooshee to Kerr Scott, March 9, 1949, Kerr Scott Gubernatorial Papers.

82. Fred W. Bonitz to Kerr Scott, March 9, 1949, Kerr Scott Gubernatorial Papers.

83. Capus Waynick, February 4, 1974, interview by Bill Finger, 4–5, SOHP; Capus Waynick, September 19, 1979, interview, 41, Waynick Papers, East Carolina University.

84. *Raleigh News and Observer*, March 13, 1949.

85. Kerr Scott, "Why I Appointed Frank Graham to the United States Senate," n.d., Oscar Coffin Papers, Southern Historical Collection.

86. *Charlotte Observer*, March 12, 1949.

87. *Charlotte Observer*, March 16, 1949.

88. Bob Scott, April 10, 1984, telephone interview by Julian M. Pleasants, in possession of the author; Ralph Scott, October 31, 1984, interview by Julian M. Pleasants, in possession of the author.

89. "Conversation with Frank Graham," June 10, 1962, 1, transcript and film on file in SOHP; Jonathan Daniels, March 9, 1977, interview by Charles Eagles, 229, SOHP; Jonathan Daniels, March 22, 1972, interview by Daniel Singal, 158, SOHP.

90. Scott, "Why I Appointed Frank Graham"; *Raleigh News and Observer*, March 24, 1949.

91. *Gastonia Gazette*, March 19, 1949; *Charlotte Observer*, March 20, 1949.

92. "Conversation with Frank Graham," 2; Scott, "Why I Appointed Frank Graham"; *Charlotte News,* March 13, 1949; *Raleigh News and Observer,* March 24, 1949.

93. *Charlotte Observer,* March 23, 1949; *University of North Carolina Alumni Review,* February 1949, 147; *Raleigh News and Observer,* March 23, 1949; *Charlotte Observer,* March 23, 1949; William C. Friday, October 17, 1984, interview by Julian Pleasants and Gus Burns, in possession of the author; William C. Friday, April 17, 1974, interview by George Hill, George Hill Papers, Southern Historical Collection.

94. *Charlotte Observer,* March 23, 1949; *Raleigh News and Observer,* March 23, 1949.

95. Scott, "Why I Appointed Frank Graham"; William D. Snider, October 30, 1984, interview by Julian Pleasants, in possession of the author; L. P. McLendon, November 2, 1984, interview by Julian Pleasants, in possession of the author.

96. William D. Snider, *Light on the Hill: A History of the University of North Carolina at Chapel Hill* (Chapel Hill: University of North Carolina Press, 1992), 202–34.

97. *Goldsboro News-Argus,* n.d. (quoted in *Charlotte Observer,* March 24, 1949).

98. *Raleigh News and Observer,* March 23, 24, 1949.

99. *Chapel Hill Weekly,* March 25, 1949.

100. *Durham Morning Herald,* March 25, 1949.

101. *Fayetteville Observer,* March 24, 1949.

102. *Charlotte News,* March 24, 1949.

103. *Carolina Times,* March 19, April 2, 1949.

104. *New York Herald Tribune,* April 10, 1949.

105. *Montgomery Journal,* March 28, 1949.

106. Harry L. Golden to Kerr Scott, March 25, 1949, Kerr Scott Gubernatorial Papers.

107. George C. Marshall to Frank P. Graham, April 5, 1949, Frank Porter Graham Papers, Southern Historical Collection.

108. Harry S Truman to Frank P. Graham, March 23, 1949, Graham Papers.

109. Unsigned Postcard to Kerr Scott, n.d., Kerr Scott Gubernatorial Papers.

110. T. Young to Kerr Scott, March 25, 1949, Kerr Scott Gubernatorial Papers.

111. Bill Scott to Kerr Scott, n.d., Kerr Scott Gubernatorial Papers.

112. "Need for More Public Services," Transcript of Radio Broadcast by Governor Scott, March 2, 1949, Ralph Scott Papers, North Carolina Department of Archives and History; Corbitt, ed., *Public Addresses,* 98–99.

113. *Raleigh News and Observer,* March 3, 1949.

114. *Raleigh News and Observer,* March 4, 1949.

115. *1949 Session Laws* (Raleigh: State of North Carolina, 1949), chap. 1249, p. 1627; *Raleigh News and Observer,* April 24, 1949; Coon, "Go Forward Governor," 50.

116. *Session Laws,* chap. 1249, p. 1628, and chap. 1020, pp. 1155–61.

117. William Bushong, *North Carolina's Executive Mansion* (Raleigh: Executive Mansion Fine Arts Committee, 1991), 73–80; "The Mansion Renovation, 1949–1953," unpublished report, n.d., Kerr Scott Private Papers.

118. *Raleigh News and Observer,* April 5, 24, 1949.

119. *Raleigh News and Observer,* March 12, 15, 16, 1949.

120. *Raleigh News and Observer,* March 12, 23, 26, 1949; *Asheville Citizen,* March 26, 1949.

121. *Raleigh News and Observer,* April 6, 7, 1949.

122. *Raleigh News and Observer,* April 7, 8, 1949.

123. *Raleigh News and Observer,* March 26, 1949, and April 1, 9, 1949.

124. *Raleigh News and Observer,* April 17, 1949.

125. W. F. Williams to Jonathan Daniels, April 6, 1949, Daniels Papers.

126. John B. Palmer to the Editor, *Raleigh News and Observer,* March 30, 1949.

127. *Session Laws,* chap. 1250, pp. 1629–36; *Raleigh News and Observer,* April 15, 16, 20, 23, 24, 1949.

128. *Raleigh News and Observer,* April 24, 1949.

129. Kerr Scott, "Report to the People," January 1, 1950, in Corbitt, ed., *Public Addresses,* 146–51; *Raleigh News and Observer,* April 24, 1949.

130. *Washington Daily News,* April 28, 1949.

131. *Raleigh News and Observer,* May 1, 1949.

132. *Raleigh News and Observer,* April 23, 1949; *St. Louis Post-Dispatch,* April 27, 1949.

133. J. S. Davis to Kerr Scott, April 28, 1949, Kerr Scott Gubernatorial Papers.

134. O. Max Gardner Jr. to Kerr Scott, April 22, 1949, Kerr Scott Gubernatorial Papers.

135. Curtiss Todd to Kerr Scott, April 25, 1949, Kerr Scott Gubernatorial Papers.

136. *New York Times,* July 3, 1949.

137. Kerr Scott to J. S. Davis, May 19, 1949, Kerr Scott Gubernatorial Papers.

138. *Raleigh News and Observer,* April 21, 25, 29, 30, May 1, 6, 1949, and July 3, 1949.

139. *Raleigh News and Observer,* July 4, 1949.

140. *Raleigh News and Observer,* July 15, 17, 1949.

141. *Fayetteville Observer,* July 14, 1949; G. C. Davidson to Kerr Scott, July 14, 1949, and Kerr Scott to G. C. Davidson, July 18, 1949, Kerr Scott Gubernatorial Papers.

142. Capus Waynick to Mr. and Mrs. Ney Evans, August 22, 1949, Waynick Papers.

143. Kerr Scott to Capus Waynick, August 30, 1949, Waynick Papers.

5. The Referendum

1. Albert Coates, *Bridging the Gap between Government in Books and Government in Action* (Chapel Hill: Professor Emeritus Fund, 1974), 145; Hugh Lefler and Albert R. Newsome, *North Carolina: A History of a Southern State* (1943), 3rd ed. (Chapel Hill: University of North Carolina Press, 1973), 614–17.

2. *Raleigh News and Observer,* May 5, 1949.

3. John Harden, *North Carolina Roads and Their Builders,* vol. 2 (Raleigh: Superior Stone Co., 1966), 55–58; Ben F. Bulla, *Textiles and Politics: The Life of B. Everett Jordan* (Durham: Carolina Academic, 1992), 63–64.

4. *Raleigh News and Observer,* April 23, 1949.

5. *Raleigh News and Observer,* April 26, 1949.

6. *Raleigh News and Observer,* April 27, 1949.

7. "Governor Scott on Schools and Roads," *University of North Carolina Newsletter,* vol. 35, no. 7 (April 13, 1949); *Raleigh News and Observer,* April 12, May 11, 1949.

8. *Raleigh News and Observer,* May 11, 1949.

9. *Raleigh News and Observer,* May 12, 1949.

10. H. Patrick Taylor Sr. to Will Edwards, May 19, 1949; H. Patrick Taylor Sr., Speech, n.d., and W. Kerr Scott to Lieutenant Governor Taylor, May 5, 1940, H. Patrick Taylor Sr. Papers, Joyner Library, East Carolina University.

11. George Pritchard to Kerr Scott, May 28, 1949, Kerr Scott Gubernatorial Papers, North Carolina Department of Archives and History.

12. Thad Stem Jr., *PTA Impact: 50 Years in North Carolina, 1919–1969* (Raleigh: North Carolina Congress of Parents and Teachers, 1969), 151–54.

13. *Raleigh News and Observer,* May 5, 1949.

14. *Raleigh News and Observer,* May 12, 1949.

15. John Marshall to Kerr Scott, May 15, 1949, Kerr Scott Gubernatorial Papers.

16. *Raleigh News and Observer,* May 15, 1949.

17. Better Schools and Roads, Raleigh, "Fact Sheet," n.d., Taylor Sr. Papers.

18. "Fifteen Questions and Answers about Governor Scott's Road Program," n.d., pp. 1–6, Ralph Scott Papers, North Carolina Department of Archives and History.

19. *Raleigh News and Observer,* May 18, 1949.

20. *Raleigh News and Observer,* May 18, 1949.

21. *Raleigh News and Observer,* May 14, 22, 1949.

22. *Charlotte News,* May 11, 1949.

23. *Durham Sun,* April 25, 1949.

24. Postcard, n.d., Taylor Sr. Papers.

25. "Citizens of Anson County Interested in Sound Government," n.d., Taylor Sr. Papers.

26. *Raleigh News and Observer,* May 15, 21, 1949.

27. *Raleigh News and Observer,* May 24, 1949.

28. *Raleigh News and Observer,* May 24, 1949.

29. *Raleigh News and Observer,* May 20, 24, 1949.

30. Kelly M. Alexander to W. Kerr Scott, June 1, 1949, Kerr Scott Gubernatorial Papers.

31. Bayard Rustin to W. Kerr Scott, June 9, 1949, Kerr Scott Gubernatorial Papers.

32. *Raleigh News and Observer,* May 21, 23, 1949.

33. *Raleigh News and Observer,* May 31, 1949.

34. W. Kerr Scott to Minnie Morgan, May 30, 1949, and W. Kerr Scott to F. F. Riggs, June 2, 1949, Kerr Scott Gubernatorial Papers.

35. W. Kerr Scott to F. L. Conrad, May 30, 1949, Kerr Scott Gubernatorial Papers.

36. H. Patrick Taylor Sr. to Will Edwards, May 19, 1949, and H. Patrick Taylor Sr. to Henry W. Jordan, May 24, 1949, Taylor Sr. Papers.

37. John Marshall to H. Patrick Taylor Sr., May 27, 1949, Taylor Sr. Papers.

38. *Raleigh News and Observer,* June 4, 1949.

39. *Raleigh News and Observer,* June 5, 6, 1949.

40. Thad Eure, *North Carolina Manual, 1951* (Raleigh: Thad Eure, 1951), 248–49; *Raleigh News and Observer,* June 5, 6, 1949.

41. Carey P. Lowrance to Kerr Scott, June 27, 1949, and Kerr Scott to Lowrance, July 11, 1949, Kerr Scott Gubernatorial Papers.

42. *Raleigh News and Observer,* June 5, 6, 1949.

43. J. M. Walker to Kerr Scott, June 6, 1949, Kerr Scott Gubernatorial Papers.

44. *Road Builders News* 26, no. 7 (July 1949): 1.

45. *Raleigh News and Observer,* June 6, 1949.

46. *Raleigh News and Observer,* June 7, 1949.

47. *Raleigh News and Observer,* June 19, 1949.

48. Anna R. Hayes, *Without Precedent: The Life of Susie Marshall Sharp* (Chapel Hill: University of North Carolina Press, 2008), 133–35.

49. Ibid., 135–36.

50. M. T. Van Hecke to Kerr Scott, May 2, 1949, and Kerr Scott to M. T. Van Hecke, May 6, 1949, Kerr Scott Gubernatorial Papers.

51. *Greensboro Daily News,* February 6, 1949.

52. Hayes, *Without Precedent,* 135–45.

53. *Raleigh News and Observer,* June 22, 1949.

54. *Raleigh News and Observer,* July 14, 20, 1949.

55. *Raleigh News and Observer,* July 8, 9, 10, 1949.

56. Kerr Scott to Harry S Truman, July 11, 1949, and Harry S Truman to Kerr Scott, July 14, 1949, President's Personal File, Harry S Truman Papers, Harry S Truman Library, Independence, MO.

57. *Asheville Citizen,* July 25, 1949; *Raleigh News and Observer,* July 13, 15, 1949.

58. W. Kerr Scott to All Heads of Departments and Institutions, July 14, 1949, Kerr Scott Gubernatorial Papers.

59. *Raleigh News and Observer,* July 29, 1949.

60. Timothy J. Minchin, *What Do We Need a Union For: The TWUA in the South, 1945–1955* (Chapel Hill: University of North Carolina Press, 1997), 81–91.

61. *Raleigh News and Observer,* June 6, 1949.

62. *Raleigh News and Observer,* June 6, 11, 15, 1949.

63. *Raleigh News and Observer,* June 16, 1949.

64. *Raleigh News and Observer,* September 20, 29, 1949.

65. *Raleigh News and Observer,* October 3, 4, 5, 6, 16, 1949.

66. *Raleigh News and Observer,* October 13, 19, 20, 25, 30, 1949.

67. Minchin, *The TWUA in the South*, 93–95; *Raleigh News and Observer*, November 28, 1949.

68. Minchin, *The TWUA in the South*, 92–93.

69. Kerr Scott to Capus Waynick, June 8, 1949, Capus Waynick Papers, Joyner Library.

70. *Raleigh News and Observer*, May 21, 1949.

71. Horace Kornegay, January 11, 1989, interview by Ben Bulla, 2–3, 12–13, SOHP.

72. Herman Parker to Kerr Scott, July 25, 1949, Kerr Scott to Herman Parker, August 2, 1949, and Kerr Scott to Jane Alexander, November 8, 1949, Kerr Scott Gubernatorial Papers.

73. Mrs. Inez Brickell to Kerr Scott, November 23, 1949, Kerr Scott Gubernatorial Papers.

74. Bessie Reid to Kerr Scott, November 21, 1949, Kerr Scott Gubernatorial Papers.

75. Joseph S. Miller to Kerr Scott, September 12, 1949, Kerr Scott Gubernatorial Papers.

76. Thurmond M. Sain to Kerr Scott, September 27, 1949, Kerr Scott Gubernatorial Papers.

77. Captain Thomas Hall to Kerr Scott, September 9, November 7, 1949, Kerr Scott Gubernatorial Papers.

78. Jesse Helms to Kerr Scott, September 17, 1949, Kerr Scott Gubernatorial Papers.

79. Kerr Scott to Jesse Helms, September 18, 1949, Kerr Scott Gubernatorial Papers.

80. Robert Rankin, *The Government and Administration of North Carolina* (New York: Thomas Y. Crowell, 1955), 80–82.

81. Ibid.

82. *Greensboro Record*, September 29, October 1, 1949.

83. Bob Terrell, *All Aboard—the Fantastic Story of Charlie "Choo Choo" Justice and the Football Team That Put North Carolina in the Big Time* (Alexander, NC: WorldComm, 1996), 125–34; Ron Fimrite, *A Long Locomotive for Choo Choo* (Chicago: Time, 1973), 48–50; *Raleigh News and Observer*, November 26, 1949.

84. Tim Peeler and Roger Winstead, *N.C. State Basketball: 100 Years of Innovation* (Raleigh: North Carolina State Athletic Department, 2011), 43–80.

85. *Raleigh News and Observer*, August 15, 1949 (quoting the *Baltimore Sun*).

86. *Raleigh News and Observer*, September 7, 8, 10, 1949.

87. *Raleigh News and Observer*, September 13, 1949.

88. Kerr Craige Ramsay to Kerr Scott, August 26, 1949, Kerr Scott Gubernatorial Papers.

89. T. C. Johnson to Capus Waynick, October 27, 1949, Waynick Papers.

90. *Shelby Daily Star*, August 29, 1949.

91. A Citizen to Kerr Scott, August 31, 1949, Kerr Scott Gubernatorial Papers.

92. *Charlotte News*, August 30, 1949.

93. John Marshall to Capus Waynick, October 20, 1949, Waynick Papers.

94. *Raleigh News and Observer,* October 1, 2, 3, 1949; John Marshall to Capus Waynick, October 20, 1949, Waynick Papers.

95. *Raleigh News and Observer,* October 11, 1949.

96. Clyde A. Erwin, "Problems That Still Remain in the Education of Negroes in North Carolina," n.d., Kerr Scott Gubernatorial Papers.

97. *Raleigh News and Observer,* November 29, 1949.

98. Hayes, *Without Precedent,* 150–53; *Raleigh News and Observer,* September 21, 1949; *Greensboro Record,* December 1, 1949.

99. *Greensboro Record,* August 11, 1949.

100. *Raleigh News and Observer,* September 1, 1949.

101. *Raleigh News and Observer,* September 21, 1949.

102. Minutes of the Meeting of the Highway Commission, October 28, 1949, Kerr Scott Gubernatorial Papers.

103. *Raleigh News and Observer,* November 22, 23, 25, 26, 27, 28, 1949.

104. David L. Corbitt, ed., *Public Addresses, Letters and Papers of William Kerr Scott, Governor of North Carolina, 1949–1953* (Raleigh: Council of State, 1957), 375–93; *Raleigh News and Observer,* January 4, 1950.

105. *Raleigh News and Observer,* January 3, 1950.

6. Crucible of Liberalism

1. Thomas Turner to Jonathan Daniels, September 12, October 19, 1949, Jonathan Worth Daniels Papers, Southern Historical Collection, University of North Carolina, Chapel Hill. See also Douglass Hunt to Kerr Scott, July 8, 1949, Frank Porter Graham Papers, Southern Historical Collection.

2. Jonathan Daniels to Santford Martin, Kemp Battle, and Charles B. Deane, August 11, 1949, Jonathan Daniels to Frank Graham, August 25, 1949, and Jonathan Daniels to John D. McConnell, September 20, 1949, Daniels Papers.

3. Charles B. Deane to Jonathan Daniels, August 19, 1949, Daniels Papers.

4. O. Max Gardner Jr. to Jonathan Daniels, September 1, 1949, Daniels Papers.

5. *Charlotte Observer,* September 21, 1949.

6. *Charlotte Observer,* October 29, 1949.

7. Dave Burgess to Jack Kroll et al., August 14, 1949, and Dave Burgess to Dan Powell, November 13, 1949, Dan Powell Papers, Southern Historical Collection.

8. Dave Burgess to Dan Powell, Weekly Report, November 21–27, 1949, Powell Papers.

9. Jonathan Daniels to Gladys Tillett, December 22, 1949, and Jonathan Daniels to Eleanor Roosevelt, December 27, 1949, Daniels Papers.

10. *Charlotte Observer,* December 14, 1949.

11. *Charlotte Observer,* December 16, 1949.

12. T. C. Johnson to Capus Waynick, December 8, 1949, Capus Waynick Papers, Joyner Library, East Carolina University.

13. Kathryn Folger, December 6, 1984, interview by Julian Pleasants, in possession of the author.

14. *Asheville Citizen,* January 7, 1950.

15. *Raleigh News and Observer,* January 9, 1950.

16. *Charlotte Observer,* January 11, 1950.

17. Gladys Tillett, Form Letter, January 13, 1950, Charles W. and Gladys Tillett Papers, Southern Historical Collection; Jeff Johnson to Gladys and Charles Tillett, January 19, 1949, Jefferson Deems Johnson Papers, Duke University Library.

18. *Asheville Citizen,* January 19, 1950; *Raleigh News and Observer,* January 19, 1950.

19. NAACP Papers, Branch Files, 1950, group 2, ser. C, box 129, Library of Congress, Washington, DC.

20. *High Point Enterprise,* January 13, 1950.

21. *Asheville Citizen,* January 31, 1950; *Raleigh News and Observer,* January 31, 1950; *New York Times,* January 31, 1950.

22. Irving C. Crawford, August 7, 1969, interview by Julian M. Pleasants, in possession of the author.

23. Holt McPherson to Clyde R. Hoey, January 14, 1950, Clyde R. Hoey Papers, Duke University Library.

24. *Asheville Citizen,* January 31, 1950; *Raleigh News and Observer,* February 1, 1950.

25. *Durham Morning Herald,* February 1, 1950.

26. *Washington Daily News,* February 4, 1950.

27. *Charlotte Observer,* February 14, 1950; James K. Dorsett Jr., December 12, 1984, interview by Julian Pleasants, in possession of the author.

28. *Elizabeth City Daily Advance,* February 18, 1950; *Raleigh News and Observer,* February 18, 1950.

29. Charles W. Tillett to Willis Smith, February 18, 1950, Tillett Papers.

30. *Charlotte Observer,* February 25, 1950; *Asheville Citizen,* February 25, 1950; *Raleigh News and Observer,* February 25, 1950.

31. *Elizabeth City Daily Advance,* February 15, 1950.

32. Sam Ragan, October 25, 1984, interview by Julian Pleasants, in possession of the author; Mayne Albright, November 30, 1984, interview by Julian Pleasants, in possession of the author; Kate Humphries, December 13, 1984, interview by Julian Pleasants, in possession of the author.

33. Frank P. Graham to Jacob Billikopf, February 24, 1950, John J. Parker Papers, Southern Historical Collection; *Elizabeth City Daily Advance,* February 16, 1950.

34. Jesse Helms, December 11, 1984, interview by Julian Pleasants, in possession of the author; Charles Tillett to Frank P. Graham, January 9, 1950, Graham Papers; Jesse Helms, *Here's Where I Stand: A Memoir* (New York: Random House, 2005), 32–34; Wil-

liam A. Link, *Righteous Warrior: Jesse Helms and the Rise of Modern Conservatism* (New York: St. Martin's, 2008), 32–35.

35. Dorsett, interview by Pleasants; J. C. B. Ehringhaus Jr., November 10, 1984, interview by Julian Pleasants, in possession of the author; Hoover Adams, May 26, 1983, interview by Julian Pleasants, in possession of the author; William T. Joyner Jr., December 12, 1984, interview by Julian Pleasants, in possession of the author; Wayne Greenhaw, *Elephants in the Cottonfields* (New York: Macmillan, 1982), 49.

36. *Norfolk Virginian Pilot*, February 27, 1950; *Asheville Citizen*, February 25, 1950.

37. *Charlotte Observer*, February 27, 1950.

38. Jonathan Daniels to Capus Waynick, February 27, 1950, Daniels Papers.

39. Jonathan Daniels to William W. Boyle Jr., February 25, 1950, Daniels Papers.

40. *Washington Daily News*, February 23, 1950.

41. Humphries, interview by Pleasants; Folger, interview by Pleasants; William W. Staton, May 24, 1983, interview by Julian Pleasants, in possession of the author; Ragan, interview by Pleasants.

42. Albright, interview by Pleasants; Folger, interview by Pleasants; Staton, interview by Pleasants; Warren Ashby, October 30, 1984, interview by Julian Pleasants, in possession of the author.

43. Thad Eure, December 11, 1984, interview by Julian Pleasants, in possession of the author.

44. Folger, interview by Pleasants; Humphries, interview by Pleasants.

45. Folger, interview by Pleasants.

46. Dave Burgess to Dan Powell, Weekly Reports, February 12–18, March 5–11, March 12–18, 1950, and Dave Burgess to Jack Kroll, March 6, 1950, Powell Papers.

47. Jeff Johnson to T. A. Hamme, March 16, 1950, and Aaron A. Moore to Jeff Johnson, March 28, 1950, Johnson Papers.

48. *Charlotte Observer*, February 28, 1950, March 31, 1950; *Asheville Citizen*, March 13, April 18, 1950.

49. *Asheville Citizen*, March 6, 1950; *Charlotte Observer*, March 30, 1950; *Greensboro Daily News*, March 30, 1950; "Frank P. Graham, Candidate for the United States Senate," n.d., pamphlet, Johnson Papers.

50. *Elizabeth City Daily Advance*, March 17, 1950.

51. *Asheville Citizen*, March 29, 1950.

52. Allen Langston to Capus Waynick, March 22, 1950, Waynick Papers.

53. "North Carolina Needs Willis Smith in the Senate," n.d., pamphlet, Allard Lowenstein Papers, Southern Historical Collection; *Greensboro Daily News*, March 20, 1950; *Charlotte Observer*, March 20, 1950.

54. Frank P. Graham to Gerald W. Johnson, August 6, 1948, Graham Papers.

55. Ehringhaus, interview by Pleasants; Joyner, interview by Pleasants; Dorsett, interview by Pleasants.

56. *The Pilot* (Southern Pines, NC), March 10, 1950.

57. *Asheville Citizen,* March 23, 1950.

58. *Raleigh News and Observer,* March 24, 1950.

59. *Charlotte Observer,* January 22, 1950; David Caute, *The Great Fear* (New York: Simon & Schuster, 1987), 60–61. See also Allen Weinstein, *Perjury: The Hiss-Chambers Case* (New York: Knopf, 1979).

60. *Asheville Citizen,* February 4, March 2, 1950; Caute, *The Great Fear,* 63.

61. Alonzo Hamby, *Liberalism and Its Challengers* (New York: Oxford University Press, 1985), 88–89; Thomas Reeves, *Life and Times of Joe McCarthy* (New York: Stein & Day, 1982), 223–26.

62. *Asheville Citizen,* February 12, 1950.

63. *Newsweek,* February 13, 1950, 11; *Charlotte Observer,* March 26, 1950.

64. Jonathan Daniels to Harry Truman, March 23, 1950, and Jonathan Daniels to Carroll Kilpatrick, March 6, 1950, Daniels Papers.

65. *High Point Enterprise,* March 7, 1950.

66. *Charlotte Observer,* February 20, March 2, 1950.

67. Jeff Johnson, Notes, n.d., Johnson Papers.

68. *Greensboro Daily News,* March 25, 1950; *Charlotte Observer,* March 25, 1950; "Life-Long Champion of Democracy," n.d., Johnson Papers.

69. *Raleigh News and Observer,* March 19, 1950.

70. *Asheville Citizen,* March 21, 1950.

71. *Asheville Citizen,* March 23, 24, 1950.

72. *Greensboro Daily News,* March 21, 1950.

73. *Goldsboro News Argus,* March 23, 1950; *Asheville Citizen,* March 24, 1950.

74. Allen Langston to Capus Waynick, March 22, 1950, Waynick Papers.

75. *Raleigh News and Observer,* March 29, 1950; *Goldsboro News Argus,* March 28, 1950.

76. *Durham Sun,* March 31, 1950.

77. *Dunn Dispatch,* March 15, 1950; *High Point Enterprise,* March 21, 23, 1950.

78. *Charlotte Observer,* April 6, 1950.

79. Newspaper Clipping, n.d., Clipping File, North Carolina Collection, University of North Carolina, Chapel Hill.

80. Original cartoon in the possession of the author.

81. *Durham Morning Herald,* March 29, 1950.

82. Jeff Johnson to Dave Burgess, May 4, 1950, Johnson Papers.

83. *Elizabeth City Daily Advance,* April 28, 1950.

84. Kerr Scott to Department Heads, February 13, 1950, Kerr Scott Gubernatorial Papers, North Carolina Department of Archives and History.

85. David M. McConnell to Jeff Johnson, April 15, 1950, Graham Papers.

86. *Newsweek,* April 17, 1950, 19.

87. Graham quoted in Lecture by William D. Snider included in "Reminiscences

of the 1950 Campaign," Frank P. Graham Jubilee Symposium, Proceedings, September 26–27, 1980, University of North Carolina, Greensboro.

88. Albright, interview by Pleasants; William C. Friday, October 17, 1984, interview by Julian Pleasants, in possession of the author.

89. *Charlotte Observer,* April 11, 1950.

90. Folger, interview by Pleasants; Ragan, interview by Pleasants; J. Melville Broughton Jr., December 12, 1984, interview by Julian Pleasants, in possession of the author; Albright, interview by Pleasants.

91. Pamphlets and Political Ads, n.d., Tillett Papers.

92. *Asheville Citizen,* April 26, 1950.

93. *Charlotte Observer,* April 28, 1950.

94. *Charlotte Observer,* April 8, 1950.

95. Smith Headquarters, Press Release, April 20, 1950, Daniels Papers.

96. Mary Coker Joslin, "Precinct Politics: The Red and the Black" (1950), 10–11, pamphlet in possession of the author.

97. Tom Schlesinger, "Frank Graham's Primary Education," *The Nation,* April 22, 1950, 368.

98. *Charlotte Observer,* May 3, 1950.

99. *Charlotte Observer,* May 9, 1950.

100. *Charlotte Observer,* May 6, 1950.

101. *U.S. News and World Report,* May 12, 1950, 13–14.

102. Jonathan Daniels to Isador Lubin, May 5, 1950, Daniels Papers.

103. *Durham Morning Herald,* May 18, 1950.

104. Warren Ashby, *Frank Porter Graham: A Southern Liberal* (Winston-Salem: John F. Blair, 1950), 260; Paul H. Douglas, *In the Fullness of Time* (New York: Harcourt Brace Jovanovich, 1972), 240–41.

105. Ashby, *Frank Porter Graham,* 260–61, 273; Albright, interview by Pleasants.

106. Advance Draft of Democratic Party Platform, May 11, 1950, Robert Gregg Cherry Papers, North Carolina Department of Archives and History; *Raleigh News and Observer,* May 12, 1950; *Elizabeth City Daily Advance,* May 11, 1950.

107. *Elizabeth City Daily Advance,* May 16, 1950.

108. Transcript of Radio Address by George Maurice Hill, May 18, 1950, 1–3, Allen Langston Papers, Duke University Library.

109. Transcript of Radio Address by D. Hiden Ramsey, May 16, 1950, Dr. Hiden Ramsey Papers, Southern Historical Collection; *Asheville Citizen,* May 17, 1950.

110. Albright, interview by Pleasants.

111. David McConnell, September 13, 1984, interview by Julian Pleasants, in possession of the author.

112. *Charlotte Observer,* May 5, 1950; *Durham Sun,* May 8, 1950; *Asheville Citizen,* May 17, 1950.

113. *Goldsboro News Argus,* May 17, 1950.

114. *Raleigh News and Observer,* May 20, 1950.

115. *Greensboro Daily News,* May 23, 1950; *Charlotte Observer,* May 23, 1950; *Raleigh News and Observer,* May 23, 1950.

116. *High Point Enterprise,* May 24, 1950; *Charlotte Observer,* May 25, 1950; *Raleigh News and Observer,* May 13, 24, 25, 1950.

117. J. E. Hall to Frank Graham, n.d., Graham Papers; Ralph W. Scott, December 31, 1984, interview by Julian Pleasants, in possession of the author; William D. Snider, October 30, 1984, interview by Julian Pleasants, in possession of the author.

118. Jonathan Daniels to Frank Logan, May 22, 1950, Daniels Papers; Snider, interview by Pleasants.

119. *Durham Morning Herald,* May 22, 1950.

120. William J. Smith, State Director of the CIO Organizing Committee, to Staff Members, May 16, 1950, Powell Papers.

121. Dave Burgess to Dan Powell, Weekly Reports, May 7–13, 15–21, 21–27, Powell Papers.

122. James T. Taylor to Jeff Johnson, May 13, 1950, Graham Papers.

123. Willie Jacobs to Frank P. Graham, May 20, 1950, Graham Papers.

124. *Charlotte Observer,* May 22, 1950.

125. *Raleigh News and Observer,* May 1, 1950.

126. *Asheville Citizen,* May 10, 1950; *Raleigh News and Observer,* May 10, 1950.

127. W. Wite to Joe Greer, May 22, 1950, Powell Papers.

128. *Charlotte Observer,* May 24, 1950; *The Carolinian* (Raleigh), May 27, 1950; *Asheville Citizen,* May 24, 1950.

129. *Raleigh News and Observer,* May 24, 1950.

130. Joyner, interview by Pleasants; Helms, interview by Pleasants; Adams, interview by Pleasants.

131. Adams, interview by Pleasants; Helms, *Here's Where I Stand,* 36.

132. Harry Golden, *The Right Time: An Autobiography* (New York: Putnam's, 1969), 271.

133. Frank P. Graham to Leroy Jones, June 11, 1949, Graham Papers; "U.S. Civil Service Commission, Ratings of Candidates in Examinations for Designation to the United States Military and Naval Academies," July 11, 1949, Graham Papers.

134. John D. McConnell to Leroy Jones, September 20, 1949, Graham Papers.

135. Adams, interview by Pleasants.

136. Albright, interview by Pleasants.

137. *Charlotte Observer,* May 6, 1950.

138. Roy Wilder Jr., September 2, 2009, interview by Julian Pleasants, in possession of the author.

139. *Raleigh News and Observer,* May 26, 1950.

140. Transcript of Radio Address by J. O. Talley Jr., May 26, 1950, Langston Papers.

141. *North Carolina Manual, 1951* (Raleigh: Office of the Secretary of State, 1951), 236; *Raleigh News and Observer,* May 29, 1950.

142. *Charlotte Observer,* May 28, 1950.

7. The Second Primary

1. *Charlotte Observer,* May 29, 1950.

2. *Greensboro Daily News,* May 29, 1950.

3. *Baltimore Sun,* May 31, 1950.

4. Dave Burgess to Dan Powell, June 1, 1950, Dan Powell Papers, Southern Historical Collection; David M. McConnell, September 13, 1984, interview by Julian Pleasants, in possession of the author.

5. *Fayetteville Observer,* June 1, 1950.

6. *Washington Daily News,* June 1, 1950.

7. *Charlotte News,* May 31, 1950; *Asheville Citizen,* June 1, 1950.

8. Nell Battle Lewis to Willis Smith, May 29, 1950, Nell Battle Lewis Papers, North Carolina Department of Archives and History.

9. *Raleigh News and Observer,* June 1, 1950; *Charlotte Observer,* June 1, 1950.

10. *Raleigh News and Observer,* June 3, 1950.

11. *Sweatt v. Painter,* 339 U.S. 637 (1950); Richard Kluger, *Simple Justice* (New York: Knopf, 1976), 281–82; *Charlotte Observer,* June 6, 1950; *Asheville Citizen,* June 6, 1950.

12. *Charlotte News,* June 7, 1950.

13. *Charlotte Observer,* June 3, 4, 1950; Hoover Adams, May 26, 1983, interview by Julian Pleasants, in possession of the author; James K. Dorsett Jr., December 12, 1984, interview by Julian Pleasants, in possession of the author; William T. Joyner Jr., December 12, 1984, interview by Julian Pleasants, in possession of the author; Jesse A. Helms, December 11, 1984, interview by Julian Pleasants, in possession of the author.

14. Helms, interview by Pleasants; Dorsett, interview by Pleasants; Ben F. Park, December 11, 1984, interview by Julian Pleasants, in possession of the author; J. C. B. Ehringhaus Jr., November 10, 1984, interview by Julian Pleasants, in possession of the author; *Charlotte Observer,* June 7, 11, 1950; Jesse Helms, *Here's Where I Stand: A Memoir* (New York: Random House, 2005), 32–37.

15. *High Point Enterprise,* June 10, 1950; *Charlotte Observer,* June 10, 1950; Joyner, interview by Pleasants; Helms, interview by Pleasants; Jesse Helms, *Here's Where I Stand,* 34–35.

16. *Elizabeth City Daily Advance,* June 7, 1950; *Greensboro Daily News,* June 8, 1950; *Asheville Citizen,* June 8, 1950.

17. *Charlotte Observer,* June 8, 1950.

18. Clyde R. Hoey to Willis Smith, June 28, 1950, Clyde R. Hoey Papers, Duke University Library.

19. *Asheville Citizen,* June 9, 21, 1950; *Greensboro Daily News,* June 9, 1950; *Raleigh News and Observer,* June 21, 1950.

20. Willis Smith to My Dear Friend, June 20, 1950, Kerr Scott Gubernatorial Papers, North Carolina Department of Archives and History.

21. *Raleigh News and Observer,* June 13, 1950; *The Pilot* (Southern Pines, NC), June 16, 1950.

22. *Rocky Mount Telegram,* June 21, 1950.

23. Harry S Truman to Jonathan Daniels, June 17, 1950, Harry S Truman Papers, Harry S Truman Library, Independence, MO.

24. Capus Waynick, November 24, 1974, interview by Bill Finger, SOHP.

25. *Elizabeth City Daily Advance,* June 16, 1950.

26. Terry Sanford, May 14, 1976, interview by Brent Glass, SOHP.

27. J. Covington Parham Jr., "Democratic Senatorial Primary of North Carolina—1950" (senior thesis, Princeton University, 1952), 218–19.

28. Lauch Faircloth, September 26, 2001, interview by Rob Christensen, in possession of the interviewer; Lauch Faircloth, December 14, 2006, interview by William A. Link, in possession of the interviewer.

29. Address of Kelly Alexander Jr., June 1, 1950, NAACP Papers, Library of Congress, Washington, DC; *The Carolinian* (Raleigh), June 10, 1950; *Fayetteville Observer,* June 2, 1950.

30. *Charlotte Observer,* June 18, 1950.

31. *Washington Daily News,* June 14, 1950; Bryan Grimes to Jeff Johnson, June 14, 1950, Frank Porter Graham Papers, Southern Historical Collection.

32. J. Melville Broughton Jr., December 12, 1984, interview by Julian Pleasants, in possession of the author; T. Clyde Auman, May 23, 1983, interview by Julian Pleasants, in possession of the author.

33. Flyer in both the Powell Papers and the Lowenstein Papers; *Raleigh News and Observer,* June 15, 1950.

34. Flier and Photographs, Lowenstein Papers.

35. Kathryn Folger, December 6, 1984, interview by Julian Pleasants, in possession of the author; Kate Humphries, December 13, 1984, interview by Julian Pleasants, in possession of the author; R. Mayne Albright, November 30, 1984, interview by Julian Pleasants, in possession of the author.

36. "White People Wake Up," flyer in both the Charles W. and Gladys Tillett (Southern Historical Collection) and the Powell Papers.

37. Pamphlet in both the Powell Papers and the Graham Papers.

38. *LaGrange News,* June 16, 1950.

39. Clipping, *Raleigh News and Observer,* n.d., Lowenstein Papers.

40. *Raleigh News and Observer,* June 22, 1950.

41. *Raleigh News and Observer,* June 27, 1950.

42. *Washington Daily News,* June 19, 1950.

43. *Elizabeth City Daily Advance,* June 17, 1950; *Raleigh News and Observer,* June 17, 1950.

44. *Asheville Citizen,* June 17, 1950.

45. Ben Roney to Charles Rogerson, June 20, 1950, Kerr Scott Gubernatorial Papers.

46. *Charlotte Observer,* June 21, 1950.

47. Julius C. Hubbard to Kerr Scott, June 10, 1950, Kerr Scott Gubernatorial Papers.

48. Emsley Armfield to the Editor, *Charlotte News,* June 20, 1950.

49. *High Point Enterprise,* June 21, 1950; *Charlotte Observer,* June 21, 1950; *Raleigh Times,* June 21, 1950.

50. *Asheville Citizen,* June 9, 1950; *Charlotte Observer,* June 14, 1950.

51. *Henderson Daily Dispatch,* n.d. (quoted in *Elizabeth City Daily Advance,* June 21, 1950).

52. *Kannapolis Daily Independent,* June 18, 1950.

53. *Greensboro Daily News,* June 21, 1950.

54. Parham, "Democratic Senatorial Primary of North Carolina," 187.

55. Dorsett, interview by Pleasants; Joyner, interview by Pleasants; Helms, *Here's Where I Stand,* pp. 32–37.

56. Frank P. Graham, July 1, 1969, interview by Julian Pleasants, in possession of the author.

57. William L. Hauser, November 20, 1989, interview by Julian Pleasants, in possession of the author; Graham, interview by Pleasants; Broughton, interview by Pleasants; *Raleigh News and Observer,* June 17, 1950; *Charlotte Observer,* June 20, 1950.

58. Graham, interview by Pleasants; Hauser, interview by Pleasants; Broughton, interview by Pleasants; *Raleigh News and Observer,* June 21, 1950.

59. Hauser, interview by Pleasants.

60. John Sanders, October 17, 1984, interview by Julian Pleasants and Gus Burns, in possession of the author.

61. Roy Wilder Jr., December 13, 1984, interview by Julian Pleasants, in possession of the author.

62. Political Ads in the Graham Papers, the Lowenstein Papers, and the personal papers in the collection of Donald McCoy, Fayetteville, NC; *Raleigh News and Observer,* June 23, 1950.

63. Willis Smith, Speech, June 22, 1950, copy in Anna Lee Dorsett Scrapbook of the Smith Family, in possession of the Smith family, Raleigh, NC; *High Point Enterprise,* June 23, 1950; *Elizabeth City Daily Advance,* June 23, 1950.

64. Samuel Lubell, *The Future of American Politics* (New York: Harper & Bros., 1952), 102, 104.

65. Jonathan Daniels, March 9, 1977, interview by Charles Eagles, 237, SOHP.

66. Lubell, *The Future of American Politics,* 104. See also Parham, "Democratic Senatorial Primary of North Carolina."

67. Adams, interview by Pleasants.

68. *Raleigh News and Observer,* June 23, 1950; *Moore County News,* June 23, 1950; *Asheville Citizen,* June 23, 1950.

69. *Asheville Citizen,* June 23, 1950.

70. *Charlotte Observer,* June 3, 1950.

71. *North Carolina Manual, 1951* (Raleigh: Thad Eure, 1951), 237–38; *Charlotte Observer,* June 25, 1950; *Asheville Citizen,* July 1, 1950.

72. William Joslin, December 12, 1984, interview by Julian Pleasants, in possession of the author; H. G. Jones, November 6, 1984, interview by Julian Pleasants, in possession of the author; *Raleigh News and Observer,* June 25, 1950; *Durham Morning Herald,* June 25, 1950; *Elizabeth City Daily Advance,* June 26, 1950; *New York Herald Tribune,* June 25, 1950.

73. William Friday, October 17, 1984, interview by Julian Pleasants, in possession of the author; Humphries, interview by Pleasants; Folger, interview by Pleasants; William A. Link, *William Friday: Power, Purpose and American Higher Education* (Chapel Hill: University of North Carolina Press, 1995), 72–73.

74. D. Hiden Ramsey to Louis Graves, June 1950, Graham Papers.

75. John Sanders to Frank P. Graham, July 6, 1950, Graham Papers.

76. Lillian Turner to Frank P. Graham, June 26, 1950, Graham Papers.

77. W. Kerr Scott to Frank P. Graham, June 27, 1950, Graham Papers.

78. W. Kerr Scott to Frank P. Graham, December 19, 1950, Kerr Scott Gubernatorial Papers and Graham Papers.

79. Frank P. Graham to Kerr Scott, June 30, 1950, Kerr Scott Gubernatorial Papers.

80. Frank P. Graham to Kerr Scott, August 7, 1950, Kerr Scott Gubernatorial Papers.

81. *Raleigh News and Observer,* June 28, 1950.

82. *Goldsboro News Argus,* June 27, 1950.

83. *Charlotte Observer,* June 26, 1950.

84. *Charlotte Observer,* June 28, 1950.

85. *Charlotte Observer,* June 27, 28, 1950; *Asheville Citizen,* June 27, 1950.

86. *Raleigh News and Observer,* August 15, 1950.

87. Victor Bryant to Jeff Johnson, July 7, 1950, Jefferson Deems Johnson Papers, Duke University Library.

88. Howard Godwin to Jeff Johnson, July 8, 1950, Johnson Papers.

89. W. H. S. Burgwyn to Kerr Scott, June 25, 1950, Kerr Scott Gubernatorial Papers.

90. John Egerton, *Speak Now against the Day: The Generation before the Civil Rights Movement in the South* (Chapel Hill: University of North Carolina Press, 1995), 532.

91. Jonathan Daniels to Harry S Truman, June 15, 1950, Truman Papers.

92. Jeff Johnson to Samuel Lubell, August 23, 1951, Johnson Papers; Jeff Johnson to Harry O'Riley, June 10, 1950, Graham Papers.

93. *High Point Enterprise,* August 17, 1950.

94. *Charlotte Observer,* June 27, 1950.

95. Lubell, *The Future of American Politics,* 124.

96. *North Carolina Manual, 1951,* 287–88.

97. Ben Dixon McNeil to Jonathan Daniels, June 30, 1950, Jonathan Worth Daniels Papers, Southern Historical Collection.

98. *Washington Evening Star,* June 29, 1950.

99. Egerton, *Speak Now against the Day,* 532.

100. *Raleigh News and Observer,* July 26, 1950.

101. Wilbur Hobby, December 18, 1973, interview by Jack Bass and Walter DeVries, SOHP.

102. Helms, *Here's Where I Stand,* 32–37.

103. *Charlotte Observer,* June 26, 1950.

104. *Durham Sun,* June 26, 1950.

105. *Raleigh News and Observer,* June 27, 1950.

106. Valerie Nicholson to Kerr Scott, July 2, 1950, Kerr Scott Gubernatorial Papers.

107. *Raleigh News and Observer,* January 7, 12, 1950.

108. *Raleigh News and Observer,* January 19, 25, 1950.

109. *Raleigh News and Observer,* January 26, 28, 1950.

110. *Raleigh News and Observer,* February 16, 1950.

111. *Raleigh News and Observer,* February 22, 1950.

112. *Raleigh News and Observer,* February 23, March 2, 1950.

113. *Raleigh News and Observer,* March 21, 1950.

114. *Raleigh News and Observer,* February 24, 1950.

115. *Raleigh News and Observer,* March 3, 4, 1950.

116. *Raleigh News and Observer,* April 28, 1950.

117. *Raleigh News and Observer,* July 22, 1950.

118. Mrs. L. H. Morris to Kerr Scott, November 7, 1950, Kerr Scott Gubernatorial Papers.

119. Tom McClure to Kerr Scott, August 26, 1949, Kerr Scott Gubernatorial Papers.

120. L. V. Sutton to Clyde R. Hoey, April 26, 1950; Clyde R. Hoey to L. V. Sutton, April 30, 1950, and September 5, 1950, Hoey Papers.

121. *Raleigh News and Observer,* September 1, 1950.

122. *Raleigh News and Observer,* August 29, 30, September 13, 27, 1950.

123. *Raleigh News and Observer,* September 15, 1950.

124. *Raleigh News and Observer,* September 27, October 26, 1950.

125. *Raleigh News and Observer,* March 3, 1950.

126. *Raleigh News and Observer,* May 19, 1950.

127. *Raleigh News and Observer,* June 27, 1950.

128. *Raleigh News and Observer,* June 7, 1950.

129. *Raleigh News and Observer,* December 20, 21, 1950.

130. *Raleigh News and Observer,* July 27, 1950.

131. *Raleigh News and Observer,* February 14, 1950.

132. *Raleigh News and Observer,* March 23, April 11, 1950.

133. Tony Tolar to W. Kerr Scott, April 10, 1950, Kerr Scott Gubernatorial Papers.

134. Boyd Harless to Kerr Scott, April 12, 1950, Kerr Scott Gubernatorial Papers.

135. J. R. Hudson to Kerr Scott, April 14, 1950, Kerr Scott Gubernatorial Papers.

136. W. Kerr Scott to Tony Tolar, April 15, 1950, Kerr Scott Gubernatorial Papers.

137. *Raleigh News and Observer,* April 16, 1950; W. Kerr Scott to John M. Gold, April 24, 1950, Kerr Scott Gubernatorial Papers.

138. *Raleigh News and Observer,* August 23, 1950.

139. *Raleigh News and Observer,* July 1, September 8, October 7, 9, 1950.

140. *Raleigh News and Observer,* October 14, 16, 1950.

141. *Raleigh News and Observer,* January 24, February 25, June 10, October 14, November 11, 1950.

142. *Raleigh News and Observer,* March 5, 1950.

143. *Raleigh News and Observer,* August 9, 10, 15, 16, September 4, 20, 21, 1950.

144. W. Kerr Scott to Ida B. Kellam, October 2, 1950, and Sarah Waggoner to Kerr Scott, October 10, 1950, Kerr Scott Gubernatorial Papers.

145. *Raleigh News and Observer,* February 10, March 5, August 2, 1950.

146. *Asheville Citizen,* March 11, 1950.

147. *Raleigh News and Observer,* August 10, 14, 1950.

148. *Greensboro Daily News,* August 12, 1950; *Carolina Times,* August 19, 1950.

149. *Raleigh News and Observer,* February 16, 1950.

150. *Raleigh News and Observer,* July 2, 18, December 29, 1950.

151. *Raleigh News and Observer,* October 2, 4, 17, 27, 1950.

152. B. Everett Jordan to W. Kerr Scott, October 9, 1950, Kerr Scott Gubernatorial Papers.

153. *Raleigh News and Observer,* November 8, 1950; *North Carolina Manual, 1951,* 240.

154. *Raleigh News and Observer,* October 17, 19, 1950; North Carolina Supreme Court to Governor W. Kerr Scott, October 18, 1950, Kerr Scott Gubernatorial Papers; David L. Corbitt, ed., *Public Addresses, Letters and Papers of William Kerr Scott, Governor of North Carolina, 1949–1953* (Raleigh: Council of State, 1957), 495–96.

155. *Raleigh News and Observer,* October 20, 21, 22, 31, 1950.

156. *Raleigh News and Observer,* June 1, 11, 1950.

157. *Raleigh News and Observer,* November 1, 1950.

8. Trials and Tribulation

1. *Raleigh News and Observer,* January 11, 24, 1951; John William Coon, "The Go Forward Governor" (M.A. thesis, University of North Carolina, 1968), 66–68; John D. Larkins Jr., *Politics, Bar and Bench: A Memoir of John Davis Larkins, Jr.: Fifty Years,* ed. Donald R. Lennon and Fred D. Ragan (New Bern, NC: Owen G. Dunn, 1980), 36.

2. Larkins, *Politics, Bench and Bar,* ix, x; *Raleigh News and Observer,* January 2, 3, 1951.

3. Kerr Scott, "1951 Biennial Message," in David L. Corbitt, ed., *Public Addresses, Letters and Papers of William Kerr Scott, Governor of North Carolina, 1949–1953* (Raleigh: Council of State, 1957), 33–51; *Raleigh News and Observer,* January 5, 1951.

4. *Raleigh News and Observer,* January 5, 1951.

5. *High Point Enterprise,* January 4, 1951.

6. H. Pat Taylor Sr. to Kerr Scott, January 7, 1951, H. Patrick Taylor Sr. Papers, Joyner Library, East Carolina University.

7. Corbitt, ed., *Public Addresses,* 54–62; *Raleigh News and Observer,* January 9, 1951.

8. *Raleigh News and Observer,* January 9, 1951.

9. *Charlotte News,* January 9, 1951.

10. *Raleigh News and Observer,* January 6, 1951.

11. Corbitt, ed., *Public Addresses,* 213–18; *Raleigh News and Observer,* February 14, 1951.

12. Corbitt, ed., *Public Addresses,* 219–33; *Raleigh News and Observer,* February 17, 1951.

13. *Raleigh News and Observer,* February 20, 24, 1951.

14. *Raleigh News and Observer,* February 21, 1951.

15. *Raleigh News and Observer,* March 14, 1951; Coon, "The Go Forward Governor," 76–78.

16. John Marshall to Capus Waynick, March 7, 1951, Capus Waynick Papers, Joyner Library.

17. *Raleigh News and Observer,* January 13, 18, 31, 1951.

18. *Raleigh News and Observer,* February 3, 8, 17, 1951.

19. Corbitt, ed., *Public Addresses,* 216–17; *Raleigh News and Observer,* February 14, 1951.

20. Corbitt, ed., *Public Addresses,* 221–23; *Raleigh News and Observer,* February 10, 17, 1951.

21. *Raleigh News and Observer,* February 22, 28, 1951.

22. *Raleigh News and Observer,* March 16, 1950.

23. Pete Daniel, *Lost Revolutions: The South in the 1950s* (Chapel Hill: University of North Carolina Press, 2000), 27–33.

24. *Raleigh News and Observer,* February 25, March 6, 28, 29, 30, 31, 1951.

25. *Raleigh News and Observer,* January 11, 16, March 22, 1951.

26. Kerr Scott to Alfred E. Driscoll, Governor of New Jersey, November 20, 1951, Kerr Scott Gubernatorial Papers, North Carolina Department of Archives and History; *Raleigh News and Observer,* February 22, March 10, 23, 1951.

27. *NCEA News Bulletin* 4, no. 2 (January 1951): 1–2.

28. *Raleigh News and Observer,* January 25, 1951.

29. R. D. Marshall to Kerr Scott, February 11, 1951, Kerr Scott Gubernatorial Papers.

30. Mrs. Dewey Kirstein Sr. to Kerr Scott, January 29, 1951, Kerr Scott Gubernatorial Papers.

31. *Asheville Citizen,* January 22, 1951; *Raleigh News and Observer,* March 30, 1951.

32. Kerr Scott to O. G. Anderson, April 4, 1951, Kerr Scott Gubernatorial Papers; *Greensboro Daily News,* April 16, 1951; *Raleigh News and Observer,* April 15, 1951.

33. *Charlotte Observer,* April 17, 1951.

34. Harry McMullan, Attorney General, to W. Kerr Scott, April 19, 1951, Audrey Ratchford to Kerr Scott, April 18, 1951, and Kerr Scott to Audrey Ratchford, April 25, 1951, Kerr Scott Gubernatorial Papers; *Raleigh News and Observer,* April 15, 1951.

35. *Raleigh News and Observer,* April 12, 14, 19, 1951.

36. *Raleigh News and Observer,* April 18, 19, 1951.

37. *Raleigh News and Observer,* September 9, 1951.

38. *Raleigh News and Observer,* July 14, October 21, 24, 1951.

39. *Raleigh News and Observer,* March 3, 14, April 3, 15, 1951; *Greensboro Daily News,* April 16, 1951.

40. *Raleigh News and Observer,* March 21, 1951.

41. *Raleigh News and Observer,* March 20, April 24, 1951.

42. *Charlotte Observer,* April 17, 1951.

43. *Raleigh News and Observer,* April 15, 16, 1951.

44. *Charlotte Observer,* April 15, 17, 1951; *Greensboro Daily News,* April 16, 1951.

45. *Raleigh News and Observer,* March 31, April 11, May 18, 1951.

46. *Greensboro Daily News,* April 16, 1951.

47. State Highway and Public Works Commission, Minutes of the Commission Meeting, March 16, 1951, 1–9, Kerr Scott Gubernatorial Papers.

48. *Raleigh News and Observer,* July 21, 1951.

49. *Raleigh News and Observer,* October 13, 23, 1951.

50. *Raleigh News and Observer,* January 23, 1951.

51. *Raleigh News and Observer,* August 31, 1951; David Cunningham, *Klansville, USA: The Rise and the Fall of the Civil Rights–Era Ku Klux Klan* (Oxford: Oxford University Press, 2013), 29–30.

52. Kerr Scott to Harry E. Stewart, September 27, 1951, and Kerr Scott to W. T. Fullwood Jr., November 27, 1951, Kerr Scott Gubernatorial Papers.

53. W. T. Fullwood Jr. to Kerr Scott, November 23, 1951, Kerr Scott Gubernatorial Papers.

54. Lee Braxton to Kerr Scott, November 21, 1951, Kerr Scott Gubernatorial Papers.

55. *Wilmington Star News,* November 23, 1951.

56. *Raleigh News and Observer,* November 26, 1951.

57. Kerr Scott to W. T. Fullwood Jr., November 27, 1951, Kerr Scott Gubernatorial Papers.

58. *Raleigh News and Observer,* March 5, 1952; Kerr Scott to A. W. McAlister, February 25, 1952, Kerr Scott Gubernatorial Papers; Cunningham, *Klansville, USA,* 30.

59. Raymond Gavins, "The NAACP in North Carolina," in *The Civil Rights Movement,* ed. Jack E. Davis (Malden, MA: Blackwell, 2001), 168–69.

60. *New York Times,* June 9, 1951; *Raleigh News and Observer,* June 9, 1951.

61. Galt Braxton to Kerr Scott, June 11, 1951, Kerr Scott Gubernatorial Papers; *Kinston Daily Free Press,* June 10, 1951.

62. H. L. Cameron, Membership Chairman of the NAACP in Sanford, to Kerr Scott, June 11, 1951, Kerr Scott Gubernatorial Papers.

63. Otis L. Hairston to Kerr Scott, June 12, 1951, Kerr Scott Gubernatorial Papers.

64. *Raleigh News and Observer,* March 28, 1951.

65. *Raleigh News and Observer,* April 25, 26, 1951.

66. *Raleigh News and Observer,* June 5, 8, 1951.

67. O. M. Powers Sr. to Kerr Scott, December 13, 1951, Kerr Scott Gubernatorial Papers.

68. Kerr Scott to O. M. Powers Sr., December 13, 1951, Kerr Scott Gubernatorial Papers.

69. Mrs. T. S. Norman to Kerr Scott, June 15, 1951, and Kerr Scott to Mrs. T. S. Norman, July 9, 1951, Kerr Scott Gubernatorial Papers.

70. *Raleigh News and Observer,* September 13, 18, 1951; *Greensboro Daily News,* September 19, 1951; L. H. Fountain to Kerr Scott, September 14, 1951 (re: Valentine), J. Andrew Warlick to Kerr Scott, September 17, 1951 (re: Bobbitt), and Larry I. Moore to Kerr Scott, September 13, 1951 (re: Gwynn), Kerr Scott Gubernatorial Papers; Anna R. Hayes, *The Life of Susie Marshall Sharp* (Chapel Hill: University of North Carolina Press, 2008), 170.

71. *Raleigh News and Observer,* June 1, 1952; *North Carolina Manual, 1957* (Raleigh: Thad Eure, 1957), 257–59.

72. *Raleigh News and Observer,* November 6, 1951.

73. Fred Flagler to Cecil Moore, August 11, 1951, and Kerr Scott to Fred Flagler, August 17, 1951, Kerr Scott Gubernatorial Papers.

74. *Raleigh News and Observer,* March 17, 1951.

75. *Raleigh News and Observer,* August 29, September 1, 1951.

76. *Raleigh News and Observer,* April 25, October 1, 1951.

77. Kerr Scott to Harry S Truman, June 8, 1951, Kerr Scott Gubernatorial Papers.

78. *Raleigh News and Observer,* October 16, 1951; Kerr Scott to Harry S Truman, October 17, 1951, and Harry S Truman to Kerr Scott, October 22, 1951, Harry S Truman Papers, Harry S Truman Library, Independence, MO.

79. *Raleigh News and Observer,* February 19, 20, 1952.

80. *Raleigh News and Observer,* January 5, 20, 1952.

81. *Raleigh News and Observer,* February 14, 1952.

82. *Raleigh News and Observer,* January 30, February 6, 1952.

83. Joseph P. Crawford to Capus Waynick, March 13, 1951, Kerr Scott Gubernatorial Papers.

84. *Raleigh News and Observer,* May 2, 1951.

85. Capus Waynick, February 4, 1974, interview by Bill Finger, 8, SOHP.

86. *Raleigh News and Observer,* September 8, 1951.

87. *Raleigh News and Observer,* September 12, 25, 1951.

88. *Raleigh News and Observer,* September 27, November 10, 1951.

89. *Raleigh News and Observer,* September 12, 1951.

90. Waynick, interview by Finger, 9; Lauch Faircloth, September 26, 2001, interview by Rob Christensen, 4, in possession of the interviewer.

91. *Raleigh News and Observer,* September 6, October 30, 1951.

92. *Raleigh News and Observer,* January 22, 23, 1951; Kerr Scott to Capus Waynick, January 28, 1952, Kerr Scott Gubernatorial Papers.

93. *Raleigh News and Observer,* May 9, 1952.

94. *Raleigh News and Observer,* January 18, 23, 26, 1952.

95. *New York Times,* May 31, June 2, 1952; *Raleigh News and Observer,* June 1, 1952.

96. *Raleigh News and Observer,* May 4, 20, 1952; *Asheville Citizen Times,* June 22, 1952.

97. *Raleigh News and Observer,* June 25, 1952.

98. *Raleigh News and Observer,* June 1, 1952.

99. Bryce R. Holt to William B. Umstead, April 30, 1952, William B. Umstead Gubernatorial Papers, North Carolina Department of Archives and History; *Raleigh News and Observer,* April 4, 5, 1952.

100. Otis M. Banks to William B. Umstead, June 3, 1953, William B. Umstead Papers.

101. *Raleigh News and Observer,* May 28, 1952.

102. *Raleigh News and Observer,* March 31, 1952.

103. *Raleigh News and Observer,* March 11, 15, 21, 22, 23, 1952; Gilbert C. Fite, *Richard B. Russell, Jr.: Senator from Georgia* (Chapel Hill: University of North Carolina Press, 1991), 281–86.

104. Howard E. Covington and Marion A. Ellis, *Terry Sanford* (Durham: Duke University Press, 1999), 114–15.

105. Ben F. Bulla, *Textiles and Politics: The Life of B. Everett Jordan* (Durham: Carolina Academic, 1992), 30.

106. B. Everett Jordan to Kerr Scott, May 15, 1952, Kerr Scott Gubernatorial Papers.

107. *Raleigh News and Observer,* May 23, 24, 26, 30, 1952.

108. *Raleigh News and Observer,* May 23, June 25, 1952; *New York Times,* May 23, 1952; Kerr Scott to J. A. McClurkin, May 27, 1952, Kerr Scott Gubernatorial Papers.

109. *Raleigh News and Observer,* June 1, 2, 1952; *North Carolina Manual, 1953* (Raleigh: Thad Eure, 1953), 209–10.

110. *Raleigh News and Observer,* February 8, 9, April 7, 29, 30, 1952.

111. *Raleigh News and Observer,* April 30, May 1, 4, 1952.

112. *Raleigh News and Observer,* May 8, 1952.

113. *Raleigh News and Observer,* June 3, 1952; W. Kerr Scott to T. C. Johnson, May 30, 1952, in Corbitt, ed., *Public Addresses,* 510.

114. *Raleigh News and Observer,* June 4, 1952; W. Kerr Scott to Landon Rosser, June 3, 1952, Kerr Scott Gubernatorial Papers.

115. Anonymous to Kerr Scott, June 4, 1952, Kerr Scott Gubernatorial Papers.

116. Mrs. Jerry Grimes to Kerr Scott, June 5, 1952, and Kerr Scott to Mrs. Jerry Grimes, June 9, 1952, Kerr Scott Gubernatorial Papers.

117. *Raleigh News and Observer,* June 6, 7, 12, 1952; Robert Rankin, *The Government and Administration of North Carolina* (New York: Thomas Crowell, 1955), 94–95; W. Kerr Scott, Governor and Director of the Budget, to D. S. Coltrane, June 6, 1952, Kerr Scott Gubernatorial Papers.

118. *Raleigh News and Observer,* June 7, 10, 1952.

119. *Raleigh News and Observer,* June 9, 10, 1952.

120. *Asheville Citizen,* June 13, 1952.

121. *Greensboro Daily News,* June 12, 1952; *Raleigh News and Observer,* June 12, 1952.

122. *Raleigh News and Observer,* June 17, 18, 19, 20, 21, 1952.

123. *Raleigh News and Observer,* May 23, 24, 1953.

124. W. Kerr Scott to Ann Bolton, July 8, 1952, and Kerr Scott to G. C. Davidson, July 8, 1952, Kerr Scott Gubernatorial Papers.

125. *Greensboro Daily News,* June 12, 1952; *Raleigh News and Observer,* June 13, 1952.

126. *Raleigh News and Observer,* August 13, 14, 15, 1952.

127. *Raleigh News and Observer,* August 27, 28, 1952.

128. *Raleigh News and Observer,* February 16, August 18, 1952.

129. Richard B. Russell to Kerr Scott, June 3, July 1, 10, 1952, and Kerr Scott to Richard Russell, June 17, 1952, Kerr Scott Gubernatorial Papers.

130. *Raleigh News and Observer,* July 9, 1952.

131. "Governor's Itinerary for National Democratic Convention in Chicago," July 19, 1952, Kerr Scott Gubernatorial Papers.

132. *Raleigh News and Observer,* July 21, 1952.

133. *Raleigh News and Observer,* July 26, August 2, 1952; Fite, *Russell: Senator from Georgia,* 291–96; Porter McKeever, *Adlai Stevenson: His Life and Legacy* (New York: William Morrow, 1989), 195–98.

134. *Charlotte Observer,* July 16, 1952; *Raleigh News and Observer,* September 6, 8, 1952.

135. *Raleigh News and Observer,* September 28, November 2, 3, 1952; Kerr Scott to R. C. Rivers, October 29, 1952, Kerr Scott Gubernatorial Papers.

136. *New York Times,* October 24, 1952.

137. Julian M. Pleasants, "Call Your Next Case," *North Carolina Historical Review* 76, no. 1 (January 1999): 66–91; *North Carolina Manual, 1953,* 211–13.

138. Kerr Scott to Capus Waynick, November 7, 1952, Kerr Scott Gubernatorial Papers.

139. *New York Times,* November 17, 1952; *Raleigh News and Observer,* November 6, 1952.

The political scientist V. O. Key Jr. recognized that the Republican Party was "strong enough to give North Carolina the earmarks of a two-party state yet not strong enough to threaten Democratic supremacy." Unlike in other southern states, in North Carolina the Republicans had enough strength to force the Democratic Party to develop a disciplined, statewide organization. Jack Bass and Walter DeVries and others identified several groups that fueled the rise of the Republican Party in the South: migrants who moved to the Sunbelt for economic reasons, citizens moving from rural areas to cities for jobs, ambitious politicians who sought to establish a true two-party system, and inhabitants who agreed with the racial and economic views of the conservative wing of the Republican Party. Many of Eisenhower's votes in 1952 came from affluent urban areas. The trend toward a two-party system had been noticed in Florida when, in the presidential election of 1948, the votes for Tom Dewey and Strom Thurmond exceeded the votes gained by Harry Truman. Although there were only fifty-one thousand registered Republicans in Florida, this election broke the Democratic Party's ironclad control of the state as conservatives began to vote with the Republicans. See V. O. Key Jr., *Southern Politics in State and Nation* (New York: Knopf, 1949); Jack Bass and Walter DeVries, *The Transformation of Southern Politics: Social Change and Political Consequences since 1945* (Athens: University of Georgia Press, 1976); and Julian M. Pleasants, "Claude Pepper, Strom Thurmond and the 1948 Presidential Election in Florida," *Florida Historical Quarterly* 76, no. 4 (Spring 1998): 439–73.

In North Carolina from 1952 to 1988, the Republican Party grew significantly in voting strength and political power. Gubernatorial elections showed a steady increase in Republican support. In 1960 Robert L. Gavin got 45.5 percent of the vote, and in 1968 James Gardner received 47.3 percent. The trend culminated with the election of Jim Holshouser in 1972, and another Republican, James G. Martin, was elected to two consecutive terms in 1984 and 1988. By 1986, the Republican Party had secured both US Senate seats, won nine of fourteen statewide races, and increased its voter registration by 143 percent. By 1996, Republicans had gained control of the state House of Representatives, held half the state's congressional seats, and increased their power at the county level. From 1968 to 1988, Republican presidential candidates carried the state, with the exception of Jimmy Carter in 1976. The party had added rural, lower-class whites who opposed the Democratic Party's stand on race to their urban business base and traditional mountain support. See Earl Black and Merle Black, *Politics and Society in the South* (Cambridge, MA: Harvard University Press, 1987); Jack D. Fleer, *North Carolina Politics: An Introduction* (Chapel Hill: University of North Carolina Press, 1968).

140. Kerr Scott to William B. Umstead, November 7, 1952, Kerr Scott Gubernatorial Papers.

141. Luther H. Hodges, *Businessman in the State House: Six Years as Governor of North Carolina* (Chapel Hill: University of North Carolina Press, 1962), 19.

142. *Raleigh News and Observer,* November 28, 1952.

143. *Raleigh News and Observer,* November 29, December 10, 1952.

144. *Raleigh News and Observer,* December 13, 1952.

145. Corbitt, ed., *Public Addresses,* 327–32; "State-Wide Radio Address from the Executive Office by Governor W. Kerr Scott," December 30, 1952, Kerr Scott Gubernatorial Papers; *Raleigh News and Observer,* December 31, 1952.

146. *Raleigh News and Observer,* January 1, 1953.

147. *Raleigh News and Observer,* January 8, 9, 1952; Hodges, *Businessman in the State House,* 17.

148. Edward L. Rankin Jr., "William Bradley Umstead," in David L. Corbitt, ed., *Public Addresses Letters and Papers of William Bradley Umstead, Governor of North Carolina, 1953–54* (Raleigh: Council of State, 1957), vi–xi.

149. *Raleigh News and Observer,* January 9, 1952; Covington and Ellis, *Terry Sanford,* 120.

150. *Raleigh News and Observer,* January 4, 9, 1952.

151. *Durham Morning Herald,* December 14, 1952.

152. *Progressive Farmer,* February 1953, 196.

153. *Raleigh Times,* January 6, 1952.

154. *Raleigh News and Observer,* December 13, 1952.

155. *Southport Pilot,* January 7, 1953.

156. *Winston-Salem Journal,* January 8, 1953.

157. *The State,* January 3, 1953, 9–11.

158. Capus Waynick to Kerr Scott, November 10, 1952, Waynick Papers.

9. The Third Primary, 1954

1. *Winston-Salem Journal and Sentinel,* January 25, 1953.

2. Lauch Faircloth, March 22, 1999, interview by Joseph Mosnier, 10, SOHP; Roy Wilder Jr., July 10, 2009, interview by Julian Pleasants, in possession of the author.

3. Transcript of Radio Broadcast, March 1, 1953, Kerr Scott Gubernatorial Papers, North Carolina Department of Archives and History.

4. Ed Rankin Jr., August 20, 1987, interview by Jay Jenkins, 42, SOHP.

5. *Raleigh News and Observer,* June 27, 28, July 11, 12, 14, 1953; Howard E. Covington and Marion A. Ellis, *Terry Sanford* (Durham, NC: Duke University Press, 1999), 126–27; Ed Rankin Jr., "William Bradley Umstead," in David L. Corbitt, ed., *Public Addresses, Letters and Papers of William Bradley Umstead, Governor of North Carolina, 1953–54* (Raleigh: Council of State, 1957), xii.

6. Terry Sanford, n.d., interview by Jack Bass and Walter DeVries, 10, SOHP.

7. *Raleigh Times,* July 13, 1953.

8. *Transylvania Times* (Brevard, NC), June 4, 1953.

9. *Raleigh News and Observer,* July 22, 1953.

10. Kerr Scott to Capus Waynick, June 12, 1953, Capus Waynick to Kerr Scott, June

16, 1953, and Kerr Scott to Capus Waynick, August 31, 1953, Kerr Scott Private Papers, North Carolina Department of Archives and History.

11. Terry Sanford to Kerr Scott, August 2, 1953, Kerr Scott Private Papers.

12. Covington and Ellis, *Terry Sanford*, 127–29; Terry Sanford, interview by UNC-TV, summer 1997, SOHP.

13. *Charlotte Observer*, August 5, 6, 1953.

14. Kerr Scott to R. Gregg Cherry, July 17, 1953, and R. Gregg Cherry to Kerr Scott, July 18, 1953, William B. Umstead Papers, Southern Historical Collection, University of North Carolina, Chapel Hill.

15. W. Kerr Scott to John D. Larkins, September 9, 1953, John D. Larkins Papers, Joyner Library, East Carolina University.

16. Kerr Scott to "Squire Truman," September 30, 1953, and Harry S Truman to Kerr Scott, October 8, 1953, Harry S Truman Papers, Harry S Truman Library, Independence, MO.

17. Kerr Scott to Inglis Fletcher, September 21, 1953, Inglis Fletcher Papers, Joyner Library; Kerr Scott to "Squire Zimmerman," September 24, 1953, William B. Umstead Papers; Kerr Scott to Tom Hawkins, October 7, 1953, Kerr Scott Senatorial Papers, North Carolina Department of Archives and History.

18. Report to Terry Sanford, n.d., Kerr Scott Private Papers.

19. *Southport Pilot*, October 13, 1953.

20. J. J. Hampton to Kerr Scott, December 5, 1953, Kerr Scott Private Papers.

21. E. L. Dillingham to Kerr Scott, December 4, 1953, Kerr Scott Private Papers.

22. *The Robesonian* (Lumberton, NC), November 16, 1953.

23. *Durham Sun*, November 18, 1953.

24. *The Robesonian* (Lumberton, NC), November 16, 1953; *Wilmington News*, November 30, 1953.

25. *Elkin Tribune*, January 1, 1954; *Goldsboro News Argus*, January 16, 1954; *Mount Holly News*, February 26, 1954; *Liberty News*, February 23, 1954; *Salisbury Post*, February 11, 1954.

26. Transcript of Radio Broadcast, n.d., Kerr Scott Private Papers.

27. Wilder, interview by Pleasants.

28. *Greensboro Daily News*, February 7, 1954; *Winston-Salem Sentinel*, February 7, 1954; *Raleigh News and Observer*, February 7, 1954; *Rocky Mount Telegram*, February 7, 1954; *Burlington Daily Times News*, February 8, 1954.

29. *Greensboro Daily News*, February 8, 1954.

30. *Newton Observer*, February 9, 1954.

31. *Dunn Daily Dispatch*, February 5, 1954.

32. *Winston-Salem Journal*, February 12, 1954; *Raleigh News and Observer*, February 10, 1954.

33. *Raleigh News and Observer*, February 8, 1954.

34. *Fayetteville Observer*, February 13, 1954.

35. *Burlington Times News,* February 27, 1954.

36. Harry Golden, *The Right Time* (New York: Putnam's, 1969), 273.

37. Kerr Scott to John A. Lang Jr., February 27, 1954, John A. Lang Jr. Papers, Joyner Library.

38. Terry Sanford to Jack Kirksey, February 18, 1954, Kerr Scott Private Papers.

39. Wilder, interview by Pleasants.

40. Terry Sanford, May 14, 1976, interview by Brent Glass, 36–45, SOHP; Bill Friday, June 28, 2010, interview by Julian Pleasants, in possession of the author.

41. Internal Memo, John Harden to J. Spencer Love, February 15, 1954, and J. Spencer Love to John Harden, February 18, 1954, John Harden Papers, Southern Historical Collection.

42. Wilder, interview by Pleasants.

43. W. M. Pence to Kerr Scott, February 27, 1954, Kerr Scott Private Papers.

44. *Greensboro Daily News,* February 27, 1954; *Kinston Daily Free Press,* March 3, 1954; *Kinston Daily News,* March 4, 1954; Covington and Ellis, *Terry Sanford,* 131.

45. *Greensboro Daily News,* March 5, 1954.

46. Kerr Scott to E. P. Bond, July 31, 1954, Kerr Scott Private Papers.

47. Covington and Ellis, *Terry Sanford,* 130–31.

48. Terry Sanford to W. A. Aldridge, March 3, 1954, Kerr Scott Private Papers.

49. Minutes of the Meeting of the Women's Division in Greensboro, March 12, 1954, Guion G. Johnson Papers, Southern Historical Collection.

50. "Kerr Scott: Tar Heel Builder," Brochure for the 1954 Senate Campaign, Kerr Scott Private Papers.

51. Kerr Scott to S. Anglin, March 29, 1954, Kerr Scott Private Papers.

52. David M. Oshinsky, *A Conspiracy So Immense: The World of Joe McCarthy* (New York: Free Press, 1983), 250–308.

53. Speech by Kerr Scott, March 5, 1954, Harry Truman Post Presidential Files, Harry S Truman Papers.

54. Harry S Truman to Kerr Scott, March 17, 1954, Truman Post Presidential Files.

55. Covington and Ellis, *Terry Sanford,* 132.

56. *Winston-Salem Journal and Sentinel,* March 23, May 23, 1954; *Durham Morning Herald,* March 28, 1954.

57. Terry Sanford to O. D. Steinback, April 21, 1954, Kerr Scott Private Papers.

58. C. A. Fink to Terry Sanford, April 26, 1954, Kerr Scott Private Papers.

59. Terry Sanford, Campaign Notebook Listing Key Workers in Each County, Terry Sanford Papers, Southern Historical Collection.

60. Thomas Kluttz to Kerr Scott, April 20, 1954, Kerr Scott Private Papers.

61. Terry Sanford to Kenneth C. Royall, April 29, 1954, Kenneth Royall to Mrs. Albert Lasker, June 8, 1954, and Kerr Scott to Kenneth Royall, April 29, May 12, 1954, Kerr Scott Private Papers.

62. Jonathan Daniels to Mrs. Max Ascoli, May 27, 1954, Jonathan Worth Daniels Papers, Southern Historical Collection.

63. John Ehle, *Dr. Frank: Life with Frank Porter Graham* (Chapel Hill: Franklin Street, 1993), 193.

64. Kerr Scott to Ralph Holt, May 24, 1954, Kerr Scott Private Papers.

65. Radio and Television Cost Estimates, Walter J. Klein Co., May 17, 1954, Kerr Scott Private Papers.

66. William B. Whitley to Laurie Nath, January 4, 1955, Kerr Scott Senatorial Papers.

67. Kerr Scott to Henry W. Jordan, April 10, 1954, Kerr Scott Private Papers.

68. *Salisbury Post,* April 22, 1954.

69. W. A. Aldridge to Terry Sanford, April 27, 1954, Kerr Scott Private Papers.

70. Ad, n.d., Harden Papers. John Harden of Greensboro, NC, was a journalist, newspaper editor, author, secretary to Governor R. Gregg Cherry, and Democratic activist. He founded the state's first full-service public relations company, John Harden and Associates. He advised Lennon on his campaign, and his papers contain significant portions of the Lennon campaign literature and correspondence.

71. "Did Governor Scott in Office Take Care of Farmer Scott?" ad, n.d., Harden Papers and Kerr Scott Private Papers.

72. Ad, n.d., Harden Papers; *Raleigh Times,* April 15, 1954; *Raleigh News and Observer,* May 28, 1950.

73. Ad, n.d., Harden Papers.

74. *Greensboro Daily News,* May 30, 1954.

75. Ad, n.d., Harden Papers.

76. Ad, n.d., Harden Papers.

77. Ad, n.d., Harden Papers.

78. *Durham Morning Herald,* May 9, 1954.

79. Clipping, *Greensboro Daily News,* n.d., Kerr Scott Private Papers.

80. *Raleigh News and Observer,* May 27, 1954.

81. Typed Manuscript, n.d., Roy Wilder Jr. Papers, Southern Historical Collection.

82. *Burlington Daily Times News,* May 7, 1954; "Tar Heel Senator," May 25, 1954, Ad, Ralph Scott Papers, North Carolina Department of Archives and History; *Hyde County Times,* May 28, 1954.

83. Ad, n.d., Ralph Scott Papers.

84. Confidential Memo no. 1, from C. A. Upchurch Jr., May 10, 1954, Harden Papers.

85. Covington and Ellis, *Terry Sanford,* 132.

86. Draft Statement, n.d., Wilder Papers.

87. Clipping, *Dunn Daily Record,* n.d., Harden Papers.

88. *Durham Sun,* May 12, 1954.

89. Confidential Memo no. 2, May 15, 1954, Harden Papers.

90. Alton Lennon to Fellow North Carolinians, May 8, 1954, Harden Papers.

91. Confidential Memo no. 3, May 22, 1954, Harden Papers.

92. Confidential Memos nos. 2 and 3, Harden Papers.

93. J. W. Ferguson to Terry Sanford, May 15, 1954, Kerr Scott Private Papers; Wilder, interview by Pleasants.

94. Alton Lennon, Speech, n.d., Harden Papers.

95. Confidential Memo no. 3, May 22, 1954, Harden Papers.

96. *Washington Daily News,* May 19, 1954.

97. David Halberstam, *The Fifties* (New York: Villard, 1993), 421–24. For greater detail on the *Brown* case, see Richard Kluger, *Simple Justice* (New York: Knopf, 1976).

98. *Shelby Star,* May 27, 1954; *The Robesonian* (Lumberton, NC), May 17, 1954; Rankin, "William Bradley Umstead," xix–xx.

99. Karl E. Campbell, *Senator Sam Ervin, Last of the Founding Fathers* (Chapel Hill: University of North Carolina Press, 2007), 83–85.

100. Rankin, interview by Jenkins, 17–19.

101. Kluger, *Simple Justice,* x.

102. W. Kerr Scott, Statement on Supreme Court Decision on Segregation, May 17, 1954, Kerr Scott Private Papers; *Raleigh News and Observer,* May 18, 1954.

103. Bob Scott, December 16, 1998, interview by Rob Christensen, in possession of the interviewer.

104. Alton Lennon, Typed Manuscript of Speech, May 19, 1954, Harden Papers; *Raleigh News and Observer,* May 19, 1954.

105. *Charlotte News,* May 19, 1954.

106. *Durham Morning Herald,* May 20, 1954.

107. Confidential Memo no. 4, May 26, 1954, Harden Papers; *Mebane Enterprise,* May 27, 1954.

108. Wilder, interview by Pleasants; Sanford, interview by Bass and DeVries, 11.

109. *Winston-Salem Journal,* May 26, 1954; copy of ad in Harden Papers.

110. Wilder, interview by Pleasants; Sanford, interview by Bass and DeVries, 12; Sanford, interview by Glass, 58–60.

111. Sworn Statement of Facts Signed by J. H. R. Greaves, May 26, 1954, Kerr Scott Private Papers; *Raleigh News and Observer,* May 28, 1954.

112. Notarized Statement, May 27, 1954, no name, Kerr Scott Private Papers; Sanford, interview by Bass and DeVries, 12–14.

113. *Raleigh News and Observer,* May 28, 1954.

114. Telegram, Terry Sanford to J. Edgar Hoover and the Special Agent in Charge of Charlotte FBI office, May 27, 1954, and Terry Sanford to H. F. Beam, Post Office Inspector, May 31, 1954, Kerr Scott Private Papers.

115. Sanford, interview by Bass and DeVries, 12–14; Sanford, interview by Glass, 60–64; *Raleigh News and Observer,* May 27, 28, 1954.

116. Terry Sanford to State Campaign Managers, June 12, 1954, Confidential Report, Terry Sanford to Warren Olney, June 30, 1954, and Howard Pitt to Terry Sanford, June 15, 1954, Kerr Scott Private Papers.

117. Terry Sanford to Martin D. Armstrong, June 15, 1954, Kerr Scott Private Papers.

118. *Raleigh News and Observer,* May 28, 29, 1954; copies of the ads in Harden Papers.

119. *Raleigh News and Observer,* May 29, 1954.

120. *Raleigh News and Observer,* May 30, 1954.

121. *North Carolina Manual, 1955* (Raleigh: Thad Eure, 1955), 247–50; *Greensboro Daily News,* May 30, 1954; *Raleigh News and Observer,* May 30, 1954; *Los Angeles Daily News,* May 31, 1954.

122. *Burlington Daily Times News,* May 31, 1954.

123. *Greensboro Daily News,* June 10, 1954.

124. *Raleigh News and Observer,* June 4, 1954.

125. *Raleigh News and Observer,* June 6, 1954.

126. Jonathan Daniels to Mrs. Max Ascoli, May 27, 1954, Daniels Papers.

127. Jonathan Daniels to Gerald W. Johnson, June 3, 1954, Daniels Papers.

128. Sanford, interview by Bass and DeVries, 13; Lynn Nisbet, *Goldsboro News Argus,* June 3, 1954.

129. *Greensboro Record,* June 1, 1954.

130. *Northhampton News,* June 2, 1954.

131. *Shelby Daily Star,* May 31, 1954.

132. *New York Times,* May 30, 31, 1954.

133. *U.S. News and World Report,* June 11, 1954.

134. Clipping, *Washington Post,* n.d., Kerr Scott Private Papers.

135. *Hickory Record,* September 7, 1954.

136. Kerr Scott to Harry Truman, June 21, 1954, Kerr Scott Private Papers.

137. Telegram, Walter Reuther to Kerr Scott, June 23, 1954, Kerr Scott Private Papers.

138. A. A. Morisey to Kerr Scott, May 31, 1954, Kerr Scott Private Papers.

139. Mrs. Hope B. Teaster to Kerr Scott, May 31, 1954, Kerr Scott Private Papers.

140. Kerr Scott to Gertrude Weil, June 29, 1954, Gertrude Weil Papers, North Carolina Department of Archives and History; Kerr Scott to F. M. Manning, July 15, 1954, Kerr Scott Private Papers.

141. Edwin Gill to Terry Sanford, June 7, 1954, Sanford Papers.

142. H. Pat Taylor Jr. to Terry Sanford, June 17, 1954, Sanford Papers.

143. Sanford, interview by Glass, 64.

144. *Hickory Record,* September 7, 1954.

145. *Raleigh News and Observer,* September 25, October 10, 17, 1954; *Raleigh Times,* August 16, 1954.

146. *Goldsboro News Argus,* October 1, 1954.

147. *North Carolina Manual, 1955,* 251–52.

148. Rankin, "William Bradley Umstead," xxii.

149. *Charlotte Observer,* September 19, 1954.

10. The Senate Years, 1954–1958

1. *Burlington Daily Times News,* November 30, 1954; *Raleigh News and Observer,* November 30, 1954; *Greensboro Daily News,* November 30, 1954; *Charlotte Observer,* December 5, 1954; *Congressional Record,* 83rd Cong., 2nd sess., vol. 100, November 29, 1954, p. 16147, and November 30, 1954, p. 16181.

2. *Salisbury Evening Post,* November 30, 1954; *Winston-Salem Journal,* November 30, 1954; Wayne Morse to "Fellow Oregonians," October 22, 1954, William McWhorter Cochrane Papers, Southern Historical Collection, University of North Carolina, Chapel Hill.

3. Bob Scott, December 18, 1998, interview by Rob Christensen, in possession of the interviewer; Bob Scott, September 18, 1986, interview by Karl Campbell, SOHP.

4. *Chapel Hill Weekly,* November 12, 1954; *Durham Sun,* November 8, 1954; *Greensboro Daily News,* November 7, 1954; Howard E. Covington and Marion A. Ellis, *Terry Sanford* (Durham, NC: Duke University Press, 1999), 144–45.

5. Noel Woodhouse to Bill Cochrane, November 8, 1954, Cochrane Papers.

6. *Chapel Hill Weekly,* November 11, 1954.

7. *Asheville Citizen,* January 11, 1955.

8. *Burlington Daily Times News,* April 17, 1958.

9. David Oshinsky, *A Conspiracy So Immense: The World of Joe McCarthy* (New York: Free Press, 1983), 416–66.

10. *Greensboro Daily News,* December 1, 1954.

11. *Congressional Record,* 83rd Cong., 2nd sess., December 2, 1954, p. 16392; Oshinsky, *A Conspiracy So Immense,* 472–94; Karl E. Campbell, *Senator Sam Ervin: Last of the Founding Fathers* (Chapel Hill: University of North Carolina Press, 2007), 89–96.

12. *Asheville Citizen,* December 3, 1954.

13. *Burlington Daily Times News,* April 17, 1958.

14. Paul Boller, *Presidential Anecdotes* (New York: Oxford University Press, 1981), 285–86.

15. Nicol Rae, *Southern Democrats in the U.S. Congress* (New York: Oxford University Press, 1994), 97–99.

16. *Greensboro Daily News,* December 7, 1954.

17. *Greensboro Daily News,* December 14, 1954.

18. Kerr Scott to Clarence Poe, January 12, 1955, Clarence Poe Papers, North Carolina Department of Archives and History.

19. *Congressional Record,* 84th Cong., 1st sess., vol. 101, June 7, 1955, p. 7713; *Durham Morning Herald,* July 10, 1955; *New York Times,* June 8, 1955; *Raleigh News and Observer,* June 10, 1955.

20. File, n.p., n.d., Kerr Scott Senatorial Papers, North Carolina Department of Archives and History.

21. *Durham Morning Herald,* July 10, 1955.

22. *Durham Morning Herald,* December 11, 1955.

23. *Winston-Salem Journal,* September 14, 1955; *Charlotte Observer,* September 15, 1955.

24. Typed Manuscript of Speech in Council Bluffs, IA, November 29, 1955, Kerr Scott Senatorial Papers.

25. *Durham Morning Herald,* July 10, 1955.

26. *Durham Morning Herald,* April 15, 1955.

27. Harry Truman to Kerr Scott, December 7, 1955, Harry Truman Post Presidential Files, Harry S Truman Papers, Harry S Truman Library, Independence, MO.

28. *Congressional Record,* 84th Cong., 1st sess., vol. 101, June 13, 1955, p. 10172.

29. *Charlotte News,* April 4, 1955.

30. *Greensboro Daily News,* April 2, 1955.

31. F. S. Royster to Scott, March 31, 1955, Kerr Scott Senatorial Papers.

32. *Sanford Herald,* October 14, 1955.

33. Kerr Scott, Statement on the Cape Fear River Project to the Subcommittee on Public Works, May 26, 1955, Ralph Scott Papers, North Carolina Department of Archives and History; Typed Manuscript of Speech in Corinth, NC, September 7, 1955, Cochrane Papers; *Winston-Salem Journal,* May 30, 1955.

34. *Greensboro Daily News,* May 29, 1955.

35. *Durham Morning Herald,* October 18, 1955; *Raleigh News and Observer,* October 18, 1955.

36. Kerr Scott to D. J. Dalton, July 28, 1956, Kerr Scott Senatorial Papers; *Raleigh News and Observer,* July 20, 21, 1956.

37. *Congressional Record,* 84th Cong., 1st sess., vol. 101, January 14, 1955 (vote no. 2818).

38. *Congressional Record,* 84th Cong., 1st sess., vol. 101, January 28, 1955 (vote no. 2822).

39. *Charlotte Observer,* April 2, 1955.

40. Kerr Scott to W. N. Berry, June 28, 1955, Kerr Scott Senatorial Papers.

41. *Congressional Record,* 84th Cong., 1st sess., vol. 101, February 9, 1955 (vote no. 2826).

42. Chester Pach and Elmo Richardson, *The Presidency of Dwight D. Eisenhower* (Lawrence: University Press of Kansas, 1991), 98–104.

43. *Congressional Record,* 84th Cong., 1st sess., vol. 101, April 1, 1955, pp. 4275–76; *New York Times,* April 2, 1955; *Greensboro Daily News,* April 2, 1955.

44. *Kings Mountain Herald,* April 5, 1955.

45. *Greensboro Daily News,* April 5, 1955.

46. *Greensboro Daily News,* January 5, 1955; *Raleigh News and Observer,* January 8, 1955; *Winston-Salem Journal,* January 16, 1955; *Durham Morning Herald,* July 1, 1956.

47. *Congressional Record,* 84th Cong., 1st sess., vol. 101, June 7, 1955 (vote no. 2872).

48. *Raleigh News and Observer,* March 12, 1955.

49. Hubert H. Humphrey to Kerr Scott, July 11, 1955, Kerr Scott Senatorial Papers.

50. *Raleigh News and Observer,* October 18, 1955; Kerr Scott to Zeno Edwards, November 8, 1955, Kerr Scott Private Papers, North Carolina Department of Archives and History.

51. *Greensboro Daily News,* October 1, 1955; *Durham Herald,* October 2, 1955.

52. Letters to Kerr Scott, November 13–19, 1955, Kerr Scott Senatorial Papers.

53. Kerr Scott to Ralph Scott, March 24, 1955, Ralph Scott Papers; *Burlington Daily Times News,* August 31, 1955; Bill Friday, June 28, 2010, interview by Julian Pleasants, in possession of the author.

54. *Rocky Mount Evening Telegram,* February 8, 1955; *Raleigh News and Observer,* March 12, 1955; Grace Furman, May 30, 2009, interview by Rob Christensen, in possession of the interviewer; Roy Wilder Jr., September 2, 2009, interview by Julian Pleasants, in possession of the author; Typed Note, n.d., Roy Wilder Jr. Papers, Southern Historical Collection.

55. Steven Niven, "Thomas J. Pearsall," in *North Carolina Century: Tar Heels Who Made a Difference,* ed. Howard E. Covington Jr. and Marion A. Ellis (Charlotte: Levine Museum of the New South, 2002), 510; William H. Chafe, *Civilities and Civil Rights: Greensboro and the Black Struggle for Freedom* (New York: Oxford University Press, 1980), 50; Covington and Ellis, *Terry Sanford,* 149–50; Davison M. Douglas, *Reading, Writing and Race: The Desegregation of Charlotte Schools* (Chapel Hill: University of North Carolina Press, 1995), 29–31; A. C. "Pete" Ivey, *Luther Hodges: Practical Idealist* (Minneapolis: T. S. Denison, 1968), 165.

56. Chafe, *Civilities and Civil Rights,* 50–52; Jeffrey D. Crow, *A History of African Americans in North Carolina* (Raleigh: North Carolina Department of Cultural Resources, 2008), 169; Luther H. Hodges, *Businessman in the State House: Six Years as Governor of North Carolina* (Chapel Hill: University of North Carolina Press, 1962), 80–90.

57. Nadine Cohodas, *Strom Thurmond and the Politics of Southern Change* (New York: Simon & Schuster, 1993), 283–86; Gilbert Fite, *Richard B. Russell, Jr.: Senator from Georgia* (Chapel Hill: University of North Carolina Press, 1991), 333–34; Pach and Richardson, *Eisenhower,* 145; Campbell, *Senator Sam Ervin,* 105–6; Herman Talmadge, *Talmadge: A Political Legacy, a Politician's Life: A Memoir* (Atlanta: Peachtree, 1987), 178.

58. Kyle Longley, *Senator Albert Gore, Sr.: Political Maverick* (Baton Rouge: Louisiana State University Press, 2004), 123–24.

59. "North Carolina's Man on the Hill," *Carolina Alumni Review* 72, no. 3 (Spring 1984): 13–15; Rob Christensen, *The Paradox of Tar Heel Politics* (Chapel Hill: University of North Carolina Press, 2008), 164.

60. Anthony Badger, "Southerners Who Refused to Sign the Southern Manifesto," in *New Deal, New South: A Badger Reader* (Fayetteville: University of Arkansas Press, 2007), 72–87.

61. Covington and Ellis, *Terry Sanford*, 168–74; Chafe, *Civilities and Civil Rights*, 52–54; Hodges, *Businessman in the Statehouse*, 91–106; Ivey, *Luther Hodges*, 167; Luther Hodges, "Personal Experiences as Governor of North Carolina," 58–59, Handwritten Notes, folder 127, box 116, Luther H. Hodges Papers, Southern Historical Collection; *Charlotte Observer*, July 15, 1956; *Greensboro Daily News*, July 24, 26, August 7, 12, September 8, 1956; *Raleigh News and Observer*, July 27, 1956; Crow, *African Americans in North Carolina*, 169–70; Douglas, *Reading, Writing and Race*, 32–34.

62. Terry Sanford, May 14, 1976, interview by Brent Glass, 79, SOHP; Covington and Ellis, *Terry Sanford*, 163–64.

63. *Raleigh News and Observer*, February 6, 1956.

64. *Courier Times*, August 23, 1956; *Charlotte Observer*, September 2, 1956.

65. *Raleigh News and Observer*, September 8, 1956.

66. Hodges, *Businessman in the Statehouse*, 90; Covington and Ellis, *Terry Sanford*, 176; *Raleigh News and Observer*, September 9, 10, 1956; *North Carolina Manual, 1957* (Raleigh: Thad Eure, 1957), 253–56.

67. *Raleigh News and Observer*, July 24, 1957.

68. Chafe, *Civilities and Civil Rights*, 54–60; Douglas, *Reading, Writing and Race*, 36–48.

69. *Winston-Salem Journal*, September 9, 1956; *New York Times*, June 19, 1956; *Raleigh News and Observer*, July 29, 1956; Kerr Scott to Lucretia Ann Street, March 6, 1958, Kerr Scott Senatorial Papers.

70. Kerr Scott to F. E. Winslow, March 21, 1956, and Kerr Scott to Henry Brandis Jr., May 3, 1955, Scott Senatorial Papers; *Winston-Salem Journal*, September 9, 1956; Stephen Ambrose, *Eisenhower the President* (New York: Simon & Schuster, 1984), 154–55; Pach and Richardson, *Eisenhower*, 59–62, 164–66.

71. Bob Scott, interview by Rob Christensen, December 18, 1998.

72. *Winston-Salem Journal*, November 21, 1956.

73. *Time*, December 10, 1954, 24.

74. Adlai Stevenson to Kerr Scott, typed notes by Roy Wilder, n.d., Wilder Papers.

75. *New York Times*, July 12, 1956; *Durham Morning Herald*, June 17, 1956.

76. John Bartlow Martin, *Adlai Stevenson and the World* (New York: Doubleday, 1977), 348–52, 391–92; *Durham Morning Herald*, August 19, 1956; John D. Larkins Jr., *Politics, Bar and Bench: A Memoir of John Davis Larkins, Jr.: Fifty Years*, ed. Donald R. Lennon and Fred D. Ragan (New Bern, NC: Owen G. Dunn, 1980), 48; Kerr Scott to Cleveland Gardner, November 9, 1956, Kerr Scott Senatorial Papers; *Raleigh News and Observer*, October 31, 1956; *North Carolina Manual, 1957*, 215.

77. Speech by Senator Kerr Scott, U.S. Senate Floor, June 13, 1956, Ralph Scott Papers; *Washington Post*, May 29, 1956.

78. *Congressional Record*, 84th Cong., 2nd sess., vol. 102, July 24, 1957, p. 14180.

79. *Congressional Record*, 84th Cong., 2nd sess., vol. 102, February 16, 1956, p. 2671, and April 11, 1956, p. 6089.

80. Speech by Kerr Scott, Benson, NC, September 21, 1956, Harry Truman Post Presidential Files; *New York Times,* September 22, 1956.

81. Edwin S. Lanier to Bill Cochrane, September 25, 1956, Cochrane Papers.

82. Collection no. 03698, pp. 340–43, Luther H. Hodges Papers; *Congressional Record,* 84th Cong., 2nd sess., vol. 102, May 10, 1956, pp. 7914–15, and July 19, 1956, pp. A5690–A5691; Kerr Scott to Ezra Taft Benson, August 19, 1955, Kerr Scott to President Eisenhower, September 12, 1955, and Wilton Peterson to Scott, September 17, 1955, Kerr Scott Senatorial Papers; *Greensboro Daily News,* September 21, 1955.

83. *New York Times,* December 4, 1955, January 11, 12, 13, February 1, 8, 1956; *Washington Post,* December 3, 1955; *Durham Morning Herald,* January 13, 18, 19, February 8, 1956; *Greensboro Daily News,* January 12, 13, 1956, February 8, 1956; *Congressional Record,* 84th Cong., 2nd sess., vol. 102, March 1, 1956, pp. 3726–32.

84. R. C. Rome to Kerr Scott, January 22, 1956, Kerr Scott Senatorial Papers.

85. *Rocky Mount Evening Telegram,* January 21, 1956.

86. *Washington Post,* January 12, 1956.

87. Typed Notes by Roy Wilder, n.d., and Robert R. Reynolds to Kerr Scott, November 28, 1957, Wilder Papers.

88. Harry Stokely to Kerr Scott, July 5, 1957, Kerr Scott Senatorial Papers.

89. *Charlotte Observer,* February 22, 1957.

90. *Charlotte Observer,* February 13, 1957.

91. *Winston-Salem Journal and Sentinel,* November 25, 1957.

92. *Charlotte News,* November 29, 1957.

93. *Raleigh News and Observer,* December 5, 1957; Kerr Scott to Bob Reynolds, December 4, 1957, Kerr Scott Senatorial Papers.

94. *Raleigh News and Observer,* June 23, 1957; *Winston-Salem Journal,* June 2, 1957.

95. Kerr Scott to Bob Hanes, June 6, 1957, Wilder Papers.

96. *Congressional Record,* 85th Cong., 1st sess., vol. 102, pp. 8959–60, 9764, 14669, 4133; Ambrose, *Eisenhower the President,* 460.

97. *Charlotte Observer,* January 25, 1957; *Asheville Citizen,* January 30, 1957.

98. *Greensboro Daily News,* January 16, 1957.

99. *Wilmington Star News,* October 9, 1957; *Winston-Salem Journal,* October 1, 1957; *Charlotte Observer,* October 1, 1957.

100. Speech by Kerr Scott on the Floor of the Senate, January 9, 1957, Harry Truman Post Presidential Files; *New York Times,* January 7, 10, 1957; *Raleigh News and Observer,* January 2, 6, 10, 1957; Pach and Richardson, *Eisenhower,* 160–61; Kerr Scott to John Simons, October 5, 1956, Kerr Scott Senatorial Papers.

101. Keith M. Finley, *Delaying the Dream: Southern Senators and the Fight against Civil Rights, 1938–1965* (Baton Rouge: Louisiana State University Press, 2008), 152–90; Pach and Richardson, *Eisenhower,* 147–49; *Raleigh News and Observer,* July 25, 1957.

102. *Greensboro Daily News,* January 3, 1957; *Raleigh News and Observer,* January 4, 1957.

103. Staley Cook to Kerr Scott, July 17, 1957, Kerr Scott Senatorial Papers.

104. Kerr Scott to Mabel Goode, March 28, 1957, and Kerr Scott to Staley Cook, July 17, 1957, Kerr Scott Senatorial Papers.

105. *Wilmington Morning Star,* March 19, 1957; *Greensboro Daily News,* March 19, 1957.

106. Copy of *Norfolk Journal and Guide,* April 1957, in J. W. Jeffries to Kerr Scott, n.d., Scott Senatorial Papers.

107. Kerr Scott to Wilbur Clark, August 8, 1957, Kerr Scott Senatorial Papers.

108. *Congressional Record,* 85th Cong., 1st sess., vol. 103, July 13, 1957, pp. 10471–75; *Durham Morning Herald,* August 8, 1957; *Raleigh News and Observer,* July 14, 1957.

109. *Congressional Record,* 85th Cong., 1st sess., vol. 103, August 29, 1957, p. 16469.

110. Finley, *Delaying the Dream,* 152–90; Pach and Richardson, *Eisenhower,* 147–49; Ambrose, *Eisenhower the President,* 497–99; Kerr Scott to Wilbur Clark, August 8, 1957, Kerr Scott Senatorial Papers; *Raleigh News and Observer,* July 25, 1957; *Winston-Salem Journal,* September 9, 1957.

111. Ambrose, *Eisenhower the President,* 414–23; Pach and Richardson, *Eisenhower,* 150–55; *Raleigh News and Observer,* September 3, 4, 5, 6, 7, 8, 20, 1957.

112. *Greensboro Daily News,* September 27, 1957; *Durham Morning Herald,* September 27, 1957; *Raleigh News and Observer,* September 26, 1957.

113. *Raleigh News and Observer,* September 25, 1957.

114. Kerr Scott to constituents, n.d., Kerr Scott Senatorial Papers.

115. Dr. Stuart Willis to Dr. George Carrington, July 22, 1949, Dr. George Carrington to Kerr Scott, July 30, 1949, and Medical Report, Dr. W. M. Nicholson to Kerr Scott, July 26, 1950, and December 23, 1953, Kerr Scott Senatorial Papers; *Burlington Daily Times News,* September 17, 1957.

116. *New York Times,* April 10, 1958.

117. *New York Times,* April 11, 1958; *Raleigh News and Observer,* April 11, 1958; *Durham Morning Herald,* April 13, 1958; *Burlington Daily Times News,* April 17, 1958.

118. *Raleigh News and Observer,* April 18, 1958; *Chapel Hill News Leader,* August 11, 1958.

119. *Greensboro Daily News,* April 17, 1958.

120. *Raleigh News and Observer,* April 17, 1958.

121. *Durham Morning Herald,* April 20, 1958.

122. *New York Times,* April 17, 1958.

123. *Raleigh News and Observer,* April 19, 1958; *Greensboro Record,* April 19, 1958; *Durham Morning Herald,* April 19, 1958; *Raleigh Times,* April 17, 1958.

124. Ralph L. Buchanan to Senator Julian Allsbrook, May 12, 1971, Ralph Scott Papers.

125. *Raleigh News and Observer,* April 18, 1958.

126. *Charlotte News,* April 18, 1958.

127. *Wilmington Star,* April 17, 1958.

128. *Morganton Citizen,* April 18, 1958.

129. *Asheville Citizen,* April 18, 1958.

130. *Congressional Record,* 85th Cong., 2nd sess., vol. 104, August 11, 1958; *Winston-Salem Journal,* August 9, 1958.

131. Katherine Jordan (wife of B. Everett Jordan), February 14, 1984, interview by Ben Bulla, 1–5, SOHP; Harold Makepeace, August 6, 1982, interview by Ben Bulla, 2–4, SOHP.

132. *New York Times,* April 20, 1958; Ben F. Bulla, *Textiles and Politics: The Life of B. Everett Jordan* (Durham: Carolina Academic, 1992), 1–10.

133. *High Point Enterprise,* April 20, 1958; *Gastonia Gazette,* April 17, 1958.

134. Makepeace, interview by Bulla, 2–4.

135. Jordan, interview by Bulla, 7.

136. *Raleigh News and Observer,* April 19, 1958.

137. *Scotland Neck Commonwealth,* April 25, 1958.

138. Charles T. Pace to Luther Hodges, May 19, 1958, folder 909, ser. 3, Luther H. Hodges Papers.

139. Terry Sanford, March 18, 1998, interview by Jack Fleer, 11, SOHP; Horace Kornegay, January 11, 1989, interview by Ben Bulla, SOHP; *Birmingham Post Herald,* April 21, 1958; *Raleigh News and Observer,* April 20, 1958.

140. *Raleigh News and Observer,* April 19, 1958; Wilder, interview by Pleasants.

11. Legacy

1. *Raleigh News and Observer,* April 15, 1950.

2. Frank Porter Graham to Leo Jenkins, October 22, 1963, Frank Porter Graham Papers, Southern Historical Collection, University of North Carolina, Chapel Hill.

3. Merle Black and Earl Black, *Politics and Society in the South* (Cambridge, MA: Harvard University Press, 1987), 26–29.

4. Paul Luebke, *Tar Heel Politics: Myths and Realities* (Chapel Hill: University of North Carolina Press, 1990), 1–123.

5. Numan V. Bartley, *The New South: 1945–1980* (Baton Rouge: Louisiana State University Press, 1995), 70–72.

6. Ralph McGill, *The South and the Southerner* (Boston: Little, Brown, 1964), 283.

7. William A. Link, *North Carolina: Change and Tradition in a Southern State* (Chapel Hill: University of North Carolina Press, 2009), 440.

8. Terry Sanford, "Remarks Accepting a Portrait of Former Governor W. Kerr Scott" (Raleigh, May 7, 1959), in *Messages, Addresses and Public Papers of Luther Hartwell Hodges, Governor of North Carolina, 1954–1961,* ed. James W. Patton (Raleigh: Council of State, 1960–1963), 164–66.

9. Memory F. Mitchell, ed., *Messages, Addresses, and Public Papers of Terry Sanford: Governor of North Carolina, 1961–1965* (Raleigh: Council of State, 1966), 5.

10. Memory F. Mitchell, ed., *Addresses and Papers of Governor James Hunt, Jr.,* 4 vols. (Raleigh: Division of Archives and History, 1977–1981), 1:93–94.

11. Ibid., 3:437.

12. *Raleigh News and Observer,* February 1, 2009; Rob Christensen, interview with Jim Hunt, April 1, 2003, in possession of the author; Rob Christensen, *The Paradox of Tar Heel Politics* (Chapel Hill: University of North Carolina Press, 2008), 236–38.

13. *Daily Tar Heel,* April 24, 1958.

BIBLIOGRAPHY

The abbreviation SOHP refers to the Southern Oral History Program, Center for the Study of the American South, University of North Carolina at Chapel Hill.

Primary Sources

Manuscript Collections

Duke University Library, Durham, NC

Clyde R. Hoey Papers
Jefferson Deems Johnson Papers
B. Everett Jordan Papers
Allen Langston Papers
John Santford Martin Papers
Political Campaign Materials, 1840–2000
Asa and Elna Spaulding Papers

Joyner Library, East Carolina University, Greenville, NC

Francis Renfrow Doak Papers
Richard T. Fountain Papers
James Y. Joyner Papers
John L. Kerr Papers
John A. Lang Jr. Papers
John D. Larkins Papers
Samuel H. Mitchell Papers
William B. Rodman Papers
H. Patrick Taylor Jr. Papers
H. Patrick Taylor Sr. Papers
Capus Waynick Papers
Francis Edward Winslow Papers

Harry S Truman Library, Independence, Missouri

Harry S Truman Papers

North Carolina Department of Archives and History, Raleigh, NC

L. Y. Ballentine Papers
Robert Gregg Cherry Papers
David S. Coltrane Papers
Ruth Current Papers
May Thompson Evans Papers
Luther Hodges Gubernatorial Papers
Nell Battle Lewis Papers
Harold Evans Minges Scrapbook
Clarence Poe Papers
Kerr Scott Gubernatorial, Senatorial, and Private Papers
Ralph Scott Papers, Restricted
Robert Walter Scott Papers
William B. Umstead Gubernatorial Papers
Gertrude Weil Papers

Southern Historical Collection, University of North Carolina, Chapel Hill

Thurmond Chatham Papers
William McWhorter Cochrane Papers
Oscar Jackson Coffin Papers
Jonathan Worth Daniels Papers
J. S. Dorton Papers
Samuel J. Ervin Papers
O. Max Gardner Papers
Frank Porter Graham Papers
Louis and Mildred Graves Papers
Robert March Hanes Papers
John Harden Papers
Luther H. Hodges Papers
E. B. Jeffress Papers
Guion G. Johnson Papers
J. Spencer Love Papers
Ben Dixon MacNeill Papers
Howard W. Odum Papers
D. Hiden Ramsey Papers
Kenneth C. Royall Papers
Terry Sanford Papers
Susie Sharp Papers
Charles W. and Gladys Tillett Papers
John Wesley Umstead Papers

William B. Umstead Papers
Lindsay Carter Warren Papers
Capus M. Waynick Papers
Roy Wilder Jr. Papers
Louis Round Wilson Papers

Interviews

Hoover Adams, May 26, 1983, by Julian Pleasants. In possession of the author.
R. Mayne Albright, November 30, 1984, by Julian Pleasants. In possession of the author.
Kelly M. Alexander, September 13, 1984. In possession of the author.
Warren Ashby, October 30, 1984, by Julian Pleasants. In possession of the author.
T. Clyde Auman, May 23, 1983, by Julian Pleasants. In possession of the author.
Harvey Beech, September 25, 1966, by Anita Foye. SOHP.
H. Clifton Blue, November 14, 1983, by Ben Bulla. SOHP.
H. Clifton Blue, October 26, 1984, by Julian Pleasants. In possession of the author.
J. Melville Broughton Jr., December 12, 1984, by Julian Pleasants. In possession of the author.
Albert Coates, August 5, 1982, by Gus Burns. In possession of the author.
Jonathan Worth Daniels, 1972. Columbia University Oral History Collection.
James K. Dorsett Jr., December 12, 1984, by Julian Pleasants. In possession of the author.
J. C. B. Ehringhaus Jr., November 10, 1984, by Julian Pleasants. In possession of the author.
Samuel J. Ervin Jr., November 9, 1984, by Julian Pleasants. Transcript of telephone conversation, in possession of the author.
Thad Eure, December 12, 1973, by Jack Bass and Walter DeVries. SOHP.
Thad Eure, December 11, 1984, by Julian Pleasants. In possession of the author.
Duncan M. "Lauch" Faircloth, July 1, 1987, and March 22, 1999, by Joseph Mosnier. SOHP.
Lauch Faircloth, September 26, 2001, by Rob Christensen. In possession of the interviewer.
Lauch Faircloth, n.d., by Bill Link. In possession of the interviewer.
Joel Fleishman, February 8, 1974, by Jack Bass. SOHP.
Kathryn Folger, December 6, 1984, by Julian Pleasants. In possession of the author.
William Friday, October 17, 1984, by Julian Pleasants and Gus Burns. In possession of the author.
William Friday, October 26 and November 19, 1990, by Bill Link. SOHP.
William Friday, June 28, 2010, by Julian Pleasants. In possession of the author.
Grace Furman, September 26, 2001, by Rob Christensen. In possession of the interviewer.
Voit Gilmore, September 20, 1989, by Ben Bulla. SOHP.
Frank Porter Graham, July 1, 1969, by Julian Pleasants. In possession of the author.
Charles P. Green, August 9, 1984, by Julian Pleasants. In possession of the author.

William L. Hauser, November 20, 1989, by Julian Pleasants and Gus Burns. In possession of the author.

Jesse A. Helms, March 8, 1974, by Jack Bass and Walter DeVries. SOHP.

Jesse A. Helms, December 11, 1984, by Julian Pleasants. In possession of the author.

George Watts Hill, January 30, 1986, by James Leutze. SOHP.

Wilbur Hobby, December 18, 1983, by Jack Bass and Walter DeVries. SOHP.

Scott Hoyman, fall 1973, by Carolyn Ashbaugh and Dan McCurry. SOHP.

Kate Humphries, December 13, 1984, by Julian Pleasants. In possession of the author.

Guion Griffis Johnson, July 1, 1974, by Mary Fredrickson. SOHP.

H. G. Jones, November 6, 1984, by Julian Pleasants. In possession of the author.

John Jordan Jr., December 12, 1984, by Julian Pleasants. In possession of the author.

Katherine Jordan, January 13, 19, 1981, and April 7, July 30, and December 14, 1982, by Ben Bulla. SOHP.

William Joslin, December 12, 1984, by Julian Pleasants. In possession of the author.

William T. Joyner Jr., December 12, 1984, by Julian Pleasants. In possession of the author.

Horace Kornegay, January 11, 1989, by Ben Bulla. SOHP.

I. Beverly Lake, September 8, 1987, by Charles Dunn. SOHP.

I. Beverly Lake, December 10, 1984, by Julian Pleasants. In possession of the author.

John Larkins, August 7, 1982, by Ben Bulla. SOHP.

Donald McCoy, December 7, 1984, by Julian Pleasants. In possession of the author.

Wesley E. McDonald, May 18, 1972, by Julian Pleasants. In possession of the author.

L. P. McLendon Jr., November 2, 1984, by Julian Pleasants. In possession of the author.

Harold T. Makepeace, August 6, 1982, by Ben Bulla. SOHP.

Harold T. Makepeace, October 25, 1984, by Julian Pleasants. In possession of the author.

Dora Scott Miller, June 6, 1979, by Beverly Jones. SOHP.

Dan K. Moore, February 19, 1982, by Ben Bulla. SOHP.

Robert Morgan, December 13, 1973, by Jack Bass and Walter DeVries. SOHP.

Ben F. Park, December 11, 1984, by Julian Pleasants. In possession of the author.

Sam Ragan, October 25, 1984, by Julian Pleasants. In possession of the author.

Sam Ragan, March 6, 1987, by Misti Turbeville. SOHP.

Edwin L. Rankin Jr., August 20, 1987, by Jay Jenkins. SOHP.

Frances Lee Reesman, November 15, 2009, by Julian Pleasants. In possession of the author.

Lawrence Rogin, November 2, 1975, by Bill Finger. SOHP.

John Sanders, October 17, 1984, by Julian Pleasants and Gus Burns. In possession of the author.

Terry Sanford, May 14, 1976, by Brent Glass. SOHP.

Terry Sanford, December 3, 1984, by Julian Pleasants. In possession of the author.

Terry Sanford, December 18, 1990, by Cindy Cheatham. SOHP.

Terry Sanford, Summer 1997. Transcript of videotaped interviews conducted by UNC-TV, SOHP.

Ralph Scott, December 20, 1973, by Jack Bass. SOHP.

Ralph Scott, April 22, 1974, by Jackie Hall and Bill Finger. SOHP.

Ralph Scott, October 31, 1984, by Julian Pleasants. In possession of the author.

Robert W. "Bob" Scott, April 10, 1984, by Julian Pleasants. Transcript of telephone conversation, in possession of the author.

Bob Scott, September 18, 1986, by Karl Campbell. SOHP.

Bob Scott, April 4, 1990, by Bill Link. SOHP.

Bob Scott, February 4, 11, 1998, by Jack Fleer. SOHP.

Bob Scott, December 18, 1998, by Rob Christensen. SOHP.

Bob Scott, September 22, 2005, by Rob Christensen and Jack Betts. In possession of the interviewers.

William D. Snider, October 30, 1984, by Julian Pleasants. In possession of the author.

Richard E. Thigpen Sr., December 5, 1984, by Julian Pleasants. In possession of the author.

Roy Thompson Jr., November 1, 1984, by Julian Pleasants. In possession of the author.

Capus Waynick, February 4, November 24, 1974, by Bill Finger. SOHP.

Capus Waynick, August 1, September 19, January 30, 1980. East Carolina University Library.

Tom Wicker, October 30, 1984, by Julian Pleasants. In possession of the author.

Roy Wilder Jr., December 13, 1984, and September 2, 2009, by Julian Pleasants. In possession of the author.

Lacy Wright, March 10, 1975, by Bill Finger and Chip Hughes. SOHP.

W. B. Wright, December 11, 1984, by Julian Pleasants. Transcript of telephone conversation, in possession of the author.

Government Sources

Federal Government

US Bureau of the Census. *United States Census of Population, 1950.* Vol. 2, pt. 33, *North Carolina.* Washington, DC: US Government Printing Office, 1952.

US Congress. *Congressional Quarterly Almanac.* Washington, DC: Congressional Quarterly News Features, 1949, 1950, 1951, 1952–58.

Congressional Record. Washington, DC. 84th, 85th, and 86th Congresses. Washington, DC.

State Government

Corbitt, David L., ed. *Public Addresses, Letters and Papers of William Kerr Scott, Governor of North Carolina, 1949–1953.* Raleigh: Council of State, 1957.

———, ed. *Public Addresses, Letters and Papers of William Bradley Umstead, Governor of North Carolina, 1953–54.* Raleigh: Council of State, 1957.

Deyton, Robert G., comp. *State of North Carolina: The Budget for the Biennium, July*

1, 1949 to June 30, 1951: Fiscal Years 1949–50 and 1950–51. Raleigh: Edwards & Broughton, 1948.

Mitchell, Memory F., ed. *Addresses and Public Papers of James Baxter Hunt, Governor of North Carolina, 1977–85.* Vol. 1. Raleigh: Division of Archives and History, 1982.

————, ed. *Addresses and Public Papers of Robert Walter Scott: Governor of North Carolina, 1969–1973.* Raleigh: Council of State, 1974.

————, ed. *Messages, Addresses, and Public Papers of Terry Sanford: Governor of North Carolina, 1961–1965.* Raleigh: Council of State, 1966.

North Carolina Almanac, 1950–51. Raleigh: Almanac Publishing Co., 1950.

North Carolina Manual, 1951, 1953, 1957. Raleigh: Thad Eure, 1951, 1953, 1957.

Patton, James W., ed. *Messages, Addresses and Public Papers of Luther Hartwell Hodges, Governor of North Carolina, 1954–1961.* Raleigh: Council of State, 1960–1963.

Poff, Jan-Michael, ed. *Addresses and Papers of Governor James Baxter Hunt: 1981–1985.* Raleigh: Division of Archives and History, 1987.

————, ed. *Addresses and Papers of Governor James Baxter Hunt: 1993–1997.* Raleigh: Division of Archives and History, 2000.

Miscellaneous

Coon, John William. "The Go Forward Governor." M.A. thesis, University of North Carolina, 1968. North Carolina Collection, University of North Carolina, Chapel Hill.

Cote, Joseph. "Clarence Hamilton Poe: Crusading Editor, 1881–1964." Ph.D. diss., University of Georgia, 1977.

Anna Lee Dorsett Scrapbook of the Smith Family, in possession of the Smith family, Raleigh, NC.

"Frank P. Graham Jubilee Symposium Proceedings." Greensboro: Office of Continuing Education, University of North Carolina, Greensboro, September 26–27, 1980.

Johnson, Samuel W. "Kerr Scott and His Fight for Improvement of North Carolina Roads." M.A. thesis, University of North Carolina, 1969.

Joslin, Mary Coker. "Precinct Politics: The Red and the Black." 1950. Pamphlet in possession of the author.

Lomax, John. "Liberalism in North Carolina since 1948." Honors essay, Political Science Department, University of North Carolina, 1991. North Carolina Collection, University of North Carolina, Chapel Hill.

MacMillan, Taylor. "Who Beat Frank Graham?" Paper, Political Science Department, University of North Carolina, 1959. North Carolina Collection, University of North Carolina, Chapel Hill.

North Carolina Democratic Party. "Official Handbook, 1950." Raleigh: State Democratic Executive Committee, 1950. North Carolina Collection, University of North Carolina, Chapel Hill.

Parham, J. Covington. "The Democratic Senatorial Primary of North Carolina—1950." Senior thesis, Princeton University, 1952.

Thigpen, Richard E., Sr. "Seventy-seven Years into the Twentieth Century: The Autobiography of Richard Thigpen, Sr." n.d. Typescript in possession of the author.

Wicker, Tom. "Frank Graham and the Progressive Tradition." Speech given September 26, 1980. Copy held by Office of Continuing Education, University of North Carolina, Greensboro.

Secondary Sources

Albright, Mayne. "O. Max Gardner and the Shelby Dynasty." *The State* 51, no. 3 (April 1983): 8–11, (July 1983): 10–13, (August 1983), 8–11, 26, and (January 1984): 14–17.

Alsop, Stewart. *The Center: People and Power in Political Washington.* New York: Harper & Row, 1968.

Anderson, Clinton. *Outsider in the Senate: Senator Clinton Anderson's Memoirs.* New York: World, 1970.

Ashby, Warren. *Frank Porter Graham: A Southern Liberal.* Winston-Salem, NC: John F. Blair, 1980.

Ashmore, Harry S. *Hearts and Minds: The Anatomy of Racism from Roosevelt to Reagan.* New York: McGraw-Hill, 1982.

Ayers, Edward. *The Promise of the New South: Life after Reconstruction.* New York: Oxford University Press, 1992.

Badger, Anthony J. "Closet Moderates: Why White Liberals Failed, 1940, 1970." In *The Role of Ideas in the Civil Rights South,* ed. Anthony J. Badger and Ted Ownby, 83–112. Oxford: University of Mississippi Press, 2002.

———. *New Deal: New South: A Badger Reader.* Fayetteville: University of Arkansas Press, 2007.

———. *Prosperity Road: The New Deal, Tobacco and North Carolina.* Chapel Hill: University of North Carolina Press, 1980.

———. "Southerners Who Refused to Sign the Southern Manifesto." *Historical Journal* 42, no. 2 (1999): 513–14.

Badger, Anthony J., and Brian Ward, eds. *The Making of Martin Luther King and the Civil Rights Movement.* London: Macmillan, 1996.

Baker, Bobby, with Larry L. King. *Wheeling and Dealing: Confessions of a Capitol Hill Operator.* New York: Norton, 1978.

Baker, Russell. *An American in Washington.* New York: Knopf, 1961.

Barkley, Alben W. *That Reminds Me.* Garden City, NY: Doubleday, 1954.

Bartley, Numan V. *The New South: 1945–1980.* Baton Rouge: Louisiana State University Press, 1995.

———. *The Rise of Massive Resistance: Race and Politics in the South during the 1950s.* Baton Rouge: Louisiana State University Press, 1969.

Bartley, Numan V., and Hugh D. Graham. *Southern Politics and the Second Reconstruction.* Baltimore: Johns Hopkins University Press, 1975.

Bass, Jack, and Walter DeVries. *The Transformation of Southern Politics: Social Change and Political Consequences since 1945.* Athens: University of Georgia Press, 1976.

Bennett, David H. *The Party of Fear: From Nativist Movements to the New Right in American History.* Chapel Hill: University of North Carolina Press, 1988.

Beyle, Thad L., and Merle Black. *Politics and Policy in North Carolina.* New York: MSS Information, 1975.

Black, Earl. *Southern Governors and Civil Rights: Racial Segregation as a Campaign Issue in the Second Reconstruction.* Cambridge, MA: Harvard University Press, 1976.

Black, Earl, and Merle Black. *Politics and Society in the South.* Cambridge, MA: Harvard University Press, 1987.

Boyd, Tim S. R. *Georgia Democrats, the Civil Rights Movement and the Shaping of the New South.* Gainesville: University Press of Florida, 2012.

Brinkley, Alan. *The End of Reform: New Deal Liberalism in Recession and War.* New York: Knopf, 1995.

Brooks, Jennifer E. *Defining the Peace: World War II Veterans, Race, and the Remaking of the Southern Political Tradition.* Chapel Hill: University of North Carolina Press, 2004.

Brooks, John. *The Great Leap: The Past Twenty-five Years in America.* New York: Harper & Row, 1966.

Bulla, Ben F. *Textiles and Politics: The Life of B. Everett Jordan.* Durham, NC: Carolina Academic, 1992.

Bushong, William. *North Carolina's Executive Mansion: The First 100 Years.* Raleigh, NC: Executive Mansion Fine Arts Committee, 1991.

Butler, Lindley J., and Alan D. Watson, eds. *The North Carolina Experience: An Interpretive and Documentary History.* Chapel Hill: University of North Carolina Press, 1984.

Campbell, Karl E. *Senator Sam Ervin: Last of the Founding Fathers.* Chapel Hill: University of North Carolina Press, 2007.

Carleton, William G. "Can Pepper Hold Florida." *The Nation,* March 4, 1950, 198–200.

Caro, Robert A. *The Years of Lyndon Johnson: Master of the Senate.* New York: Knopf, 2002.

Carter, Hodding, Jr. *Southern Legacy.* Baton Rouge: Louisiana State University Press, 1950.

Cash, W. J. *The Mind of the South.* New York: Vintage, 1941.

Caute, David. *The Great Fear: The Anti-Communist Purge under Truman and Eisenhower.* New York: Simon & Schuster, 1987.

Cecelski, David. *Along Freedom Road: Hyde County, N.C. and the Fate of Black Schools in the South.* Chapel Hill: University of North Carolina Press, 1994.

Chafe, William H. *Civilities and Civil Rights: Greensboro, N.C. and the Black Struggle for Freedom.* New York: Oxford University Press, 1980.

Chappell, David. *Inside Agitators: White Southerners in the Civil Rights Movement.* Baltimore: Johns Hopkins University Press, 1994.

Cheney, John L., ed. *North Carolina Government, 1585–1974: A Narrative and Statistical History.* Raleigh, NC: Secretary of State, 1981.

Christensen, Rob. *The Paradox of Tar Heel Politics*. Chapel Hill: University of North Carolina Press, 2008.

Cimbala, Paul, and Barton C. Shaw, eds. *Making a New South: Race, Leadership and Community after the Civil War*. Gainesville: University Press of Florida, 2007.

Claiborne, Jack, and William Price, eds. *Discovering North Carolina: A Tar Heel Reader*. Chapel Hill: University of North Carolina Press, 1991.

Clancy, Paul R. *Just a Country Lawyer: A Biography of Senator Sam Ervin*. Bloomington: Indiana University Press, 1974.

Clare, Rod. "Resisting the Doldrums: The League of Women Voters in North Carolina." *North Carolina Historical Review* 86, no. 2 (April 2009): 180–207.

Clayton, Bruce. *W. J. Cash: A Life*. Baton Rouge: Louisiana State University Press, 1991.

Clifford, Clark. *Counsel to the President: A Memoir*. New York: Random House, 1991.

Coates, Albert. "East Is East and West Is West—but Which Is Which?" *Popular Government,* August 1948, 7.

———. *The Story of the Institute of Government*. Chapel Hill, NC: privately published, 1981.

Cochrane, Bill. "North Carolina's Man on the Hill." *Carolina Alumni Review,* Spring 1984, 13–14, 26–30.

Cohodas, Nadine. *Strom Thurmond and the Politics of Social Change*. New York: Simon & Schuster, 1993.

Cooper, Christopher A., and H. Gibbs Knotts, eds. *The New Politics of North Carolina*. Chapel Hill: University of North Carolina Press, 2008.

Covington, Howard E., Jr. *The Good Government Man: Albert Coates and the Early Years of the Institute of Government*. Chapel Hill, NC: University Library, 2010.

Covington, Howard E., Jr., and Marion A. Ellis, eds. *The North Carolina Century: Tar Heels Who Made a Difference*. Charlotte, NC: Levine Museum of the New South, 2002.

———. *Terry Sanford: Progress, Politics and Outrageous Ambitions*. Durham, NC: Duke University Press, 1999.

Crabtree, Beth. *North Carolina Governors: Brief Sketches*. Raleigh, NC: State Department of Archives and History, 1958.

Crow, Jeffrey D., et al., eds. *A History of African Americans in North Carolina*. Raleigh, NC: Department of Cultural Resources, 2002.

Cummings, Richard. *The Pied Piper: Allard Lowenstein and the Liberal Dream*. New York: Grove, 1987.

Dabney, Dick. *A Good Man: The Life of Sam J. Ervin*. Boston: Houghton Mifflin, 1976.

Dallek, Robert. *Lone Star Rising: Lyndon Johnson and His Times*. New York: Oxford University Press, 1991.

Daniel, Pete. *Lost Revolution: The South in the 1950s*. Chapel Hill: University of North Carolina Press, 2000.

Daniels, Jonathan. *Tar Heels: A Portrait of North Carolina*. New York: Dodd, Mead, 1947.

Donovan, Robert J. *The Presidency of Harry Truman, 1945–48*. New York: Norton, 1977.

———. *Tumultuous Years: The Presidency of Harry Truman, 1949–1953.* New York: Norton, 1982.

Douglas, Davison M. *Reading, Writing and Race: The Desegregation of Charlotte Schools.* Chapel Hill: University of North Carolina Press, 1995.

Douglas, Paul H. *In The Fullness of Time.* New York: Harcourt Brace Jovanovich, 1972.

Drescher, John. *Triumph of Good Will: How Terry Sanford Beat a Champion of Segregation and Reshaped the South.* Jackson: University Press of Mississippi, 2000.

Drukman, Mason. *Wayne Morse: A Political Biography.* Portland: Oregon Historical Society Press, 1997.

Drury, Allen. *A Senate Journal: 1943–1955.* New York: Da Capo, 1972.

Eagles, Charles. *Is There a Southern Political Tradition?* Jackson: University Press of Mississippi, 1996.

———. *Jonathan Daniels and Race Relations: The Evolution of a Southern Liberal.* Knoxville: University of Tennessee Press, 1982.

Egerton, John. *Shades of Gray: Dispatches from the Modern South.* Baton Rouge: Louisiana State University Press, 1991.

———. *Speak Now against the Day: The Generation before the Civil Rights Movement in the South.* Chapel Hill: University of North Carolina Press, 1995.

Ehle, John. *Dr. Frank: Life with Frank Porter Graham.* Chapel Hill, NC: Franklin Street, 1993.

Ellis, Tom. "An Interview with Tom Ellis." *Tar Heel: The Magazine of North Carolina,* March 1980, 33–34, 47–48, 50.

Evans, Roland, and Robert Novak. *Lyndon B. Johnson: The Exercise of Power.* New York: New American Library, 1966.

Ferrell, Robert H., ed. *Off the Record: The Private Papers of Harry S Truman.* New York: Penguin, 1980.

Fimrite, Ron. "A Long Locomotive for Choo Choo." *Sports Illustrated,* October 15, 1973, 44–52.

Fine, Fred. "Notes on the 1950 Elections." *Political Affairs,* May 1950, 136–37.

Fite, Gilbert. *Richard B. Russell, Jr.: Senator from Georgia.* Chapel Hill: University of North Carolina Press, 1991.

Fleer, Jack D. *Governors Speak.* Lanham, MD: University Press of America, 2007.

———. *North Carolina Government and Politics.* Lincoln: University of Nebraska Press, 1994.

———. *North Carolina Politics: An Introduction.* Chapel Hill: University of North Carolina Press, 1968.

Fontenay, Charles L. *Estes Kefauver: A Biography.* Knoxville: University of Tennessee Press, 1980.

Frederickson, Kari. *The Dixiecrat Revolt and the End of the Solid South, 1932–1968.* Chapel Hill: University of North Carolina Press, 2001.

Gavins, Raymond. "The NAACP in North Carolina during the Age of Segregation and the Civil Rights Movement." In *The Civil Rights Movement*, ed. Jack E. Davis, 156–71. Malden, MA: Blackwell, 2001.

Gilmore, Glenda. *Defying Dixie: The Radical Roots of Civil Rights, 1919–1950*. New York: Norton, 2008.

Golden, Harry. *The Right Time: An Autobiography*. New York: Putnam's, 1943.

Goldfield, David R. *Promised Land: The South since 1945*. Arlington Heights, IL: Harlan Davidson, 1987.

Goulden, Joseph C. *The Best Years: 1945–1950*. New York: Atheneum, 1976.

Graham, Katherine. *Personal History*. New York: Knopf, 1997.

Grantham, Dewey. *The Democratic South*. New York: Norton, 1963.

Griffith, Barbara. *The Crisis of American Labor: Operation Dixie and the Defeat of the CIO*. Philadelphia: Temple University Press, 1981.

Griffith, Robert. *The Politics of Fear: Joseph R. McCarthy and the Senate*. Lexington: University of Kentucky Press, 1970.

Guillory, Ferrel. "Political and Economic Paradox in North Carolina." *Raleigh News and Observer*, July 8, 1990.

Halberstam, David. *The Fifties*. New York: Villard, 1993.

Hamilton, Virginia Van der Veer. *Lister Hill: Statesman from the South*. Chapel Hill: University of North Carolina Press, 1987.

Harden, John. *North Carolina Roads and Their Builders*. Vol. 2. Raleigh: Superior Stone, 1966.

Havard, William C. *The Changing Politics of the South*. Baton Rouge: Louisiana State University Press, 1972.

Hayes, Anna R. *Without Precedent: The Life of Susie Marshall Sharp*. Chapel Hill: University of North Carolina Press, 2008.

Heard, Alexander. *A Two Party South?* Chapel Hill: University of North Carolina Press, 1952.

Hero, Alfred O., Jr. *The Southerner and World Affairs*. Baton Rouge: Louisiana State University Press, 1965.

Hobbs, Huntington S., Jr. *North Carolina: An Economic and Social Profile*. Chapel Hill: University of North Carolina Press, 1958.

Hodges, Luther H. *Businessman in the State House: Six Years as Governor of North Carolina*. Chapel Hill: University of North Carolina Press, 1962.

Ivey, A. G. *Luther H. Hodges: Practical Idealist*. Minneapolis: T. S. Denison, 1968.

Katznelson, Ira, et al. "Limiting Liberalism: The Southern Vote in Congress." *Political Science Quarterly* 108 (1993): 283–306.

Keech, William R. *The Impact of Negro Voting: The Role of the Vote in the Quest for Equality*. Chicago: Rand McNally, 1968.

Key, V. O., Jr. *Southern Politics in State and Nation*. New York: Knopf, 1949.

Klarman, Michael. "How *Brown* Changed Race Relations." *Journal of American History* 81 (1994): 81–118.

Kluger, Richard. *Simple Justice: The History of* Brown v. Board of Education *and Black America's Struggle for Equality.* New York: Knopf, 1976.

Korstad, Robert R., and James L. Leloudis. *To Right These Wrongs.* Chapel Hill: University of North Carolina Press, 2010.

Kousser, J. Morgan. *The Shaping of Southern Politics.* New Haven, CT: Yale University Press, 1974.

Lamus, Alexander P. *The Two Party South.* New York: Oxford University Press, 1984.

Larkins, John D., Jr. *Politics Bar and Bench: A Memoir of John Davis Larkins, Jr.: Fifty Years.* Edited by Donald R. Lennon and Fred D. Ragan. New Bern, NC: Owen G. Dunn, 1980.

Latham, Earl. *The Communist Controversy in Washington: From the New Deal to McCarthy.* Cambridge, MA: Harvard University Press, 1976.

Lawson, Steven F. *Black Ballots: Voting Rights in the South, 1944–1969.* New York: Columbia University Press, 1976.

Lefler, Hugh, and Albert Ray Newsome. *North Carolina: The History of a Southern State.* 1943. 3rd ed. Chapel Hill: University of North Carolina Press, 1973.

Leidholdt, Alexander S. *Battling Nell: The Life of Southern Journalist Cornelia Battle Lewis.* Baton Rouge: Louisiana State University Press, 2009.

Lerche, Charles O. *The Uncertain South: Its Changing Patterns of Politics in Foreign Policy.* Chicago: Quadrangle, 1964.

Link, William A. *Righteous Warrior: Jesse Helms and the Rise of Modern Conservatism.* New York: St. Martin's, 2008.

———. *William Friday: Power, Purpose and American Higher Education.* Chapel Hill: University of North Carolina Press, 1995.

Lubell, Samuel. *The Future of American Politics.* New York: Harper & Bros., 1952.

———. "Has Truman Lost the South?" *Look,* October 24, 1950, 129–36.

Luebke, Paul. *Tar Heel Politics: Myths and Realities.* Chapel Hill: University of North Carolina Press, 1990.

Marshall, F. Ray. *Labor in the South.* Cambridge, MA: Harvard University Press, 1967.

Marshall, John. "Governor Scott's Go Forward Program Is Completed." *The State* 20, no. 31 (January 3, 1953): 9–11.

Martin, John Bartlow. *Adlai Stevenson and the World.* New York: Doubleday, 1977.

———. *The Deep South Says Never.* New York: Ballantine, 1957.

Matthews, Donald R. *U.S. Senators and Their World.* New York: Vintage, 1960.

Matthews, Donald R., and James W. Prothro. *Negroes and the New Southern Politics.* New York: Harcourt, Brace & World, 1966.

Matusow, Allen J. *Farm Policies and Politics in the Truman Years.* Cambridge, MA: Harvard University Press, 1967.

McCoy, Donald R. *The Presidency of Harry S Truman.* Lawrence: University Press of Kansas, 1984.

McCullough, David. *Truman.* New York: Simon & Schuster, 1992.

McGill, Ralph. *The South and the Southerner.* Boston: Little, Brown, 1964.

McLaurin, Melton A. *The N.C. State Fair: The First Fifty Years.* Raleigh, NC: Office of Archives and History, 2003.

McMillen, Neil R., ed. *Remaking Dixie: The Impact of World War II on the American South.* Jackson: University Press of Mississippi, 1997.

Miller, Merle. *Lyndon: An Oral Biography.* New York: Putnam, 1980.

Minchin, Timothy J. *What Do We Need a Union For: The TWUA in the South, 1945–1955.* Chapel Hill: University of North Carolina Press, 1997.

Mobley, Joseph A., ed. *The Way We Lived in North Carolina.* Chapel Hill: University of North Carolina Press, 2003.

Morrison, Joseph L. *Governor O. Max Gardner: A Power in North Carolina and New Deal Washington.* Chapel Hill: University of North Carolina Press, 1971.

———. *W. J. Cash: Southern Prophet.* New York: Knopf, 1967.

Morton, Hugh. *Making a Difference in North Carolina.* Raleigh, NC: Light Works, 1988.

Oshinsky, David M. *A Conspiracy So Immense: The World of Joe McCarthy.* New York: Free Press, 1983.

Parramore, Thomas C. *Express Lanes and Country Roads: The Way We Lived in North Carolina, 1920–1970.* Chapel Hill: University of North Carolina Press, 1983.

Pearson, Drew, and Tyler Abell, eds. *Diaries: 1949–1959.* New York: Holt, Rinehart, 1974.

Phillips, Cabell. *The Truman Presidency: The History of a Triumphant Succession.* Baltimore: Penguin, 1969.

Pleasants, Julian M. *Buncombe Bob: The Life and Times of Robert Rice Reynolds.* Chapel Hill: University of North Carolina Press, 2000.

———. "Call Your Next Case: H. F. 'Chub' Seawell, the Gubernatorial Election of 1952 and the Rise of the Republican Party in North Carolina." *North Carolina Historical Review* 66, no. 1 (January 1991): 66–101.

———. "The Last Hurrah: Bob Reynolds and the U.S. Senate Race in 1950." *North Carolina Historical Review* 65, no. 1 (January 1988): 52–75.

———. "Many Campaigns of the Pinetown Pig Breeder." *The State* 53, no. 10 (March 1986): 10–12.

Pleasants, Julian M., and Augustus M. Burns. *Frank Porter Graham and the 1950 Senate Race in North Carolina.* Chapel Hill: University of North Carolina Press, 1990.

Poe, Clarence H. *My First Eighty Years.* Chapel Hill: University of North Carolina Press, 1963.

Powell, William S. *North Carolina through Four Centuries.* Chapel Hill: University of North Carolina Press, 1989.

Powers, Richard Gid. *Secrecy and Power: The Life of J. Edgar Hoover.* New York: Free Press, 1987.

Rae, Nicol E. *Southern Democrats in the U.S. Congress.* New York: Oxford University Press, 1994.

Rankin, Robert S. *The Government and Administration of North Carolina.* New York: Thomas Y. Crowell, 1955.

Reed, John Shelton. *The Enduring South: Subcultural Persistence in Mass Society.* Chapel Hill: University of North Carolina Press, 1986.

Reeves, Thomas C. *The Life and Times of Joe McCarthy.* New York: Stein & Day, 1982.

Roland, Charles P. *The Improbable Era: The South since World War II.* Lexington: University of Kentucky Press, 1975.

Salmond, John A. *Miss Lucy of the CIO: The Life and Times of Lucy Randolph Mason, 1882–1959.* Athens: University of Georgia Press, 1988.

———. *Southern Struggles: The Southern Labor Movement and the Civil Rights Struggle.* Gainesville: University Press of Florida, 2004.

Sanford, Terry. *Storm over the States.* New York: McGraw-Hill, 1967.

Scales, Junius, and Richard Nickson. *Cause at Heart: A Former Communist Remembers.* Athens: University of Georgia Press, 1987.

Schlesinger, Tom. "Frank Graham's Primary Education." *Nation,* April 22, 1950, 368.

Seawell, Herbert F., Jr. *Satire in Solid Skitches.* Carthage, NC: self-published, printed by Edwards & Broughton, 1974.

Sharpe, William P. *A New Geography of North Carolina.* Raleigh, NC: Sharpe, 1954.

Snider, William D. *Light on the Hill: A History of the University of North Carolina at Chapel Hill.* Chapel Hill: University of North Carolina Press, 1992.

———. "North Carolina Highway and Road System." In *North Carolina Almanac, 1950–51.* Almanac Publishing Co., 1950.

Sosna, Morton. *In Search of the Silent South: Southern Liberals and the Race Issue.* New York: Columbia University Press, 1982.

Speck, Jean. *The Gentleman from Haw River.* N.p.: privately printed, 1990.

Stem, Thad. *PTA Impact: Fifty Years in North Carolina, 1919–1969.* Raleigh: Congress of Parents and Teachers, 1969.

Stone, I. F. *The Haunted Fifties.* New York: Random House, 1963.

Sullivan, Patricia. *Days of Hope: Race and Democracy in the New Deal Era.* Chapel Hill: University of North Carolina Press, 1996.

Talmadge, Herman E., with Mark Royden Winchell. *Talmadge: A Political Legacy, a Politician's Life: A Memoir.* Atlanta: Peachtree, 1987.

Taylor, Gregory S. *The History of the North Carolina Communist Party.* Columbia: University of South Carolina Press, 2009.

Terrell, Bob. *All Aboard: The Fantastic Story of Charlie "Choo-Choo" Justice and the Football Team That Put North Carolina in the Big Time.* Apex, NC: World Com, 1996.

Tindall, George B. *The Emergence of the New South: 1913–1945.* Baton Rouge: Louisiana State University Press, 1967.

Trawick, Gary E., and Paul B. Wyche. "Kerr Scott." In *100 Years, 100 Men, 1871–1971,* ed. C. C. Crittenden et al. Raleigh, NC: Edwards & Broughton, 1971.

Troxler, Carole W., and William M. Vincent. *Shuttle and Plow: A History of Alamance*

County. Burlington, NC: Alamance County Historical Association, 1999.

Turner, Herbert S., comp. *The Scott Family of Hawfields.* Durham, NC: Seeman, 1971.

Turner, Walter R. *Paving Tobacco Road: A Century of Progress.* Raleigh, NC: Department of Transportation, 2010.

Walker, Anders. *The Ghost of Jim Crow: How Southern Moderates Used* Brown v. Board of Education *to Stall Civil Rights.* New York: Oxford University Press, 2009.

Walser, Richard G. *North Carolina Parade: Stories of History and People.* Wendell, NC: Broadfoot's, 1979.

———. *Tar Heel Laughter.* Chapel Hill: University of North Carolina Press, 1974.

Ward, Jason Morgan. *Defending White Democracy: The Making of a Segregationist Movement and the Remaking of Racial Politics, 1936–1965.* Chapel Hill: University of North Carolina Press, 2011.

Wicker, Tom. *Facing the Lions.* New York: Viking, 1973.

Wilder, Roy, Jr. *You All Spoken Here.* New York: Viking Penguin, 1984.

Index

Page numbers in *italics* refer to photographs.

New Directions in Southern History

Series editors
Michele Gillespie, Wake Forest University
William A. Link, University of Florida

CPSIA information can be obtained at www.ICGtesting.com
Printed in the USA
BVOW03*2351010215

385717BV00002B/3/P

9 780813 146775